The Parties Respond

D1124742

TRANSFORMING AMERICAN POLITICS
Lawrence C. Dodd, Series Editor

Dramatic changes in political institutions and behavior over the past two decades have underscored the dynamic nature of American politics, confronting political scientists with a new and pressing intellectual agenda. The pioneering work of early postwar scholars, while laying a firm empirical foundation for contemporary scholarship, failed to consider how American politics might change or to recognize the forces that would make fundamental change inevitable. In reassessing the static interpretations fostered by these classic studies, political scientists are now examining the underlying dynamics that generate transformational change.

Transforming American Politics will bring together texts and monographs that address four closely related aspects of change. A first concern is documenting and explaining recent changes in American politics—in institutions, processes, behavior, and policymaking. A second is reinterpreting classic studies and theories to provide a more accurate perspective on postwar politics. The series will look at historical change to identify recurring patterns of political transformation within and across the distinctive eras of American politics. Last and perhaps most importantly, the series will present new theories and interpretations that explain the dynamic processes at work and thus clarify the direction of contemporary politics. All of the books will focus on the central theme of transformation—transformation in both the conduct of American politics and in the way we study and understand its many aspects.

TITLES IN THIS SERIES

The Parties Respond

CHANGES IN THE AMERICAN PARTY SYSTEM

EDITED BY

L. Sandy Maisel
Colby College

Westview Press
BOULDER • SAN FRANCISCO • OXFORD

FOR JOYCE

Transforming American Politics

All rights reserved. No part of this publication may be reproduced or transmitted in any form or by any means, electronic or mechanical, including photocopy, recording, or any information storage and retrieval system, without permission in writing from the publisher.

Copyright © 1990 by Westview Press, Inc.

Published in 1990 in the United States of America by Westview Press, Inc., 5500 Central Avenue, Boulder, Colorado 80301, and in the United Kingdom by Westview Press, Inc., 36 Lonsdale Road, Summertown, Oxford OX2 7EW

Library of Congress Cataloging-in-Publication Data
The Parties respond : changes in the American party system/edited by
  L. Sandy Maisel.
    p. cm.—(Transforming American politics series)
  Includes bibliographical references.
  Includes index.
  ISBN 0-8133-0881-X. ISBN 0-8133-0882-8 (pbk.)
  1. Political parties—United States. I. Maisel, Louis Sandy,
1945–   . II. Series.
JK2261.P29 1990
324.273—dc20   90-12521
                                                                     CIP

Printed and bound in the United States of America

The paper used in this publication meets the requirements
of the American National Standard for Permanence of Paper
for Printed Library Materials Z39.48-1984.

10   9   8   7   6   5   4   3   2   1

Contents

PART SIX
TOWARD THE FUTURE

Acknowledgments

A book such as this one reflects the efforts of many people. Those of us who teach courses on political parties and elections in the United States have long recognized the need for a collection of essays bringing together the work of scholars who study various aspects of partisan politics. But it was Larry Dodd, the editor of the series of which this book is a part, who took the additional step of asking for a proposal to address that need. This book has benefited greatly from his comments at all stages, from conceptualization through final editing. Let me also say that I have never worked with an editor who has been as thoughtful, helpful, and supportive as Jennifer Knerr. For those of us who have worked with Jennifer, she has come to define the ideal against which other editors should be measured. I feel very much the same way about the others at Westview who have aided in the production of this book, especially Christine Arden, Jeanne Campbell, Amy Eisenberg, and Ellen Kresky.

As an editor myself, I cannot say enough for my friends and colleagues who have contributed the essays of which this book is composed. They shared my view that a book such as this one was important. They permitted me to define the approach they would take in covering their topics. They put this topic on the top of their research agendas, so that we could meet our deadline and produce the book on schedule. To each of the contributors I am deeply indebted. The same can be said of those who worked with me in readying this book for the publisher. As I have said often in the past, I am fortunate to work with a secretary like Patricia Kick. I also want to thank Nancy Morrione for her assistance in editing, and especially Gretchen Anglund, perhaps the best under-graduate research assistant with whom I have ever worked, as she provided immeasurable aid throughout this entire project.

I completed this work on Thanksgiving morning; under other cir-cumstances I would have spent that time with my family. Over the years Dana, Josh, and Dylan have come to understand that I am not always the easiest father to be around when I am finishing a project. I hope they all know that I appreciate their acceptance and understanding of my need to be alone in a quiet place.

This book is dedicated to my wife, Joyce. How simple the transformations in the party system seem when compared to the changes that take place in the individual and shared lives of a married couple. I hope Joyce realizes how lucky I consider myself to be to share the learning and joys of those changes with her.

L. Sandy Maisel
Waterville, Maine

Prologue

Americans have always loved to hate political parties. From George Washington's Farewell Address, through the rhetoric of the Progressives, to the pleadings of this generation's good-government lobbies, reformers have warned against the evils of party—the mischief of factions, the pernicious dealings of the smoke-filled room, the purveyors of personal favor.

The persistence of American political parties through nearly two centuries of criticism stands as a testimony to their role in our system of government. Despite the fact that they are never mentioned in the Constitution, parties have had an impact on virtually every aspect of American political life.

The role of political parties has deserved particular attention in recent decades as they have responded to ongoing transformations in American politics. Think of the environment in which political parties operate. In broadest terms, parties seek to attract voters to support candidates for office, based on allegiance to the party label and on agreement with the policy positions supported by the party. They do so within a legal and political context that is constantly changing because of world events, a context that varies from state to state and even from community to community within states. Rarely in this nation's history have those changes been as marked as during the past thirty years.

Thirty years ago the civil rights movement was the major social and political force in the nation. In 1954 the Supreme Court had ruled, in *Brown v. Board of Education*, that separate was no longer legally equal; but government officials throughout the South were resisting integration as a matter of public policy, and northern society was nearly as segregated as southern. Politics reflected a society in which racial taboos still dominated. James Meredith had to be accompanied by federal marshalls when he integrated the University of Mississippi over the objections of Governor Ross Barnett in 1962; Sidney Poitier broke another racial barrier when he starred in and won the Best Actor Oscar for *Lilies of the Field* in 1963, a feat matched in television by Bill Cosby's Emmy-winning starring role in "I Spy" two years later (see Weisbrot, 1990).

A variety of Jim Crow laws kept black Americans from voting throughout the South; in Mississippi, fewer than 10 percent of the black population were registered to vote when John Kennedy was elected president. Even in the supposedly liberal North, few black politicians successfully sought elective office, and virtually none was elected except in areas where they constituted a racial majority.

The civil rights movement began to change American society in important ways. In 1964 the Twenty-Fourth Amendment to the Constitution banned the Poll Tax, a lingering example of Jim Crowism. The Voting Rights Act of 1965 led directly to a dramatic increase in black participation in the political process; at the time of the passage of that act, fewer than 100 African Americans held elective office. According to the Joint Center for Political Studies in Washington, that number is now approaching 7,000, including 4,000 in the South. And the political parties have had to respond to those changes. The changes have been so profound that the chief beneficiary of a rule change to increase the influence of southern states in the Democratic party's nominating process was Jesse Jackson, a black minister whose political roots were in the civil rights movement that brought about these changes.

But the civil rights movement has not been the only force influencing American politics in recent decades. Indeed, the Vietnam War dominated the political landscape for nearly ten years. Its political legacy included not only the Twenty-Sixth Amendment to the Constitution, which gave those old enough to fight in Vietnam the right to choose the governing officials who make foreign policy, but also a generation of young people who were uncertain if electoral politics and the traditional political parties could meet their needs. And, again, as the political landscape was transformed, parties had to respond.

The women's movement also had a profound impact. Thirty years ago most of the women active in electoral politics were widows of prominent politicians. Even the legendary Margaret Chase Smith (R-ME), so prominent early in the 1950s for her defiance of Senator Joseph McCarthy (R-WI), first sought office to fill a seat vacated by the death of her husband. But the role of women in American society and American politics was fundamentally transformed in the 1970s and 1980s. Female politicians, many of them initially drawn to politics through their participation in the civil rights and anti-Vietnam movements, became more and more prominent. And just as the civil rights movement led to increased participation by black voters, to increased concern for political issues of particular concern to racial minorities, and to an increase in the number of black office holders, so too did the women's movement lead to the mobilization of women as active political participants, to definable differences (the so-called gender gap) between male and female voters, to a concern for issues of gender from the Equal Rights Amendment (ERA) to abortion to improved day-care facilities, and to an increase in prominent female politicians. Once again the parties had to respond as the body politic underwent a transformation.

Other changes could be added to this list—the Supreme Court rulings requiring apportionment schemes that, to the extent possible, equalized the value of votes, the increase in the numbers of Hispanic and Asian Americans, an increased public concern about ethics in government largely as a result of the Watergate affair, the movement of the nation's population from the Snowbelt states to the Sunbelt states with consequent shifts in the size of congressional delegations—but the lessons remain the same. As the nation has undergone dramatic changes, the political parties, as institutions that must function within this changing context, have had to respond.

And there is no doubt that the parties—as well as the politicians who run under party labels, and the institutions in which they serve— *have* responded. Some of their responses have been abrupt and some more subtle. Some have been successful and some have failed. Some have been welcomed and some criticized. By any account, however, the list of reforms, many of which were promulgated during the turbulent 1970s, is impressive—major changes in the committee and seniority systems in the Congress, Government in Sunshine laws and sunset legislation to close the books on unneeded programs, imposition of more stringent ethical standards in the Congress and the executive branch, redefinition of the relationship between the executive and the legislature as they work on the federal budget and conduct foreign policy, public funding of presidential campaigns and restrictions on the financing of congressional campaigns and campaigns in nearly every state, restructuring of the delegate-selection process for national conventions (reflecting a move toward more popular and less organization influence), and, finally, the reactions to those reforms, such as affirmative action programs for women and minorities.

The Democrats and the Republicans have not always responded in the same way to these changes in American politics; partisan differences on some reforms have been pronounced. But the parties have been involved in all of these matters, and neither party in 1990 comes even close to what it was in 1960 in terms of organization, membership, how it appeals to the electorate or serves its candidates, and its impact on governing. This book examines the parties' responses.

The essays written for this volume examine contemporary political parties. But the historical context of that examination is important as well. As Joel Silbey persuasively argues in the opening essay, the centrality of the party role has varied significantly over time. Not only the intensity of that role but also the locus of its impact have shifted.

The essays that follow Silbey's historical introduction do not examine political parties as a whole; rather, each chapter looks at one aspect of the role played by these resilient institutions as they have adapted to a changing political context. For instance, the second through fourth chapters look at party organization. The next two chapters focus on the role of the party in the electorate; the four after that examine the role of parties in the more broadly defined electoral arena. The three subsequent chapters on the role of party in government recognize the fact that party as an institution has more than an electoral role. And the final two essays speculate on how this role will change in the decades ahead.

The fifteen essays that make up this book represent the most recent thinking by leading scholars; yet they have been written with an undergraduate audience in mind. They not only cover the varying aspects of this topic from differing perspectives, but they also employ a range of research methods so that students can be exposed to the various modes of analysis used by contemporary researchers.

In Chapters 2 and 3, John Bibby and Paul Herrnson examine political parties as organizations in search of a role, at the state and national levels, respectively. In each case, the question is whether these organizations, perceived as weak and ineffectual, can find a niche through which they can regain the influence they once had. And in each case, the answer is a qualified "yes." In Chapter 4, Walter Stone, Ronald Rapoport, and Alan Abramowitz refer to surveys of state convention delegates in their examination of the views of political activists who influence party decisions. When activists in the two parties, among them the party leaders, emphasize different issue positions and thus become further separated in ideological terms, their positions might well presage similar differences among their followers.

In Chapters 5 and 6, Warren Miller and Morris Fiorina analyze the relationship between parties and voters. Using national survey data from the presidential elections of the 1980s, Miller refutes the arguments of those who claim that the electorate has lost its allegiance to the major political parties. He maintains that the voters (as opposed to citizens who do not vote) retain party as an important referent group, and that the evidence points to a realignment toward the Republicans that began during the Reagan administration and was cemented in the election of 1988. Fiorina, looking at how voters decide on the array of choices with which they are presented on each election day, and contrasting the elections of the 1980s with those a half-century earlier, concludes that elections, once party-centered, are now office-centered (i.e., voters view presidential elections and congressional elections in different ways) and person-centered (i.e., voters relate to those candidates they come to know). Now that ticket-splitting and divided government are accepted parts of the electoral scene, the traditional concept of realignment caused by divisive issues is no longer meaningful.

The next four chapters concern the role of political parties in the conduct of elections. In Chapter 7, Sandy Maisel, Linda Fowler, Ruth Jones, and Walter Stone present a model to explain candidate decision-making and explore the limitations of the role that party can play in determining who will be candidates in state and local elections. The authors also speculate on how that role can be enhanced. In Chapter 8, Elaine Kamarck demonstrates the effect of national party rules on the strategies and outcomes of recent presidential nominations. She concludes with a discussion of the party context in which future nominating contests will occur. In Chapter 9, Frank Sorauf and Scott Wilson explore the means by which political parties have responded to the evolving cash economy of modern campaigns. As modern campaigns require more money and less manpower, parties have found a new niche; but Sorauf and Wilson reveal evidence that this new role may prove to be as transitory as previous ones. Then, in Chapter 10, Gary Orren and Bill Mayer examine the functions of the media and political parties as intermediaries between public officials and the electorate. They conclude with a discussion of the challenge that the media must face in walking the line as private institutions that serve public purposes.

Decades ago, V. O. Key directed political scientists to look at the role of political parties in government as well as in the electoral arena. In Chapters 11 and 12, accordingly, Barbara Sinclair and David Brady analyze the complex impact of party on Congress. Drawing on her experiences as a participant observer, Sinclair shows evidence of re-emerging strength in party leadership in the process by which the legislature defines the policy agenda and structures the two chambers. But Brady claims that, despite evidence of increased party voting in recent Congresses, structural factors and many of the same political factors on which Fiorina commented lead one to conclude that one must increasingly look at cross-party coalitions in order to understand legislative behavior. Cal Mackenzie, in Chapter 13, then argues that party is much less a resource on which presidents can draw to staff their administrations than it once was, largely because party leaders do not tend to be as concerned about issues as they are about the techniques of winning office. Thus, the party in government connection has been further weakened.

In Chapters 14 and 15, E. J. Dionne and Sandy Maisel conclude with a look to the future. Dionne explores the first year of the Bush administration and raises questions about its implications for future partisanship. And Maisel speculates on the evolution of political parties—in their various roles—as the twenty-first century approaches.

Taken together, these fifteen essays paint a fascinating picture of American political parties. Parties in the role of institutions have adapted as the nation has changed over two centuries. But as parties are not monolithic, any analysis must take into account not only their complexity but also the various points at which they affect the American polity. The authors of these chapters come to the topic from different perspectives—not only as political scientists but also as historians, journalists, and activists, as students not only of political parties but also of organizations, of voting behavior, of elections, of the Congress, and of the presidency. Only by looking at the entire picture can one begin to understand the complexity of American political parties, the ways they have responded to a changing country, and the reasons for which they have persisted as they have.

PART ONE

Parties in the American Context

1

The Rise and Fall
of American Political Parties
1790–1990

JOEL H. SILBEY

The 1790s were contentious years in American politics. The recently ratified Constitution had established a new national political arena with a central government of great potential, power, and authority. The efforts of Treasury Secretary Alexander Hamilton to invigorate the federal government were not universally supported, however. Given all that was at stake and the geographic extent of the political battlefield, those opposing the Hamiltonian initiatives as detrimental to their own interests came together under the banner of Jeffersonian Republicanism in time to contest the congressional elections of 1794. Two years later they bitterly fought to wrest the presidency away from their still-dominant enemies (Chambers, 1963). These dramatic contests, occurring early in our history as a nation, were only the forerunners of ever-recurring conflict in American life and the constant need to mobilize in the battle for political power.

From the 1790s onward there were few national or state elections held in the absence of political parties, which organized and energized the regular combat taking place between the different interests on the scene. In their electoral functions and appearance, these political parties have seemed to enjoy great stability over 200 years. Analysts have distinguished five distinct party systems, however: (1) the original Federalist-Republican system, which lasted until about 1815; (2) a Democratic-Whig system, between 1828 and the 1850s; (3) the first Republican-Democratic system, from 1860 to 1896; (4) a second such system, lasting between 1896 and 1932; and (5) the New Deal party system, after 1932. These analytic distinctions are based on the lineup of the particular interests and social groups supporting each party—not occasionally and haphazardly, but in a sustained, repetitive fashion in election after election throughout the years of a particular party system. Each system has been bounded by an electoral realignment in which major shifts in voting choice occurred among these groups—shifts powerful enough, and long-lasting enough, to fundamentally change the shape of subsequent party warfare (Chambers and Burnham, 1975; Kleppner et al., 1981).

In addition to these electoral shifts, sharp variations and significant changes have occurred in the reach and importance of political parties throughout our history. Given contemporary attitudes toward parties, their role, power, and, most critically, the centrality of their place in the American political system, we might consider a somewhat different delineation of the changing shape of the partisan dimension in the American political universe. According to this view, the chronology consists of (1) a pre-party era from the 1790s to the late 1830s; (2) a party era from the 1830s to the 1890s; (3) a post-party era from the 1890s to the 1950s; and (4) a nonparty era ever since (Silbey, 1991).

The justification for arranging American party history in this way grows out of the different kinds of political institutions, norms, and behavior that have *predominated* in each era. Thus, although two parties have always been on the scene, only once—from 1838 to 1893—did parties totally dominate the American political landscape. Before 1838 they were incompletely developed and seen as foreign, unwelcome, and, one hoped, temporary intrusions into public affairs. Since the 1890s, they have been in sharp decline throughout the nation's political system, plummeting to their present position of limited relevance to most people in a nonparty, candidate-centered age (Formisano, 1974; Wallace, 1968, 1973; Wattenberg, 1986).

FACTIONS ORGANIZED AROUND TEMPORARY ISSUES

The original attempts to establish national parties in the 1790s, for example, were incomplete. These first parties were only partially accepted by politically involved people, and they ultimately foundered, not just as electoral coalitions but as institutions having any role at all to play in American politics. They were neither deeply rooted in the political soil nor all-encompassing in their influence and importance. To be sure, some coordinated efforts were made to select candidates, manage campaigns, attract voters, and bring legislators and other office holders under the discipline of party. From Washington to the state capitals, party labeling and party coordination of political activities took place, as did the polarized articulation of contrasting policies. All of these practices were repeated in successive election campaigns and in meetings of Congress and the state legislatures. Federalists and Republicans seemed to be everywhere (Banner, 1970; Fischer, 1965; Banning, 1978; Goodman, 1964).

Nevertheless, there was always an intermittent, ad hoc quality to all of these efforts and a casual attitude toward the partisan forms. Although these early combatants had much ideological vigor, they were quite deficient organizationally. There was little coordination of party warfare between the national level and the political battles in the states. The network of institutions needed to mobilize voters and to present each party's policy stances was only partially developed and erratic in its activities and relevance. In some places, such as New York and North Carolina, these institutions were built quite early and were used extensively. Elsewhere, party organization was not even rudimentary (Formisano, 1974, 1981, 1983). Early political development remained elite focused rather than popular. The voting behavior of the relatively small electorate remained quite volatile and was only occasionally party oriented throughout the years of Federalist-Republican battles. It was not until later years that election days were characterized by sustained partisan alignments and behavior (Benson, Silbey, and Field, 1978; Bohmer, 1978; McCormick, 1982).

The full development of political parties in the United States was hampered in this early period by a powerful mindset against them, combined with little appreciation of their potential usefulness in an expansive, pluralist society. There was a profound distrust of any institution that organized and sustained domestic political conflict. Such distrust originated in the still-potent eighteenth-century fear that recurrent internal conflict endangered all republics. Parties, by organizing such conflict, made matters worse and jeopardized a nation's very survival (Shalope, 1972; Watts, 1987).

According to some scholars of this early period, therefore, even to label the institutions of the 1790s as parties distorts the record, given the strong evidence of their weakness, incompleteness, and irrelevance as well as the hostility toward them. Indeed, as one such scholar has written, "until the idea exists that parties are legitimate, that there are necessary divisions within a complex society, that there are continuous, enduring group conflicts that can and should be organized in a sustained, partisan political fashion, [it is] anachronistic" to call what existed in the decade and more after the Constitution "anything but factions organized around temporary issues" (Benson, 1981:24). In a pre-party era, Federalists and Republicans could be little else.

ESSENTIAL TO THE EXISTENCE OF OUR INSTITUTIONS

The failure to establish political parties as a normal part of American politics lasted for about a half-century after the ratification of the Constitution. The era ended because political activities had increased in scope and vigor, thus demanding a more extensive, powerful, and permanent system to deal with the problems of American politics. As the nation continued to grow after 1815, as incipient sectional tensions and regional rivalries became more vocal, as social antagonisms grew along religious and nationality lines, and as different economic interests renewed their battles to control government and its policies, it soon became clear that the pressing political needs of a pluralist nation of great size and many conflicts required political institutions beyond the Constitution and the limited forms of organization that had occasionally been present (Formisano, 1971; McCormick, 1967; Shade, 1981; Silbey, 1991).

The push for parties came out of three streams: the need to manage and guide a rapidly growing electorate; the need to bring together like-minded interests and factions into coalitions in order to win elections; and the need to enact specific policies in an arena where real differences over public policy existed alongside perceptions of serious public danger if the wrong policies, people, or groups dominated. For ten years after 1815, political excitement increased in intensity in America—initially at the state and local levels, stimulated by battles over economic development and social cohesion, and then in renewed contests over national problems and the presidency. As these conflicts developed, they involved more people than ever before, inasmuch as suffrage requirements for adult white males had eased up dramatically. Political leaders had to give sustained attention to dealing with a larger electorate that had spread much further geographically than ever before and had been aroused by the renewal of a wide range of bitter policy and group conflicts (Nichols, 1967; McCormick, 1967; Benson, 1961; Williamson, 1960; Watson, 1981).

These political leaders were successful in finding a way to deal with their political problem. At first, the impulse toward both mass politics and collective political organization originated with outsider movements such as the Anti-Masons, which took the lead, ahead of the conventional political leadership, in their willingness to mobilize the masses. Their example was not lost for very long on many astute political observers, who were searching for ways to structure the changing political landscape. New York's Martin Van Buren and his well-organized associates—the Albany Regency—learned from what was happening around them, made the case for parties, and acted collectively, accepting the direction and discipline that such action entailed. As Michael Wallace (1973:138) has argued, "for the individualism so dear to Whig and Republican theory [they] . . . substituted an almost servile worship of organization." A Van Buren lieutenant, Churchill Cambreleng, set forth the new tone clearly and forcefully in a speech before Congress in 1826: Political parties, he argued, are "indispensable to every Administration [and] . . . essential to the existence of our institutions; and if . . . an evil, [they are ones] we must endure, for the preservation of our civil liberty." But parties "never yet injured any free country. . . . The conflict of parties is a noble conflict—of mind to mind, genius to genius" (*Register of Debates*, 1826:1546; Remini, 1951; Benson, 1961).

The original organizational impulse and the assault on ideological antipartyism culminated in the election of Andrew Jackson in 1828. But that victory, far from being an end to party development, was in fact the beginning. In the subsequent decade, the intellectual defense of parties and the building up of partisan institutions utterly transformed the political scene into something quite different from anything that had preceded it. The excitement of the process by which the Jackson administration defined itself, and the persistent battles over the presidential succession and economic policy that followed, completed the movement toward a partisan-dominated nation (Benson, 1961; Formisano, 1971; Watson, 1981).

Whatever hesitancies some politically involved Americans continued to have about these organizations, and however intense the demands of these organizations for the subordination of the individual in the collective, more and more political leaders played by the new political rules in order to achieve their specific policy goals. The party impulse spread into the camp of Jackson's opponents. Still deeply imbued with the old-style antiparty attitudes of an earlier era, the Whigs (reluctantly at first) adopted the style of, and argument for, political parties. Ultimately, many of them became powerful articulators of the necessity for party. They built up their organization as well and even celebrated the political parties (Silbey, 1991).

This development meant more than rhetorical acceptance and behavioral exhortation. What occurred moved from intermittence, individualism, and voluntarism to persistence, structure, and organized professionalism. Parties sank very deep roots into the system, among leaders and followers alike, and came to shape all but a small part of the American political world. Organizationally, their arrival meant the building of patterned, systematic institutions to do the necessary work. Elections were frequent in nineteenth-century America. Parties were always nominating, running, or preparing to nominate or run some candidate for one or another of the great array of elected offices. As they emerged, parties designated candidates at every level, replacing individual and group free-wheeling with disciplined processes of choice. They collectively shaped what they would say and controlled all other aspects of the mobilization of the electorate. Party organizations grew into a regular array of committees, legislative caucuses, and conventions, designed to hammer out decisions about candidates, priorities, and programs, to run the actual campaigns, and to bring the voters to the polling booth on the day appointed.

These institutions had a symmetrical shape across time and place. Their organization was decentralized, but they looked, and generally acted, the same everywhere. Wherever parties were present, their constituent elements and responsibilities remained constant from state to state across the country (McCormick, 1967; Gienapp, 1982; Silbey, 1991).

The heart and soul of nineteenth-century party organization were the conventions that were held at every political level from the local to the national. Conventions had occasionally met earlier in American history, but it was only from the late 1830s onward that they became a widespread and normal part of the political scene. Each level of activity replicated the pattern whereby people were called together to hammer out policy initiatives, choose candidates, and select delegates to the next highest level convention. Topping all such activities was the national convention held every four years. All of these meetings, at every level, were cloaked with tremendous power. Their authority in party affairs was considered to be total, as they represented the place where major decisions were made about all things (Thornton, 1978; Silbey, 1991).

Once the conventions were over and the party's candidates had been chosen, with their arguments clarified and formalized, the Whigs and Democrats proceeded to disseminate each campaign's political discourse through a growing network of partisan newspapers, pamphleteering, and organized mass rallies. The parties' platforms originally codified each party's stance. In the debates that followed, Whigs and Democrats presented quite polarized images to the voters. They remained forever nose to nose. Party leaders drew on a rich pool of ideas about policies to sharpen differences among the voters overall and to draw together their own tribes. In their platforms, newspaper editorials, and campaign speeches, they enshrined the religious, nationality, sectional, and cultural animosities between groups, reflected the most up-to-date differences over the economic direction of the newly liberated, rapidly developing society, and provided a way for politically involved Americans to understand the world and its problems. The party leaders also became adept at mobilizing the tensions that were present and at bringing them together into large policy frameworks. In sorting out the political world, they defined what was at stake and linked the different outlooks and perspectives into a whole (Benson, 1961; Howe, 1979; Silbey, 1991).

Each political party in this dialogue aggregated society's many interests and social groups in a selective way, reaching out not to everyone but only to a portion of the electorate. What resulted, in the 1840s, was a party of social homogeneity and governmental vigor in all things, economic and social—the Whigs. Another party, the Democrats, espoused social and ethnic pluralism and was suspicious of too much government activity in human affairs. Both parties clearly and repeatedly articulated the differences between them. They hammered home, once again, how "utterly irreconcilable" they were—"as opposite to each other as light and darkness, as knowledge and ignorance" (*Louisville Journal*, 1852; Benson, 1961; Holt, 1978).

The extent of party organization varied across the country and was never as complete or as tight as party leaders desired. But despite all of their reservations and the incompleteness of the structure, the ideal of comprehensiveness was always sought. The many elements constituting an efficient model were present, if not quite as developed as they would yet become. More to the point, I suggest, was the trajectory of party development and the similarity of party operations across the nation. There was a more widespread commitment than ever before, a movement in a particular direction, and a shift in values toward collectivities as the means to promote and achieve political goals. The atmosphere and mechanics of each campaign became the same everywhere (Shade, 1981; Silbey, 1991).

More critical still, popular voting behavior became extremely party driven from the end of the 1830s, as the battles over policies penetrated popular consciousness and the parties' mobilization machinery matured. Turnout at the polls dramatically increased over earlier levels in response to each party's extensive mobilization activities. When voters cast their ballots, their sustained commitment to a party in election after election became the norm in a way that was never the case before. Each succeeding election was viewed not as a separate contest involving new issues or new personalities but as yet another opportunity to vote for, and reaffirm, an individual's support for his or her party and what it represented. As the editor of the Albany *Argus* put it in the 1840s, "the first duty of a Democrat is to vote; the next to vote the regular ticket." Each voter did both much more often than not (Albany *Argus*, 1846; Kleppner, 1979; Formisano, 1971; Benson, 1961).

By the beginning of the 1840s the American people were worshipping more and more at the "shrine of party." Their commitment to the parties moved beyond instrumentalist calculation of the rewards of specific policies or the benefits to be gained from particular candidates. Each party's popular support was rooted in the intense, deep, persistent loyalty of individual voters to their party home. The electoral pattern furthered such commitment. Party warfare split Americans decisively and evenly. The battles between Whigs and Democrats, and later between the Republicans and Democrats, were highly competitive. Close electoral contests were the rule. Indeed, their closeness reinforced the drive to organize and turn out the vote and to expand, even further, the commitment to individual parties and to the party system as a preferred mode of organizing the nation's political affairs and settling its major problems (Silbey, 1967, 1977, 1985; Gienapp, 1982).

As a result, parties had great vitality in the 1840s and thereafter. They were everywhere. For the first time, they were considered both natural and necessary. They came to control all but a small part of American politics, and they staffed the government through their patronage operations. Once in office, the party leaders were expected to carry out the policies their party stood for—as, indeed, they attempted to do. Although elaborate policymaking was unknown in the middle of the nineteenth century, whatever efforts were made occurred in response to party promises and arguments. Finally, both the appeals of the two major parties and the loyalty of voters and leaders to them occurred at a national level. Whatever sectional tensions existed in the United States, as the parties developed, both the Whigs and the Democrats were able to attract support and make their influence felt, regardless of the pressures to divide along other gradients (Silbey, 1967; McCormick, 1986; Formisano, 1981; Shade, 1981).

Two major disruptions of the political system—first the electoral realignment of the 1850s and then the Civil War—demonstrated that the passionate commitment to one's party had limits. The increase in ideological intensity along sectional lines in the 1850s and 1860s shook the political nation severely. It was a destructive, chastening experience for those in command of the traditional political channels. Nevertheless, when the smoke cleared after a series of intense voter shifts after the death of one party and the rise of another, the essential structure of American politics remained largely as before. Electoral coalitions were reshaped, sectional tensions became the norm, and one party—the Republican party—was no longer national in its reach. But the central reality of partisan-defined and -shaped political activities stood firm. The nation's agenda and institutions, as well as the reactions of both leaders and voters to the events of the day, continued to reflect the dominance of existing patterns of two-party politics and the intense loyalties that had been such a crucial aspect of them since the late 1830s (Gienapp, 1987; Silbey, 1977, 1991).

After the Civil War, the reach of political parties expanded further than ever before as the party era continued to make its way in American life. New partisan forms, such as the urban political machine, developed to meet new needs. But, in general, the structures, appeal, and meaning of parties remained much as they had been for the preceding thirty years. Much emphasis was put on reinforcing party loyalty and eliciting automatic partisan responses to new issues and conflicts, whatever their nature. Even as society began to change dramatically from an agricultural to an industrial-urban one, Democrats and Republicans continued to confront each other in the well-disciplined, predictable phalanxes of people deeply committed to powerful, closely competitive institutions designed to fulfill group and individual needs (Kleppner, 1979; Jensen, 1971; McSeveney, 1971; McCormick, 1981).

The extent of the partisan imperative in nineteenth-century American politics was demonstrated, finally, by the behavior of the many challenges to the Democratic-Whig-Republican hegemony. From the beginning of this partisan political era, there were regular protests against the central tenets of the political nation from people ever impatient with or continually frustrated by the national parties, their advocacy, and their command of the system. Yet, the way in which these challenges interacted with politics suggests their adherence to many of the central political values of their era, despite their persistent outsider questioning, stance, and self-image. Between 1838 and the early 1890s, minor parties organized and campaigned much as the major political parties did; they also nominated candidates, thought about who they wished to appeal to, and sought to mobilize particular voters behind their policies. Most held national conventions and issued national platforms. Somewhat more sporadically, they called state, district, and local conventions as well. They staged campaign rallies and organized to get out the vote. They issued pamphlets and published party newspapers. In emulating their enemies to the extent that they did, they underscored the power of the partisan impulse on this particular political landscape (Holt, 1973; Kleppner, 1979).

TOO IMPORTANT TO BE LEFT TO POLITICIANS

This party era lasted into the 1890s. With the electoral realignment of that decade, the role of the parties began to shift dramatically. Launched against them was a full-scale assault that included shrewd (and ultimately successful) legislative efforts to weaken their organizations, their command of the landscape, and the powerful partisanship that had made the system what it was. Parties found themselves less able than before to resist the reformist onslaught. As a result, the equilibrium between them and their challengers was upset. The churning and destabilization of the electoral landscape led to profound systemic disintegration. From the 1890s on, the nation's politics started to become nonpartisan. The vigor of American electoral politics, rooted in the passionate confrontations between two well-developed and dominant parties, gave way to an antiparty, and ultimately nonparty, way of carrying on political activities. America's political ways went from focusing specifically on the ceremonies and rituals of partisan polarization to appealing, organizing, and working beyond parties. As that happened, Americans went from strong commitment to one party and angry dissatisfaction with the other to vituperative dissatisfaction with all parties (McCormick, 1981; Burnham, 1965, 1970; McGerr, 1986).

There was no sudden upheaval or coup d'etat. The new era opened with an extended period of transition during which many of the institutions, values, and approaches of the past continued to be important. At the national level, after 1896, the Democrats vigorously contested the new Republican electoral hegemony in the traditional manner. The two parties' internal processes of defining themselves, resolving their divisions, and choosing their candidates also remained largely as they had been. The same was true of their external behavior during campaigns as well as their approach to government staffing, responsibilities, and policy-making. But with the loss of electoral competitiveness in many parts of the country in the 1890s, the fires of political confrontation cooled. Organizing elements became flabby as the losers in one-sided electoral situations lost workers, coverage, heart, and vigor. As a result, politics shifted into new channels. At the same time, as a major element of the nation's transformation, an alternate vision of political propriety developed and then took firm hold. The basic ambivalence this vision manifested toward the political world evolved into a powerful negativism stimulated by what was seen as excessive political expediency and increasingly sordid partisan manipulation of democratic politics. Coupled with the rise of new, very powerful external forces that were reshaping the society, this negativism eventually imposed its view of propriety on the American system (Benson, 1955; Hays, 1957, 1959; McCormick, 1981).

As Richard Jensen has succinctly noted, the Progressives sought, early in the new era, "to banish all forms of traditionalism—boss control, corrupt practices, big business intervention in politics, 'ignorant' voting and excessive power in the hands of hack politicians" (Jensen, 1978:27). For the Progressives, political reform, especially the concerted attack on the parties, was a prerequisite to all else they wished to accomplish. Party politics was corrupt, irrational, and unprincipled. And so they redefined politics as a detached search for objective, and therefore correct, policies—a search unrelated to the passions, rituals, self-interest, and deception connected with political parties (Hays, 1957; Wiebe, 1967; Ranney, 1975).

In the first decade and a half of the twentieth century, the Progressives and their allies were able to take a series of legislative actions that attacked and ultimately uncoupled several of the links between parties and voters. They energized the efforts under way since the 1880s to reform election laws—especially, to institute voter registration and gov-ernment-controlled official ballots. Their successful passage of a large number of such legislative initiatives had a major impact on the political system. Nonpartisan electoral reforms weakened the partisan imperative by challenging, first, the politicians' control of nominations and the election process and, then, the party-dominated, unrestrained wheeling and dealing over policy priorities (Kousser, 1974; McCormick, 1981).

At the same time, in the economic realm the Progressives successfully promoted the growth of government power and a shift in focus from generalized, distributive policies to new regulative channels, which demanded technical expertise, well-developed budgeting and financial skills, and an ability to deal with sophisticated control mechanisms—rather than the more generalist negotiating talents of party leaders, which had previously dominated a simpler, more limited government apparatus and its activities. As a result, there was a steady increase in the number of, and activities by, specialized nonpartisan interest groups, each of which sought to shape specific government policies without the mediation of political parties. In addition, government eventually took over responsibility for matters the parties had traditionally controlled, social welfare being one prime example. The nonpartisan civil service continued to expand—challenging, and ultimately weakening, the partisan patronage resources that had been so important to party operations (Benson, 1955; McCormick, 1981; Wiebe, 1967).

All of this indicated the success, over several decades, of what Daniel T. Rodgers calls "the explosion of scores of aggressive, politically active pressure groups into the space left by the recession of traditionally political loyalties" (1982:114). This nonpartisan occupation had significant long-range effects on the political nation. The emerging organizational society of technicians, bureaucrats, and impersonal decisionmakers had no faith in, or commitment to, mass politics—especially as expressed through the parties. Although no one group was solely responsible for the changes that occurred, all reforming groups, whatever their interests, aims, and nature, shared a commitment to move in the same direction. As their numbers and reach increased, their vision grew to be quite popular. The Progressives' political agenda was antipartisan in direction and vigorously pushed (McCormick, 1981; Hays, 1957, 1959).

The range of changes under way worked its way through the political nation slowly. The impact of each of the pressures was cumulative. From the first, the reform challenge meant that parties had competition at the center of the political world for the first time since the 1830s. For decades well into the 1940s, however, there were different balances between old and new. In some areas, parties retained vestiges of influence and a capacity to shape events, as evidenced by the electoral vigor of the urban political machines and the success of their policy initiatives. For a time, during the New Deal years, there was evidence that political parties still had a strong kick, reminiscent of an earlier time and perhaps suggestive of a return to dominance by them. An electoral realignment in the 1930s not only restored the Democrats to power with a new agenda but also invigorated voter loyalties, fired by the Depression and the Rooseveltian response. These loyalties took deep hold and shaped much about electoral politics and something about policy, as well, for a generation thereafter. The era from the 1890s into the 1950s, therefore, was a mixed, post-party one in which, amid the signs of party decay in government affairs, policymaking, and the structure of electoral involvement, partisanship still anchored much voter choice as it had in the past (Campbell et al., 1960; Burnham, 1970; Andersen, 1979; Silbey, 1991).

ANARCHY TEMPERED BY DISTRUST

But the partisan honeymoon of the 1930s and 1940s, however powerful and dramatic, was only a deviation from the long-range pattern of party collapse. The decline of political parties resumed and quickened as the New Deal began to fade from popular memory after World War II. Other, extraparty elements became even more firmly entrenched on the landscape. Over time, parties as organizers and as symbols of the battles over public policies lost more and more of their relevance. Party control of the electoral process continued to weaken. Shifts in the way political information was presented—moving from partisan to nonpartisan sources—had been under way throughout the twentieth century. Party newspapers, with their relentless, clear, direct, and unambiguous message, gave way to a different journalistic style serving a broader clientele. Cheap, sensationalist, nonpartisan, and often cynical about politics, newspapers came into their own at the turn of the century. But they failed to provide quick and easily absorbed partisan guides, as their predecessors had done—an oversight that had a long-term effect (McGerr, 1986; Burnham, 1970, 1982).

This transformation accelerated greatly with television's rise in the 1950s. In its style of presentation and dominance of the scene, television even more sharply cut off much of the partisan shaping of what was at stake—a central factor in mobilizing voters into loyal party channels in the nineteenth century. Parties had once been able to argue that all political legitimacy lay with them. Independent newspapers and television challenged that assumption in both direct and indirect ways. Television, to the parties' detriment, emphasized imagery and personality against the allegedly artificial styles and deceptive auras of the political parties; it also ignored or downplayed the distinguishing features of parties that made them important to the political process (Ranney, 1983).

In the post–World War II years, as well, the size, reach, and influence of the federal government became the central fact of the political nation. With this growth of state power, a partisan-directed model of activities and behavior lost its last vestiges of importance among many Americans. Instead, the interest group pattern, unmediated by partisan priority-setting and influence, finally replaced it. The well-entrenched, nonpartisan, economic interest groups began to forge and make permanent the kinds of links with the legislative and administrative branches that they had been groping toward since the end of the partisan political nation in the 1890s. Their earlier belief that parties were a barrier to their best interests was succeeded by a growing sense of the irrelevance of parties to their activities at any level. From the 1930s on, the expansion of nonpartisan interest groups accelerated, reaching well beyond their original economic base among the new industrial forces to encompass any segment of the society that sought government assistance. By the 1960s, every policy impulse had its own organization that moved readily into the legislative and administrative arenas, largely as if parties did not exist. Many different groups, with many different agendas and enthusiasms, articulated issues, mobilized voters, financed campaigns, and organized legislative and administrative support for their limited goals. These in turn became vested interests in their areas of concern and dominant as articulators of specific demands. The result was a cacophony of voices, continuous discordant battling, and, often, policy fragmentation (Lowi, 1979).

At the same time, in the 1960s, the legitimacy of parties was subjected to a renewed assault, echoing a theme once dominant and now reborn with a virulence and power long forgotten. All of the earlier deficiencies of parties, from corruption to elite manipulation and the denial of democracy, were once again widely rehearsed. Much media commentary took up the assault and gave it a repetitive reality, especially during such unpleasant episodes as the Democratic National Convention of 1968. This unrelenting negative commentary took a toll. Its intellectual offensive against parties, coupled with the massive shifts in communications—and both resting on the Progressives' changing of the playing field and the rules of the game—added up in such a way as to impel the creation of a new nonparty political nation (Ranney, 1975; Burnham, 1982).

All of the antiparty tendencies at play, which had become quite clear by the end of the 1950s, determined the course of the next decade. A *New York Times* reporter later argued that John F. Kennedy, at the outset of the 1960s, was "the last great representative of the politics of loyalty, human intermediation, compromise and tradition" (1980:E19). With his death, the parties' last bastion—the electoral arena—gave way. Throughout the 1960s, there was certainly a profound shift in the ways in which mass politics was organized, its rituals were displayed, and its supporters were mobilized. Party-dominated mass meetings, conventions, and campaign rallies continued, but they were in a prolonged state of decay and became increasingly irrelevant to the country's political business. The parties' ability to coalesce a range of interests was gone. Although national party conventions still nominated and labeled candidates, they had less and less influence over the actual process of choosing who the party would put forward. Delegates were no longer the key players they once had been. They had lost their bargaining, reviewing, and reflecting power. In Richard Jensen's apt summing up, more and more "candidates for office selected themselves" (1981:219) by mobilizing the nonpartisan resources on the political scene. This situation affected the subsequent runs for office as well. In many campaigns, party labels became less prevalent than they once had been. Increasingly, candidates preferred to run as individuals, emphasizing their personal qualities rather than their adherence to party norms.

The impact of the successful century-long assault against parties on the way the American voter engaged in politics was enormous and emblematic of the whole thrust of the post-1893 American political nation. First, individual involvement in the electoral system changed dramatically over the years. American voters in 1990 no longer behaved as their ancestors did in 1890. The size of the electorate expanded throughout the twentieth century as various legal and social constraints on the participation of particular social groups fell away. But while that was happening, popular interest in politics waned. It could be reinvigorated from time to time, as in the New Deal years, but once again the trend line was clear: downward, toward popular nonparticipation. All of the destabilizing elements at work against political parties was coterminous with a massive fall-off in voter involvement, demonstrated most starkly by the steep decline in turnout at the polls over the course of the twentieth century. By the 1980s, in fact, a sizable "party of nonvoters" existed on the American scene. This group was, at best, sporadically mobilized; it consisted of people eligible to vote but who usually did not do so (Burnham, 1965, 1970, 1982).

Added to popular deinvolvement was popular partisan dealignment. When they did come to the polls, the voters demonstrated that they had become increasingly unstuck from party moorings and caught up, instead, in what Burnham (1973:39) refers to as a "volcanic instability." The all but automatic identification with parties became the minor key in voter behavior. Whatever the power of certain economic or other issues to reawaken such party identification for a while, such issues became less and less influential as time passed. Whatever their differences, whatever distinct ideological and policy stances they fostered, parties could no longer draw voters to them as they had once routinely done. The electorate, in Everett Ladd's terms, less and less considered "voting for 'my party' a sociological or psychological imperative" (1985:2). Each election, at every level of political activity, became a new throw of the dice; and the electorate behaved differently each time, with the ordering of choice among many voters between the parties increasingly unpredictable from contest to contest. "The politics of the 1930s and 1940s resembled a nineteenth century battlefield," one scholar wrote, "with two opposing armies arrayed against each other in more or less close formation; politics today is an altogether messier affair, with large numbers of small detachments engaged over a vast territory, and with individuals and groups frequently changing sides" (King, 1978:372).

Given all this volatility and the absence of strong, widespread partisan influences across the voting universe, electoral strategy had to shift. Candidates, already themselves free from many party constraints, no longer ran for office primarily by mobilizing the party faithful, if they did so at all. There were no longer enough of them to do so. Rather, their efforts centered on appealing to uncommitted, or partially committed, voters. Campaign advertising almost never identified candidates with their party, emphasizing their personal attributes instead. Who or what an individual was, rather than a party's policy stance or deeply rooted partisan loyalties, became the centerpiece of political affairs. In those offices where incumbents seemed all but immune from overturn, such as the House of Representatives, such campaigning turned more and more on the emphasis of extreme personal deficiencies (King, 1978; Brady, 1988).

All this was of a piece. By the late 1980s there could be no uncertainty about current differences from America's political past. The contrast is marked, indeed. The nineteenth-century political nation reflected a culture that sought first to bring people into the system and then to tame them and their desires through disciplined collectivities. America's powerful individualism, it was felt, needed such discipline. Toward the end of the twentieth century, the political process powerfully highlighted that individualism, becoming a system in which a premium was placed on the seeking of individual rather than party-defined objectives. The reputation of political parties continued to plummet—irreversibly, it seemed. Parties were increasingly considered "at best interlopers between the sovereign people and their elected officials and, at worst, rapacious enemies of honest and responsible government" (Ranney, 1978a:24). Few people seemed to disagree or care. All of this negativism was a very far cry from the celebrations of parties and their role that had once filled the American scene so forcefully.

PART TWO

The Evolving State of Party Organization

2

Party Organization at the State Level

JOHN F. BIBBY

In the face of a changing and often unfriendly environment, political parties in the American states have demonstrated adaptability and resiliency. This capacity to cope with the forces of political change has meant, of course, that the parties have undergone substantial alteration. Indeed, today's state party bears little resemblance to either the old-style organization of the late nineteenth century or the organizations that existed in the 1950s and 1960s.

The state party organization at the turn of the century was often a hierarchically run operation that was closely tied to local machines, fed by federal, state, and local patronage, and frequently supported and influenced by corporate interests. In many of the states, these old-style party organizations were capable of controlling nominations and providing the resources needed to conduct general election campaigns. They placed great emphasis on mobilizing their supporters on election day. In this activity, they were greatly assisted by an absence of popular cultural support for independent voters, who evaluated candidates on their merits. Independents were often called "mugwumps" and scorned as "traitors" and "corrupt sellers of their votes." Walter Dean Burnham has characterized turn-of-the-century organizations as "militarist" in the sense that they drilled their supporters to turn out and vote a straight party ticket (Burnham, 1970:72–23).

Progressive reformers early in this century sought to undermine the organizations' bases of power by instituting the direct primary system of nomination to diminish their control over nominations, the civil service system of public employment to severely limit their patronage, and corrupt-practices legislation to cut off some of their sources of financing (Mayhew, 1986:212–237). These reforms, particularly the direct primary, had the desired effect. The hierarchically organized state party organization had largely passed from the scene by the 1920s. The Republican and Democratic state party organizations that replaced them had vastly reduced influence over nominations and gradually lost the ability to direct state-level campaigns. By the early 1960s state party organizations were in a weakened condition in all but a few states (Key, 1956:271; Epstein, 1986:144–153).

Since the 1960s state parties have demonstrated their adaptive capacity when faced with new challenges and competitors for influence. These potentially party-weakening influences have included (1) a weakening of partisan ties among the voters—that is, a dealignment of the electorate; (2) the emergence of candidate-centered campaigns run by candidates' personal organizations, instead of by party organizations; and (3) the rise of political action committees (PACs) as a major source of political money. Republican and Democratic parties at the state level have also been affected by the process of party organizational change occurring at the national level, especially the development of strengthened national party committees.

After exploring the legal and electoral environment in which state party organizations must operate, this essay describes the processes of adaptation and change that have occurred within these organizations during the decades of the 1970s and 1980s. The development of more professionalized state party organizations capable of providing campaign assistance to their candidates is analyzed to demonstrate the remarkable durability of the organizations. The changing national-state party relationship and the implications of the heightened levels of intraparty integration are also explored.

THE CHANGING LEGAL ENVIRONMENT OF STATE PARTIES

In most Western democracies, political parties are considered to be private associations much like the Rotarians, Elks, or Sons of Norway and, as such, have been permitted to conduct their business largely unregulated by government. American political parties, however, can be likened to public utilities in the sense that they perform essential public functions (e.g., making nominations, contesting elections, organizing the government) that have sufficient impact upon the public to justify governmental regulation (Epstein, 1986: Ch. 6).

State governments' most significant regulatory device has been the requirement that the parties nominate their candidates via the direct primary. Before the direct primary was instituted, party leaders could exert substantial influence over party nominating caucuses and conventions. By involving ordinary voters in the selection of party nominees, the direct primary has reduced the capacity of party leaders to control nominations. It has also encouraged candidates to form personal campaign organizations in order to win primary elections.

But the state regulatory process goes well beyond party nominating procedures. State laws determine the eligibility criteria a party must meet in order to be listed on the general election ballot, regulate who can vote in partisan primaries, and govern campaign finances. State regulations frequently extend to matters of internal organization such as procedures for selecting officers, composition of party committees, dates and locations of meetings, and powers of party committees. Only five states (Alaska, Delaware, Hawaii, Kentucky, and North Carolina) do not specify in state law some aspect of the parties' internal organizational operations (Advisory Commission of Intergovernmental Relations, 1986:128). Although the content of statutory regulation varies from state to state, the net effect of state laws has been to mold state parties into quasi-public agencies and to limit party leaders' flexibility in devising strategies to achieve organizational goals.

The legal status of political parties as quasi-public entities that are subject to extensive governmental regulation is, however, currently in the process of modification as a result of a series of Supreme Court decisions (Epstein, 1986:189–199; 1989:239–274). These decisions have extended to parties the rights of free political association protected by the First and Fourteenth Amendments. By according constitutional protection to parties, the Court has struck down a series of state-imposed restrictions upon political parties.

In the case of *Tashjian v. Connecticut* (93 L. Ed. 514 [1986]), the Court ruled that Connecticut could not prevent voters registered as independents from voting in a Republican primary, if the state Republican party wanted to allow independents as well as registered Republicans to vote in partisan primaries. Although the Connecticut case has potential long-term implications for state regulatory policy, its immediate consequences appear to be quite limited. Only a few state parties have sought to open their primaries to independents, as they are clearly authorized to do under the *Tashjian* decision. Nor is there any realistic likelihood that state parties will use the power seemingly granted them in *Tashjian* to abolish state-mandated direct primaries. The direct primary is simply too popular and well ingrained in the political culture (Epstein, 1989:260–274).

In 1989 the Supreme Court followed its *Tashjian* decision by further limiting state regulatory authority over parties in a case arising under California laws (*Eu v. San Francisco County Democratic Central Committee*, 109 S. Ct. 1013 [1989]). Asserting that California statutes violated the political parties' rights of free association, the Court struck down state laws that banned party organizations from endorsing candidates in primary elections (pre-primary endorsements), limited the length of state party chairmen's terms to two years, and required that the state party chairmanship be rotated every two years among residents of northern and southern regions of the state.

In these cases, the Supreme Court has clearly indicated that there are limits on the extent of regulation that may be imposed by the states. In the future, party leaders should therefore have greater flexibility to advance their organizations' interests. It is unlikely, however, that political parties will ever by completely "privatized" and allowed to operate as strictly private organizations.

THE STATE ELECTORAL ENVIRONMENT

There is great diversity among the states in terms of the election laws, the strength of their political parties, political traditions, and citizens' partisan, ideological, and policy orientations. This diversity should not, however, obscure the common features of the electoral environment within which every state party must operate. Common to all the states are candidate-centered campaigns, an increasing role for PACs in funding campaigns, heightened interparty competition for state-wide offices, and high rates of reelection for incumbent members of Congress and state legislators.

Candidate-Centered Campaigns

Candidates run under party labels that help them attract votes from among the party adherents in the electorate, but there is nothing that forces them to let the party organizations run or participate in their campaigns (Sorauf, 1980:252). Indeed, there are substantial obstacles to party control of campaigns.

Candidates are encouraged to rely on their own personal campaign organizations by the direct primary system of nominations. Party organizations can rarely guarantee victory in the primaries for favored candidates. The direct primary, therefore, imposes a personal responsibility upon each candidate to create a campaign organization capable of winning the primary. This candidate organization is carried over to the general election because the resources of the party organization are seldom sufficient to ensure victory. The large numbers of offices that are contested as well as the frequency of elections in America strain and dilute the effectiveness of even the most dedicated and sophisticated party organizations.

Candidate independence from party organizations is also encouraged by the reduced role played by party affiliation in voter choices on election day. Voters commonly split their tickets—for example, by voting Republican in presidential elections but for Democrats in congressional and state office elections. In the American political culture, it is frequently advantageous not to be perceived as closely tied to a political party. Many voters glorify the candidate who stands above party.

Technological advances in campaigning have further stimulated candidates to rely on personal campaign organizations. Major races and even some state legislative contests now utilize polling, television and radio advertising, direct mail, computer-based targeting of precincts and voters, and professionalized campaign planning, management, and fund raising. Although party organizations can provide some of these services on a limited basis, candidates gain access to these campaign tools primarily by hiring political consultants. Indeed, campaign consulting has grown into a major industry. The firms that provide these services operate on a national scale.

The Growth of PACs

Most commentary on the role of PACs in campaigns has focused on their role in congressional elections and their tendency to support incumbents. The expanding role of PACs is not, however, transforming campaigns only for the Senate and House; it is affecting races of state offices as well. The level of PAC financing of state-level campaigns varies from state to state depending upon state regulations. But, as is true in congressional elections, PACs have provided an increasing share of campaign dollars in state contests. In New York, for example, 60 percent of the $11 million raised during a five-year period in the 1980s for state legislative races came from PACs (Kerr, 1988:1, 7). Well-financed state-level PACs provide not only direct contributions to candidates for state office but also in-kind campaign services (Jones, 1984:172–213). State PACs also follow the congressional-level pattern of contributing primarily to incumbents. In 1986, for example, 80 percent of incumbent California legislators' receipts came from PACs and businesses, whereas only one-third of the much smaller amounts of money raised by challengers came from these sources (Sorauf, 1988:265).

PACs, of course, are potential competitors with the parties for a role in campaigns. By contributing directly to candidates rather than to parties, and by providing a major source of campaign financing to candidates, PACs encourage candidate-centered politics.

State-Level Competitiveness and Incumbent Reelection in Congressional and Legislative Races

Interparty Competition in Statewide Races. Across the country it is now possible for either party to win statewide elections. This is particularly true in presidential contests. For example, in 1988 the winning margin in twenty-one states was 54 percent or less of the popular vote, and in an additional fourteen states it was between 55 and 59 percent. Both the Republicans and the Democrats also have the capacity to win U.S. Senate and gubernatorial elections in virtually every state. This is true even of former one-party bastions such as the states of the Confederacy, where since 1966 only Georgia and Mississippi have failed to elect at least one Republican governor, and only Arkansas and Louisiana have failed to elect a Republican U.S. senator. Similarly, in traditional citadels of Republicanism such as Kansas, Maine, Nebraska, and North Dakota, the Democrats have won the governorship more frequently since the 1970s than the GOP. There is even evidence that, in the once solidly Democratic South, electoral competitiveness is seeping into lower-level state constitutional offices. In 1988 the GOP won statewide elections for Supreme Court judge, secretary of state, lieutenant governor, and railroad commissioner in Florida, North Carolina, and Texas.

Incumbent Advantage in Congressional and State Legislative Races. The results of most congressional and state legislative contests can be summarized in two words—"incumbents win"! Accordingly, only a limited proportion of House and state legislative seats normally change party control from election to election. Incumbent advantages make it difficult for both parties to recruit strong challengers to take on incumbents. This difficulty diminishes meaningful electoral competition and means that intense campaigns tend to be waged either in the small number of constituencies in which an incumbent may be considered vulnerable or in open seats, where no incumbent is seeking reelection.

Parties that for decades were the traditional minority parties within a state have had their greatest difficulty in achieving a competitive status in congressional and state legislative elections. For example, in spite of strong showings in gubernatorial elections, Democrats since 1968 have never controlled the Kansas Senate or the South Dakota House, and Republicans do not control a legislative chamber in the entire South. Indeed, GOP legislators are a rare commodity in Alabama, Arkansas, Louisiana, and Mississippi.

The pattern of meaningful competition in statewide elections and incumbent reelection in congressional and state legislative contests is related to the increasingly candidate-centered nature of American politics. Inasmuch as statewide races tend to emphasize individual candidates instead of party affiliations, it is possible for either Democrats or Republicans to win gubernatorial and Senate contests in each of the fifty states. At the same time, incumbent members of the House and state legislatures have been able to use their offices to build both personal followings among the voters and personal campaign organizations (often heavily funded by PAC funds) to gain a high level of electoral security. It is within this two-tiered electoral system that state party organizations must operate.

STRENGTHENED STATE PARTY ORGANIZATIONS

In the late 1960s and early 1970s the conventional wisdom among political observers was that parties were in a state of decline. There was even speculation about the possibility of partyless politics (Burnham, 1970). The likely future of parties seemed to be captured by the *Washington Post's* ranking political reporter, David Broder, who entitled his 1971 book *The Party's Over* (Broder, 1971). The prophets of party demise, however, have been proven wrong. Since the 1960s American state party organizations have become more professionalized and organizationally stronger in the sense that they can provide campaign services to their candidates. They still do not control nominations because of the direct primary, but many are playing an important role in campaigns. The state parties have also become more closely integrated with the national party organizations and are being utilized by those organizations in presidential, senatorial, and congressional elections.

Striking parallels exist between party development within the states and the resurgence of party organizations that has occurred at the national level (see Chapter 3 of this volume). Like the Republican and Democratic National Committees, state central committees have strengthened their fund-raising capacities and developed the ability to provide services to candidates. There are also parallels between the major campaign role now played nationally by the congressional and senatorial campaign committees and the emergence of the state legislative campaign committees as the principal party campaign resource in legislative races. In addition, both national and state parties have adapted to the growth of PACs by seeking to channel PAC funds to their candidates.

The Strengthening of State Party Organizations

The indicators of improved state party organizational strength include (1) permanent party headquarters, (2) professional leadership and staff, (3) adequate budgets, and (4) programs to maintain the state party structure, assist local party units, and support candidates and officeholders (Cotter et al., 1984:13–40; Advisory Commission on Intergovernmental Relations, 1986).

Permanent Headquarters. In the 1960s state party headquarters often had an ad hoc quality and led a transitory existence. As the state party was frequently run out of the home or office of its chairman, the headquarters moved from city to city depending upon the residence of its leader. As late as the 1970s, 10 percent of the headquarters lacked a permanent location (Huckshorn, 1976:254). The practice of moving the headquarters to the chairman's hometown has now been virtually abandoned. In its place, more and more state parties operate out of modern office facilities equipped with computer-based technology. The Florida Republicans operate a particularly high-tech headquarters, packed with computer hardware, telephone banks, and printing facilities, that in 1988 was funded by a budget of $6 million (Barnes, 1989:70; Sabato, 1988:91).

Professional Staffing. In the 1950s and 1960s it was common for a state headquarters to operate with minimal staff—often just a secretary or an executive director plus volunteers. Modern campaigning and party building, however, require more extensive and professional staffing. Virtually all state parties now have full-time professional leadership. Approximately 30 percent of state chairmen work full time in their positions, and almost all state parties have either a full-time chairman or an executive director (Cotter et al., 1984:16–19; Crotty, 1985:97).

The level of headquarters staffing fluctuates between election and nonelection years, and depends upon the financial condition of the party. The basic trend since the 1960s, however, has been growth in the size of staffs and greater division of labor and specialization within the headquarters. In addition to the chairman and executive director, a reasonably well-staffed headquarters is likely to include the positions of finance director, political director, comptroller, communication director, field operatives, and clerical personnel. Although the state parties have made substantial progress in developing more professional staffs, they constantly face the problem of high turnover in leadership and staff positions. For example, state chairmen serve an average of only two to three years, and staff members normally stay in their positions for less than two years (Cotter et al. 1984:18).

Budgets. Since the 1960s state party budgets have increased and, in some of the states (e.g., California, Florida, Indiana, New Jersey, and New York), annual budgets in excess of $1 million are now quite common. The state parties themselves have become more sophisticated in their fund-raising activities. When Alexander Heard published his classic study of campaign finance in 1960, he reported that two-thirds of the Republican state committees had centrally organized fund-raising operations and that the Democrats had generally failed to develop regularized fund-raising operations (Heard, 1960:218–222, 228–229). In the 1980s the Republican state committees continued to be more systematic and regularized in their fund raising, often having professional fund raisers on their staffs to operate direct-mail (sustaining-membership) programs as

TABLE 2.1
Assistance Provided by State Parties to Candidates
for State Office

Assistance/Service Provided	Republican	Democratic
Financial Contributions	90%	70%
Fund-raising Assistance	95	63
Polling	78	50
Media Consulting	75	46
Campaign Seminars	100	76
Coordinating PAC Contributions	52	31

Source: Advisory Commission on Intergovernmental Relations (1986:115).

well as large giver programs. The Democrats have continued to lag behind the GOP in developing regularized fund-raising programs, but they have made considerable progress since Heard did his study. Democratic state committees place greater emphasis than do the Republicans on fund-raising dinners, public funding through state income tax check-off systems, a small number of large contributors, unions, and such techniques as party-sponsored bingo games.

Party Activities: Party Building and Candidate Support. Since the 1960s state parties have expanded their activities in both party building and candidate support. In the sphere of party building, a larger share of Republican and Democratic parties now have regularized fund-raising operations, conduct voter identification/list maintenance/get-out-the-vote programs, publish newsletters, assist local party units, engage in issue development, and utilize public opinion polling.

The parties are also active in providing assistance to their candidates. Table 2.1 reports the results of a 1984 survey of state central committee activities conducted by the Advisory Commission on Intergovernmental Relations (ACIR). According to the ACIR, both Republican and Democratic state committees reported that they had provided a wide array of campaign assistance to candidates for state office. The Republicans were more likely to be involved in assisting their candidates than the Democrats.

Although the state parties are organizationally stronger and provide a broader array of campaign services than in the past, their role in campaigns is supplementary to that of the candidates' own personal campaign organizations. The job of the party is normally to provide technical services—polling, funds, get-out-the-vote services—as well as volunteers. For example, Republican state organizations frequently have major programs to make certain that their supporters cast absentee ballots when they will be out of town on election day. In 1988 the Florida GOP state organization spent $200,000 to send instructions on how to get an absentee ballot to 1 million voters (Babcock, 1988:A35).

Campaigning in the American states, however, is not party centered but candidate centered. Party organizations thus rarely manage campaigns. Instead, the candidates normally have their own headquarters and their own organization, which in statewide campaigns usually includes a group of advisers, a campaign manager, a research staff, campaign and media consultants, press aides, a field staff, a scheduler, fund raisers, and volunteers. An example of an unusually well-developed candidate organization was that of Senator Lloyd Bentsen (D-TX) in 1988. Bentsen's personal organization included field coordinators and co-coordinators in all of Texas's 254 counties, 100,000 volunteers, phone banks capable of contacting 2.8 million voters in key precincts, and a steering committee of 2,700 that read "like a Who's Who of every community in the state" (Kilday and Edgar, 1988:34A).

Republican-Democratic Differences. On the various indicators of party organizational strength considered in this section, Republican state committees generally score higher than do the Democrats. This is true in all sections of the country and normally the case even where the Republicans are a traditional minority party (Cotter et al., 1984:26–30; Jewell and Olson, 1988:63–70).

This Republican organizational strength advantage is also present at the national level (Reichley, 1985:175–202; Kayden and Mahe, 1985). It reflects not only a basic difference between the parties but also the fact that the party organization tends to be a more important campaign resource for Republican candidates than for Democrats. Democratic candidates and state organizations are more apt than their Republican counterparts to rely on the assistance of allied organizations such as labor unions, teachers, and social action groups (Cotter et al., 1984:137–141).

Party Organizational Strength and Votes. The organizational strength of state parties affects their ability to mobilize voters on election day. An analysis of gubernatorial elections has shown that the party with an organizational strength advantage over the opposition gains an incrementally higher percentage of the vote (Cotter et al., 1984:100–101). But improved party organizational strength does not necessarily lead to electoral victories. The relationship between party organizational strength and votes is complex and often indirect. In some cases, strong party structures—such as those of the Indiana Republicans, the Minnesota Democrats, and the Republicans and Democrats of Pennsylvania—have clearly contributed to their parties' electoral victories. In these instances, electoral success and the presence of meaningful competition have provided incentives to maintain the viability of party organizations. However, in other states in which one party has enjoyed a long history of electoral success, the dominant party may have little incentive to develop or maintain its organization. This was true of the Democratic party in the South until it was recently challenged by an emerging Republican party. It is frequently the electorally weaker of the two parties that has the greater incentive to build an effective party organization as a first step toward gaining electoral victories. This has been the pattern of the Republican party in the South, where, after a period of organization building in the early 1960s, it now challenges the once-dominant Democratic party in statewide and some congressional and legislative elections. Party organizational strength, therefore, can have long-term consequences. A strong party structure can provide the infrastructure for candidates and activists to continue competing until political conditions become more favorable. The Republicans of Florida, a long-time minority party in the state, provide an example. The party's organizational strength helped it take advantage of favorable circumstances to elect a governor in 1986 and U.S. senators in 1980 and 1988, and to gain a majority in the state's congressional delegation in 1988.

The Expanding Role of State Legislative Campaign Committees and Leadership PACs

The expanding role of state legislative campaign committees parallels the greatly increased involvement of the senatorial and congressional campaign committees at the national level (see Chapter 3). State legislative campaign committees, composed of incumbent legislators, operate in both the upper and lower chambers of most state legislatures. These committees have become the principal party-support institution for legislative campaigns in many states (Jewell and Olson, 1988:218–220). Indeed, they have become so active that in some states, especially for the Democrats, they have become their party's strongest state organization (e.g., the Democratic legislative campaign committees in Illinois and Wisconsin).

To raise money, legislative campaign committees often take advantage of the access of incumbent legislators and party leaders to PACs, lobbyists, and large contributors. Accordingly, the levels of expenditure by these committees can be substantial. For example, the Ohio Republican State Senate Caucus spent more than $1 million on a 1988 television-radio drive (Edsall, 1989:A14); in 1986 the California Democratic assembly campaign committee spent $2.5 million and the Republicans spent $1.2 million; and in 1986 races for the New York lower house, the Democratic campaign committee spent $944,000 and the Republican committee spent $633,000 (Gierzynski and Jewell, 1989).

Legislative campaign committees are much more than incumbent-protection institutions. They tend to follow a strategy designed to achieve or maintain majority status in the legislative chambers. Resources are concentrated upon challengers to opposition party incumbents, open seat races, and incumbents in electoral trouble (Gierzynski and Jewell, 1989; Stonecash, 1988:477–494; Jones and Borris, 1985:89–106). The ability of these committees to help cause a change in party control of legislative chambers is, however, limited by the incumbents' substantial electoral advantages.

Unlike the situation with state central committees, in which the Republicans tend to be organizationally stronger, the Democratic legislative campaign committees do not seem to operate at a disadvantage. The explanation for the strength of these legislative campaign committees appears to stem from the Democrats' control of significantly more legislative chambers than the GOP. They have been able, therefore, to use incumbency and the power that goes with chamber control to raise more money for legislative campaigns than that raised by the Republicans. In addition to providing campaign contributions, state legislative campaign committees supply such services as campaign staff, telephone banks, mass mailings, campaign consultants, media support, and brochure preparation. The role of the legislative campaign committee was captured in a statement by the Speaker of the Wisconsin Assembly, who also served as chairman of the Democratic assembly campaign committee.

> We raised about $150,000 this year [1984] to help Democrats running in marginal seats. In most cases we recruited the candidate. We provide training through campaign schools. We provide personnel and logistical support, issue papers, press releases, speakers for fund raisers, fund raisers themselves, and phone banks; we pay for the recount if it's a close race; we pay for the lawyer if it goes to court; if they have kids, we pay for the baby-sitter. . . . We do everything a political party is supposed to do. (Loftus, 1985:100)

The legislative campaign committees in some states are able to involve legislative staff personnel, who are paid with state funds, in campaign activity. For example, in New York it is possible for legislative employees to work on campaigns so long as they perform some state duties while on the state payroll. Some have even worked mainly as key operatives in local party headquarters away from the state capitol (Lynn, 1987:6E).

A further basis for the enhanced role of the state legislative party has been the emergence of PACs controlled by legislative leaders. The most striking examples of this phenomenon have occurred in California, where the Speaker of the Assembly, Democrat Willie Brown, contributed $1.7 million to seventeen candidates in 1984. His contributions exceeded those of the regular party organization outside the legislature (Sorauf, 1988:268).

Adapting to the PACs

PACs have customarily been considered a threat to political parties. However, simultaneous with their rise, state central committees have gained organizational strength and legislative campaign committees have become increasingly important. As has been true at the national level, state parties have learned to adapt to a political environment in which PACs are major players. The state parties have worked closely with PACs and have helped channel PAC funds to party candidates. In these efforts, the state party organizations have been aided by the fact that many state-level PACs are run by attorneys or accountants, who are not specialists in electoral politics, or by lobbyists, who are specialists in the legislative process but not in statewide election strategies. The parties, therefore, have been in a position to provide political intelligence about where PAC contributions would have maximum impact and to introduce the PACs to "friendly" legislative candidates. Ruth Jones, the leading expert on state campaign finance, has observed that by channeling PAC money to candidates, the parties have gotten "new funds into legislative campaigns that carried the imprimatur of the party at no direct expense to the party coffers" (Jones, 1984:197). State parties have also achieved coordination with PACs in providing in-kind services to candidates.

THE CHANGING RELATIONSHIP BETWEEN THE NATIONAL AND STATE PARTY ORGANIZATIONS

Until the late 1970s, most political scientists stressed fragmentation and dispersion of power as prominent characteristics of American parties. For example, V. O. Key (1964:334), the leading scholar of political parties in the postwar period, described the relationship between national and state parties as independent and confederative. The Republican and Democratic National Committees were dependent on state parties for financing and so lacking in power that a landmark study characterized them as "politics without power" (Cotter and Hennessy, 1964). During the 1970s and 1980s, however, the national committees were transformed into substantially more powerful institutions capable of exerting considerable influence over their state affiliates. This increased national party influence has resulted in greater integration and interdependence between the national and state party structures. It has also led to a strengthening of state parties as the national parties have poured resources into their state affiliates, utilizing them to achieve national party objectives.

Enforcement of National Party Rules

Since 1968 the Democratic party has intensified its efforts to ensure the loyalty of state parties toward the national ticket. Through a series of party reform commissions, the national party has developed detailed rules governing the method by which the state parties must select their national convention delegates. It has also implemented a National Democratic Charter, which contains prescriptions concerning the organization and operation of state parties. These national party rules have been vigorously enforced upon state parties, even against prominent party officials. For example, in 1972 an Illinois national convention delegation that had been handpicked by the leader of the Chicago Democratic organization, Mayor Richard J. Daley, was not seated at the convention because of failures to follow national party rules of delegation selection. Similarly, when Wisconsin Democrats failed in 1984 to comply with national party rules that banned the use of the state's traditional open presidential primary system to select national convention delegates, they were forced by the Democratic National Committee (DNC) to select their delegates via a party caucus system. The national committee's power to require compliance with its rules has been upheld in a series of Supreme Court decisions (e.g., *Cousins v. Wigoda*, 419 U.S. 477 [1975]; *Democratic Party of the United States v. Wisconsin ex rel La Follette*, 450 U.S. 107 [1981]).

In contrast to the Democrats, the GOP has not sought to gain influence over its state affiliates through rules enforcement. Instead, it has maintained the confederate legal structure of the party, and the Republican National Committee (RNC) has assumed a relatively permissive posture toward its state parties withs regards to delegate-selection procedures and internal organization. Party centralization and integration have moved forward within the GOP by different means, however. The national party has gained power through providing assistance to its state organizations and their candidates (Bibby, 1981:102–155).

Providing Financial and Technical Assistance to State Parties

The RNC's efforts to provide assistance to state parties started in a modest way while Ray C. Bliss was serving as national chairman (1965–1969). They were greatly expanded by Chairman Bill Brock (1977–1981) and further augmented by his successors. The RNC has developed multimillion-dollar programs to provide cash grants, professional staff, data-processing services, and consulting services for organizational development, fund raising, campaigning, media, and redistricting. Major investments of money and personnel have been made to assist state parties in voter-list development and get-out-the-vote efforts.

Beginning in 1978 the RNC entered the arena of state legislative elections. In its initial effort, it spent $1.7 million to support legislative candidates and has continued the program in successive election cycles, distributing $2 million to candidates in 1988 (Bibby, 1979:219–236; Republican National Committee, 1989:14). This state-level effort has been supplemented by programs designed to persuade Democratic legislators to switch parties and join the GOP.

In addition to its state-level activities, the RNC has sought to strengthen the party at the grass roots. In 1985 it sponsored mass mailings (1.2 million pieces) to key states, urging Democratic voters to switch their party registrations. And in 1986 it embarked upon a local party-building drive that included cash grants totaling $400,000 to 110 key county party organizations (Bibby, 1986:90; Republican National Committee, 1986:20).

The RNC's fund-raising advantage over the DNC enabled it to begin its program of assisting state parties well before the DNC followed suit. Its continuing financial advantage also has meant that the RNC's efforts have been much more extensive than those of the DNC. Under DNC Chairman Paul Kirk (1985–1989), however, significant strides were made to broaden the services provided to state parties. Kirk created and funded a Democratic Party Election Force of trained professionals in sixteen key states. In those states, the DNC paid for a full-time political operative and fund raiser. In exchange for these services, recipient state parties were required to sign agreements committing them to continue DNC-sponsored party-building programs and to cooperate with the DNC in matters relating to presidential nominating procedures and national campaigns (Broder, 1986:A23).

Kirk also followed the Republican example by creating a national party program of financial and technical assistance to state legislative candidates. But the Republican and Democratic incursions into state legislative politics reflect significant differences between the parties. The Republican effort is clearly a *party* operation carried out directly by the national party organizations in conjunction with the state parties. By contrast, the Democrats' state legislative effort was a consortium of national-level Democratic party committees (the DNC and the Democratic Senatorial and Congressional Campaign Committees), state parties, and nonparty groups allied with the Democrats. These nonparty organizations included the American Federation of State, County, and Municipal Employees, the National Committee for an Effective Congress, and Democrats for the 80s (Pamela Harriman's PAC). This organizational difference between the parties is consistent with the pattern observed at the state level. Party organizations tend to be a more important campaign resource for Republican than for Democratic candidates; and nonparty groups play a much larger role in supporting Democratic candidates and in directly supplementing the activities of the Democratic party than is true for the GOP (Cotter et al., 1984:137–141). The state Democratic party in Ohio, for example, typically receives $150,000 to $200,000 from labor unions in an election cycle (Balz, 1990a).

The state party assistance programs of both the RNC and the DNC are contributing to the increased organizational strength that state parties have exhibited since the 1960s. Although the Democrats have moved to overcome the Republicans' head start, the GOP state party assistance activities continue to be more extensive. In 1986, for example, the party's three national-level committees—the RNC, the National Republican Senatorial Committee, and the National Republican Congressional Committee—implemented a $10 million program to assist state parties in the development and maintenance of lists of Republican-oriented voters. The duration and extensive nature of the RNC's state assistance programs no doubt contribute to the aforementioned organizational strength advantage of the Republican state parties over those of the Democrats.

National-to-State Party Fund Transfers and the FECA

Massive transfers of funds were made in the 1980s from national party organizations to state and local organizations. In addition, the national organizations also channeled direct contributions from large givers to party organizations in states considered crucial to winning presidential, senatorial, and House elections. It is estimated that, in 1988, $45 to $60 million was solicited for the state parties to support the campaigns of George Bush and Michael Dukakis. National-to-state party fund transfers and the routing of contributions to state parties are encouraged by the Federal Election Campaign Act (FECA), which imposed strict limits on the amount of money national party organizations can contribute or expend on behalf of candidates for federal office. At the same time, the FECA does permit state and local party organizations to spend without limit on "party building activities" such as voter registration, get-out-the-vote drives, bumper stickers, phone banks, and facilities. Since national party organizations are now capable of raising more money than the strict FECA spending limits permit them to spend legally on federal elections, they have transferred their "surplus" funds to state and local parties for "party-building" activities. In 1988 the money transferred to state and local parties was primarily to run voter identification and get-out-the-vote campaigns for Republican and Democratic presidential nominees. These programs were directed by the RNC and DNC, which operated through the state parties. As a result, state party organizations in key states started operating with unusually large budgets and field staffs. The Democrats' Campaign '88 operation in California, for example, had a paid staff of 500 with a budget of $5 million; and in Ohio, the Republican state organizations sent out 4 million pieces of mail and made 1.5 million telephone contacts with voters (Taylor, 1988a:A16; 1988b:A24).

Further evidence of the extent to which state parties are being integrated into national party election strategies is the emerging pattern of state party contributions to senatorial and congressional elections outside their own borders. For example, in a special Wyoming House election in 1990, fifteen state Democratic parties made the maximum FECA-allowable contribution of $5,000 to their party's nominee, whereas ten GOP state parties contributed to the Republican candidates. These out-of-state contributions are encouraged by the national party organizations (Balz, 1990b).

With the FECA encouraging the national party organizations to channel funds to state parties in an effort to influence the outcome of federal elections, the state parties are being integrated into the national campaign structure to play a significant role in presidential, Senate, and House elections. Accordingly, the distinction that is commonly made between the candidate's personal organization and the party organization has been blurred at the state level. Unless the FECA is changed, it appears that large national-to-state party fund transfers will continue for the foreseeable future.

Party Integration and Nationalizing Campaign Efforts

As earlier noted, the national party committees have used their resources and legal authority to nationalize the parties' campaign efforts. Leon Epstein has characterized this process as being analogous to the categorical grant-in-aid programs that the federal government has used to enlist state governments in achieving national policy objectives. Like the federal government, which requires state and local governments to comply with federal guidelines in order to receive grants-in-aid, the RNC and DNC attach conditions—albeit quite flexible ones—to the assistance they give to state parties and candidates (Epstein, 1986:223). In the process, the national parties have achieved greatly increased influence over their state parties. After the 1988 election, Robert A. Farmer, the DNC's chief fund raiser, was quite candid about the national party's desire to centralize campaign decisionmaking. He said that his organization discouraged large contributors from giving directly to state parties and instead "tried to funnel everything into the DNC to have greater control over . . . electoral strategy" (Berke, 1988:23).

Through their programs of financial and technical assistance to state parties, the RNC and DNC have reversed the direction of resource flow from what it was prior to the 1970s. In the past, funds flowed from the state parties to the national committees, and with those funds went substantial state party influence over the activities of the national committees. As Alexander Heard accurately observed, however, "any changes that freed the national party committees of financial dependence on state organizations could importantly affect the loci of party power" and enable the parties to develop "a more cohesive operational structure" (Heard, 1960:294). The power shift that Heard foresaw in 1960 has occurred. Now that the national committees are able to raise unprecedented amounts of money and then allocate some of those funds to their state affiliates, the RNC and DNC have gained substantial autonomy as well as leverage over the state parties.

National-to-state transfers of funds and technical assistance have also meant that substantially heightened levels of integration have been achieved between the two strata of party organizations. This heightened level of intraparty integration as well as the nationalizing of party campaign efforts that has occurred since the 1970s constitute changes of major proportions in the American party system. No serious observer of American political parties can any longer assert, as did the author of the leading 1960s text on the subject, that "no nationwide party organization exists. . . . Rather, each party consists of a working coalition of state and local parties" (Key, 1964:315). Thanks in part to the assistance provided by the national party committees, state parties have undergone a process of strengthening. At the same time, however, they have grown increasingly dependent on the national party organizations and have lost some of their traditional autonomy.

STATE ELECTIONS AND NATIONAL POLITICS

Although state parties are organizationally stronger now than they were in the 1960s, their electoral fortunes are affected by factors over which they have little control, including national-level influences such as economic conditions, presidential popularity, and public perceptions of the national parties. And as partisan loyalties are normally kindled in the fires of presidential campaigns, it is extremely difficult for a state party to sustain a public image in state politics that is at odds with its national image. An example can be found in the Democratic parties in the South, which have normally sought to project a policy posture to the right of the national party and its presidential nominees. This disparity between the national party and state parties, along with the changing population and economy of the region, allowed Republican presidential candidates—Eisenhower, Nixon, and Goldwater—to win key southern states in the 1950s and 1960s. These Republican inroads were followed by significant ·Republican victories in gubernatorial, senatorial, and congressional elections after the mid-1960s. Although the Republicans have made only limited gains in state constitutional offices and state legislatures, the electoral alignment of southern voters is becoming increasingly congruent with that of the rest of the nation.

Analyses of the relationship between presidential and state legislative election outcomes have shown that state legislative elections are affected by the drawing power of the parties' presidential candidates (Campbell, 1986:45–65). In an effort to insulate state elections from such national influences, almost three-quarters of the states have scheduled elections for governor and state constitutional offices, as well as for the state legislature in nonpresidential election years. Despite the reformers' best intentions, national economic and political conditions continue to intrude and to play a significant role even during these off-year elections (Chubb, 1988:113–154). In every off-year election since World War II (with the exception of 1986), the president's party has lost governors, just as it has also lost seats in the House of Representatives. The magnitude of gubernatorial losses, however, has often been much greater than in the House. For example, in the 1982 midterm elections, the GOP sustained a net loss of seven governorships—30 percent of the governorships it had held going into the election. By contrast, its loss of twenty-six congressional seats that year constituted only 14 percent of pre-election House GOP membership. The vulnerability of governors in midterm elections reflects both the competitive nature of statewide races in most states and the high visibility of governors within their states. As the most visible figures on midterm election ballots, they are likely to be held accountable for the state of their states and to be convenient targets for discontented voters (Bibby, 1983:111–132).

THE ADAPTABLE AND ENDURING STATE PARTY

State parties emerged from the 1980s substantially changed and stronger than they had been two decades earlier. They adapted to the challenges posed by candidate-centered campaigning and the development of PACs as major candidate-support mechanisms. They also became more closely integrated into the national parties' campaign structures. A series of judicial decisions hold the potential for freeing them from the most onerous of state regulations so that they will have greater flexibility in achieving their objectives.

Although this record of adaptability and durability of state parties is impressive, the American political environment is not conducive to strong

European-style parties capable of controlling nominations and running political campaigns. From a cross-national perspective, therefore, American state parties appear to be rather modest political organizations that supplement the personal campaign organizations of candidates.

Probably the most significant question concerning the future of the state parties relates to the evolution of their relations with increasingly strong national party organizations. The national parties now give extensive assistance to and exert unprecedented influence over their state affiliates. Their priorities, however, are not necessarily identical to those of the state organizations—a situation that is apt to be a source of continuing tension. Furthermore, national party finances may not continue to grow as they did in the 1970s and 1980s. As a result, the national committees may not be able to provide assistance to the states at the level or with the regularity that the state parties have come to expect. Such a development would slow the process of party integration and perhaps cause some weakening of the state parties. Given their resiliency, however, there seems to be little doubt that state party organizations will continue to be significant participants in the electoral process.

3

Reemergent National Party Organizations

PAUL S. HERRNSON

Once characterized as poor, unstable, and powerless, national party organizations in the United States are now financially secure, institutionally stable, and highly influential in election campaigns and in their relations with state and local party committees. The national party organizations—the Democratic and Republican national, congressional, and senatorial campaign committees—have adapted to the candidate-centered, money-driven, "high-tech" style of modern campaign politics. This essay examines the development of the national party organizations, their evolving relations with other party committees, and their role in contemporary elections.

PARTY ORGANIZATIONAL DEVELOPMENT

Origins of the National Parties

The birth and subsequent development of the national party organizations were the outgrowth of forces impinging on the parties from the broader political environment and of pressures emanating from within the parties themselves. The Democratic National Committee (DNC) was formed during the Democratic national convention of 1848 for the purpose of organizing and directing the presidential campaign, promulgating the call for the next convention, and tending to the details associated with setting up future conventions (Cotter and Hennessy, 1964). The Republican National Committee (RNC) was created in 1856 at an ad hoc meeting of future Republicans for the purposes of bringing the Republican party into existence and conducting election-related activities similar to those performed by its Democratic counterpart. The creation of the national committees was an important step in a process that transformed the parties' organizational apparatuses from loosely confederative structures to more centralized, federal organizations.

The congressional campaign committees were created in response to electoral insecurities that were heightened as a result of factional conflicts that developed within the two parties following the Civil War. The National Republican Congressional Committee (NRCC) was formed in 1866 by Radical Republican members of the House who were feuding with President Andrew Johnson. The House members believed they could not rely on either the president or the RNC for assistance, so they created their own campaign committee to assist with their elections and to distance themselves from the president. As is often the case in politics, organization begot counterorganization. Following the Republican example, pro-Johnson Democrats formed their own election committee—the Democratic Congressional Campaign Committee (DCCC).

Senate leaders created the senatorial campaign committees in 1916 after the Seventeenth Amendment transformed the upper chamber into a popularly elected body. The Democratic Senatorial Campaign Committee (DSCC) and the National Republican Senatorial Committee (NRSC) were founded to assist incumbent senators with their reelection campaigns. Like their counterparts in the House, the Senate campaign committees were established during a period of political upheaval—the Progressive Movement—to assuage members' electoral insecurities in an era of exceptionally high partisan disunity and political instability.

The six national party organizations have not possessed abundant power during most of their existence. Flowcharts of the party organizations are generally pyramid-like, with the national conventions at the apex, the national committees directly below them, the congressional and senatorial campaign committees (also known as the Hill committees) branching off the national committees, and the state and local party apparatus below the national party apparatus (see, e.g., Frantzich, 1989). However, power is not, and has never been, distributed hierarchically. Throughout most of the parties' history, and during the height of their strength (circa the late nineteenth and early twentieth centuries), power was concentrated at the local level, usually in countywide political machines. Power mainly flowed up from county organizations to state party committees and conventions, and then to the national convention. The national, congressional, and senatorial campaign committees had little, if any, power over state and local party leaders (Cotter and Hennessy, 1964).

Local party organizations are reputed to have possessed tremendous influence during the golden age of political parties. Old-fashioned political machines had the ability to unify the legislative and executive branches of local and state governments. The machines also had a great deal of influence in national politics and with the courts. The machines' power was principally rooted in their virtual monopoly over the tools needed to run a successful campaign. Party bosses had the power to award the party nominations to potential candidates. Local party committees also possessed the resources needed to communicate with the electorate and mobilize voters (Bruce, 1927; Merriam, 1923; Sait, 1927; Sorauf, 1980).

Nevertheless, party campaigning was a cooperative endeavor during the golden age, especially during presidential election years. Although individual branches of the party organization were primarily concerned with electing candidates within their immediate jurisdictions, party leaders at different levels of the organization had a number of reasons to work together (Ostrogorski, 1964; Schattschneider, 1942). The party leaders recognized that ballot structures and voter partisanship linked the electoral prospects of their candidates. They further understood that electing candidates to federal, state, and local governments would enable them to maximize the patronage and preferments they could exact for themselves and their supporters. In addition, they were conscious of the different resources and capabilities possessed by different branches of the party organization. The national party organizations, especially the national committees, had the financial, administrative, and communications resources needed to coordinate and set the tone of a nationwide campaign (Merriam, 1923; Sait, 1927; Bruce, 1927; Kent, 1923). Local party committees had the proximity to voters needed to collect electoral information, conduct voter registration and get-out-the-vote drives, and perform other grass-roots campaign activities (Merriam, 1923). State party committees had relatively modest resources, but they occupied an important intermediate position between the other two strata of the party organization. State party leaders channeled electoral information up to the national party organizations and arranged for candidates and other prominent party leaders to speak at local rallies and events (Sait, 1927). Relations between the national party organizations and other branches of the party apparatus were characterized by negotiation and compromise rather than by command. Party organizations in Washington did not dominate party politics during the golden age. They did, however, play an important role in what were essentially party-centered election campaigns.

Party Decline

The transition from a party-dominated system of campaign politics to a candidate-centered system was brought about by legal, demographic, and technological changes in American society as well as by reforms instituted by the parties themselves. The direct primary and civil service regulations instituted during the Progressive era deprived party bosses of their ability to handpick nominees and reward party workers with government jobs and contracts (see, e.g., Key, 1958; Roseboom, 1970). The reforms weakened the bosses' hold over candidates and political activists, and encouraged candidates to build their own campaign organizations.

Demographic and cultural changes reinforced this pattern. Increased education and social mobility, declining immigration, and a growing national identity contributed to the erosion of the close-knit, traditional ethnic neighborhoods that formed the core of the constituency of the old-fashioned political machines. Voters began to turn toward nationally focused mass media and away from local party committees for their political information (Ranney, 1975; Kayden and Mahe, 1985; McWilliams, 1981). Growing preferences for movies, radio, and televised entertainment underscored this phenomenon by reducing the popularity of rallies, barbecues, and other types of interpersonal communication at which old-fashioned political machines excelled.[1] These changes combined to deprive the machines of their political bases and to render many of their communications and mobilization techniques obsolete.

The adaptation of technological innovations developed in the public relations field to the electoral arena further eroded candidates' dependence on party organizations. Advancements in survey research, computerized data processing, and mass media advertising provided candidates with new tools for gathering information about voters and communicating messages to them. The emergence of a new corps of campaigners—the political consultants—enabled candidates to hire nonparty professionals to run their campaigns (Agranoff, 1972; Sabato, 1981). Direct-mail fund-raising techniques helped candidates raise the money needed to pay their campaign staffs and outside consultants. These developments helped to transform election campaigns from party-focused, party-conducted affairs into events that revolved around individual candidates and their campaign organizations.

At the outset, the party reforms introduced by the Democrats' McGovern-Fraser Commission and the Federal Election Campaign Act of 1971 (FECA) and its amendments also appeared to weaken party organizations and to reinforce the candidate-centeredness of American elections. The McGovern-Fraser reforms, as well as the reforms instituted by later Democratic reform commissions, were designed to make the presidential nominating process more open and more representative. One of their effects was to make it more difficult for long-time "party regulars" to attend national party conventions or to dominate other party activities. They also made it easier for issue and candidate activists who had little history of party service (frequently labeled "purists" or "amateurs") to play a larger role in party politics.

Moreover, the rise of the "purists" led to tensions over fundamental issues such as whether winning elections or advancing particular policies should have priority (Wilson, 1962; Polsby and Wildavsky, 1984). Heightened tensions made coalition building among party activists and supporters more difficult. Intraparty conflicts between purists and professionals, and the purists' heavy focus on the agendas of specific candidates and special interests, also resulted in the neglect of the parties' organizational needs. The reforms were debilitating to both parties, but they were more harmful to the Democratic party, which had introduced them (Ranney, 1975; Polsby, 1983; Polsby and Wildavsky, 1984).

The FECA, too, had some negative effects on the parties. Its contribution and expenditure limits, disclosure provisions, and other regulatory requirements forced party committees to keep separate bank accounts for state and federal election activity. The reforms had the immediate effect of discouraging state and local party organizations from participating fully in federal elections (Price, 1984; Kayden and Mahe, 1985). The FECA also set the stage for the tremendous proliferation of political action committees (PACs) that began in the late 1970s. The Federal Election Commission's SunPAC Advisory in 1976 opened the way for PACs to become the major organized financiers of congressional elections (Alexander, 1984).

The combination of progressive reforms, demographic and cultural transformations, new campaign technology, recent party reforms, and campaign finance legislation reduced the roles that party organizations played in elections and fostered the evolution of a candidate-centered election system. Under this system, candidates typically assembled their own campaign organizations, first to compete for their party's nomination and then to contest the general election. In the case of presidential elections, a candidate who succeeded in securing the party's nomination also won control of the national committee. The candidate's campaign organization directed most national committee election activity. In congressional elections, most campaign activities were carried out by the candidate's own organization both before and after the primary. The parties' seeming inability to adapt to the new "high-tech," money-driven style of campaign politics resulted in their being pushed to the periphery of the election process. These trends were accompanied by a general decline in the parties' ability to structure political choice (Carmines, Renten, and Stimson, 1984; Beck, 1984), to furnish symbolic referents and decisionmaking cues for voters (Burnham, 1970; Ladd and Hadley, 1975; Nie, Verba, and Petrocik, 1976 [1979]; Wattenberg, 1984), and to foster party unity among elected officials (Deckard, 1976; Keefe, 1976; Clubb, Flanigan, and Zingale, 1980).

The Reemergence of National Party Organizations

Although the party decline was a gradual process that took its greatest toll on party organizations at the local level, party renewal occurred over a relatively short period and was focused primarily in Washington, D.C. The dynamics of recent national party organizational development bear parallels to changes that occurred in earlier periods. The content of recent national party organizational renewal was shaped by the changing needs of candidates. The new-style campaigning that became prevalent during the 1960s placed a premium on campaign activities that required technical expertise and in-depth research. Some candidates were able to run a viable campaign using their own funds or talent. Others turned to political consultants, PACs, and special interests for help. However, many candidates found it difficult to assemble the money and expertise needed to compete in a modern election. The increased needs of candidates for greater access to technical expertise, political information, and money created an opportunity for national and some state party organizations to become the repositories of these electoral resources (Schlesinger, 1985).

Nevertheless, national party organizations did not respond to changes in the political environment until electoral crises forced party leaders to recognize the institutional and electoral weaknesses of those organizations. As was the case during earlier eras of party transformation, crises that heightened office holders' electoral anxieties furnished party leaders with the opportunities and incentives to augment the parties' organizational apparatuses. Entrepreneurial party leaders recognized that they might receive payoffs for restructuring the national party organizations so that they could better assist candidates and state and local party committees with their election efforts.[2]

The Watergate scandal and the trouncing that Republican candidates experienced in the 1974 and 1976 elections created a crisis of competition that was the catalyst for change at the Republican national party organizations. The Republicans lost 49 seats in the House in 1974, had an incumbent president defeated two years later, and controlled only twelve governorships and four state legislatures by 1977. Moreover, voter identification with the Republican party (which had previously been climbing) dropped precipitously, especially among voters under 35 (Malbin, 1975).

The crisis of competition drew party leaders' attention to the weaknesses of the Republican national, congressional, and senatorial campaign committees. After a struggle that became entwined with the politics surrounding the race for the RNC chair, William Brock, an advocate of party organizational development, was selected to head the RNC. Other party-building entrepreneurs were selected to chair the parties' other two national organizations: Representative Guy Vander Jagt of Michigan took the helm of the NRCC in 1975, and Senator Robert Packwood of Oregon became chair of the NRSC in 1977.[3] The three party leaders initiated a variety of programs aimed at promoting the institutional development of their committees, increasing the committees' electoral presence, and providing candidates with campaign money and services. All three leaders played a major role in reshaping the missions of the national parties and in placing them on a path that would result in their organizational transformation.

The transformation of the Democratic national party organizations has been more complicated than that of their Republican counterparts because DNC institutionalization occurred in two distinct phases. The first phase of DNC development, which is often referred to as *party reform* and associated with party decline, was concerned with enhancing the representativeness and openness of the national committee and the presidential nominating convention. The second phase, which resembles the institutionalization of the Republican party organizations and is frequently referred to as *party renewal*, focused on the committee's institutional and electoral capabilities.

Democratic party reform followed the tumultuous 1968 Democratic National Convention. Protests on the floor of the convention and in the streets of Chicago constituted a factional crisis that underscored the deep rift between liberal, reform-minded "purists" and "party regulars." The crisis and the party's defeat in November created an opportunity for major party organizational change. The McGovern-Fraser Commission, as well as later reform commissions, introduced rules that made the delegate-selection process more participatory and led to the unexpected proliferation of presidential primaries; increased the size and demographic representativeness of the DNC and the national convention; instituted midterm issue conferences (which were discontinued by Paul Kirk after his selection as DNC Chair in 1984); and resulted in the party's adoption of a written charter. Some of these changes are believed to have been a major cause of party decline (see, e.g., Crotty, 1983).

Other changes may have been more positive. Upon adopting the decisions of the McGovern-Fraser Commission, the DNC took on a new set of responsibilities that concerned state party compliance with national party rules governing participation in the delegate-selection process. The expansion of DNC authority in the delegate-selection process has resulted in the committee's usurpation of the power to overrule state party activities connected with the process that are not in compliance with national party rules.[4] Thus a fundamental shift has occurred in the distribution of power between the national committee and the state party organizations. Indeed, Democratic party reform transformed the DNC into an important agency of intraparty regulation and increased committee influence in party politics.

The second phase of Democratic national party institutionalization followed the party's massive defeat in the 1980 election. The defeat of incumbent President Jimmy Carter, the loss of 34 House seats (half of the party's margin), and the loss of control of the Senate constituted a crisis of competition that was the catalyst for change within the Democratic national party organizations. Unlike the previous phase of national party development, Democratic party renewal was preceded by widespread agreement among DNC members, Democrats in Congress, and party activists that the party needed to increase its competitiveness by imitating the GOP's party-building and campaign service programs (Cook, 1981).

The issue of party renewal was an important factor in the selection of Charles Manatt as DNC chair and Representative Tony Coelho as DCCC chair in 1981. It also influenced Democratic senators' choice of Lloyd Bentsen of Texas to chair the DSCC in 1983. All three party leaders were committed to building the national party organizations' fund-raising capabilities, improving their professional staffs and organizational structures, and augmenting the Republican party-building model to suit the specific needs of Democratic candidates and of state and local Democratic committees. Like their Republican counterparts, all three Democratic leaders played a critical role in promoting the institutionalization of the Democratic national party organizations.

INSTITUTIONALIZED NATIONAL PARTIES

The institutionalization of the national party organizations refers to their becoming fiscally solvent, organizationally stable, and larger and more diversified in their staffing; it also refers to their adoption of professional-bureaucratic decisionmaking procedures. These changes were necessary to the development of the national parties' election-related and party-building functions.

Finances

National party fund raising improved greatly in the late 1970s and 1980s. During this period the national parties raised more money from more sources and using more varied approaches than ever before. The information presented in Table 3.1 indicates that the Republican com-

TABLE 3.1
National Party Receipts, 1976–1988 (in millions)

Party	1976	1978	1980	1982	1984	1986	1988
Democrats							
DNC	$13.1	$11.3	$ 15.4	$ 16.5	$ 46.6	$ 17.2	$ 52.3
DCCC	.9	2.8	2.9	6.5	10.4	12.3	12.5
DSCC	1.0	.3	1.7	5.6	8.9	13.4	16.3
Total	$15.0	$14.4	$ 20.0	$ 28.6	$ 65.9	$ 42.9	$ 81.1
Republicans							
RNC	$29.1	$34.2	$77.8	$ 84.1	$105.9	$ 83.8	$ 91.0
NRCC	12.2	14.1	20.3	58.0	58.3	39.8	34.5
NRSC	1.8	10.9	22.3	48.9	81.7	86.1	65.9
Total	$43.1	$59.2	$120.4	$191.0	$245.9	$209.7	$191.4

Source: Federal Election Commission.

mittees raised more money than did their Democratic rivals in all seven election cycles, but also that, following the 1980 election, the Democrats began to narrow the gap in fund raising. The GOP's financial advantage reflects a number of factors. The Republican committees began developing their direct-mail solicitation programs earlier and have taken a more business-like approach to fund raising. The greater wealth and homogeneity of their supporters has also made it easier for the Republican committees to raise money. Finally, the Republicans' minority status has provided them with a powerful fund-raising weapon. Negative appeals, featuring attacks on those in power, are generally more successful in fund raising than are appeals advocating the maintenance of the status quo (Godwin, 1988). Although Republican fund raising appears to have reached a plateau and the Democrats have made strides in improving their fund-raising programs, there is some question as to whether the Democratic national party organizations will be able to catch up to the GOP committees.

Most national party money is raised in the form of direct-mail contributions of less than $100. Telephone solicitations also are used to raise both small and large contributions. Traditional fund-raising dinners, parties, and other events experienced a revival as important vehicles for collecting large contributions from individual donors during the 1988 election. Sometimes individuals will contribute to a party organization's building fund or some other nonfederal, "soft money" account such as the Republicans' Victory '88 or the Democratic Victory Fund.[5] These "soft money" accounts enable wealthy individuals to make contributions in excess of the FECA's contribution limits (Drew, 1983; Sorauf, 1988; Jackson, 1988). In 1987, for example, Joan Kroc, heiress to the McDonald's fast-food chain, gave the DNC a check for $1 million in "soft money" (Jackson, 1988).

PACs also give substantial sums of money to the national party organizations. Many PACs pay dues of up to $5,000 per year to belong to one of the national committees' labor or business councils such as the DCCC's Speaker's Club, the DSCC's Leadership Council, the NRCC's Congressional Leadership Council, the NRSC's Senate Trust Club, or some other "club" created by one of the national party organizations for the purpose of raising large contributions. In return for their donations, club members get the opportunity to meet with members of Congress and other prominent party officials. Club members also receive electoral briefings from the committees and other useful "perks." The existence of these clubs is indicative of the symbiotic nature of the relationships that exist between the national parties and many PACs (Sabato, 1984; Herrnson, 1988).

Infrastructure

Success in fund raising has enabled the national parties to invest in the development of their organizational infrastructures. Prior to their institutionalization, the national party organizations had no permanent headquarters. For a while, the four Hill committees were quartered in small offices in congressional office buildings. Upon leaving congressional office space they became transient, following the national committees' example of moving at the end of each election cycle in search of cheap office space. The national parties' lack of permanent office space created security problems, made it difficult for them to conduct routine business, and did little to bolster their standing in Washington (Cotter and Hennessy, 1964).

All six national party organizations are now housed in party-owned headquarters buildings located only a few blocks from the Capitol. The headquarters buildings furnish the committees with convenient locations for carrying out fund-raising events and holding meetings with candidates, PACs, journalists, and campaign consultants. They also provide a secure environment for the committees' computers, records, and radio and television studios. The multimillion-dollar studios, each of which is owned by one of the congressional campaign committees, allow the parties to produce professional-quality campaign commercials for their candidates (see, e.g., Herrnson, 1988).

Staff

Each national party organization has a two-tiered structure consisting of members and professional staff. The members of the Republican and

Democratic national committees are selected by their state parties, and the members of the Hill committees are selected by their colleagues in Congress. The national parties' staffs have grown tremendously in recent years. Republican committee staff development accelerated following the party's Watergate scandal, whereas the Democratic party experienced most of its staff growth after the 1980 election. In 1988 the DNC, DCCC, and DSCC employed 160, 80, and 50 full-time staff members respectively, whereas their Republican counterparts had 425, 80, and 88 full-time employees.[6] Committee staffs are divided along functional lines; different divisions are responsible for administration, fund raising, research, communications, and campaign activities. The staffs have a great deal of autonomy in running the committees and are extremely influential in formulating their campaign strategies. In the case of the NRCC, for example, committee members have adopted a "hands-off" attitude toward committee operations similar to that of a board of directors (Herrnson, 1989).

The Parties' Relations with PACs and Political Consultants

Although it was initially believed that the rise of political consultants and the proliferation of PACs would hasten the decline of parties (Sabato, 1981; Crotty, 1984; Adamany, 1984), recent evidence suggests that political consultants and PACs are seeking to cooperate with the political parties rather than to destroy them (Herrnson, 1988; Sabato, 1988). National party organizations, consultants, and PACs frequently work together in pursuit of their common goals. Fund raising constitutes one area of party-PAC cooperation; the dissemination of information and the backing of particular candidates constitute others. National party organizations handicap races for PACs and arrange "meet and greet" sessions for PACs and candidates. They also mail, telephone, and "fax" large quantities of information to PACs in order to keep them abreast of developments in competitive elections. PAC managers use party information when formulating their contributions strategies.

Relations between the national party organizations and political consultants have also become more cooperative. During election years, the national parties facilitate contacts and agreements between their candidates and political consultants. The parties also hire outside consultants to assist with polling and advertising, and to furnish candidates with campaign services. During nonelection years, they hire private consultants to assist with long-range planning. These arrangements enable the parties to draw upon the expertise of the industry's premier consulting firms and provide the consultants with steady employment, which is especially important between election cycles.

The symbiotic relationships that have developed among the national parties, political consultants, and PACs can be further appreciated if we look at the career paths of people working in electoral politics. Employment at one of the national party organizations can now serve as a stepping stone in the career of a political operative. It has become increasingly common for consultants to begin their careers by working for a candidate, a small firm, or a PAC, then to be hired by one of the national party organizations, and finally to leave the party organization to form their own political consulting firm or to accept an executive position with a major firm or PAC. Finding employment outside of the national parties rarely results in the severing of relations between consultants and the national party organizations. Parties often hire past employees, and their firms, to conduct research, give strategic or legal advice, or provide campaign services to candidates. The "revolving door" of national party employment provides political professionals with opportunities to gain experience, make connections, establish credentials that can help them move up the hierarchy of political consultants, and maintain profitable relationships with the national parties after they have gained employment elsewhere.

Party Building

The institutionalization of the national party organizations has provided them with the resources to develop a variety of party-building programs. The vast majority of these programs are conducted by the two national committees. Many current RNC party-building efforts were initiated in 1977 under the leadership of Chairman Brock. Brock's program for revitalizing state party committees consisted of (1) appointing regional political directors to assist state party leaders in strengthening their organizations and utilizing RNC services; (2) hiring organizational directors to help rebuild state party organizations; (3) appointing regional finance directors to assist state parties with developing fund-raising programs; (4) making computer services available to state parties for accounting, fund raising, and analyzing survey data; and (5) organizing a task force to assist parties with developing realistic election goals and strategies. Brock also established a Local Elections Campaign Division to assist state parties with creating district profiles and recruiting candidates, to provide candidate training and campaign management seminars, and to furnish candidates for state or local office with on-site campaign assistance (Bibby, 1981; Conway, 1983).

Frank Fahrenkopf, RNC chair from 1983 to 1988, expanded many of Brock's party-building programs and introduced some new ones. The national committee continues to give Republican state parties financial assistance and to help them with fund raising.[7] An RNC computerized information network created during the 1984 election cycle furnishes Republican state and local party organizations and candidates with issue and opposition research, newspaper clippings, and other sorts of electoral information. RNC publications, such as "First Monday" and "County Line," provide Republican candidates, party leaders, and activists with survey results, issue research, and instructions on how to conduct campaign activities ranging from fund raising to grass-roots organizing. Moreover, NRCC and NRSC agency agreements with Republican state party organizations enable the two Washington-based committees to make the state parties' share of campaign contributions and coordinated expenditures in House and Senate elections. Agency agreements enable the state parties to spend their money on party-building functions and party-focused campaign activities (Federal Election Commission, 1984; Jacobson, 1985).

The DNC's party-building activities lagged behind those of its Republican counterpart and did not become significant until the 1986 election. During that election Chairman Paul Kirk created a task force of thirty-two professional consultants who were sent to sixteen states to assist their Democratic state committees with fund raising, computerizing voter lists, and other organizational activities. In 1988 the task force went to another sixteen states to help modernize and strengthen their Democratic state committees. The task force is credited with improving Democratic state party fund raising, computer capacities, and voter registration and mobilization programs. Nevertheless, the Democrats remain behind the Republicans in many areas. The DNC has still not created a Republican-style computer information network for state and local party committees, and the Democratic congressional and senatorial campaign committees could not afford to enter into agency agreements with as many state party committees as did rival GOP committees during the 1988 election.[8]

National committee party-building programs have succeeded in strengthening, modernizing, and professionalizing many state and local party organizations. Agency agreements between the Hill committees and state party organizations further contribute to these efforts by encouraging state parties to spend their money on organizational development, state and local elections, and generic party campaigning rather than on House and Senate elections. These programs have altered the balance of power within the parties' organizational apparatuses. The national parties' ability to distribute or withhold party-building or campaign assistance gives them some influence over the operations of state and local party committees. The DNC's influence is enhanced by its rule-making and -enforcement authority.[9] As a result of these developments, the traditional flow of power upward from state and local party organizations to the national committees has been complemented by a new flow of power downward from the national parties to state and local parties. The institutionalization of the national party organizations has enabled them to become more influential in party politics and has led to a greater federalization of the American party system (Wekkin, 1985).

NATIONAL PARTY CAMPAIGNING

The institutionalization of the national parties has provided them the wherewithal to play a larger role in elections, and national party campaign activity has increased tremendously since the 1970s. Yet the electoral activities of the national parties, and of party organizations in general, remain constricted by electoral law, established custom, and the level of resources in the parties' possession.

Candidate Recruitment and Nominations

Most candidates for elective office in the United States are self-recruited and conduct their own nominating campaigns (see Chapter 7). Both the DNC and the RNC have a hand in establishing the basic guidelines under which presidential nominations are contested, but their role is defined by the national conventions and their recommendations are subject to convention approval. The rules governing Democratic presidential nominations are more extensive than are those governing GOP contests, but the state committees of both parties have substantial leeway in supplying the details of their delegate-selection processes.

Neither the DNC nor the RNC expresses a preference for candidates during its party's presidential nomination. Such activity would be disastrous if a candidate who was backed by a national committee were to be defeated, inasmuch as the successful, unsupported candidate would become the head of the party's ticket as well as its titular leader. Accordingly, candidates for the nomination assemble their own campaign staffs and compete independent of the party apparatus in state-run primaries and caucuses. Successful candidates arrive at the national convention with seasoned campaign organizations composed of experienced political operatives.

The national party organizations, however, may get involved in selected nominating contests for House, Senate, and state-level offices. They actively recruit some candidates to enter primary contests and just as actively discourage others from doing likewise.[10] Most candidate-recruitment efforts are concentrated in competitive districts, but party officials will sometimes encourage a candidate to enter a primary in a district that is safe for the opposite party so that the general election will be uncontested. National party staff in Washington and regional coordinators in the field meet with state and local party leaders to identify potential candidates and encourage them to enter primaries. Party staff use polls, the promise of party campaign money and assistance, and the persuasive talents of party leaders, members of Congress, and even presidents to influence the decisions of potential candidates.[11] The DSCC is credited with playing an important role in recruiting Joseph Lieberman, who defeated incumbent Lowell Weicker in Connecticut in 1988, and with discouraging William Press from challenging Leo McCarthy in California's Democratic Senate primary. Its Republican counterpart is credited with convincing Conrad Burns and Connie Mack to undertake their successful bids in Montana and Florida. The NRSC, however, was unable to discourage Representative Hal Daub from challenging incumbent David Karnes in Nebraska's Republican primary. The DCCC and NRCC are believed to have had a major hand in persuading about two dozen candidates to run for the House in 1988, even though the Iran-Contra scandal impeded Republican party recruitment efforts (Klinge, 1989). Neither House campaign committee exerted much energy in their efforts to pare down the field of candidates in contested primaries during 1988. NRCC and DCCC spokespersons have explained that "negative recruitment" is rarely practiced in House races because the party staffs are principally occupied with locating candidates to run against incumbents.

National party candidate recruitment and primary activities are not intended to do away with the dominant pattern whereby self-selected candidates assemble their own campaign organizations to compete for their party's nomination. Nor are these activities designed to restore the turn-of-the-century pattern whereby local party leaders select the party's nominees. Rather, most national party activity is geared toward encouraging or discouraging the candidacies of a small group of politicians who are considering running in competitive districts. Less focused recruitment methods attempt to arouse the interests of a broader group of party activists by informing them of the campaign assistance available to candidates who make it to the general election.

National Conventions

The national conventions are technically a part of the nominating process. After the 1968 reforms were instituted, however, the conventions lost control of their nominating function and became more of a public relations event than a decisionmaking one. Conventions still have plat-

form-writing and rule-making responsibilities, but these are overshad-
owed by speeches and other events designed to attract the support of
voters.

The public relations component of the national conventions reached
new heights during the 1980s. Contemporary conventions are known
for their technologically sophisticated video presentations and choreo-
graphed pageantry. Convention activities are designed so that they can
be easily broken down into sound bites suitable for television news
programs. National committee staff formulate strategies to ensure that
television newscasters put a desirable "spin" on television news coverage.
Party public relations activity at national conventions reached a new
plateau in 1988, when the DNC's Harriman Communications Center set
up its Convention Satellite News Service, which featured satellite uplink
capabilities, and former CBS News anchor Ike Pappas reported activity
from the convention floor. Television correspondents from around the
nation were invited to use the Harriman Center's facilities to interview
delegates and members of Congress, or to report to their local stations.
Television stations also were given the opportunity to incorporate Pappas's
news reports into their nightly news shows (Grove, 1988; Kontnik, 1989;
McCurry, 1989). Both parties increased media opportunities for local
stations in an attempt to compensate for the cutbacks in coverage
scheduled by the major networks.

The national parties also conduct less visible convention activities to
help nonpresidential candidates with their bids for office. In 1988, for
example, congressional and senatorial candidates had access to party
television and radio taping facilities. The Hill committees also sponsored
"meet and greet" sessions to introduce their most competitive challengers
and open-seat candidates to PACs, individual big contributors, party
leaders, and the press (Thompson, 1988; Ward, 1989; Rintye, 1989). The
atrophy of the national conventions' nominating function has been
partially offset by an increase in its general election-related activities.

The General Election

Presidential Elections. Party activity in presidential elections is restricted
by the public-funding provisions of the FECA. Major party candidates
who accept public funding are prohibited from accepting contributions
from any other sources, including the political parties. The amount that
the national parties can spend directly on behalf of their presidential
candidates is also limited. In 1988 George Bush and Michael Dukakis
received $46.1 million apiece in general election subsidies, and each of
the national committees were allowed to spend approximately $8.3
million directly on behalf of their candidates. Both parties spent just

under the legal maximum (Federal Election Commission, 1988a, 1988b, 1989).

The legal environment reinforces the candidate-centeredness of presidential elections in other ways as well. Rules requiring candidates for the nomination to compete in primaries and caucuses guarantee that successful candidates will enter the general election with their own sources of technical expertise, in-depth research, and connections with journalists and other Washington elites. These reforms have combined with the FECA to create a regulatory framework that limits national party activity and influence in presidential elections.

Nevertheless, the national parties play an important role in presidential elections. The national committees furnish presidential campaigns with legal and strategic advice and public relations assistance. National committee opposition research and archives serve as important sources of political information. The money that the national committees spend directly on behalf of their candidates can boost the total resources under the candidates' control by more than 15 percent. The national committees also assist their candidates' campaigns by distributing "soft money" to state parties so they can finance voter-mobilization drives and party-building activities. In 1988 the DNC and the RNC are each estimated to have raised between $20 million and $30 million in "soft money" (Barnes and Cohen, 1988; Cook 1988). Most of these funds were distributed in accordance with the strategies of their presidential candidates. "Soft money" enabled the national parties to wage a coordinated campaign that supplemented, and in some cases replaced, the voter-mobilization efforts of presidential and other candidates.

Congressional Elections. The national party organizations play a larger role in congressional elections than in presidential campaigns. The national parties contribute money and campaign services directly to congressional candidates. They also provide candidates with transactional assistance that helps them obtain campaign resources from political consultants and PACs. Most national party assistance is distributed by the Hill committees to candidates competing in close elections, especially those who are nonincumbents. This arrangement reflects the committees' goal of maximizing the number of congressional seats under their party's control (Jacobson, 1985–1986; Herrnson, 1989).

The FECA limits party activity not only in presidential elections but in congressional races as well. National, congressional, and state party organizations are allowed to contribute $5,000 apiece to House candidates. The parties' national and senatorial campaign committees are allowed to give a combined total of $17,500 to Senate candidates; state party organizations can give $5,000. National party organizations and state party committees also are allowed to make coordinated expenditures on

TABLE 3.2
Party Contributions and Coordinated Expenditures
in the 1988 Congressional Elections[a]

	House		Senate	
	Contributions	Coordinated Expenditures	Contributions	Coordinated Expenditures
Democratic				
DNC	$ 120,000	$ 30,000	$ 0	$ 0
DCCC	593,849	2,251,449	0	0
DSCC	0	0	418,620	6,197,037
State & Local	400,475	342,363	70,219	310,820
Total	$1,118,740	$2,623,812	$488,839	$ 6,507,857
Republican				
RNC	$ 291,480	$ 0	$ 0	$ 0
NRCC	1,429,856	3,868,586	55,731	0
NRSC	195,000	0	520,960	10,247,724
State & Local	553,310	51,389	111,695	6,992
Total	$2,469,646	$3,919,975	$688,386	$10,254,716

[a]Includes only general election activity. Figures are calculated from a preliminary version of campaign finance data, which may be subject to minor revision.

Source: Federal Election Commission.

behalf of their candidates. Unlike the independent expenditures of PACs, party-coordinated expenditures are made in cooperation with candidate campaign committees, giving both the party and the candidate a measure of control over them. Originally set at $10,000 per committee, the limits for coordinated expenditures on behalf of House candidates have been adjusted for inflation and reached $23,050 in 1988. The limits for coordinated expenditures in Senate elections vary according to the size of a state's population and are also indexed to inflation. They ranged from $46,100 in the smallest states to $938,688 in the most populous state (California) during the 1988 election cycle (Federal Election Commission, 1988a). The national parties give virtually every competitive House or Senate candidate the maximum contribution, and most also benefit from a large coordinated expenditure. The Hill committees routinely enter into agency agreements that allow them to make some of their national and state party committees' coordinated expenditures.[12]

The figures in Table 3.2 indicate that most party money, especially in Senate elections, is distributed as coordinated expenditures, thus reflecting the higher legal limits imposed by the FECA. Republican party organizations spent more than Democratic party organizations in 1988, but the gap between the parties is narrower than it was in previous elections (Federal Election Commission, 1989). National-level GOP committees outspent their Democratic rivals by substantial sums. The bulk

TABLE 3.3

Average Party Spending in the 1988 Congressional Elections[a]

	House			Senate		
	Incumbent	*Challenger*	*Open Seat*	*Incumbent*	*Challenger*	*Open Seat*
Democratic						
DNC	$ 291	$ 596	$ 1,739	$ 0	$ 0	$ 0
DCCC	8,101	9,297	19,116	0	0	0
DSCC	0	0	0	154,291	257,728	272,568
State & Local	1,490	3,215	5,497	2,299	7,873	50,675
Total	$ 9,882	$13,108	$26,352	$156,590	$265,601	$323,243
Percent[b]	2.2%	6.3%	5.0%	4.2%	10.9%	12.2%
(N)	(189)	(109)	(23)	(14)[c]	(12)	(5)[d]
Republican						
RNC	$ 504	$ 1,010	$ 4,477	$ 0	$ 0	$ 0
NRCC	12,430	18,304	48,935	0	3,000	1,789
NRSC	213	698	3,636	313,890	320,153	366,617
State & Local	1,098	2,403	5,550	3,560	2,346	6,794
Total	$14,246	$22,415	$62,599	$317,451	$325,500	$375,200
Percent[b]	3.2%	13.9%	13.9%	7.5%	17.6%	12.6%
(N)	(164)	(129)	(22)	(12)	(15)	(6)

[a]Includes only general election contributions and coordinated expenditures for elections in which one or more party organizations spent money; the averages would be lower, obviously, if all races were included. Figures are calculated from a preliminary version of campaign finance data, which may be subject to minor revisions.

[b]Denotes percentage of candidate-controlled money (candidate receipts and party coordinated expenditures) composed of party money.

[c]Spark Matsunaga (HI) took no party money.

[d]Herbert Kohl (WI) took no party money.

Note: Some numbers do not add up because of rounding.

Source: Federal Election Commission.

of national party spending is done by the four Hill committees. Both national committees spent only small amounts in House elections and made no direct expenditures in Senate contests.

The figures for the NRCC and NRSC call attention to a relatively new phenomenon known as "crossover spending," which occurs when a senatorial campaign committee spends money in House elections or a congressional campaign committee spends money in Senate races. It is generally the result of shared polling or some other coordinated campaign activity that is conducted by one of the campaign committees in cooperation with the other campaign committee, a Senate candidate, or one or more House candidates who typically reside in the same state.

Table 3.3 provides further insights into the parties' role in campaign finance. The figures demonstrate that Republican candidates generally receive more assistance from party committees than do Democratic candidates. Both parties spend substantial sums in open-seat races. They spend the next largest amount in races waged by challengers. Substantially less is spent in connection with incumbent campaigns. The percentage figures indicate that the importance of party money varies with candidate status. Party money accounts for more than 10 percent of the general election funds spent by or on behalf of Republican nonincumbent candidates for the House and nonincumbent candidates of both parties for the Senate. An impressive 17.6 percent of the funds spent by or on behalf of Republican Senate challengers was furnished by party committees.

The national parties target most of their money to candidates in close races. Challengers who show little promise and incumbents in safe seats are usually given only token sums. In 1988, for example, the parties spent more than $40,000 in connection with each of 107 House candidacies and spent no money in connection with 178 others (Federal Election Commission, 1989). The discrepancies in party spending in Senate elections were even greater, reflecting party strategy as well as the FECA's contribution and spending limits. At one extreme, the Democratic party spent no money in the Hawaii contest between Democratic incumbent Spark Matsunaga and Republican challenger Maria Hustace.[13] At the other, the parties spent approximately $1.9 million each in the California race between Republican incumbent Pete Wilson and Democratic challenger Leo McCarthy, accounting for 21.4 percent and 12.9 percent, respectively, of all the money spent in the campaign over which the candidates had some control.[14]

Even though individuals and PACs still furnish candidates with most of their campaign funds, political parties currently constitute the largest single source of campaign money for most candidates. Party money comes from one or, at most, a few organizations that are concerned with one goal—the election of their candidates. Individual and PAC contributions, on the other hand, come from a multitude of sources that are motivated by a variety of concerns. In addition, it is important to recognize that dollar-for-dollar national party money has greater value than the contributions of other groups. National party contributions are often given early and function as "seed money" that candidates use to generate more funds. National party contributions and coordinated expenditures often take the form of in-kind campaign services that are worth many times more than their reported value. Moreover, national party money and transactional assistance help candidates attract additional money from PACs.

The national parties also furnish many congressional candidates with campaign services ranging from legal advice to assistance with campaign advertising.[15] The national parties distribute most of their services to competitive contestants, especially those who are nonincumbents. National party help is more likely to have an impact on the outcomes of these candidates' elections than on those of incumbents holding safe seats or of nonincumbents challenging them.

The national parties provide a variety of management-related campaign services. They hold training colleges for candidates and campaign managers, introduce candidates and political consultants to each other, and frequently provide candidates with in-kind contributions or coordinated expenditures consisting of campaign services. The national parties also help congressional campaign committees file reports with the Federal Election Commission and perform other administrative, clerical, and legal tasks. Most important, the national parties furnish candidates with strategic assistance. In 1988 the DCCC had eight field workers and the NRCC had ten who visited campaign headquarters to help their candidates develop campaign plans, respond to attacks, and perform other crucial campaign activities (Maddox, 1989; Bates, 1989).

The national party organizations assist congressional candidates with gauging public opinion by distributing newsletters that analyze voter attitudes toward party positions and report the mood of the national electorate. The Hill committees, too, conduct district-level analyses of voting patterns exhibited in previous elections to help congressional candidates locate where their supporters reside. They also conduct surveys for their most competitive candidates. These surveys help the candidates ascertain their levels of name recognition, electoral support, and the impact that their campaign communications are having on voters. In 1988 the DCCC conducted benchmark surveys for five nonincumbents and tracking polls for ten of its most competitive contestants, whereas the NRCC conducted vulnerability studies for more than fifty nonincumbents and tracking polls for thirty of its strongest contenders.[16]

National party assistance in campaign communications takes many forms. All six national party organizations conduct issue and opposition research. DNC and RNC research revolves around traditional party positions and the issue stands of incumbent presidents or presidential candidates. Congressional and senatorial campaign committee research is more individualized. The Hill committees send competitive candidates issue packets hundreds of pages long that detail the issues likely to attract press coverage and win the support of specific voting blocs. The packets also include suggestions for exploiting an opponent's weaknesses.

In addition, the national party organizations furnish candidates with assistance in mass media advertising. In 1988 the DCCC's Harriman Center produced 660 television commercials for 125 House candidates.[17] The NRCC directly serviced fewer campaigns, producing a total of only 300 television commercials, but it arranged for many other House candidates to receive media assistance from professional consultants at its expense.[18] The Republican committee also provided House candidates with more comprehensive media packages than did its Democratic counterpart. The NRCC helped develop advertising themes, wrote scripts, and arranged for its candidates' advertisements to be aired on local stations (Klinge, 1989; Pessel, 1989). Democratic candidates, in contrast, were given use of the Harriman Center's recording facilities and technical staff, but had to supply their own creative talent (Kontnik, 1989). The DSCC and NRSC generally do not get as deeply involved in their candidates' campaign communications. They offer advice and criticism, and occasionally pretest their candidates' television and radio advertisements. The senatorial campaign committees play more of an advisory role because Senate campaigns have enough money and experience to hire premier consultants on their own.

The national parties help their congressional candidates raise money from individuals and PACs both in Washington and in their election districts. The Hill committees help congressional candidates organize fund-raising events and develop direct-mail lists. The Hill committees' PAC directors help design the PAC-kits that many candidates use to introduce themselves to the PAC community, mail campaign progress reports, "fax" messages, and spend countless hours on the telephone with PAC managers. The goals of all this activity are to get PAC money flowing to the party's most competitive candidates and away from their candidates' opponents. National party endorsements, communications, contributions, and coordinated expenditures serve as decisionmaking cues that help PACs decide where to invest their money. National party services and transactional assistance are especially important to nonincumbents running for the House because nonincumbents typically do not possess fund-raising lists from previous campaigns, are less skilled at fund raising than incumbents, have none of the clout with PACs that comes with incumbency, and begin the election cycle virtually unknown to members of the PAC community.

State and Local Elections. The national parties' state and local election programs bear similarities to those for congressional elections. The DNC and RNC work with state party leaders to recruit candidates, formulate strategy, and distribute campaign money and services. They also hold workshops to help state and local candidates learn the ins and outs of modern campaigning, recommend professional consultants, and disseminate strategic and technical information through party magazines and briefing papers.

Important differences also exist between national party activity in state and local contests and that in congressional elections. First, the parties give less campaign money and fewer services to state and local candidates, as a reflection of the smaller size of state legislative districts. Second, national committee strategy for distributing campaign money and services to state and local candidates incorporates considerations related to presidential elections and reapportionment. The Hill committees, by contrast, focus almost exclusively on factors related to individual candidates' prospects for success. Last, the national committee staffs go to great lengths to locate state and local candidates worthy of assistance, whereas the Hill committee staffs are inundated with requests for campaign assistance by candidates for Congress (Victor, 1989; Messick, 1989; Chalmers, 1989).

Party-focused Campaigning. In addition to the candidate-focused campaign programs discussed earlier, the national parties conduct generic, or party-focused, election activities designed to benefit all candidates on the party ticket. The most visible of these activities were the party-focused television commercials first aired by the RNC in 1980. Commercials such as the Republicans' "Going to Work" or the Democrats' "Children" advertisements are designed to convey a message about an entire political party and to activate voters nationwide.

More traditional forms of party-focused campaigning include rallies and other grass-roots events. Party-sponsored voter registration and get-out-the-vote drives reached unprecedented levels during the 1980s. Most of these activities are spearheaded by the national committees and conducted in cooperation with congressional, senatorial, state, and local party committees and candidates. The RNC and the Reagan-Bush campaign dwarfed Democratic voter-mobilization efforts in 1984 by investing in excess of $10 million to register more than 4 million previously unregistered Republican identifiers and to contact almost 30 million households (Herrnson, 1988). Following that election, the Democrats expended tremendous energy in their efforts to catch up with the GOP. By 1988 DNC field operatives had helped state party organizations in thirty-two states to develop computerized voter files and to formulate plans to register new voters and get them to the polls. DNC staff members estimate that these efforts resulted in the registration of more than 2 million new Democratic voters and claim that the Democratic party is close to establishing parity with the Republicans in the area of voter mobilization (Chalmers, 1989; McCurry, 1989; Dean, 1989). The RNC staff members do not agree with this appraisal, but they acknowledge that the Democrats have reduced the Republican lead in voter mobilization.

CONCLUSION

American political parties are principally electoral institutions. They focus more on elections and less on initiating policy change than do parties in other Western democracies (Epstein, 1986). American national party organizations were created to perform electoral functions. They developed in response to changes in their environment and the changing needs of their candidates. National party organizational change occurs sporadically. Electoral instability and political unrest have occasionally given party leaders opportunities to restructure the national parties. The most recent waves of party organizational development followed the turbulent 1968 Democratic convention, the Republicans' post-Watergate landslide losses, and the Democrats' traumatic defeat in 1980. These crises provided both opportunities and incentives for party entrepreneurs to restructure the roles and missions of the national, congressional, and senatorial campaign committees.

As a result of this restructuring, the national parties are stronger, more stable, and more influential than ever in their relations with state and local party committees and candidates. National party programs have led to the modernization of many state and local party committees. The national parties also play an important role in contemporary elections. They assist presidential candidates with their campaigns. They give congressional candidates campaign contributions, make coordinated expenditures on their behalf, and provide services in areas of campaigning that require technical expertise, in-depth research, or connections with political consultants, PACs, or other organizations possessing the resources needed to conduct a modern campaign. The national parties provide similar types of assistance to candidates for state and local offices. Although most national party activity is concentrated in competitive districts, candidates of varying degrees of competitiveness benefit from party mass media advertisements and voter-mobilization drives. Indeed, the 1980s witnessed the reemergence of national party organizations as important players in party politics and elections.

NOTES

I thank Robert Biersack for his assistance in compiling Tables 3.1, 3.2, and 3.3.

1. The development of radio and especially television was particularly influential in bringing about an increased focus on candidate-centered election activities. These media are extremely well suited to conveying information about tangible political phenomena, such as candidate images, and less useful in providing information about more abstract electoral actors such as political parties (Ranney, 1983; Graber, 1984; Robinson, 1981; Sorauf, 1980).

2. For further information about the roles that political entrepreneurs played in restructuring the national party organizations during the 1970s and 1980s, see Herrnson and Menefee-Libey (1988).

3. Senator Ted Stevens (R-AK), who chaired the committee during the 1976 election cycle, was not very committed to building up the committee (Herrnson and Menefee-Libey, 1988).

4. This power has been upheld by a number of court decisions, including the U.S. Supreme Court's decisions in *Cousins v. Wigoda* and *Democratic Party of the U.S. v. Wisconsin ex rel LaFollette*. The DNC, however, has retreated from strict enforcement of some party rules. For example, it decided to allow Wisconsin to return to the use of its open primary to select delegates to the national convention following the 1984 election (Epstein, 1986).

5. "Soft money" cannot be spent directly on behalf of federal candidates. The national parties use it to purchase equipment and other organizational resources, to strengthen local party organizations, and to finance voter registration and get-out-the-vote drives. It should be noted that some of the Republicans' Victory '88 accounts were "hard money" accounts, which were subject to FECA regulations, rather than "soft money" accounts. The term *soft money* was coined by Elizabeth Drew (1983).

6. These figures do not include staff employed by either the Democrats' Campaign '88 Committee or the Republicans' Victory '88 Committee. Estimates were provided by party committee staff members.

7. The NRSC also provides selected state party organizations with financial assistance.

8. The 1988 election was the first in which the DSCC and DCCC had the money to make contributions and coordinated expenditures on behalf of Democratic state party committees in every state having a competitive Senate race and in most competitive House races (Chlopak, 1989).

9. As explained in Note 4, the DNC has not been inclined to fully exercise this power.

10. For further information on the candidate-recruitment activities of the national party organizations, see Herrnson (1988).

11. The national parties have given money and campaign assistance to few candidates competing for contested primary contests since the 1984 election cycle. Prior to the 1984 election, the Republican national party organizations backed a number of candidates in contested primaries. Protests registered by state and local party activists in 1984 led RNC members to pass a rule prohibiting committee involvement in House and Senate nominating contests and led the NRCC to institute a policy requiring primary candidates to have the support of their state delegation in the House and of local party leaders before they are given support. The NRSC continues to get involved in a small number of primaries. The DCCC's bylaws bar it from becoming involved in contested primaries, and the DNC and DSCC rarely get involved in them.

12. The coordinated expenditure limit for states with only one House member is $46,100 (Federal Election Commission, 1988a).

13. The Republicans spent $5,000 in this race.

14. These figures exclude independent expenditures by PACs, which are made without the candidates' knowledge or consent, as well as party spending on party-focused television commercials, voter-mobilization drives, and other forms

of party-focused campaigning. The figures are calculated on the basis of those reported in Federal Election Commission (1989).

15. For further information on national party campaign services, see Herrnson (1988), especially Chapters 3 and 4.

16. Benchmark surveys are used early in the election cycle to collect basic information, such as the partisan composition of the electorate and the candidate's level of name recognition. Vulnerability studies are also used early in the election cycle to assess the candidate's level of name recognition and the intensity of public opinion on salient issues, whereas tracking polls are used in the last few weeks of the election to provide an overview of the impact of campaign communications (O'Donnell, 1989; Klinge, 1989).

17. The Harriman Center also produced ads for twelve Senate candidates as well as for a small number of candidates in local elections (Visclosky, 1989).

18. The NRCC's media center also produced ads for a small group of Senate, state, and local candidates (Klinge, 1989; Pessel, 1989).

4

The Reagan Revolution and Party Polarization in the 1980s

WALTER J. STONE
RONALD B. RAPOPORT
ALAN I. ABRAMOWITZ

The process of party change has long been of interest to scholars and other close observers of American politics. The immediate prospect of a partisan realignment, with its far-reaching consequences for the co-alitional makeup of the parties, the leadership of the nation, and the policy agenda of national institutions, has excited interest since the mid-1960s (Burnham, 1970). Realignment, however, is only the most extreme form of partisan change. Changes of a less dramatic nature such as leadership turnover, increased partisan identification with the minority party, and major party reform may have substantial short-term effects on American politics, and may even contribute to an eventual realignment. Since the election of 1980, questions about the effects of the Reagan presidency on partisan change have divided scholars. Some see a realignment as having occurred, others see a realignment at the presidential level only, and still others see the Reagan years as only a temporary aberration. (See Chapter 5.)

In 1980 Ronald Reagan and the Republican party won the presidency from an incumbent Democratic president. The fact that the Republicans also won control of the U.S. Senate for the first time since 1952 suggests that the 1980 election had broader repercussions than those implied by a mere changing of the guard at the White House. Ronald Reagan, moreover, was not just another Republican candidate. He identified himself with the Republican party's conservative wing on economic, social, and foreign policy issues in order to present a clear set of policy alternatives to the traditional Democratic (and Republican) programs.

After winning the presidency, Reagan quickly set to work enacting his agenda, particularly in the areas of economic and foreign policy. He was successful in getting Congress to reduce domestic welfare expenditures by significant amounts, in cutting taxes, and in increasing the nation's budgetary commitment to defense. In doing so, Reagan polarized the parties in Congress. Congressional Republicans were solidly in support of his programs and congressional Democrats were in opposition. Indeed, under Reagan, the indices of partisan polarization in congressional roll-call voting computed by *Congressional Quarterly* reached their highest levels in years (Stanley and Niemi, 1988).

When Reagan won reelection over Walter Mondale in 1984 by landslide proportions, it was clear that he had changed the course of his party and of electoral politics at the national level. The presidential election of 1988 confirmed his success. Who would have guessed that a liberal nominee of the Democratic party, only eight years after Reagan's defeat of Carter, would have to devote so much attention to the question of how to balance the national budget? In addition, much of George Bush's success in sweeping to victory in a spirited nomination battle, and then easily besting Michael Dukakis in November, was attributable to the record popularity of Ronald Reagan.

Whether a true realignment accompanied the Reagan revolution remains unclear at this juncture. Reagan's personal victories did not penetrate the party system to the degree that Franklin Roosevelt's triumph in 1932 transformed the American parties. Reagan actually left office with eight fewer Republican senators than had accompanied him to victory in 1980. Republicans could not win control in the House of Representatives, nor did they make substantial gains in the number of seats they held. The Republican party gained ground in the electorate but failed to capture the loyalty of most party identifiers in the public, and its hold on state and local offices is still substantially the same as it has been throughout the post–World War II period. The Republican party remains a minority party in American politics, except at the presidential level.

However, those quick to dismiss the Reagan years as a passing phenomenon tied solely to the presidential career of its leader would do well to look more closely. Presidential politics, especially as practiced by Ronald Reagan, can have an enormous effect on the attitudes and perceptions of the public and the party system generally, particularly when the president has a unified set of policy initiatives to sell. Presidents occupy a position of extraordinary public visibility and legitimacy, and recent chief executives have not been reluctant about using their office to influence public opinion (Edwards, 1983). Indeed, as Samuel Kernell argues, Ronald Reagan was particularly willing to "go public" by appealing to his popular constituency in order to influence members of Congress and other decisionmakers (Kernell, 1986).

Our concern in this essay is with the effects of the Reagan years on the party system, particularly the activist strata of the political parties. Those individuals who are intensively involved in presidential nomination campaigns are of interest to us because they form important links between presidential politics and the party system as a whole. They help initiate and promote significant change in the issues they favor and the candidates they support. They are also particularly sensitive to, and likely to take positions on, policy initiatives promulgated by political leaders such as the president. In times of political change, it is these activists who are likely to help define and differentiate policy alternatives (Carmines, 1986). Thus, when these individuals change, the implications for the political system can be wide ranging. For example, were it not for the dramatic changes that took place among the activists participating in the Democratic presidential nomination campaigns between 1968 and 1972, George McGovern never could have captured the nomination. McGovern's candidacy, though doomed to failure, not only helped extend legitimacy to the opposition to the Vietnam war but also changed the direction of the Democratic party's foreign policy. And were it not for similar changes after 1976, the Republican party would have been unable to make the transition from the Nixon and Ford wings of the party to the Reagan ascendancy in 1980 (Miller and Jennings, 1986). Thus, an immediate consequence of change among nomination activists is that parties can shift directions rather dramatically in their choice of a presidential nominee and in the platform issues they endorse.

Changes in the activist core of a party reflect outward to the electorate by altering the bases of policy debate both between and within the parties. Party activists are well placed to influence opinion in the electorate and in the halls of government. Activists are more interested and conversant in political debate than most of the public, particularly during times of change. They also interact with the people in government and in party decisionmaking positions. Accordingly, changes among those active in party affairs can be expected to change party behavior in government.

There is every reason to expect substantial change in the form of polarization between the parties in response to the Reagan years. Democrats were faced with a formidable opponent who could not only claim record personal popularity but who sought to use that popularity to promote a policy "revolution." The brand of liberalism promoted by Democrats since their New Deal heyday was clearly in jeopardy. And the Reagan reforms in domestic and foreign policy appeared to be working: Prosperity seemed at hand throughout most of the Reagan presidency, and the drift in American foreign policy during the Carter years appeared to be arrested.

Democrats had to confront the problem of how to recapture the public philosophy. How much of the Reagan agenda should they accept? How could they best protect their domestic constituencies and priorities against what many activists saw as an all-out assault from the right? The answers were not obvious. Unless it was clear that the shift to the right had been accepted by rank-and-file voters, there was little incentive for Democratic activists or candidates to accept Reagan's policies. And, although Reagan maintained record personal popularity, his policies did not. Support for the Contras was low, and there was a growing consensus for cutting the military budget and for increasing at least certain categories of domestic social spending. Sensing these developments, congressional Democrats had hardened their opposition (and Republicans their support) during Reagan's last term, thereby producing the highest level of party polarization in the House throughout Reagan's entire term. In addition, as 1988 got under way there was a clear feeling of uncertainty about the future among the public. How could the Democrats best confront these problems and opportunities so as to become competitive once again at the presidential level?

Republicans also had a problem, albeit a less unpleasant one. Conservative activists had succeeded in nominating one of their own in 1980, and had seen him achieve enormous successes. They had realized gains in Republican partisanship over the previous eight years and, in Ronald Reagan, had a remarkably popular spokesman (Wattenberg, 1990). However, the downward reach of Republican gains to states and localities was limited, and Reagan's popularity masked substantial disagreement over his issue positions. Could the Republican party make its bid for realignment and dominance when much of its policy agenda was rejected by a majority of the American public?

There were also potential intraparty ideological difficulties for the Republicans coming into 1988. The moderate wing of the party had resisted much of the original Reagan agenda. Would this faction, which had supported a relatively moderate George Bush in 1980, be able to forget its commitment to the Equal Rights Amendment and its opposition to a constitutional amendment banning abortion, particularly when Bush shifted his positions on these issues in 1988?

Thus, as 1988 began, partisan prospects for both parties were unclear. Although the Democrats were confronting serious electoral problems, particularly at the presidential level, the lack of policy consensus in the mass public meant that there was little pressure on Democratic activists to shift to the right in issue position or candidate choice. For the Republican activists who had labored so hard for the Reagan victories, there was no incentive to compromise in the wake of an eight-year success story. Thus, we postulate that a pattern of increasing polarization between the parties occurred throughout the Reagan years, rather than a pattern of relative moderation.

To examine this possibility, we must probe for evidence about the response of the parties to the Reagan years. We shall do so by examining the activist stratum of the parties for evidence of change between 1980 and 1988. Our supposition is that if we can uncover significant areas of change, we can offer more informed speculation about the lasting effects of the Reagan presidency on the American two-party system.

THE 1980–1988 PARTY ACTIVIST SURVEY

In order to look at change over the Reagan presidency, we must be able to compare samples of Democratic and Republican activists from 1980 and 1988. Because of turnover in the activist ranks, activists participating in 1988 are not the same people who were activists in 1980. Therefore, to address the sources of change in the parties, we must be able to identify those who have circulated into the activist stratum as well as those who have dropped out. In addition, we must be able to follow activists from 1980 into 1988 to see how these individuals changed (or remained constant) in their attitudes throughout the Reagan years. Our research design allows us to trace the attitudes and behaviors of individual activists throughout the eight-year period, as well as to identify newcomers to the parties in 1988 and those who dropped out after 1980.

In 1980 and 1988 we surveyed Democratic and Republican state convention delegates during the presidential nomination campaign in Iowa and Virginia. These cross-section samples of the state conventions are the centerpiece of our analysis of party change. In both states, delegates to the state conventions were selected as the result of a process that began with local assemblies of the party faithful. Delegates to the state convention represent the culmination of the presidential selection process in their state, and they select from their midst delegates to attend the national presidential nominating conventions. By comparing our cross-sectional survey of 1980 delegates with the 1988 cross-sectional survey of the same stratum in the parties, we can observe the net pattern of change over the eight-year period.[1]

The second component of our design involves a panel of individuals whom we followed from the original 1980 survey and then resurveyed in 1988. The panel feature of the design allows us to monitor how activists responded to the Reagan years. It also permits us to compare those who dropped out of the activist stratum with those who remained active.[2]

Of course, a study of two states cannot capture the full measure of party change at the national level, and national samples would be preferable to our samples of activists in Iowa and Virginia. However, American parties are based on state organizations, and conducting a set of similar surveys in all fifty states would be prohibitively expensive. In addition, we purposely selected two states that exhibit important differences in the areas of political culture and history. By studying these two states, we hope both to capture a healthy portion of response in the parties to the Reagan presidency and to speculate in a reasonable way beyond the limits of our particular data.

ISSUE CHANGE BETWEEN 1980 AND 1988

Political parties are institutions devoted to winning control of public office and affecting the course of government policy. Ultimately, therefore, one of the most important dimensions of change one can examine is change in the policy preferences of those intensely active in the parties. Our analysis of issue change depends on five common items from our 1980 and 1988 questionnaires. We asked respondents to place themselves on a liberal-conservative scale, and we requested their opinions on four specific issues: a constitutional amendment to prohibit abortions, defense spending, affirmative action, and a constitutional amendment to require a balanced budget. The liberal-conservative scale is designed to capture change in the broad philosophical orientations of the parties, whereas the issue items track narrow-gauge patterns of change. The issues are linked primarily to domestic problems because foreign policy problems have tended to be more episodic. The defense spending question taps respondents' attitudes toward increasing defense expenditures relative to domestic spending, an issue that has endured throughout the Reagan years.

In general, our analysis reveals that the parties became more polarized throughout the Reagan years. Many studies have found that Democratic and Republican party activists tend to adopt issue stands substantially more different from each other than is the case among Democrats and Republicans in the electorate (McClosky, Hoffman, and O'Hara, 1960; Miller and Jennings, 1986; Baer and Bositis, 1988). Not only did we find differences between activists in 1980, but these issue differences between the parties grew during the Reagan years. This increased polarization has important consequences for the nature of presidential campaigns, for the ability of the parties to reconcile their differences in Congress, and for the clarity of choice offered to the electorate. Partisan polarization may also be a sign of impending realignment as the parties sharpen

TABLE 4.1
Issue Opinions Among Democratic and Republican State Convention Delegates,
1980 and 1988

	1980		1988	
	Democrats (N=3181)	Republicans (N=2737)	Democrats (N=1379)	Republicans (N=1366)
Political Philosophy				
−Liberal	60%	6%	68%	3%
+Conservative	18	80	13	92
Index of Opinion:	(−42)	(+74)	(−55)	(+89)
Abortion Amendment				
−Oppose	65%	52%	70%	31%
+Favor	25	37	24	64
Index of Opinion:	(−40)	(−15)	(−46)	(+33)
Increase Defense Spending				
−Oppose	48%	10%	78%	18%
+Favor	36	83	17	75
Index of Opinion:	(−12)	(+73)	(−61)	(+57)
Affirmative Action				
−Favor	64%	20%	75%	32%
+Oppose	19	58	16	56
Index of Opinion:	(−45)	(+38)	(−59)	(+24)
Balanced Budget Amendment				
−Oppose	56%	28%	41%	9%
+Favor	23	56	46	86
Index of Opinion:	(−33)	(+28)	(+5)	(+77)

Note: On all issue items in this table, the "liberal" position is scored negatively.

Source: Authors' Party Activist Survey, 1980 and 1988.

their differences on a range of issues and carry those differences to the electorate in presidential campaigns (Pomper, 1972; Beck, 1979).

In Table 4.1 we present a profile of the parties' stands on the issues in 1980 and 1988 based on our cross-sectional surveys of the two states' nominating conventions. We have indicated the percentage of each party taking the liberal position on the item (scored −1) and the percentage adopting the conservative position (scored +1). We have also indicated the difference between the percentage within the party adopting a liberal position on an issue and the percentage adopting the conservative view. We label this percentage difference the "index of opinion," as it captures the dominant opinion in the party. A negative index score indicates a predominantly liberal opinion. An index score of -100 would mean that 100 percent of the party membership adopted the liberal view. A positive score (up to a maximum of $+100$) indicates that conservatives dominate the party.

One can immediately see that the parties tend to have very distinct centers of gravity, such that most Democrats adopt the liberal position on the issues and most Republicans prefer the conservative position. Take the parties' positions on the general liberal-conservative scale as an example. Sixty percent of Democrats in 1980 adopted the liberal position, whereas only 18 percent said they were conservative in their overall political philosophy. The preponderance of liberals among the 1980 Democrats is reflected in an index of opinion score of -42. Republicans were even more homogeneous: Fully 80 percent of their number adopted a conservative philosophy, and only 6 percent said they were liberal. The absolute value of the Republican index of opinion is larger than among Democrats because of the greater unity in the GOP, and it is positive rather than negative, of course, because Republicans overwhelmingly take the conservative view.

There are important differences among the issues that bear comment. For example, given the 1980 Republican national party platform stance in favor of a constitutional amendment to limit abortions, it may come as a surprise that a majority of Iowa and Virginia Republican activists in 1980 actually took the liberal side and opposed the idea. Compare the abortion results in 1980 with those on defense spending in the same year. Republicans were overwhelmingly in favor of increasing defense spending relative to domestic spending, whereas Democrats were more closely divided on the question. Democrats also opposed increases in defense spending, but just barely.

Of course, the major purpose to which we direct our analysis is uncovering and explaining patterns of change. The items in Table 4.1 enable us to sketch the nature of party change among state convention delegates through the Reagan years. From the data in that table we have calculated measures of party polarization and party change on the issues between 1980 and 1988 (see Table 4.2).

The data in Table 4.2 show that the parties became more polarized throughout the Reagan years. We calculated from Table 4.1 the differences between the parties' indexes of opinion to provide a simple measure of party polarization in each year. Consider political philosophy in 1980 as an example. The Democrats scored -42 whereas the Republican score was $+74$. The polarization or difference between the parties in 1980 was thus 116, which reflects the substantial philosophical gap between activists in the two parties. This gap on the liberal-conservative scale increased substantially over the next eight years to 144. If every Democrat

TABLE 4.2
Partisan Polarization and Issue Opinion Change, 1980 and 1988

	Party Polarization			Direction of Issue Change[b]	
	1980	*1988*	*Change*[a]	*Democrats*	*Republicans*
Political Philosophy	116	144	+28	−13	+15
Abortion	25	79	+54	−6	+48
Defense Spending	85	118	+33	−49	−16
Affirmative Action	83	93	+10	−14	−4
Balanced Budget	61	72	+11	+38	+49

[a]Positive changes indicate increasing polarization.
[b]A negative score indicates change in the liberal direction; a positive score indicates change in the conservative direction.

Source: Authors' Party Activist Survey, 1980 and 1988.

were a liberal (for a score of −100) and every Republican were a conservative (for a score of +100), the polarization score would reach the maximum of 200. The differences between the parties by 1988 were approaching the theoretical maximum on general political philosophy, a factor that may have contributed to the divisive quality of the 1988 presidential campaign.

There was also an increase in party polarization on each of the specific issues included in our study. The greatest increases in polarization between the parties occurred on the abortion and defense spending issues. On affirmative action and the balanced budget amendment items, the parties differed more from one another in 1988 than they had in 1980, but the increase in polarization was much less than on the other issues.

The data on party change shown in Table 4.2 indicate how the polarization occurred. The indicators of party change are merely the signed or algebraic differences between the indexes of opinion for each party reported in Table 4.1. Thus, for example, the 1980 index of opinion for Democrats on defense spending was −12. In 1988 Democratic delegates had on average become dramatically more liberal, such that the index of opinion had changed to −61. The change in Democratic opinion on defense spending was therefore −49, reflecting the fact that delegates in 1988 were on the whole much more liberal than their colleagues had been in 1980. The negative change scores indicate movement in the liberal direction; positive scores indicate movement toward a more conservative position.

On the liberal-conservative and abortion items, polarization occurred because the parties moved in opposite directions throughout the eight-year period. The increase in polarization on abortion was greatest because of the dramatic shift to the right by the Republicans coupled with a leftward drift among Democrats. The same pattern, whereby the parties moved in opposite directions, occurred on the liberal-conservative item—and, of course, the result was an increase in polarization.

On the remaining issues, however, the parties moved in the same direction; but polarization nonetheless increased. Thus our finding that the differences between the parties increased throughout the 1980s does not imply that the parties always moved in opposite directions. Indeed, there was a substantial increase in polarization on defense, even though both parties moved in a liberal direction. However, the Democratic party, which consistently represents the liberal view, moved more strongly in the liberal direction than did the Republican party. On the balanced budget amendment, the Republicans increased their support to a greater degree than did the Democrats, even though both parties showed more support than they had in 1980. Whether because the parties moved in opposite directions, or because the movement of one party in one direction exceeded that of the other, party polarization is the story of the parties' responses to the Reagan years.

Our results on party polarization bear some comment before we move to a more thorough accounting of party change in the 1980s. Ronald Reagan made no apologies for his conservative views in his tries for the Republican nomination before 1980, in his successful campaign for that nomination in 1980, or in his presidential campaigns in 1980 and 1984. His conservative philosophy was not merely the source of inflamed campaign rhetoric. Because Reagan was a staunch conservative, and because he vigorously promoted his views as president, it is not surprising to see that the parties polarized in response to his presidency. His successes and popularity could be expected both to increase the legitimacy of his brand of conservatism among activists in his own party and to excite greater opposition among Democrats. This pattern of increased polarization, which is evident on abortion and political philosophy, appears to be consistent with the increased polarization that occurred in Congress during the Reagan years.

On the need for a balanced budget amendment, both parties moved in a conservative direction in response to Reagan. For Republicans, such a move may have meant that Reagan had convinced more of his fellow partisans of the need for that part of his program. Given the large budget deficits of the Reagan presidency, which resulted from cuts in taxes combined with increased defense expenditures, the budget deficit had to be confronted by both parties. Many Democrats may have become convinced of the need for a balanced budget amendment to curb what they viewed as the excesses of another president like Ronald Reagan. Reagan's doubts about affirmative action programs, and especially his concern with continued increases in military spending, appear to have lost ground in both parties. Understandably, Democrats switched to a rejection of the president's positions on these issues at a greater rate than did Republicans; but even among Republican activists, there was significant erosion of the consensus in favor of continued defense expenditures at the expense of domestic priorities.

Party polarization resulted from different processes, depending upon the issue, but it was an overarching reality of the parties' responses to the Reagan years. Reagan was a president who sought to make a difference. One important effect of his efforts was to drive the parties further apart during his tenure in Washington.

ACCOUNTING FOR PARTY CHANGE ON THE ISSUES

We now consider two sources of change in attempting to account for the broad pattern of increased polarization between the parties on the issues. First, the polarization we have observed could have resulted from circulation effects among activists in both parties. That is, relatively moderate activists might have dropped out of the delegate stratum, perhaps because of the heightened ideological climate of political debate. If dropouts in each party were replaced by newcomers further apart on the issues, the net effect on the parties would be increased polarization. A second possibility is that the change in polarization was due to conversion effects. In this event, those who dropped out as delegates would have been very similar to delegates who were newcomers. The increased partisan polarization would have resulted from conversion among individuals who remained active as delegates. In the case of conversion, we would have observed delegates in each party who remained active throughout the period moving apart either because they moved in opposite directions or because one party's cohort moved more than the other's. The implication is that the Reagan presidency had its greatest effects on those who remained active as delegates in their party.

The reality is doubtless a mix of both circulation and conversion effects. By examining the data with these two patterns in mind, we can ascertain the nature of that mix and come to a better understanding of the effects of the Reagan years on the parties.

Circulation Effects

Table 4.3 permits us to describe circulation effects by comparing those who remained active as state convention delegates in 1984 and 1988 ("continuing delegates") with the two circulating cohorts: "Dropouts" are those who dropped out of the delegate stratum of their party following the 1980 election, and "newcomers" are those new to the

TABLE 4.3
1988 Opinions of Circulating Cohorts of Delegates
Compared with Activists Who Continued as Delegates

	Continuing Delegates	Dropouts	Newcomers	Net Circulation Effect
Democrats				
Philosophy	−50	−45	−40	+5
Abortion	−68	−51	−40	+11
Defense Spending	−74	−60	−59	+1
Affirmative Action	−68	−36	−59	−23
Balanced Budget	−50	+1	+31	+30
N=	(231)	(377)	(676)	
Republicans				
Philosophy	+86	+72	+96	+24
Abortion	+15	−5	+53	+58
Defense Spending	+46	+13	+62	+49
Affirmative Action	+29	+14	+20	+6
Balanced Budget	+75	+56	+86	+30
N=	(158)	(274)	(678)	

Source: Authors' Party Activist Survey, 1980 and 1988.

delegate stratum since 1980. Our 1980–1988 panel allows us to compare the 1988 opinions of those who continued to be active as delegates with those who dropped out as state convention delegates. We employ the 1988 cross-section surveys to identify "newcomers" since, by definition, they are not available to our 1980–1988 panel. Note that the entries in Table 4.3 are based entirely upon 1988 opinions. Thus we analyze the dropouts' 1988 opinions in order to ascertain which direction the state conventions would have taken had the dropouts remained as delegates.

In the case of both Democrats and Republicans, the comparisons of activists who continued as delegates with their 1980 colleagues who dropped out show a clear pattern. On the liberal-conservative scale, and on each of the four issue items, activists who remained as delegates were more extreme in their 1988 opinions than those who had dropped out—a finding that is true, without exception, for both parties. The regularity with which relatively moderate Democrats and Republicans tended to drop out of the delegate stratum in their respective parties is striking. It may be that the dropouts generally felt less strongly committed on the issues than those who continued. And as a result of their lower commitment on the issues, they may have been less willing to endure the continuing costs of prolonged party activity and accordingly reduced their commitment to partisan activity.

In order to determine how the parties were affected by dropouts and replacements, we must consider the effects of newcomers on each party. Among Democrats, the replacement effect was less pronounced because newcomers were similar to the dropouts they replaced. Among Republicans, the effect was greater because newcomers were not only more conservative than those who had dropped out; they were also more extreme than the continuing cohort of delegates on every issue save affirmative action. Thus, circulation tended to moderate the Democratic party's position by making the party less liberal, whereas the Republican party was made more extreme in its conservatism as a result of circulation.

We ascertained the net effect of circulation into and out of the delegate stratum by calculating the difference between dropouts and newcomers in each party (see the "Net Circulation Effect" column in Table 4.3). Take abortion as an example. Among Democrats, the net effect of circulation on this issue was to move the party in a conservative direction ($+11$) because newcomers were less liberal (-40) than were the dropouts they replaced (-51). On defense spending, the net effect of circulation was almost zero because the dropouts and newcomers had virtually the same opinions on the issue. On the balanced budget issue, circulation moved the Democrats noticeably to the right. Newcomers on that issue were much more conservative than dropouts ($+31$ and $+1$ respectively), whereas on affirmative action, the party was moved in a liberal direction by circulation because the newcomers were considerably more liberal than those who dropped out. As Table 4.3 shows, the circulation effect on philosophy, abortion, and defense spending was much greater among Republicans than among Democrats. The result for Republicans, then, was a cumulative pattern rather than the offsetting pattern we observed for Democrats. Relatively moderate Republican dropouts, had they remained active in 1988, would have kept the party in a less conservative position than that favored by continuing activists. When the dropouts were replaced by newcomers even more extreme than the continuing group of delegates, the party was pushed markedly to the right.

Circulation of activists out of and into the parties, therefore, contributed to the increase in polarization that we have seen between Democrats and Republicans. Whereas the Democrats shifted only slightly to the right as the net result of circulation, the Republican shift to the right was far greater. The result was an increase in polarization because the Republican move to the right was much more dramatic than the relatively slight moderating effect among Democrats.

Conversion Effects

Circulation is not the whole of the party-change story. But it does contribute substantially to party change given the permeability of the

TABLE 4.4
Conversion Effects Among Continuing Delegates, 1980 and 1988

	Democrats (N=231)			Republicans (N=158)		
	1980	1988	Net Change	1980	1988	Net Change
Philosophy	−54	−50	+4	+78	+86	+12
Abortion	−43	−68	−25	−10	+15	+25
Defense Spending	−25	−74	−49	+74	+46	−28
Affirmative Action	−48	−68	−20	+45	+29	−16
Balanced Budget	−59	−50	+9	+44	+75	+31

Source: Authors' Party Activist Survey, 1980 and 1988.

party system. Over the eight-year period under discussion, a considerable amount of turnover occurred among state convention delegates in Iowa and Virginia. In both parties, only 30 percent of our 1980 panel respondents indicated that they continued to participate as delegates in both 1984 and 1988. Thus, the circulation effects described in Table 4.3 may seem to account for the lion's share of party change over the period.

Conversion effects are important because they help account for the pattern of party change, but they are also of interest in their own right. The conversion effects that result when the same individuals change their positions on the issues may seem unlikely among activists since they are much more interested in politics than the average citizen. They also tend to be much more committed to the ideological and issue opinions they hold, to follow campaigns and party affairs more closely, and to care much more deeply about political outcomes (Rapoport, Abramowitz, and McGlennon, 1986; Stone, Abramowitz, and Rapoport, 1989). Activists are likely to have given considerable thought to the opinions they hold and may change them reluctantly, even in the face of powerful political forces. At the same time, they may alter their opinions precisely because they are closer to politics and are in a position to respond to changing events and personalities. Reagan's perceived successes as president may have converted many Republicans who were initially suspicious of his policy goals or personal abilities. Those same "successes" may have pushed Democratic activists further away from the president in their opinions. Such a pattern of individual change would have contributed to the polarization we observed throughout the Reagan years.

Table 4.4 presents the indexes of opinion in 1980 and 1988 for Democratic and Republican activists who continued as state convention delegates throughout the period. It is interesting to note that on only one item in the set—abortion—did continuing delegates move in opposite directions. On the whole, Democrats became more liberal and Republicans became more conservative. On political philosophy, continuing delegates in both parties shifted slightly to the right. Democrats executed a modest shift to the right on the balanced budget amendment—a shift that was outrun by a more dramatic change in the conservative direction on that issue among Republicans. On defense spending, Democrats made a dramatic move to the left and became nearly unanimous in their opposition to further cuts in domestic programs to fund defense expenditures. Republicans, by contrast, shifted from an overwhelming consensus in favor of more defense spending in 1980 to a more liberal aggregate position in 1988. Finally, on affirmative action, both parties moved modestly to the left.

Summarizing Issue Change

We can summarize our analysis of issue change in the 1980s, first, by combining our estimates of the net circulation and conversion effects in each party to provide an estimate of total change and, then, by assessing the effects of both sources of change on party polarization (see Table 4.5.).[3] The net circulation and conversion effects are merely brought forward from Tables 4.3 and 4.4 respectively. The "total change" estimate in each party is based on the proportion of delegates circulating into the party conventions in 1988 and the proportions remaining active throughout the period. In both parties, 70 percent of the delegates from our 1980 sample dropped out, whereas 30 percent were "continuing." Therefore, we calculate the total change in Table 4.5A as the effect of circulation discounted by the proportion of the delegates circulating in and out (.7), plus the effect of conversion discounted by the proportion of our sample continuing as delegates throughout the period (.3).

Notice that circulation and conversion effects do not always work in tandem. On abortion for the Democrats and on defense spending for Republicans, circulation had the effect of making the party more conservative. The liberalizing effect of conversion on abortion among Democrats completely offset the circulation effect to yield an estimated change of zero. Among Republicans on defense spending, the conservative effects of circulation outweighed the liberalizing effects of conversion, leaving the party noticeably more conservative than it would have been had the full 1980 cohort of delegates remained active through 1988.

The estimates of the sources of partisan polarization (see Table 4.5B) are simply cross-party comparisons of the net circulation effects and the net conversion effects on party differences. Once again, these net effects are discounted by the proportions of activists in our sample who circulated and/or continued as delegates through the period. A positive score indicates that polarization increased on the item, whereas the zero on

TABLE 4.5
Sources of Change and Party Polarization Among Delegates Between 1980 and 1988

		(A) Summary of Change	
	Total Change =	.7(Circulation Net) +	.3(Conversion Net)
Democrats			
Philosophy	+5	+5	+4
Abortion	0	+11	−25
Defense Spending	−14	+1	−49
Affirmative Action	−22	−23	−20
Balanced Budget	+24	+30	+9
Republicans			
Philosophy	+20	+24	+12
Abortion	+48	+58	+25
Defense Spending	+26	+49	−28
Affirmative Action	−1	+6	−16
Balanced Budget	+30	+30	+31

		(B) Sources of Partisan Polarization	
	Total Polarization =	.7(Polarization from Circulation) +	.3(Polarization from Conversion)
Philosophy	+15	+19	+8
Abortion	+48	+47	+50
Defense Spending	+40	+48	+21
Affirmative Action	+21	+29	+4
Balanced Budget	+7	0	+22

Source: Authors' Party Activist Survey, 1980 and 1988.

the balanced budget item indicates no change in polarization due to circulation. The total polarization effect is calculated by taking the difference between the total effects of circulation and conversion in the Democratic party and the total effects of both sources of change in the Republican party.

Our estimates of the effects of change on party polarization support the claim that the Reagan years saw the parties move apart. On every issue save the balanced budget amendment, both circulation and conversion had the effect of increasing the differences between the parties. And even on the balanced budget item, the net polarizing effect of conversion left the parties further apart in 1988 than in 1980, despite the failure of circulation to contribute to that trend. Thus, even when the effect of change was to move the parties in the same direction (as on the philosophy, affirmative action, and balanced budget items), the parties nonetheless moved further apart than they had been in 1980 (see Table 4.2) or would have been had all 1980 activists continued as delegates through 1988.

In short, the Reagan years drove a deeper wedge between the parties on the issues we have studied. A full explanation of this increase in polarization would take us beyond the purpose of this essay. However, we would be remiss not to consider the links between the issue changes we have observed and the changes in party leadership. Hence we turn next to an analysis of change in candidate coalitions to unravel further the nature and sources of party change in the 1980s.

CANDIDATE CHANGE IN THE 1980s

In one sense, candidate-centered analysis of change is trivial. Jimmy Carter was the Democratic party's incumbent nominee for the presidency in 1980; he was not a candidate in 1988. Because there was a completely different cast of characters vying for the Democratic presidential nomination, change took place. Such change is common in American presidential politics, especially within the losing party. If parties are permeable among the activist ranks, they are in constant turmoil in the candidate ranks as individual fortunes rise and fall with electoral outcomes and public opinion polls.

More interesting than the changing of the guard brought on by the American electoral calendar is the response of the activist core of each party to candidate change. Thus we are drawn back to our concern with issues and with the effects of circulation and conversion, for candidate change is a primary mechanism for promoting party change. For example, it remains an open question as to whether the Republican party after Reagan will be the same party as it was during the Reagan years. Certainly the candidacy of Pat Robertson was designed to reshape the party by capitalizing on the new right's political agenda. On the Democratic side, Jesse Jackson has made no bones about his desire to recruit new participants into the party and thereby work significant change. Therefore, we can look to candidate factions for important clues about sources of internal conflict within the parties, as well as for a fuller understanding of the forces at work creating party change.

We begin by noting the distribution of candidate preferences among respondents to our 1980 and 1988 cross-sections (Table 4.6). Preferences among state convention delegates in the two states do not necessarily reflect the preferences of lower-level activists in the party, nor do they reflect the preferences of the nation as a whole. Because our surveys were conducted in Iowa and Virginia, two states with strong Robertson support, it is not surprising that Bush was the preferred candidate of only a minority of Republican activists in our sample and that Pat

TABLE 4.6

Candidate Preference Among Delegates, 1980 and 1988

	1980			1988	
	Democrats (N=3111)	Republicans (N=2702)		Democrats (N=1102)	Republicans (N=1331)
Carter	71%	—	Dukakis	45%	—
Kennedy	23	—	Gephardt	11	—
Other Democrats	6	—	Gore	10	—
			Jackson	11	—
			Simon	16	—
			Other Democrats	8	—
Reagan	—	59%	Bush	—	33%
Bush	—	24	Dole	—	20
Other Republicans	—	17	Kemp	—	9
			Robertson	—	33
			Other Republicans	—	5
	100%	100%		100%	100%

Source: Authors' Party Activist Survey, 1980 and 1988.

Robertson had a following equally as large. Because our major interest is not to explain the candidate preferences of the parties in 1988 *per se* but to note the continuities and discontinuities between candidate factions at the beginning and end of the Reagan years, of greater importance is the fact that substantial proportions of our samples preferred candidates other than the eventual nominee in each party. By tracing patterns of candidate support, we can observe some of the effects of party factionalism that attend candidate-based conflict within the parties.

The two major candidate factions within the Democratic party in 1980 were tied to Jimmy Carter and Senator Edward Kennedy. Carter had been elected president in 1976 as a moderate southerner with a strong commitment to civil rights. He was challenged for his party's nomination in 1980 by Senator Kennedy on several grounds linked both to his personal style of leadership and to his policy agenda. Carter was perceived by many Democrats to be an ineffective president who had failed to manage the economy and whose policies abroad were contributing to drift and confusion. Edward Kennedy in particular accused Carter of abandoning the liberal agenda of Franklin Roosevelt and Lyndon Johnson. Kennedy's challenge fell considerably short of winning the nomination, but it did succeed in drawing ideological and issue-based battle lines within the party.

The Republican fight for the nomination in 1980 was also waged between ideological factions within the party. Ronald Reagan stood for staunch conservatism in domestic and foreign affairs, whereas George

TABLE 4.7
Factional Continuity Among Continuing Delegates, 1980 and 1988

| | (A) Democrats | |
	1980 Preference for Carter (N=552)	1980 Preference for Kennedy (N=170)
1988 Candidate Preference:		
Dukakis	27%	26%
Gephardt	13	18
Gore	22	4
Jackson	8	19
Simon	17	19
Other Democrats	12	14
	100%	100%

| | (B) Republicans | |
	1980 Preference for Reagan (N=343)	1980 Preference for Bush (N=129)
1988 Candidate Preference		
Bush	47%	73%
Dole	22	21
Kemp	21	2
Robertson	6	1
Other Republicans	3	3
	100%	100%

Source: Authors' Party Activist Survey, 1980 and 1988.

Bush appealed to a more moderate brand of Republicanism. In the 1980 nomination campaign especially, Bush supported the Equal Rights Amendment and made clear his severe reservations about Reagan's economic policy. Ideology does not offer anything like a complete explanation of candidate support among activists in nomination campaigns (Stone and Abramowitz, 1983), but when candidates make appeals to ideological constituencies within their party, it is important to trace those factions in order to monitor party change. Table 4.7 begins that tracing by showing the 1988 candidate preferences of the principal 1980 candidate factions within each party in our 1980–1988 panel.

The remarkable thing about the 1980 Democratic factions is how similar they were in the areas of candidate preferences to those in 1988. There are vestiges of the ideological split between Kennedy and Carter in the greater proportions of Kennedy partisans who preferred the liberal Jesse Jackson in 1988, and in the relatively large number who favored the centrist southerner Albert Gore among Carter supporters. Nonetheless, the slight edge for Richard Gephardt in the 1980 Kennedy faction is not easily explained on ideological grounds, nor are there sharp differences in the proportions of Kennedy and Carter supporters favoring the liberal Paul Simon. Likewise, the proportions favoring Michael Dukakis were equal among both the Carter and Kennedy factions.

Factional continuity is much clearer in the Republican party, in part because George Bush was a candidate in both 1980 and 1988. In our panel, Bush retained almost three-quarters of his supporters from his first run for the GOP nomination. It is of particular interest that less than half of Reagan's faction preferred that the vice-president run on his own eight years later. Both of the 1980 camps contributed equally to the Robert Dole effort, but a far larger proportion of 1980 Reagan supporters than Bush partisans from that year preferred the conservative Jack Kemp. Likewise, although Pat Robertson did not attract much support from any of the 1980 delegates, he fared better among those who had preferred Reagan than among Bush supporters. Thus there is some evidence of ideological continuity on the Republican side as well, inasmuch as Reagan supporters were much more likely to be attracted to the conservative candidacies of Kemp and Robertson than were those who had preferred George Bush in 1980. But the continuity among Bush supporters from 1980 onward is particularly striking since, by all appearances, the George Bush who ran a campaign designed to capture the moderate wing of the Republican party in 1980 was not the same candidate who captured the nomination of a more conservative GOP eight years later.

A second way of identifying factional patterns associated with the candidates is to examine the issue preferences of each candidate's supporters. Table 4.8 presents the index of opinion for each candidate's supporters on the political philosophy and issue items in 1980 and 1988. The results in this table were taken from our cross-section surveys of the state conventions in each year. The factional structure in 1980 was very clear in both parties. Reagan supporters were substantially to the right of Bush partisans on every item in the set, and Kennedy Democrats were plainly to the left of their co-partisans, who preferred to renominate Jimmy Carter. In 1988 the scenario was somewhat murkier, if only because there were more candidates with substantial support for the nomination in each party. The pattern among Republicans was that Bush attracted partisans who, on averge, were to the right of Dole supporters but were less conservative than the Kemp and Robertson camps. On most of the issues, the differences among the factions were not terribly large (abortion among the Republicans was the glaring exception). The Bush faction in 1988 adopted a position that, on balance, was just a shade on the liberal side in opposition to a constitutional amendment

TABLE 4.8

Index of Opinion Scores for Major Candidate Factions, 1980 and 1988

	(A) Republicans					
	1980		1988			
	Reagan	Bush	Bush	Dole	Kemp	Robertson
N =	(1647)	(565)	(509)	(294)	(130)	(407)
Philosophy	+92	+49	+87	+75	+96	+99
Abortion	+11	−58	−10	−3	+68	+94
Defense Spending	+86	+62	+58	+26	+74	+76
Affirmative Action	+50	+23	+32	+8	+52	+17
Balanced Budget	+62	+1	+72	+71	+82	+89

	(B) Democrats						
	1980		1988				
	Carter	Kennedy	Dukakis	Gephart	Gore	Jackson	Simon
N =	(2102)	(675)	(479)	(118)	(97)	(115)	(169)
Philosophy	−29	−79	−53	−31	00	−66	−77
Abortion	−36	−50	−54	−21	−38	−55	−59
Defense Spending	+4	−52	−62	−58	−28	−60	−77
Affirmative Action	−37	−65	−55	−35	−21	−62	−68
Balanced Budget	−26	−42	−1	+28	+12	−12	−12

Source: Authors' Party Activist Survey, 1980 and 1988.

prohibiting abortion. Indeed, the potential for conflict over the abortion issue within the GOP was reflected in the huge disparity between Bush and Robertson supporters.

The Democratic party's nominee, Governor Michael Dukakis, like his counterpart in the Republican party, attracted supporters who, on average, were between the extremes of the factional structure in his party. On most issues, the index of opinion among Dukakis supporters reveals them to be firmly situated in the liberal camp. But both Jesse Jackson and Paul Simon attracted Democratic activists who were more liberal on average than those who supported the Massachusetts governor. At the same time, Richard Gephardt and Senator Albert Gore attracted followers who were generally more moderate than the Dukakis faction.

Perhaps the most important findings in Table 4.8 for understanding party change are the differences between the 1980 Bush supporters and his backers in 1988. On every issue except defense spending, the Bush faction in 1988 was markedly more conservative then its counterpart in 1980. And on defense spending, the liberal drift in the Bush faction (−4) was not as great as the change in the Republican party as a whole (−16). Thus, although we can say that Bush was more moderate than two of his competitors in 1988, he was certainly attracting a more

TABLE 4.9
Perceptions of Reagan and Bush Ideological Positions Among Delegates,
1980 and 1988

	1980		1988	
	Democrats (N=2810)	Republicans (N=2688)	Democrats (N=1152)	Republicans (N=1297
Reagan	+88	+96	+89	+96
Bush	+59	+38	+89	+79

Source: Authors' Party Activist Survey, 1980 and 1988.

conservative following than he did in 1980. Of course, he lost the nomination to Ronald Reagan in 1980, and in the eight years since that loss his party drifted markedly to the right. It was nearly inevitable, then, that Bush's supporters in 1988 would be more conservative.

But knowing that the average Bush supporter in 1988 was much more conservative than his average supporter in 1980 tells us only part of the story. How did the candidate himself change over the period, and what forces created his 1988 supporting coalition? In an attempt to answer these questions, we asked our respondents in 1980 and 1988 to place Ronald Reagan and George Bush on the same liberal-conservative scale used to classify the activists' own political philosophy. We then coded their placements of Reagan and Bush in the same manner as we had done the issue coding earlier: −1 for a liberal placement, +1 for a conservative placement, and 0 for a placement in the middle of the scale. Table 4.9 presents the indexes of opinion calculated for the placements of Ronald Reagan and George Bush in 1980 and 1988.

Both Democratic and Republican activists in 1980 understood the difference between Ronald Reagan's brand of conservatism and that of George Bush. The dominant opinion in both parties was that Reagan was a conservative, whereas Bush's placement was much more moderate. Particularly among Republicans, Bush was seen as moderately conservative and Reagan as very conservative (remember, the most conservative index of opinion is +100). In 1988 Republicans placed Reagan at exactly the same place they had in 1980, and Democrats were almost perfectly consistent with their 1980 placement of Reagan. But the change in Bush's placement was dramatic. Among Democrats the index of opinion on the ideological placement of Bush had changed by +30 points, and among Republicans it had changed +41. Democrats actually perceived Bush and Reagan as being at the same point on the liberal-conservative scale in 1988, whereas Republicans still saw Bush as more moderate than his mentor. Nevertheless, the gap between them was much less than it had been in 1980.

Very clearly, Bush's years in the vice-presidency under Ronald Reagan altered the activists' perception of his political philosophy. Although he had vigorously challenged some of Reagan's positions in 1980, the 1988 Bush brand of conservatism was seen as indistinguishable from Reagan's by Democrats and as only slightly more moderate by Republicans. In the 1988 campaign, Bush stood four-square against further taxation, having changed his position on the Reagan economic program from scoffing about "voodoo economics" to pugnacious attacks on the "tax and spend" Democrats and invitations to "read my lips." And although Bush had supported the ERA and had been cautiously in favor of abortion on demand, he took a strong anti-abortion stand in 1988. Bush's shift to the right during Reagan's terms seems to have been genuine, and our activist respondents probably perceived the magnitude of that shift correctly.

Can candidate change in the Republican party help explain the issue change we have observed? Table 4.10 shows the index of opinion scores for 1980 and 1988 in terms of candidate faction in the two elections. Although activists understood that George Bush had moved sharply to the right between 1980 and 1988, it cannot be said that he persuaded his 1980 supporters to move with him on the issues. On political philosophy, abortion, and the balanced budget, continuing Bush supporters moved to the right, but to a degree that was roughly consistent with the general conservative movement among continuing Republican activists. Notice also that the Bush supporters who continued from 1980 were considerably more liberal than the Reagan partisans who turned to Bush as their candidate in 1988. The continuing Bush supporters were also more liberal than Bush supporters generally (see Table 4.8).

These results suggest that Bush shifted between 1980 and 1988 to a position more compatible with his party. In doing so, he may have lost part of his 1980 coalition to the slightly more moderate Robert Dole. Notice that the 1980 Bush supporters who switched to Dole were more liberal on every item than those who stayed with the vice-president in 1988. At the same time, although Bush picked up a healthy proportion of conservative Reagan supporters, the more conservative of Reagan's 1980 supporters tended to prefer Jack Kemp in 1988. This makes perfect sense inasmuch as the one candidate remaining from 1980 changed his position in the eyes of activists far more than did the average Republican delegate. In moving to the right, Bush became more acceptable to the conservative wing of his party. But most true-blue conservatives opted for Kemp (or Robertson) as a standard-bearer in keeping with their ideology and issue opinions. Had the vice-president retained the relatively moderate stance he adopted in 1980, he might have had a much more difficult time securing the nomination. As matters stood in 1988, the

TABLE 4.10
Index of Opinions by Candidate Coalitions Among
Republican Delegates, 1980 and 1988

Candidate Preference:	Bush '80—Bush '88 (N=105)		Reagan '80—Bush '88 (N=158)	
	1980 Opinion	1988 Opinion	1980 Opinion	1988 Opinion
Philosophy	+51	+69	+93	+92
Abortion	−65	−42	−7	+9
Defense Spending	+61	+19	+91	+68
Affirmative Action	+23	+12	+56	+30
Balanced Budget	−2	+51	+43	+79

Candidate Preference:	Bush '80—Dole '88 (N=28)		Reagan '80—Dole '88 (N=77)	
	1980 Opinion	1988 Opinion	1980 Opinion	1988 Opinion
Philosophy	+55	+59	+94	+90
Abortion	−45	−44	+18	+14
Defense Spending	+50	+6	+74	+22
Affirmative Action	+34	−26	+30	+16
Balanced Budget	−11	+12	+74	+79

Candidate Preference:	Reagan '80—Kemp '88 (N=73)	
	1980 Opinion	1988 Opinion
Philosophy	+96	+98
Abortion	+33	+54
Defense Spending	+89	+68
Affirmative Action	+62	+53
Balanced Budget	+85	+72

Source: Authors' Party Activist Survey, 1980 and 1988.

Republican party was represented by a candidate who had artfully shifted his positions (or, depending on the perspective, had cynically manipulated his image) in order to be in step with his party. He did so, however, without any apparent ill-effects on his general election chances against the Democratic nominee. Most remarkable, perhaps, Bush was able to execute his move to the right while holding onto the bulk of his moderate 1980 supporting coalition.

CONCLUSION

The eight years of the Reagan presidency saw the parties grapple with a number of potential sources of internal conflict. Between 1980 and 1988 the Democrats continued in vain their search for national leadership and an agenda that would allow them to recapture the White House. Republicans benefited from an extraordinarily popular leader whose policy agenda was clear, if not the source of the president's popularity. Change in the Republican party appeared, for the most part, to be occurring in the direction of Ronald Reagan's ideological inclinations. The Republican party was more conservative in 1988 than it had been in 1980 in its general political philosophy, on the abortion issue, and on the question of a balanced budget amendment. On affirmative action and defense spending, it moderated its position between 1980 and 1988. The Democrats appeared to be reacting to Reagan on defense spending, abortion, affirmative action, and political philosophy. Only on the balanced budget amendment did Democratic activists change in a direction favored by the outgoing president.

It was no surprise to find that the parties moved apart as a result of the Reagan years. A president with great personal popularity and a strong ideological commitment, coupled with the widespread feeling that his program was working, likely moved his party toward his own views. An important consequence of Ronald Reagan's presidency was that the stakes in political conflict were raised. The Democratic failure to win the White House in any of the three elections throughout the decade meant losing not merely the symbolic and material accoutrements of office but also the wide range of policy goals to which the Democratic party had long-standing commitments.

Factionalism within the parties was partially linked to the presence of particular candidates. This connection was most evident among Republicans, as we were able to observe the effects of continuity in the persons of Ronald Reagan and George Bush. Among our panel respondents, Ronald Reagan was consistently viewed as staunchly conservative. George Bush, however, migrated quite dramatically to the right between his first run at his party's nomination in 1980 and his successful campaign in 1988. Surprisingly, despite Bush's rightward shift, he retained a large majority of his more moderate supporters from 1980. To be sure, there was evidence of ideological factionalism in both parties tied to candidate support, but ideological conflict within the parties does not appear to rigidly categorize activists. Democratic supporters of the centrist Jimmy Carter in 1980, for example, supported Michael Dukakis for the nomination in 1988 at the same rate as did supporters of the liberal Edward Kennedy. Ideological and issue distinctions among the candidates in both parties were evident; but in the absence of the continuity provided by the continuation of the same individual as a candidate, a fair amount of reshuffling of activist loyalties appears to have taken place.

As the activist stratum we have studied is highly permeable, we found considerable coming and going among our delegates in the 1980s.

Circulation has the potential to work substantial changes in an American political party simply because there is so much of it: Recall that fully 70 percent of delegates in our two states dropped out between 1980 and 1988. Thus an incredibly potent source of change is made available to those who would attempt to influence national politics through the presidential selection process. Ronald Reagan's own career attests to the efficacy of this avenue of change. As the Reagan years recede and the parties respond to new issues and new leadership, change is likely to continue. For example, we found that the overwhelming majority of supporters of Pat Robertson in 1988 were newcomers not only to activity as state convention delegates but to party activity of any sort. With additional changes in the presidential arena sure to come, many of these activists may also drop out. But the point holds true nonetheless: The parties are available for the taking. Whether the agenda for change is a liberal one associated with a George McGovern or a Jesse Jackson, or a conservative one associated with a Ronald Reagan or a Pat Robertson, the mobilization of new activists into the presidential nomination campaign is a viable strategy for influencing the direction of a party.

Of course, the Robertson phenomenon, however episodic, must itself be considered part of the Reagan legacy. Reagan prepared the way for a new-right candidate whose appeal was directed primarily to "amateurs" strongly motivated by religious ideals. That legacy may well continue to influence politics within the Republican party for years to come. By the same token, the Democratic party must continue its struggle to find a coherent response to the Reagan challenge. An important part of the resulting clash between the parties is very likely to be continued polarization with more visible differences between the Democratic and Republican camps. In times of partisan change up to and including realigning change, the parties differentiate themselves clearly as they search for new bases of support and new ways of confronting the opposition. There are tantalizing hints of such a pattern of change in our data—a pattern that conforms with the polarizing change in the Congress. The Reagan years doubtless had continuing effects on the American party system. Among the possible results are long-term party polarization and realignment. If those results include a clearer sense of where the parties differ, coupled with a revitalized debate over national priorities, the parties will emerge as stronger arbiters of the nation's political life.

NOTES

An earlier version of this chapter was presented at the Annual Meeting of the American Political Science Association, Atlanta, Georgia, August 31–September

3, 1989. We are grateful to the National Science Foundation for support of the party activist surveys and to Lonna Atkeson and Jay McCann for valuable research assistance.

1. We distributed questionnaires at the Democratic and Republican state conventions in Iowa and Virginia in both 1980 and 1988. The response rate in 1980 was 62.9 percent, with 2,780 Democrats and 3,385 Republicans responding. In 1988 we received 1,438 questionnaires from Democrats and 1,393 from Republicans, for a 60.6 percent response rate. The n's are smaller in 1988 than in 1980 because we sampled delegates in the latter year, whereas in 1980 we distributed questionnaires to all in attendance.

2. The panel component of the design required that we trace respondents from the 1980 cross section eight years after the original survey. Of the 3,645 1980 respondents for whom we had names and addresses, we were able to trace 2,842, or 78 percent, successfully. Of these, we received responses from 1,522, or 53.6 percent. For an extraordinarily long panel of eight years, this is a very satisfying response, but it was inevitably a small subset of the full 1980 cross section. In examining the distributions of all variables in the file of the full 1980 cross section compared with our panel subset, we found remarkably few significant differences. The panel was almost perfectly representative on the 1980 issue items of the larger cross section.

3. The estimates of net change and polarization in Table 4.5 do not match the estimates in Table 4.3 because the latter are based on direct comparisons of the 1980 cross section with the 1988 cross section. In Table 4.5, our estimates of circulation effects take into account the change in opinion among dropouts by basing the calculations on their 1988 opinion. Because the dropouts changed their opinions between 1980 and 1988, our analysis does not merely disaggregate the cross-sectional change reported in Table 4.3.

PART THREE

The Changing Relationship Between Parties and Voters

5

The Electorate's View of the Parties

WARREN E. MILLER

In 1952, at the same time the University of Michigan's Survey Research Center was conducting its first major study of electoral behavior in an American presidential election, V. O. Key, Jr., was bringing out the third edition of his classic text, *Politics, Parties, and Pressure Groups* (Key, 1952). In the opening paragraphs of Chapter 20, "Electoral Behavior: Inertia and Reaction," Key drew two broad conclusions about the American electorate: "In substantial degree the electorate remains persistent in its partisan attachments. The time of casting a ballot is not a time of decision for many voters; it is merely an occasion for the reaffirmation of a partisan faith of long standing. . . . A second main characteristic evident in electoral behavior is that under some conditions voters do alter their habitual partisan affiliations. To what condition is their shift in attitude a response?" Latter-day political scientists have spent the better part of four decades testing these two conclusions and trying to answer Key's single question. Under the impetus of the Michigan research, "party identification" replaced "habitual partisan affiliation," but the basic terms of the query into the nature of the citizens' enduring partisan attachments have remained very much as Key identified them.

The results of the first four major Michigan studies of the national electorate were entirely in line with Key's first assertion as well as with his preoccupation with persistence and inertia as attributes of mass electoral behavior. From 1952 to 1964 national survey data, bolstered by a study that plotted individual change over time, documented a great persistence in citizens' identifications with the Democratic and Republican parties. There was a brief upturn in Democratic support in 1964, but it disappeared four years later, drawing perhaps too little attention to a condition under which partisan attitudes had shifted. Other than that temporary perturbation, Democrats enjoyed a consistent 15- to 18-point edge over Republicans. During the same period, the measures of the strength or intensity of partisan attachments seemed to confirm the thesis of partisan stability; in election after election, strong identifiers outnumbered nonpartisans by virtually identical margins of about 25 percentage points.

Without destroying the suspense or giving away the story line (as the latter is not without its complexities), I think it fair to note that the period from 1952 to 1964 is now often referred to as the "steady state" era (Converse, 1976). A series of inquiries into this era established party identification as distinctly different from the partisan character of the single vote, both in concept and in operational measure. The role of party identification as a predisposition that powerfully influences citizens' perceptions and judgments was spelled out (Campbell, Converse, Miller, and Stokes, 1960). And in some reifications or glorifications of more sober analysis, party identification was sometimes referred to as the "unmoved mover," or the "first cause" of electoral behavior. Certainly, the evidence was all that V. O. Key could have hoped for as documentation of his hypothesis that partisan attachments had great stability at the level of the individual as well as that of the aggregate.

At the same time, the theme of party realignment continued to attract attention among political analysts. This was particularly so among Republican enthusiasts who saw in the Eisenhower victories (and the initial Republican congressional successes that accompanied them) the possibility of a resurgence for the Republican party. The narrow Kennedy victory in 1960, in the face of a presumably daunting Democratic plurality in the eligible electorate, added fuel to the Republican fire and, at least in part, aided the Republican nomination of Goldwater in 1964 on the premise that he would mobilize latent conservative Republican sympathies and bring an end to the Democratic hegemony (Converse, Clausen, and Miller, 1965).

Although the Goldwater candidacy was something less than a triumph of Republican expectations, another four years later the Republican Nixon *was* elected and, for the first time since systematic modern measurement had dominated social scientific analysis of electoral behavior, the bedrock of party identification cracked. The partisan balance was not disturbed and the Democratic dominance was unchanged, but the strength and intensity of partisanship declined. First in 1968, then in 1972, and finally again in 1976, each successive reading taken at election time revealed fewer strong partisans and more citizens devoid of any partisan preference.

PARTY ALIGNMENT, 1952–1980

Fortunately for the stability of the country, it was largely political scientists and not national leaders who reacted to the decline in the fortunes of party in the electorate. Political scientists, however, made

TABLE 5.1
Partisan Balance of Party Identifications
by Gender, Region, and Race, 1952–1988

Year	National Electorate[a] D	I	R	B	White Males South	Non-South	White Females South	Non-South	Blacks
1952	47	26	28	19	56	8	53	4	37
1956	44	28	29	15	55	6	45	−3	31
1960	45	26	30	15	39	3	38	2	27
1964	52	24	25	27	43	15	45	14	65
1968	45	31	25	20	28	5	36	8	83
1972	41	36	23	18	21	4	23	9	59
1976	40	38	23	17	25	6	21	3	64
1980	40	37	23	17	15	4	20	12	67
1984	37	36	27	10	13	−4	15	0	59
1988	35	37	23	7	−1	−6	19	−6	56
80–88	−5	0	5	−10	−16	−10	−1	−18	−11

[a]D: Democrat; I: Independent; R: Republican; B: Balance
Note: Entries for the first three columns are strong and weak party identifiers (D and R) and independents. Subsequent entries are the proportions of Republican identifiers, strong and weak, subtracted from the proportions of Democratic identifiers, strong and weak.

Source: Data for the entire eligible electorate were taken from the Michigan Survey Research Center of the Center for Political Studies, National Election Studies series.

the most of it, and many made far too much of it (Burnham, 1975). Even though persuasive evidence of a national party realignment was not to appear for another twenty years,[1] the literature on parties, elections, and electoral behavior from 1968 on was replete with analysis and discourse on party dealignment and realignment. When such analysis rested on a proper disaggregation of national totals and the examinations of subsets of citizens experiencing real change under local political conditions, the facts are not in dispute. Change *was* occurring in the South (Beck, 1977). Hindsight makes it particularly clear that change in party identification had begun among white southerners as early as 1960 and was simply accentuated and accelerated in the late 1960s under the combined impetus of Goldwater's "southern strategy," Johnson's promotion of civil rights legislation such as the Voting Rights Acts of 1964 and 1965 as a part of his vision of the Great Society, and the economic as well as foreign policies of the Democratic party leaders in the 1970s and 1980s (Black and Black, 1987).

The most vivid contrast between the changes occurring in the South and the virtually total absence of change outside the South is provided in the comparison of white males in Table 5.1. In 1952 the one-party nature of the post–Civil War South was reflected in the fact that self-declared Democrats outnumbered Republicans among southern white males by 68 to 12.[2] The McGovern candidacy in 1972 saw that margin reduced to 42 to 21; and 1988 witnessed a virtual dead heat, 29 to 30. Apparently the Democratic candidacies of Johnson and Carter had slowed the tides of change without completely stemming them. Outside the South, there is no evidence among men or women of a trend either away from the Democrats or toward the Republicans until 1984. The year of Johnson's election, 1964, saw a brief surge of Democratic sympathies that was immediately followed by a decline, or return to "normalcy," among white citizens. Even so, the two regional patterns stand in stark contrast to each other.

The changing distributions of the party identifications of black citizens is, of course, a story unto itself. The figures in Table 5.1 understate the spectacular changes in the contributions of blacks to recent political history because they do not reflect the changes in the politicization and mobilization of blacks during the 1950s and 1960s.

The aggregation of the various patterns created by differences in gender, race, and region appears in the first columns of Table 5.1. The net result, nationally, does reflect meaningful year-by-year differences, but it also supports the overall conclusion that prior to 1984 there was little manifestation of a realignment that would end Democratic dominance of popular partisan loyalties.

Despite occasional election-day evidence of some resurgence of Republican affinities, and despite reports of increased Republican organizational strength, the dominance of Democrats over Republicans in the eligible electorate across the nation did not waver throughout the 1960s or 1970s. Even despite the election and reelection of Richard Nixon in the 1968 and 1972 presidential elections, the data on the underlying partisan balance of party identification did not change. Not even in 1980—when Ronald Reagan made it five out of eight wins for Republican candidates for the presidency, and with another Republican landslide making history with the defeat of an incumbent (Democratic) president—was there a suggestion of basic changes in partisan sentiments outside the South.

In order to reconcile all the evidence of stability and change in party identification and in the vote between 1952 and 1980, it is necessary to separate the analyses of the *directional balance* of partisanship between Democrats and Republicans from the study of changes in the *strength* of party identification (i.e., the ratio of strong partisans to nonpartisans).

CHANGES IN THE STRENGTH OF PARTISANSHIP

The story of the apparent decay and rebirth of partisanship is fascinating and complex, and it rests on evidence surrounding the elections of the 1980s. The first *national* decline in the strength of party identification after 1952 occurred in 1968, coincident with a retreat among white citizens outside the South from the partisan Democratic high of 1964. The drop in strength of party identifications was apparent in national estimates and was widely interpreted as an indication that strong partisans were rejecting old loyalties and taking on the role of nonpartisans. A relatively simple analysis of changes in the relationship between the partisanship and the age of citizens might have forestalled—or at least modified—such interpretations. It is true that the decline in the strength of partisanship was reflected in a temporary diminution of partisan intensity among *older* citizens, but the portent for the future, as well as the reason for the apparent decline in party fortunes, was contained in the contrast between the partisanship of the youngest and the oldest cohorts.

In keeping with established regularities that had found strength or intensity of party identification very much a function of increasing age, by 1968 the oldest cohorts, who were literally dying off (like those who had preceded them and like those who were to follow), were the strongest carriers of partisan attachment. Their "replacements," the young cohorts newly eligible to vote, not only followed the pattern of having the weakest of partisan attachments but, in 1968, far exceeded their counterparts from previous years in the extent to which they were nonpartisans, and were not strong partisans when they had any partisan inclinations at all.

Throughout the 1950s and early 1960s the youngest members of the eligible electorate had been less partisan than their elders, but, as Table 5.2 indicates, they had always counted many more strong partisans than nonpartisans in their ranks, usually by a margin of 10 to 20 percentage points (compared to margins of 45 to 55 points among the oldest cohorts). In 1968, however, the entering cohort of those eligible to vote for president for the first time actually contained more nonpartisans than strong party identifiers.

To the extent that 1968 ushered in an antiparty era of weak party control and weak party loyalties, the consequence was immediately and massively evident among the young; but it was scarcely reflected at all in the partisanship of the middle-aged and older cadres. Indeed, by 1972 the strength of party sentiments among citizens more than sixty years old had pretty much returned to the levels of 1960–1964. Among the very large number of citizens in their late teens and twenties, however, nonpartisans clearly outnumbered strong partisans. By 1972 these youngest cohorts made up a full 33 percent of the total electorate. The contribution of the young to national estimates of the strength of partisan sentiments was the primary source of the apparent nationwide

TABLE 5.2

Strength of Partisanship by Four-Year Age Cohorts, 1952–1988

Age in 1952	Year of First Vote for President	1952	1956	1960	1964	1968	1972	1976	1980	1984	1988	Age in 1988
	1988										4	18-21
	1984									2	7	22-25
	1980								−6	6	15	26-29
	1976							−11	−8	11	14	30-32
	1972						−11	−3	0	13	14	33-36
	1972						−1	−10	2	8	18	37-40
	1968					−4	−5	−3	11	11	15	41-44
	1964				19	0	1	−6	4	10	22	45-48
	1960			11	25	16	1	−6	18	23	27	49-52
	1956		16	25	24	18	3	4	25	28	31	53-56
21-24	1952	25	14	20	32	15*	12	4	24	34	36	57-60
25-28	1948	27	24	27	34	13	20	27	18	24	28	61-64
29-32	1944	26	23	24*	25	15	20	16	19	31	34	65-68
33-36	1940	28	23	28	37	12	20	25	28	35	32	69-72
37-40	1936	32	25	29	27	27	29	25	24	33	41	73-76
41-44	1932	29	32	32*	40	30	23	23*	42	40	27	77-80
45-48	1928	27	34	32	36*	38	25	41	33	37	32	81 +
49-52	1924	38	36*	36	43	37	34	35*	41	41		
53-56	1920	41	36	40	40	38*	38	52	33			
57-60	1916	49	40*	39	55	45	32	23				
61-64	1912	40	40*	46	53	48	37					
65-68	1908	39	40	52	41	33						
69-72	1904	51	55	58	36							
73-76	1900	40	52	56								
77-80	1896	41	60									
81 +	1892	40										
National Totals		31	27	27	30	19	12	9	13	18	21	

Note: Entries represent differences between the proportion of strong party identifiers and the proportion of Independent-Independents. The 10 entries (out of 165) marked by * have been "smoothed" by replacing those entries with the average of those in adjoining years and cohorts, when that single entry was markedly inconsistent with the entries for adjoining years and cohorts. The assigned values for these cells, reading by column are: 36 was 24, 40 was 30, 40 was 53, 24 was 15, 32 was 21, 36 was 53, 15 was 28, 38 was 31, 23 was 3, and 35 was 18. This "smoothing" attempts to remove the most obvious instances of sampling error by substituting innocuous entries for those that are otherwise anomalous.

Source: All of the data are based on the Michigan Survey Research Center of the Center for Political Studies, National Election Studies series.

decline in strength of party identification that continued until sometime after the election of 1976.

In examining the full set of four-year cohort data, following each new entering class across the thirty-six years and ten presidential elections covered by the Michigan data and presented in Table 5.2, we may reasonably conclude that the traumas of the late 1960s and early 1970s— failed presidencies, international frustrations, domestic turmoil, and the disruptive effects of civil rights protests, anti–Viet Nam demonstrations, and counterculture happenings—did create a period effect felt throughout the electorate. The strength of partisan sentiments among the older cohorts rebounded in 1972 and 1976, but in the 1980s these sentiments did not continue to advance to the high mark set by the oldest cohorts thirty years earlier. At the same time, the larger impact of the antipolitics decade seems to have been a generational effect: The young reacted to the events of the period more sharply and possibly even more permanently than did the older cohorts. It was the refusal and delay of the young in accepting partisan ties, not the lasting rejection of loyalties once held by their elders, that produced the indicators of dealignment in the mid-1970s.

It now seems clear that too many of the scholarly discussions of dealignment and realignment—given the aggregate figures, which showed fewer strong partisans and more nonpartisans—inaccurately attributed the cause of this change. They simply *assumed* that dealignment had occurred because old partisans actively rejected former party loyalties in favor of dealignment, professing no support for either party in preparation for switching party loyalties. The absence of party loyalty among the large numbers of young people, with no implications of rejection, conveys a quite different sense. This is an important distinction because the post-1976 evidence points to an increase in the incidence of party attachments among the young and the strengthening of their partisan sentiments.

Indeed, particularly where the strength of partisan sentiments is concerned, a pervasive upturn since the 1970s has been led by the same young cohorts whose original entry into the electorate was dominated by nonpartisans. Each of the younger cohorts who contributed so much to the apparent national dealignment has experienced a dramatic increase in both the incidence and the intensity of partisan sentiments in each of the elections of the 1980s as the political climate normalized. Their level of attachment in 1988 remained much below the norm that we associate with their generational counterparts in the 1950s, but primarily because they started from such an abnormally low point when they first entered the electorate. They have in fact made a large contribution to the national indications of renewed partisanship.

In 1988 strong partisans outnumbered nonpartisans in the younger cohorts by larger margins (14 or 15 points) than nonpartisans had outnumbered strong partisans (9 or 11 points) twelve years earlier. And by 1988 the post-1976 cohorts numbered more than 25 percent of the total electorate. Between 1976 and 1988 the eight youngest cohorts from 1972 increased their strength of partisanship by an average of 26 points; the remaining eight oldest cohorts in 1988 had gone up only 6 points in the same twelve years. At the same time, the composition of the electorate does continue to change over time inasmuch as old cohorts, whose normally quite intense feeling of party loyalty strengthened as they aged, continue to leave the electorate. Their departure has slowed the overall rate of recovery in national strength of partisanship, which otherwise would have reflected more clearly the increase in partisanship being contributed by the younger cohorts since 1976.

In sum, many arguments that took indicators of the declining strength of party identification in 1972 or 1976 as indicators of impending party realignment erred in the interpretation of these indicators. The actual *reduction* of intensity of individual partisan commitments was real, but it was very limited in magnitude and constituted a very brief episode for older members of the electorate. For the younger members, the turmoil of the late 1960s and early 1970s delayed but did not forestall their development of party loyalties. The magnitude of the delaying effect on them was so great, and they have been such a large and growing part of the electorate, that their simple lack of partisanship has been the largely unrecognized primary source of the indications of what was called dealignment but what was, in reality, nonalignment. To be sure, a nonalignment of the young may be followed by a first-time alignment that will differ from that of the old, and that might ultimately reshape the party alignment of the entire electorate. But the dynamics of partisan change that follow from such a beginning will probably be quite different from those anticipated or imagined when it was thought that an experienced electorate was rejecting its old loyalties in preparation for switching a *re*alignment involving switching parties by the individual citizen.

SOME IMPLICATIONS OF NEW ALIGNMENTS

Before considering further the topic of the realignment of national partisan sympathies, we may find it useful to reflect on some of the implications of the period effects and generational differences that have just been suggested. The very introduction of the idea of cohort analysis emphasizes the consequences of compositional change of the electorate during a period of political turbulence. Notwithstanding the rapid but ultimately incomplete rejuvenation of partisanship among older voters between 1972 and 1976, the concern with the changing composition of the electorate begs the direct question of Key's basic interest in individual-level stability and change in partisanship.

In approaching that question, we should first note that the observed generational differences that appeared rather suddenly in 1968 suggest that we modify some of the traditional as well as revisionist notions of the origins of party identification. Historically, party identification was thought to have been shaped by national traumas and watershed events such as the Civil War of the nineteenth century or the Great Depression of the 1930s. The lasting effects of such realigning epochs were thought to be carried by the influence of parents on the social and political attitudes of the successor generations. Early evidence for this view was provided by the recall of parental predisposition and supplemented by insightful arguments that described a waning transmission of the first causes through successive generations that are more and more remote from the shaping cataclysms (Beck, 1977). This latter theme was, of course, intended to account for the diminution of partisanship—the dealignment that logically might precede realignment.

The evidence of cohort differences in partisanship that we have reviewed would, of course, be consonant with the thesis that new disruptions of the party system simply accentuate the decay of family traditions and familial transmission of party loyalties. But it is more than this. The very abruptness of the cohort differences that appeared in 1968 suggests an active intrusion of new events into the process whereby partisanship is acquired among the young. This disruption of familial lines of inheritance may or may not have lasting effects that produce real discontinuities in the partisanship of the electorate. But it certainly produces short-term change, which was not anticipated in the early theories of political socialization. And the rapid recovery of partisanship among the older cohorts, with a much slower rate of development and growth in the younger (filial) generations, creates a generational gap that belies a pervasive influence of the older over the younger (Jennings and Niemi, 1981). In short, whatever the role of the family in shaping and preserving party traditions, the events of the late 1960s and early 1970s had an impact of their own on the partisan predispositions of the younger cohorts entering the electorate. Those most affected were not *re*aligned, and not even *de*aligned. They simply entered the electorate more often *un*aligned, with no partisan preference.

Moreover, the immediacy of that impact of events on young people did not allow for the habituation to behavioral patterns that has become a choice explanation of the origins of party identification (Fiorina, 1981). The notion that acts of crossing partisanship—Democrats voting for

Eisenhower in 1952 and 1956, for Nixon in 1968 and 1972, or for Reagan and Bush in 1980, 1984, and 1988—have an impact on one's sense of party identification is not at issue. Rather, as with generational differences and family tradition, the sharp break with the partisanship of entering cohorts prior to 1968 makes the absence of partisanship in the new cohorts of 1968 more of a comment on the immediate impact of historical context than an extension of either family influence or rational-choice theory as the explanation for new partisan identities.

The amassing of new data that captures variations in historical context has enriched our understanding of the origins of party identification and partisanship. As an aside, we should note that the growing evidence of a multiplicity of origins may upset some old orthodoxies, but it does not necessarily address the question of whether the significance, meaning, and consequence of party identification are similarly enriched or altered. The meaning of "I generally think of myself as a strong Democrat/ Republican" *may* vary with the origin of the sentiment, but that possibility must be the subject of much future research. In the meantime, we simply note the proliferation of evidence that party identification, in its origins, is a fascinating and many-splendored thing.

POLITICAL ENGAGEMENT AND PARTISAN STABILITY

The extent to which the incidence, strength, and direction of party identification vary with the context experienced by the identifiers is further illuminated if we define *context* in terms of the political depth of the partisan engagement of the individual citizen. We have already noted some of the correlates of the political context at one's time of coming of political age. We have also noted how aging, or experience, inoculates one against change in later years of life. An even more dramatic insight into the durability of partisanship is provided when we subdivide citizens into voters and nonvoters.

Let us turn first to national assessements of the strength of partisanship. In the "steady-state" elections of 1952–1964, strong partisans among voters outnumbered those with no partisan preference by a ratio of 39 to 7; among nonvoters the comparable averages were 26 percent (strong partisans) and 8 percent (no partisan preference). At the height of the excitement about dealignment (1968–1976), the ratio of strong partisans to nonpartisans was still 30 to 10 among voters; however, it had reversed to 16 (strong) to 19 (no preference) among nonvoters. In the elections of the 1980s, the ratio for voters was back to 35 (strong preference) to 8 (no preference); for nonvoters it was still 18 to 17. Thus there *was* some weakening of the aggregate indicators of the strength of partisanship among voters; indeed, the role of the young nonpartisan cohorts in changing the partisan composition of the entire electorate has already been noted. However, the dramatic change in the intensity of partisan sentiments that began in 1968 and persisted through the 1980s occurred primarily among nonvoters—that is, nonparticipants in the presidential elections of the period. The high point of contrast occurred in 1976, when strong partisans still outnumbered nonpartisans among *voters* by a ratio of 28 to 11; among nonvoters, however, the ratio was reversed, 12 to 22. Of course, the contrast was occasioned in part by the disproportionate incidence of young people among the nonvoters of that year, as in every election year.

In other words, the cry of alarm that the partisan sky was falling, with all of the strong implications for the future of the electoral process, was occasioned by indicators emanating primarily from the nonparticipants in presidential politics. A "dealignment" of these apathetic nonparticipants might also have deserved comment and even some analytic thought, but unfortunately it was the mistaken belief that future elections would no longer be shaped by a continuation of the party identifications of the past that commanded the attention of most analysts and commentators. Both the diagnosis (alienation of the voters) and the prognosis (realignment of partisanship at the polls) were flawed because it was largely the nonvoters who constituted the source of the alarming (or promising) indicators of impending change.

Now that we have separated voters and nonvoters in order to reexamine the aggregate indicators of partisan dealignment, it is a natural extension to turn directly to the theme of party realignment. This, in turn, results in still more evidence of the persistence of party identification, even as we introduce the first description of a significant shift in the numerical balance of the two parties. Table 5.3 indicates that prior to 1984 there was little hint in the national party identification distributions among voters of an impending realignment that would see the Republican party in the ascendancy. Indeed, the only visible departure from a thirty-year span of Democratic pluralities of some 14 percentage points occurred during and after the election of 1964. In that year, still an underanalyzed episode, party loyalties shifted and enhanced the "steady-state" Democratic margin by a full 10 points. Despite the chaos of the Democratic nominating convention in Chicago in 1968, and perhaps as a partial explanation of Hubert Humphrey's near victory in the fall election with strong black support, the preelection Democratic plurality of party identifications in that year remained visibly above the norms of the 1950s and 1970s. By 1972, however, and again despite the limited national appeal of the Democratic candidate, George McGovern, a kind of normalcy had returned to the two-party competition for party loyalties. The proportion of voters with no party identification had increased by a

TABLE 5.3
Party Identification of Voters, 1952–1988[a]

Year	Democrat	Independent	Republican	Partisan Balance
1952	45	23	30	+15
1956	44	24	32	+12
1960	45	22	32	+13
1964	52	20	28	+24
1968	45	28	28	+17
1972	40	31	28	+12
1976	39	34	27	+12
1980	41	32	27	+14
1984	37	30	32	+5
1988	36	30	33	+3

[a]In 1980, 1984, and 1988 the distinction between voters and nonvoters was validated by the National Elections Studies staff. For all other years the distinction relies on the self-reports of individuals.

Source: All of the data are based on the Michigan Survey Research Center of the Center for Political Studies, National Election Studies series.

third over that of the late 1950s, but those numbers drew almost equally from Democrats and Republicans. The Democratic margin of party loyalties in 1972 and 1976 was virtually identical to that in 1956 and 1960. And that margin persisted through Reagan's first candidacy and his defeat of Jimmy Carter in 1980.

Between 1980 and 1988, however, at least a limited version of the long-heralded partisan realignment took place. After eight elections, bracketing a span of twenty-eight years, during which Democrats out-numbered Republicans by almost identical margins among those voting for president, the Democratic edge virtually disappeared in the election of 1988. The Democratic plurality dropped from a "normal" 14 points in 1980 to no more than 3 points in 1988. A tentative explanation—or at least a description—of that change will be offered shortly. In the meantime, it is worth noting that the 11-point decline among voters was accompanied by a bare 4-point shift among nonvoters. The disparity stemmed, in part, from the fact that the Democratic edge among nonvoters actually appeared to *increase* between 1984 and 1988 (from 14 to 17 points), whereas it continued to erode among voters. This difference and others between the politically engaged portion of the eligible electorate and those less involved provide direction to our next effort to account for the equalizing realignment in the 1980s.

Just as the disaggregation of the eligible electorate into voters and nonvoters casts a very different light on the historical ebb and flow of partisan sentiments, so a deeper probing into differences in the level of political engagement *among voters* amplifies our understanding of those sentiments. In general, there is clear if not dramatic evidence that those voters who are the least engaged by, or sophisticated about, politics are the most volatile in their political attitudes, including their political identities. A simplified version of the measure of "levels of conceptualization" introduced in *The American Voter* (Campbell, Converse, Miller, and Stokes, 1960) can be used to sort voters into two groups: the more politicized (at the higher two levels) and the less politicized (at the lower two levels). Doing so is a step toward further refining our sense of the conditions under which party identification is persistent and stable, and of the circumstances under which voters alter their habitual party affiliations.

On the average, interelection shifts in the partisan balance of party identification among the voters classified as reflecting the higher levels of conceptualization amounted to changes of only 2 or 3 percentage points between 1952 and 1988. Among the remaining less politicized voters, the same average shift across the nine pairs of elections approximated 5 or 6 points. On average, the changes are not great in either case; hence they reflect the relative stability of party identification among voters, if not always among nonvoters.

However, closer examination reveals that the apparent greater volatility among the less sophisticated, or less engaged, voters is almost entirely the product of two election eras: 1960 to 1964 and 1980 to 1984. Between 1960 and the 1964 Johnson landslide there was an astronomical 35-point shift in party identification favoring the Democrats within the ranks of the less sophisticated voters. This shift erased a 13-point Republican margin in 1960 and produced a 22-point Democratic lead four years later in 1964. The proportion of Democratic identifiers increased by 19 percentage points (from 37 to 56, with 406 and 450 cases in 1960 and 1964 respectively), whereas the proportion of Republicans dropped 16 points (from 50 to 34). It should be noted that this massive exchange took place among voters during such a brief period that turnover in the composition of the electorate cannot be held responsible. There is nothing in the literature on party identification that provides a theoretical basis for anticipating such a high incidence of change.

Moreover, while the less engaged 40 percent of the voters in 1964 were moving precipitously toward the Democrats and away from the Republicans, the more engaged 60 percent were moving in the opposite direction. Although the net figures for changes in party identification among the more sophisticated voters (6 points between 1960 and 1964) did not depart from *their* average change of 5 points across nine pairs of elections, the direction of change favored Barry Goldwater and the Republicans rather than Lyndon Johnson, the Great Society, and the Democrats.

There was clearly something about the period from 1960 to 1964 that evoked very different responses from the more politicized and less politicized voters. This anomaly clearly merits greater attention than it has received because the election of Lyndon Johnson in 1964 marked the one and only significant net shift in the balance of party loyalties among voters between the first Eisenhower election of 1952 and the second Reagan election thirty-two years later in 1984. It is true that the overall Democratic gain of 11 points among voters in 1964 was not a lasting gain; by 1974 things were back to the three-decade norm. Nevertheless, the 1964 Democratic landslide was both a political event of significance and an occasion to learn more about the conditions under which party identifications change.

A similar pair of changes took place though to a lesser degree and somewhat different in kind, between 1980 and 1984. Among the more sophisticated voters the proportion of self-declared Democrats dropped 2 points as the proportion of Republicans went up 3 points between the two Reagan elections. Among the less sophisticated voters the Democratic loss was 6 and the Republican gain was 7. An even greater contrast occurred on election day. Despite the pro-Republican shift in party identification, the more sophisticated voters increased their 1984 Democratic vote over their 1980 record, from 53 percent Republican and 47 percent Democrat to 48 percent Republican and 52 percent Democrat (a majority voted for Walter Mondale). In contrast the less sophisticated voters turned their 1980 vote, which favored Reagan by a margin of 63 percent Republican to 37 percent Democrat into an 80 to 20 percent rout on his behalf in 1984. By these calculations, Reagan was reelected by the less sophisticated voters. It is, however, of at least equal interest to the student of political change to note that, once again, the more politicized and less politicized voters moved in opposite directions in response to changing events in the world of national politics. Nevertheless, the contrasts in these reponses should not be overdrawn. Apart from the two election periods just discussed, the parallelism between the two sets of voters has been notable in election after election over a period of thirty years.

THE REALIGNMENT OF 1980–1988

The 1980–1988 realignment among voters apparently took place in two phases, each phase affecting one of the two somewhat different groups of voters we have just noted. Between 1980 and 1984 at least some changes in party loyalties took place pretty much across the board, but the shifting loyalties were concentrated in two familiar sectors. First, young voters shifted more to the Republican side than did the old, again suggesting greater malleability or susceptibility to the winds of change among the less experienced voters. At the same time, among young and old alike, the voters with fewer resources for coping with complex matters of politics swung more heavily to the Republicans. Thus it was the less well educated young people who changed the most: A Democratic margin of 23 points dwindled to 9 points, resulting in a 14-point shift between 1980 and 1984. Among the better-educated older voters, a small 3-point plurality of Republicans grew to an 8-point margin, a shift of only 5 points.

During the second phase of the realignment, there was a further shift to the Republicans in only one sector of the voting population. In Table 5.3 we noted that, across the entire voting population, the Republicans gained only 2 points between 1984 and 1988. Apparently, all of that gain was concentrated in the ranks of the older, better-educated voters. These voters—precisely the group that had been most resistant to the national move into the Republican camp between 1980 and 1984—went from a modest 40 to 32 Republican margin in 1984 to a solid 46 to 28 plurality in 1988. If the first phase of the realignment was a tribute to the charismatic attraction that Ronald Reagan held for the less involved, less political of the voters, the second phase seems to have engaged the more ideologically predisposed voters who had come to appreciate that Reagan really was a conservative Republican president (Miller, 1986).

It is possible, of course, that the realignment of the Reagan years may vanish as swiftly as did the increment that Lyndon Johnson's election gave to the Democrats in 1964. Certainly every national leader is well aware of the speed with which short-run disaster can overtake long-term expectations. But barring the unforeseen cataclysm, it seems more likely that the realignment of the late 1980s is a relatively durable part of the Reagan legacy to American politics. The rationale for such a forecast derives from a basic perspective on the nature of democratic political processes. That perspective, in turn, brings this essay full circle as we move on to another insight expressed by V. O. Key, Jr.—in this case, his metaphor of the electoral process as an echo chamber in which voters echo the message of political leaders. The more elaborate version of Key's perspective is presented as the conclusion to *Public Opinion and American Democracy* (Key, 1961). Key posits political leadership as the wellspring of mass politics and argues that it is the political elite, the subculture of activists, that articulates the alternatives that shape public opinion.

The political elite, including political leaders such as presidents, also gives definition to the political party. (Recall Chapter 4.) There are many reasons for the half-century dominance of American politics by the Democratic party, but not the least of these is the sense of habitual party affiliation that came to many citizens from voting four times for Franklin Delano Roosevelt as the leader of the Democratic party, three times to reaffirm a preference for having him continue as president. At this remove it is difficult to reconstruct the public opinion of fifty years ago, but the incomparable longevity of Roosevelt's presidential leadership must have contributed much to the contemporary meaning of being a "New Deal Democrat."

As we search for the roots of party identification, we may easily forget that following Truman, FDR's vice-president, Eisenhower's hallmark in the public presentation of self was his emphasis on bipartisanship. And although his signal contribution to postwar domestic politics may well have been his conversion of the Republican party from the party of isolationism and America First to the party of internationalism and the United Nations, his legacy was not the redress of the partisan balance in the electorate. It was Eisenhower, not Stevenson, who warned in 1960 of the future dangers of the military-industrial complex. And only rare commentators foresaw a party realignment at the end of Eisenhower's term.

I have already commented on the Kennedy-Johnson era, but it is worth noting again that in the aftermath of New Frontier, Camelot, and Great Society euphoria there were the hot summers and burning riot-torn cities of the late 1960s, Woodstock and the counterculture, and protests against Viet Nam and for civil rights. As an antidote to the repressions of the 1950s, American foreign policy, and the heritage of racial discrimination, the decade of protest was undoubtedly overdue; but it was not calculated to endear the Democratic establishment to Main Street America any more than to the hearts of the protestors. In hindsight it is remarkable that the Democratic party did not suffer more as a consequence of the rejection of its leadership in 1968 and 1972, but in fact there was little subsequent evidence of realignment.

The Nixon era, like the Eisenhower years, constituted another opportunity foregone throughout eight years of presidential leadership for the Republican party. Nixon's personal triumph was almost unequalled in his reelection in 1972, but that outcome, Watergate, and the Committee to Reelect the President were all well separated from the Republican party—thus possibly preventing a "failed presidency" from actually disadvantaging Nixon's party.

Carter presided over yet another failed presidency, in large part because he was not the party's leader. He campaigned as an outsider from Plains, Georgia, and he presided as an outsider. Like Johnson, he benefited from his regional identification, and he momentarily stopped the southern white flight from his party with his 1976 campaign when he ran against the Washington establishment. He did not appear to hurt his party—at least not at the grass-roots level, where party identification flourishes—but he scarcely took honors as the revitalizing leader of the party in the electorate.

Ronald Reagan was the only president of the postwar era who took office as an avowed partisan and an unvarnished idealogue; held office for eight years, during which he championed his conservatism *and* his Republicanism; and retired at the end of two full terms with a legacy of goodwill sufficient to elect his successor. The textbooks say that the president is the titular head and leader of the party. Reagan may not have satisfied all the factions within the Republican party, but not because he wasn't an articulate Republican spokesman and an active campaigner openly partisan on the election trail as well as in Washington. And despite trials and tribulations that would have ended some careers, he remained popular to the end and retired from office with the country relatively at peace with itself and others.

In a more detailed account of the changes in party identification between 1980 and 1984, I attribute much of the 1980–1984 change to Reagan's personal popularity among the less experienced and less sophisticated sectors of the electorate (Miller, 1986). That analysis explicitly examined and rejected the hypothesis that it was the Reagan administration's conservatism rather than its Republicanism that provided the foundation for changing partisanship. Four years later, in 1988, it appeared that his sustained personal popularity as president prevented any visible backsliding on the part of the recent converts to Republicanism.

Another relatively elaborate analysis of the 1988 election (Shanks and Miller, 1989) provides two sets of evidence that conform to our interpretation of the two-stage sequence of realignment. In the first place, there is pervasive and powerful evidence of Reagan's contribution to the Bush victory. The election was in some ways a retrospective triumph for Reagan—a triumph of popular satisfaction with his policies, with the general state of the world and of the nation as he left office, and with his performance (Shanks and Miller, 1989). In the absence of evidence to the contrary, there seems no reason not to attribute the carryover of the 1984 increases in Republican party identification to Reagan's carryover popularity.

The second pertinent finding from this election analysis is of a different order. Across the three elections preceding 1988, the distribution of ideological predispositions among voters had not changed from the 13-point margin of self-designated conservatives over self-designated liberals. In 1988 that margin increased by 8 points. In disaggregating voters by age and education, as we have done to locate those who changed their party identification, we find that the older, better-educated voters who had a 15-point increase in their Republican margin (from a slim 34 to 31 in 1980 to a solid 46 to 28 in 1988) between 1980 and 1988 experienced a very substantial 17-point increase in their conservatism during the same interval. Among the better-educated young voters, a comparable increase in conservatism was associated with a full 7-point increase in Republicanism. By contrast, among the less well-educated voters, whose pro-Republican shift occurred entirely between 1980 and 1984 (in response to Reagan's popularity), there was no 1980–1988 increase in conservative predispositions at all. In 1988 the less well-educated voters were more Republican than they had been in 1980, but they were not more conservative; the better-educated voters were both more Republican *and* more conservative.

My analysis of the 1988 elections thus supports the thesis that a significant first phase of the 1980–1988 realignment occurred between 1980 and 1984 among the less experienced and less sophisticated voters who responded to Reagan's personal leadership with an increase in Republicanism. A smaller but perhaps more meaningful second phase then occurred between 1984 and 1988, particularly among the older and better-educated voters who ultimately responded favorably to the Reagan administration's emphasis on conservatism. Thus ideology and personality, articulated and presented by the same presidential party leader, may have reshaped the sense of party loyalty among different sections of the voting public. I am persuaded by this two-pronged explanation of the 1980–1988 realignment because it seems to fit a relatively broad view of the origins of party identification and yet makes explicit the importance of presidential leadership for party as well as for country.

My rendering of the recent history of the persistence of partisan attachments and my examination of the conditions under which voters alter their habitual partisan affiliations are somewhat incomplete. Except for my limited speculation about recent presidencies, I have virtually ignored party in government as a partner in the shaping of mass partisan sentiments. And my disaggregations of the mass did not reach up to either the political activists or the nongovernmental elites that are so much a part of our political processes. Nonetheless, my accumulated resources have permitted explorations and reconstructions that were not available to earlier generations of scholars. The old question "What is a political party?" is answered as before: It is people, the people's leaders, and the symbols they present for public approval. The old question "What causes stability and change in the people's attachment to party?" is now, more than ever, an important question with a very complex set of possible answers.

NOTES

1. At least since the time of Key's seminal article, "A Theory of Critical Elections" (Key, 1955:3–18), analysts have used the concept of political alignment

to describe the composition of the competing sides in electoral competition. Realignment occurs when changes take place in the competitive balance between the parties. Realignment may also be *geographic*, as regional alignments change; *group-based*, as social or economic groups shift their party support; or simply *numerical* as one party grows in size relative to the other. The idea of individual or groups not taking sides is inherent in the concept of nonalignment, just as moving from support for one side to a middle ground between the parties is described as dealignment. For a good summary discussion, see Sorauf and Beck (1988).

2. In 1952, 80 percent of southern white males identified with one or the other of the two major parties (68 percent Democratic, 12 percent Republican). The Democratic advantage, as shown in Table 5.1, was 56 percent.

6

The Electorate in the Voting Booth

MORRIS P. FIORINA

In the 1984 elections Ronald Reagan rolled to an overwhelming victory, carrying every state but Minnesota, the home of his opponent, Walter Mondale. Unfortunately for the president's fellow Republicans, however, the Reagan tide did not wash over other offices on the ticket. The Republicans captured only 182 seats in the House of Representatives— a disappointing 14-seat gain—and although they narrowly retained control of the Senate, they lost 2 seats. At the state level the Democrats took consolation in the fact that they emerged from the elections holding almost 60 percent of the state legislative seats and thirty-four of the fifty governorships.[1] Although a few particularly hopeful or fearful commentators continued to talk about party realignment and the Reagan revolution, for most commentators the 1984 elections indicated that the promise or threat of 1980 had been aborted.

In the 1936 elections Franklin D. Roosevelt rolled to an overwhelming victory, carrying every state but Maine and Vermont. The Democrats enlarged their already overwhelming majorities in the House and Senate, adding seven senators and twelve representatives.[2] At the state level the Democrats emerged from the election with full political control of 29 states. Thus, the 1936 elections resoundingly reinforced the verdict of 1932, verifying that a new era of Democratic hegemony had indeed dawned.

These two elections half a century apart differ both in their antecedents and their consequences. But for the purposes of this essay, the most important difference lies in the individual voting behavior that generated the differing outcomes. In the 1930s the electorate behaved much as it had behaved for the preceding century. It was a *party-oriented* electorate. The great majority of those citizens who supported FDR at the top of the ticket also supported Democratic candidates further down the ticket. Conversely, the preponderance of the minority who supported Alf Landon also cast votes for other Republican candidates. In the 1980s, however,

116

various trends produced an electorate that is both more *office oriented* and more *person oriented.*[3] A significant proportion of the citizenry—at least one-quarter and probably more than one-third—picked and chose among the names on the ticket and ended up casting their votes for both Democrats and Republicans.[4] And even some of those who cast a straight ticket undoubtedly did so less out of blind party loyalty than because on other grounds they happened to prefer all the candidates of one party to all those of the other.

This essay contrasts the voting behavior of the contemporary electorate with its more partisan counterpart of a generation ago. Ideally, one would compare elections of the 1980s with those of the 1930s, but lack of data makes that impossible. Hence the partisan electorates used as a contrast with the contemporary electorate are those of 1952–1960. Given that signs of change were already apparent in the 1950s (Alford and Brady, 1989), the comparisons in this essay undoubtedly underestimate the differences between contemporary American voters and their more partisan counterparts of earlier historical periods.

THE AMERICAN VOTER, THEN AND NOW

In 1960 Campbell, Converse, Miller, and Stokes published their monumental treatise, *The American Voter*. Relying on data from the 1952 and 1956 elections, the four Michigan researchers advanced a tripartite explanatory scheme: Voting behavior was motivated by attitudes toward the candidates, the issues, and the parties, with the first providing most of the variation over time, the third accounting for most of the regularity of behavior, and the second apparently trailing the other two in importance. The Michigan team did not provide any separate analyses of voting for offices other than president; rather, they made the implicit assumption that voting for lesser offices was a simpler, paler reflection of the presidential vote decision. After all, most voters could not recall even the names of the House candidates and had very little information about House races; moreover, from the presidential level downward, the importance of partisanship appeared to grow stronger (Stokes and Miller, 1962). Hence "the American voter" described the most general case— one that subsumed the simpler forms of voting behavior.

By the mid-1970s students of voting behavior had come to recognize the need for revising the prevailing model. The importance of issue attitudes appeared to have grown, and party identification seemed to be somewhat less the unmoved mover than it had been two decades previously. Thus it was only natural that Nie, Verba, and Petrocik (1976) entitled their revisionist treatise *The Changing American Voter*. Nevertheless, the revisionists retained the implicit notion that voting was singular; there was no explicit questioning of the notion that presidential voting behavior was only the most developed form of a particular kind of behavior known as voting.

More than a decade has passed since the revisionist heyday, but no new general treatise on American voting has appeared.[5] Rather, in the 1980s students of voting behavior dropped all pretense of a general, unified treatment of voting. Following an outpouring of research on congressional elections, researchers have implicitly come to accept the notion that voting behavior is simply *different* across different offices: One cannot usefully treat the congressional voting decision as a special case of the presidential voting decision. Of course, one can still speak generally of attitudes toward the candidates, parties, and issues, but the specific realizations of these concepts differ greatly across offices. Discussions of congressional voting behavior emphasize incumbency, campaign spending, and the (in)visibility of challengers—concepts that are far down the list in any discussion of presidential voting.[6]

Today, research on presidential and congressional elections proceeds largely along independent tracks.[7] Although points of contact exist, different researchers are prominent in each arena and different agendas structure research in each arena. That is the natural approach to the study of an electorate that has become more person and office oriented. Still, an instructive way to highlight the changes that have occurred in American voting behavior is to chronicle the decay in the association between presidential and House voting behavior across time.

The Loosening of the Ties That Bind

Table 6.1 presents the most graphic indicator of the increasing independence of the presidential and House vote. At the turn of the century only a handful of congressional districts registered pluralities for the presidential candidate of one party and the congressional candidate of another. There was a slight upward trend in the frequency of split outcomes throughout the first half of the century, a noticeable jump at mid-century, and still another sharp increase in the most recent elections. On average, the elections that followed the social upheavals of the 1960s have seen more than a third of all congressional districts turn in a split decision for the presidency and the House—most commonly a verdict for a Republican president and a Democratic member of Congress.[8]

Our interest, of course, is in the individual behavior that underlies the aggregate trend. Individual-level data are not available for the first half of the century, but from 1952 on, the rise in individual ticket splitting has clearly been a major contributor to the increasing proportion of split outcomes. Ticket splitting in the 1950s hovered at the 15-percent

TABLE 6.1

Percentage of Congressional Districts Carried by House
and Presidential Candidates of Different Parties

Year	Percent
1900	3
1908	7
1916	11
1924	12
1932	14
1940	15
1948	21
1952	19
1956	30
1960	26
1964	33
1968	32
1972	44
1976	29
1980	34
1984	44
1988	34

Sources: The data for 1900 to 1986 were compiled from various sources and are reported in Ornstein, Mann, and Malbin (1987); the 1988 figures were compiled by the author.

level and then jumped sharply in the late 1960s to its current level of approximately 25 percent (see Figure 6.1). Ticket splitting seems to be especially productive of split outcomes when presidents are reelected.[9]

When we begin to delve beneath the individual ticket-splitting series, matters become more complicated. There is every reason to believe that individual ticket splitting has been a response to different factors at different times. For example, ticket splitting was very difficult before the adoption of the Australian ballot at the turn of the century. Prior to that time the parties printed their own ballots, listing only their own nominees. Splitting one's ticket thus involved crossing out and writing in names, or turning in two (or possibly more) ballots with votes marked on each. As party ballots were often color coded and ballots were not marked in secret, ticket splitting was evident to party poll watchers. Thus, splitting one's ticket was both physically and psychically difficult. Institutional and procedural barriers were not the only obstacle to ticket splitting, however. Even after the Australian ballot reforms, the estimated rate of ticket splitting rose only slightly (Rusk, 1970). And, of course, the sharp rise in ticket splitting in the late 1960s has no obvious procedural or institutional basis.

Political historians have argued that the political culture of the late nineteenth century was quite different from that of the early twentieth century, and especially from the contemporary political culture.[10] In the late nineteenth century *independent* was more a term of derogation than one of commendation. An independent was someone who lacked the courage of his party convictions ("hers" weren't permitted to vote). Partisans, on the other hand, were people of principle. Thus, even after ticket splitting became physically and psychologically easier, straight-ticket voting remained the prevailing norm. In contrast, the modern political culture exalts political independence: "Vote for the person, not the party" is a maxim inculcated in recent generations of American schoolchildren. But while political cultural explanations are consistent with some of the broad differences between voting in the nineteenth and twentieth centuries, they too fail to account for much of the interesting detail.

For one thing, partisan voting has not steadily declined over the course of the twentieth century. On the contrary, partisanship undoubtedly increased during the 1930s. And far from parties losing their ability to organize the electorate, there was more unified government in the first half of the twentieth century than *either* before or since (Fiorina, 1990). As late as 1958, 85 percent of all American voters were loyally voting for the House candidate of their party. That, however, is the contemporary high-water mark; the loyalty of partisans in House elections has dropped significantly since then (see Table 6.2). The exact numbers in these series are subject to some dispute inasmuch as they depend on whether one classifies those who say they are independent but lean toward a party as partisans or as independents.[11] But even strong partisans are less likely to support the House candidate of their party today than they were a generation ago.

What seems clear is that, regardless of changes in the political culture, party identification in the population was a stronger correlate of voting in the 1930s and 1940s than it is today. Although the increased independence of the contemporary electorate has clearly been exaggerated, during the period covered by the American National Election Studies there has been a general weakening in the strength of partisanship (see Figure 6.2).[12] In addition there has been a decline in the capacity of partisanship to "structure" the vote. In other words, even those who report that they are strong partisans today are less likely to support their party's candidates across the board than they were a generation ago. In speaking of the erosion of partisanship, I refer to the sum of both processes—more independents, fewer strong partisans, and a lessened partisan impact on voting for different offices. Thus, with the abolition of procedural/institutional barriers to ticket splitting, only

TABLE 6.2

Party-line Voting in Presidential and Congressional Elections,
(as Percentage of All Voters), 1956–1988

Year	Presidential Elections			House Elections		
	Party-line Voters	Defectors	Pure Independents	Party-line Voters	Defectors	Pure Independents
1956	76	15	9	82	9	9
1958				84	11	5
1960	79	13	8	80	12	8
1962				83	12	6
1964	79	15	5	79	15	5
1966				76	16	8
1968	69	23	9	74	19	7
1970				76	16	8
1972	67	25	8	75	17	8
1974				74	18	8
1976	74	15	11	72	19	9
1978				69	22	9
1980	70	22	8	69	23	8
1982				76	17	6
1984	81	12	7	70	23	7
1986				72	22	6
1988	81	12	7	74	20	7

Source: Ornstein, Mann, and Malbin (1987: Table 2-17).

psychological barriers such as partisanship remained. When the latter began to erode, a space was opened in which other factors might affect the vote.

Filling the Space

A lesser reliance on partisanship does not logically entail a decline in straight-ticket voting. The diminished role of partisanship simply enhanced the opportunity for other factors to affect votes, especially the votes of independents and of those with weak partisan leanings. But these factors could just as easily have led to an *increase* in straight-ticket voting. Consider presidential coattails, for example. Some congressional votes are the product of decisions to vote a particular way for president. A presidential nominee who raises his party's congressional vote total by a large amount is said to have long coattails.[13] If voters had come to focus more and more on their presidential vote decision as their partisanship weakened, then straight-ticket voting might have remained constant or might even have increased as voters associated their votes for lower offices with their votes for president. In other words, coattails could have replaced partisanship.

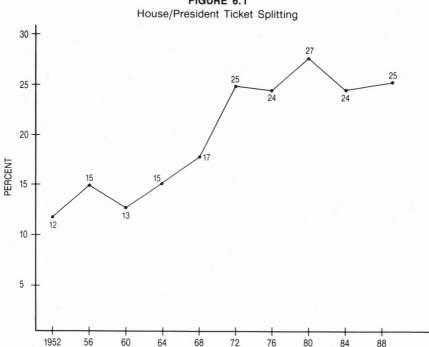

FIGURE 6.1
House/President Ticket Splitting

Source: Compiled by the author on the basis of data from Michigan Survey Research Center of the Center for Political Studies, National Election Studies series.

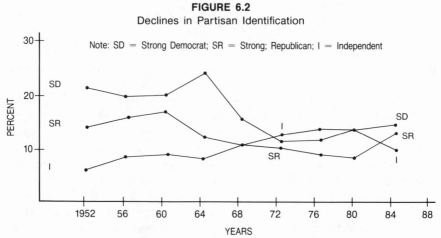

FIGURE 6.2
Declines in Partisan Identification

Note: SD = Strong Democrat; SR = Strong; Republican; I = Independent

Source: Compiled by the author on the basis of data from Michigan Survey Research Center of the Center for Political Studies, National Election Studies series.

TABLE 6.3
The Effect of Presidential Votes and Incumbency
on Votes for House Candidates, 1956–1980

| | Seats with Incumbents | |
| | Presidential | |
Year	Votes	Incumbency
1956	.38	.09
1960	.47	.13
1964	.47	.15
1968	.50	.17
1972	.31	.24
1976	.24	.34
1980	.24	.34

Source: Ferejohn and Fiorina (1985).

In fact, the importance of presidential coattails has declined over time (Ferejohn and Calvert, 1984). The influence of presidential votes on congressional votes is now less than half what it was three decades ago (see Table 6.3). Rather than associate their House votes more closely with their presidential votes and the numerous national factors that determine the latter, voters increasingly seem to be casting their House votes on some different basis.

The most obvious other basis is incumbency. The importance of incumbency status has approximately quadrupled over the course of the past generation, with a particularly sharp upsurge in the late 1960s (see Table 6.3)—precisely the time during which the split-ticket voting series showed its sharpest increase. Incumbents have always had some advantage; they are proven winners, after all. But during the 1960s the electoral value of being an incumbent increased sharply.[14] Too much has been written on this topic to summarize here (for comprehensive surveys, see Beth, 1981–1982, 1984). Suffice it to say that numerous reinforcing developments have rendered careful incumbents all but invulnerable. Incumbents have permanent personal staffs, district offices, and travel and communications budgets that would cost challengers as much as a million dollars per year to duplicate; the growth of government has enabled them to provide impressive levels of nonpartisan constituency services; and they are able to raise hundreds of thousands of dollars in campaign contributions from political action committees (PACs) and other contributors.[15] For these and other lesser reasons, House incumbents have been able to transform their offices into 435 political machines.

The important point is that these 435 political machines are all geared toward one thing: to reelect the member of Congress. They are not principally geared toward electing a Democratic or Republican majority, a conservative or liberal, or a Bush supporter or opponent. Individuation is the name of the game. And to the extent that voters can be induced to play that game, voting for Congress becomes that much more independent of voting for president.

So, the erosion of partisanship in the contemporary era did not logically imply a decline in partisan behavior. Citizens could have decided to focus on the office of the presidency, but they did not. Instead, they appear to have compartmentalized their decisions, relying on one set of considerations when deciding how to vote for president, another set of considerations when deciding how to vote for members of the House, and perhaps still a third set of considerations when deciding how to vote for senators. And this process of differentiation continues when attention turns to various state and local offices.

To summarize everything discussed thus far, we can now compare presidential-congressional voting in 1952 and 1960 with that in 1980 and 1988 (see Table 6.4). In 1952 and 1980 the electorate turned out unpopular Democratic administrations and elected candidates of the minority Republican party—along with a congressional majority in the first case, but not in the second. In 1960 and 1988 incumbent vice-presidents attempted to succeed popular presidents—unsuccessfully in the first case as the Democrats won an across-the-board, if narrow, victory. In contrast is the contemporary pattern of 1988—a comfortable Republican presidential victory coupled with an equally comfortable Democratic win in the House.

The major points of the preceding discussion are apparent in light of the following statistical results:[16]

1. The capacity of party identification to "structure" the vote across offices has declined: The difference between self-identified Democrats and Republicans in presidential voting has widened, if anything, but it has narrowed significantly in congressional voting.[17]
2. The importance of House incumbency has increased: In the 1960 House equation, incumbency is barely significant for Democrats and effectively zero for Republicans, whereas it is the single most important variable in the later equations.[18]
3. The impact of party evaluations (measured on a scale running from -10 to $+10$) declines over time in the presidential equations. Wattenberg (1990) has shown that fewer people offer party evaluations; this analysis reveals that those who do so are motivated less by such evaluations when casting their *presidential* votes. At the same time, the importance of party evaluations in House voting appears to have grown: The smaller proportion of people who

TABLE 6.4
Comparison of Voting Models

	1952	1960	1980	1988
President				
Constant	.33[b]	.49[b]	.38[b]	.38[b]
Democratic ID	.27[b]	.17[b]	.23[b]	.32[b]
Republican ID	−.05	−.18[b]	−.10[b]	−.11[b]
Party Likes & Dislikes	.04[b]	.03[b]	.02[b]	.02[b]
Candidate Likes & Dislikes	.04[b]	.05[b]	.06[b]	.04[b]
n	1181	885	845	1159
R^2	.59	.61	.58	.63
% Correctly Predicted	89	89	87	89
House				
Constant	.15[b]	.25[b]	.35[b]	.46[b]
Democratic ID	.26[b]	.15[b]	.07	.00
Republican ID	−.07[a]	−.17[b]	−.08[b]	−.24[b]
Party Likes & Dislikes	.00	.00	.01	.02[b]
Presidential Vote	.55[b]	.49[b]	.24[b]	.22[b]
Dem. Incumbent	—	.08[a]	.25[b]	.28[b]
Rep. Incumbent	—	.05	−.13[a]	−.17[b]
n	972	706	668	793
R^2	.63	.61	.39	.56
% Correctly Predicted	87	88	78	85

[a] $p < .05$
[b] $p < .01$

Source: Compiled by author on the basis of data from Michigan Survey Research Center of the Center for Political Studies, National Election Studies series.

advance party evaluations take more account of them when casting their House votes than did the larger proportion a generation ago.[19]

4. The impact of presidential vote choice (coattails) on the House vote in the 1980s was less than half what it was in 1952 and 1960.

5. As a consequence of the first four points, the presidential and congressional votes responded largely to the same factors in 1952 and 1960, but not in 1980 and 1984. Even without incumbency in the equation, the president and House equations predict virtually the same percentage of votes correctly in 1960, whereas without incumbency the 1988 House prediction is almost 10 percent poorer than the presidential prediction, and the 1980 prediction is almost 10 percent poorer even with incumbency in the equation. In sum, the factors that produce an association between presidential votes

and House votes operate less consistently today than a generation ago.

WHY THE CHANGES?

The preceding section describes the changes that have taken place in voting behavior in national elections over the past generation. But description is not explanation. The glue that unified the electoral behavior of previous generations—voter partisanship—has weakened, allowing voters to respond in a more differentiated way to the individual candidates and the offices they contest. Why has partisanship weakened? To discuss the possible answers, we must first understand the nature of partisanship.

In the original Michigan formulation, a voter's party identification was viewed as a psychological affiliation generally fixed early in life and highly resistant to change thereafter (Campbell et al., 1960, Ch. 7). Later research has given the concept a more instrumental interpretation. Party identification is now thought to reflect (at least in part) the similarity between a voter's opinions and the policy positions of the favored party (Jackson, 1975; Franklin and Jackson, 1983) as well as the voter's evaluation of the relative performance of the parties when they held office (Fiorina, 1981). Under these interpretations the partisanship of an electorate can be explained in fairly simple terms. Figure 6.3 depicts a simple two-dimensional policy space, where the horizontal dimension indexes left-right positions on economic policy issues and the vertical dimension indexes dove-hawk positions on issues of foreign policy. There is a large cluster of voters in the southwest corner of the space and another cluster in the northeast corner. If one party consistently locates near each cluster and implements policies favored by that cluster when in office, then over time we would expect to see the voters in each cluster develop an identification with the party nearer them. Socialist doves would consistently oppose laissez-faire hawks, voters would believe that elections have major implications for the future course of their society and that their party would better handle the most important problems facing their society, and most voters would vote straight tickets.

On the other hand, for whatever reason (owing, perhaps, to the influence of highly ideological but unrepresentative party activists), the parties might both locate far from the voter clusters (see Figure 6.4). Socialist doves might then be attracted by the economic positions of the socialist hawk party but be repelled by its foreign policy positions; conversely, they might be attracted to the foreign policy positions of the free-market dove party but be repelled by its economic policies. Free-market hawk voters would be in an analogous situation of attraction-repulsion. In this system one would not expect to see voters develop

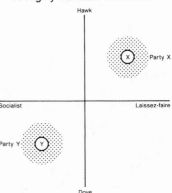

FIGURE 6.3
A Highly Partisan Electorate

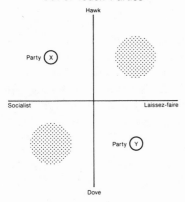

FIGURE 6.4
Out-of-Touch Parties

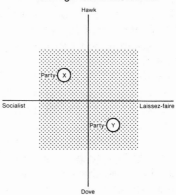

FIGURE 6.5
A Heterogeneous Electorate

strong party affiliations: Even though they would agree that there are important differences in what the parties stand for, most of them would be cross-pressured by the positions and performances of the contending parties.

Figure 6.5 depicts yet a third situation. Now the voters are a heterogeneous lot, scattered evenly throughout the policy space. Wherever the parties locate, they will have no great appeal to most of the voters. Here, too, the electorate is thus unlikely to develop strong party affiliations: Whether the parties locate far apart or very near each other, most voters will not see them as terribly relevant for their own policy choices.

A highly partisan electorate, then, is likely to be one in which voters are clearly divided by one or a small number of lines of cleavage and, equally important, one in which the parties make clear appeals to voters on one side or the other of the cleavage(s). Conversely, both voter heterogeneity and parties that are out of touch with large concentrations of voters are factors that are not conducive to the development of a strongly partisan electorate.

The explanation of the weakening of partisanship in the United States appears to be found in some combination of Figures 6.4 and 6.5.[20] In the New Deal party system, voters and parties were divided relatively clearly along economic lines, with the Democrats taking a clear stand in favor of government intervention and the Republicans taking an equally clear position of general opposition to government intervention. After the outbreak of World War II foreign policy largely ceased to be a matter of partisan disagreement, and for many years the issue of race was kept off the agenda.

This simple equilibrium ended in the mid-1960s, however, as the Vietnam War divided the Democratic party's elite and race and social issues drove a wedge between working class whites, on the one hand, and blacks and cause groups, on the other. Changes in the nomination process that enabled the nationally unattractive George McGovern to win the nomination in 1972, as well as the disappointing economic performance of the Carter administration in 1976–1980, further eroded the accumulated political capital of the Democratic party. The cumulative impact of these developments can be seen in the erosion of Democratic partisanship from its 1964 high—in retrospect, the last hurrah of the New Deal Democrats (see Figure 6.2).[21] Apparently the Democratic losses came less from the outright desertion of older partisans than from the failure of their children to take on the expected Democratic coloration (see Chapter 5 of this volume).

Meanwhile, the Republican party was experiencing its own difficulties, even though these were evidently less harmful to their electoral prospects than those of the Democrats. The Republican geographic base broadened and deepened under the impetus of social and economic change. The racial issue enabled the Republicans to become the preferred presidential party of the South and to capture a significant number of House and Senate seats. The growth of the sunbelt added population and wealth to areas already favorable to Republicans. At the same time, they were able to harness the energies of some of the cause groups that formed largely in reaction to Democratic policies—the complex of groups generally referred to as the "new right." These and other lesser developments made the party considerably more internally heterogeneous than in the past, but to date the splits have not emerged on the electoral level to anything like the degree that they have in the Democratic party. In fact, the mid-1980s saw a slight increase in Republican partisanship (see Figure 6.2), thus apparently reflecting the relative success of the Reagan administration in controlling inflation, promoting economic growth, and strengthening America's position in the international arena. Despite media hyperbole, however, these changes have been relatively minor.

PROSPECTS FOR CHANGE

In six of the past nine presidential elections, the American people have divided control of the House, Senate, and presidency between the two parties. Not only is this a more frequent occurrence than during any previous era in our history, but government divided by presidential elections rather than by midterms is historically unprecedented (Fiorina, 1990). With the erosion of partisanship, the shortening of presidential coattails, and the rise of incumbency—in short, with the increasing orientation of the electorate to specific offices and candidates—divided government has become the normal condition of modern American government. With divided government comes operational problems of efficiency and accountability, problems I will not discuss here given that they have already received detailed and thoughtful treatment in the literature (Sundquist, 1988). The question with which I will conclude this essay has to do with prospects for change. Partisanship has waned whereas individuation has waxed. What are the prospects for a reversal of this trend? "Not very good" is the short answer.

Political historians suggest that, in the past, the partisan loyalties of the electorate were reinvigorated on a large scale in a number of critical realignments of the electoral system (Burnham, 1970). A severe condition or crisis can shake up existing party affiliations that may already be under stress if the condition is a chronic one. If a governing party successfully deals with the condition or crisis, it earns the lasting support of the electorate (Clubb, Flanigan, and Zingale, 1980). The Republican response to secession and the Democratic response to the Great Depression provide the classic illustrations. In the aftermath of such political con-vulsions, national forces in elections run unusually high (vis-à-vis local forces) and the newly ascendant party enjoys high cohesion in government (Brady, 1988). These factors are mutually reinforcing in that high cohesion supports strong leadership and major policy shifts, which in turn elevate national issues in the minds of the public.

Theorists of critical elections have undoubtedly idealized the process. But if they are correct in broad outline, there is little hope for a major realignment today, for the simple reason that the process of electoral disaggregation has gone so far that it is difficult to see how a national trauma in the contemporary period could produce a realignment along the lines of earlier historical examples. If an economic recession more serious than anything experienced in the 1970s and 1980s were to occur, who would be blamed? The Republican president? Or the Democratic Congress? In 1929 the Republicans "enjoyed" full control of the national government; when catastrophe struck there was no question of where to lay the blame. Similarly, the depression of the 1890s struck when the Democrats were in full control. And, of course, some southern states began to secede precisely because the elections of 1860 gave full control of national institutions to the Republicans. While it is true that eras of divided government preceded the realignments of the Civil War and the 1890s, though not the New Deal (Fiorina, 1990), in each case the precipitating event or crisis occurred when one party controlled all three national elective institutions.

In the absence of unified government, the best chance for realignment would appear to be a crisis that would be the clear responsibility of a Republican president—the assumption being that there are more con-ditions for which the president might be tagged with full responsibility than the Congress. Foreign policy is the most obvious example. An extremely unpopular war, or some disastrous international setback that clearly reflected on presidential leadership, would produce the necessary clear responsibility. However, past realignments have not been the result of wars and foreign policy setbacks, although there have been ample "opportunities." And certainly no one could seriously hope for inter-national catastrophe as the remedy for the American electoral disag-gregation.

So far as reasonable observers can judge, then, the present era of the independent voter, oriented toward specific offices and candidates, will be with us for the foreseeable future. For that era to pass, events that probably cannot be predicted, and certainly are not desired, would have to transpire.

NOTES

1. Of course, only thirteen states now elect their executives in presidential election years, so Democratic domination of the governors' mansions largely reflected a good showing two years earlier.

2. The 12-seat House gain by itself may seem small, but it came on the heels of the only midterm election since the Civil War in which the party of the incumbent president gained 9 seats and followed a gain of 97 seats in 1932 and of 53 seats in 1930.

3. Note that "person" does not mean "personality." One may support a particular candidate on the basis of his or her issue stands, past performance, and other reasons more substantial than "personality."

4. One can make only rough estimates about levels of split-ticket voting across time. In the 1980s somewhat more than a quarter of all voters in American National Election Studies (ANES) surveys reported splitting their tickets between presidential and House candidates. When senatorial, gubernatorial, and state/ local voting are considered, the total obviously must increase. A reliable base of survey data for the 1930s is not available, but president-House ticket splitting in 1956 occurred in only 15 percent of the votes. Given that a Democratic House was elected in that year, it is reasonable to presume that the 1936 ticket-splitting figure must have been significantly lower.

5. More than modesty leads me to subsume my own *Retrospective Voting in American National Elections* (1981) under this generalization. Following Ladd and Burnham, I argued in the final pages of this work that electoral behavior was becoming sufficiently disaggregated as to make a unified treatment problematic.

6. There is much less research on state and local elections, but it bears a similar implication: The forces at work in such elections require attention to variables other than those required to describe presidential voting.

7. The principal exception to this generalization would be the study of economic voting, in which researchers move easily between voting for president and voting for Congress.

8. An increase has also been noted in the number of states that are simultaneously represented by a senator from each party. This phenomenon does not reflect ticket splitting in a single election, of course, but it does indicate some electoral instability from election to election. See Poole and Rosenthal (1984:Figure 1).

9. For statistical aficionados the regression equation that predicts split outcomes from ticket splitting (1952–1988) is

% split = 14.4 + .94(% ticket splitting),
adj R^2 = .37 (all coefficients p < .05).

When presidential reelection interacts with ticket splitting, the equation is a much superior

% split = 15 + .68(% ticket splitting) + .50(% ticket splitting) $\times$ reelection
adj R^2 = .83 (all coefficients p < .01).

10. For a thoughtful recent discussion, see McGerr (1986).

11. The figures in Table 6.2 are conservative, however. If independents who lean toward a party were classified as true independents, the figures for party-line voting would obviously be lower.

12. In their study of temporal changes in party identification, Raymond Wolfinger and his students have shown that the shifts have been much smaller than usually argued. See Keith et al. (1987).

13. In the popular press, a president's coattails are sometimes measured by the number of *seats* his party gains in Congress. Given the vagaries of the translation of votes into seats in single-member simple-plurality electoral systems as well as the strong evidence of change in that translation over time, seat totals do not yield accurate estimates of the strength of presidential coattails.

14. Jacobson (1987) has noted that, although incumbent vote totals went up sharply, incumbent reelection rates (already above 90%) increased only a little.

15. Note, however, that the sharp increase in the apparent advantage of incumbency preceded the PAC explosion by ten years or so.

16. Probit estimates are technically more appropriate, but their implications generally differ little from those of regression estimates when the dependent variable splits in the 60:40 range. The advantage of regression is that coefficients can be directly compared across equations. These regression results are fully compatible with probit results that are not reported. References to the percentage correctly predicted by the models denote the unreported probit results.

17. Democratic and Republican effects are measured relative to Independents (the omitted category). Other things being equal, Independents and Republicans were very close in 1952, whereas in 1960 Independents were midway between Republicans and Democrats. In the 1980s Independents were closer to Republicans in their presidential voting but closely resembled Democrats in their House voting.

18. As the Survey Research Center did not code the congressional district of the respondent in 1952, incumbency status cannot be entered into the equations for that year.

19. Space limitations prevent any further exploration of this finding, but it probably reflects the increased distinctiveness of the congressional parties as southern Democrats have become more like other Democrats in their voting patterns. See Rohde (1989).

20. Shively (1979) proposed yet another instrumental theory of partisanship with roots in Downs (1957). Party identification can serve as a means for economizing on decisionmaking costs; one need only ascertain the candidate's party label and vote accordingly. This theory can also account for the erosion of partisanship: As the electorate became better educated and as media coverage of politics increased, voters were presumably less in need of a simple means of making decisions. But the theory is also fully compatible with the performance-evaluation and policy-compatibility theories of partisanship discussed in the text. As voters become less enamored of the parties, for any of the reasons discussed in connection with Figures 6.4 and 6.5, the party affiliation of the candidate would become a less useful guide to voting.

21. At first glance this account might appear to be at odds with that of Wattenberg (1986), who discounts negative voter reaction to the parties as an explanation for the weakening of voter partisanship. Although he concedes that voter repulsion from the parties was evident in 1968 (p. 60), Wattenberg argues that the more general and important factor is that voters increasingly believe the parties are irrelevant. I think that there is a subtle but plausible way to reconcile Wattenberg's careful analysis with the more conflict-based account offered in the text and in much of the literature. Wattenberg focuses on leadership, arguing that "the link between issues and parties depends heavily on the candidate's actions, that is, his or her treatment of issues in partisan terms. . . . It is thus crucial to note that for a variety of institutional reasons candidates now have substantially less incentive to foster the link between themselves and the parties, as well as between political issues and the parties" (p. 74). Yes, but might there be something beyond "institutional reasons"? In 1960 John Kennedy wrapped himself in the Democratic party mantle because he expected to gain from it; Richard Nixon avoided the Republican tag because he expected to be hurt by it. Realizing that the party label carries too much harmful baggage, recent candidates of both parties have deemphasized it, thus contributing to the trend described by Wattenberg. Neutral feelings or no, the experience of the 1988 campaign strongly suggests that negative associations from the past can be reactivated very easily.

PART FOUR

The Electoral Arena

7

The Naming of Candidates: Recruitment or Emergence?

L. SANDY MAISEL
LINDA L. FOWLER
RUTH S. JONES
WALTER J. STONE

On the Tuesday after the first Monday in November, in even-numbered years, Americans go to the polls to elect tens of thousands of public officials. Although many officeholders are elected on other days in other years, at no time is the vast expanse of our multitiered, federated system, which features separate legislative, executive, and judicial branches, so evident to even the most casual observer as it is on these election days.

Each state's entire delegation to the U.S. House of Representatives is elected every two years; Senate elections are held in approximately two-thirds of the states. Forty-five of the states elect representatives to the lower house of their state legislature every two years; thirteen states elect members of their upper house every two years; most of the other states elect state senators for four-year terms, with senatorial elections divided between presidential and nonpresidential election years; forty-seven of the fifty states elect governors for four-year terms, thirty-three of those in nonpresidential election, even-numbered years and five in odd-numbered years.[1] A common feature of all of these elections, save the elections to Nebraska's unicameral legislature, is that they are partisan elections; that is, candidates are listed on the ballot by political party.

Fewer commonalities exist for other elections held on the same day. Some states hold a series of statewide elections—for lieutenant governor, attorney general, treasurer, and like offices. In some states, county, municipal, and special district (e.g., school board and water district board) elections are held on the same day, while in others they are held on different days in the same year or in different years. In some states certain judicial posts are filled by election—on the same day or not—

whereas in other states all judicial posts are filled by appointment. In some states all or some of the elections held are partisan, although roughly three-quarters of American towns and cities now conduct local elections on a nonpartisan basis (Sorauf and Beck, 1988:57; Welch and Bledsoe, 1986). The picture that emerges from this review is one of a vast array of elections, many of them held on the same day, many of them between candidates of political parties, to fill the offices that hold the executive, legislative, and at times judicial powers at the national, state, and local levels.

Representative democracy in the United States depends on competition for office (Dahl, 1956; Downs, 1957; and many others). If there is no competition for office, then the citizenry cannot replace those who are implementing policies with which they disagree. A healthy party system plays the role of guaranteeing this competition for office. According to V. O. Key (1964:10), "The electoral practices of democracies are associated with party systems which propose to the electorate a choice." Similarly, as Frank Sorauf (1964:10) has noted, "The parties facilitate the popular participation, the representation of interests, and the presentation of alternatives on which the processes of democracy depend." In the vast number of elections that are partisan, parties play this role by nominating candidates to contest for office.[2] That is, they create competition for office, and they structure choice for the voters.

However, all parties do not perform this task equally well in all contexts. In this essay, we shall explore the role that political parties, in differing political environments, play in selecting candidates for office. To anticipate the argument, we first examine the relative success of parties in providing electoral competition. We then explore the structural limitations on political parties and the ways in which contemporary parties have worked to increase their influence and thus their effectiveness in guaranteeing competition. Next we turn to the choices made by potential candidates for office. We present a model that defines the role a party can and does play in determining whether effective competition for office will exist. We conclude with some speculative thoughts about the emerging role of political parties in selecting candidates for office.

PARTY EFFECTIVENESS IN CANDIDATE RECRUITMENT

One measure of competition—certainly not the only one, and perhaps not the most important one, but one frequently used nonetheless—is the extent to which those in office lose bids to retain power. A telling observation shared by politicians (from both the left and the right), political journalists, and political scientists is that more elected officials lost their positions in the 1989 elections in the Soviet Union than in the 1988 American congressional elections. In the last two congressional elections, more than 98 percent of incumbent members of the House of Representatives seeking reelection have been reelected. Indeed, in recent decades it has been routine for more than 90 percent of those seeking to retain their seats in the House to do so successfully. The current Era of the House Incumbent opened with the Democrats in control. Despite shifting party fortunes in the control of the presidency, the Democrats have continuously held the majority in the House of Representatives since 1954. These are impressive indications of limits on competition. But, of course, they deal with only one office.

Noncontested Elections

An even more extreme measure of the absence of competition is provided by the number of uncontested elections. Clearly, if one or the other of the major parties does not run a candidate for office, no partisan competition exists—and the party without a candidate has not fulfilled its task. Figures 7.1 and 7.2 present data on uncontested races for U.S. senator and governor respectively. The total number of seats to be contested is always low, and that number varies from year to year depending on state election cycles. Even taking this into account, we note that most of those seats are contested between major party candidates. In the early years covered by these data, southern Democrats ran unopposed in a number of races. In Georgia, Mississippi, Alabama, and South Carolina, in year after year and race after race, no Republican candidate was on the ballot. But southern Republicanism was given a boost by the party's continuing control of the White House in the 1950s and by the candidacy of Barry Goldwater in 1964; the impact of the rejuvenation of the Republican party in the South, frequently described in presidential elections, is readily apparent from these data for other races at the top of the statewide ballot. Only twice since 1964 have southern Republicans not run a candidate for governor; only six times have incumbent Democratic senators not been opposed.

More to the point, all of the statewide races for governor or senator in the South since 1976 have been contested by the Republicans. Republicans have fielded candidates in all elections for governor in the northern states and in all for senator, with the exception of the 1976 reelection of Robert Byrd in West Virginia. Similarly, Democrats have run candidates against incumbent Republicans in all of the races in the last decade, except for the 1986 reelection of Governor James Thompson (R-IL).[3] Thus, for these highly visible and prestigious offices, the problem of lack of contests has never been large and now seems to have all but disappeared.

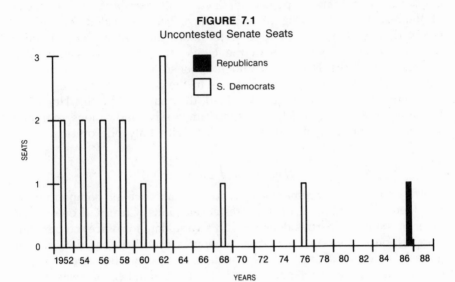

FIGURE 7.1
Uncontested Senate Seats

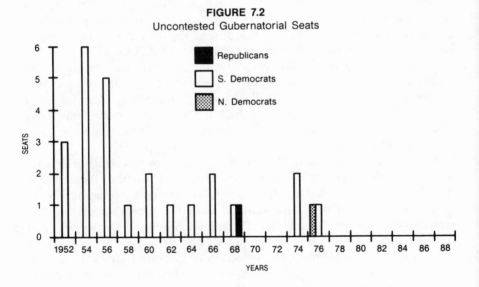

FIGURE 7.2
Uncontested Gubernatorial Seats

FIGURE 7.3
Elections to the House of Representatives Without a Candidate of
One of the Major Parties, 1950–1988

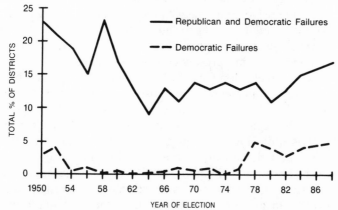

Source: Figure compiled from data reported in Schlesinger (1985)
and Fowler and Maisel (1990).

The contrast between the competition in gubernatorial and senatorial elections and the lack of such competition in other elections is marked. In each of the last two congressional elections, more than 15 percent of the seats have not been contested by one or the other of the major parties. Although this percentage may seem alarming, the number of uncontested seats is not out of line with those in the first years of this century and are in fact lower than those during the period in midcentury when the Republican party did not exist throughout much of the South (Schlesinger, 1985:1159). However, a number of factors should be noted. First, the data for the most recent years suggest the beginning of an increase in the number of uncontested seats, following a relatively stable period that lasted for approximately two decades. Second, as Figure 7.3 shows, the candidates for noncontested seats are not found in the same regions as they once were. The number of southern Democrats in the House who do not face Republican competition has been declining, whereas in the North the number of Republicans not facing Democratic competition has been increasing slightly and that of northern Democrats not facing Republican competition has been rising even more. Recent years have seen a rejuvenation of Republican fortunes in the South, with a decrease in the number of seats in which Democrats run uncontested, whereas the party has become increasingly unable (or unwilling) to contest congressional seats in other regions.

Table 7.1 presents data for state legislative elections. Until very recently, systematic data on state legislative races were unavailable. However, the Inter-University Consortium for Political and Social Research has undertaken a comprehensive State Legislative Elections Project, which has brought heretofore fugitive data to light. The data in Table 7.1 are from thirteen states (arrayed geographically) for which the data are now readily available.[4] The first column presents the average percentage of incumbent legislators seeking reelection from 1978 through 1986; the second column presents the average percentage of those seeking reelection who have won. Although the results vary somewhat from state to state and between the houses of the legislatures, it is abundantly clear that turnover due to retirement is quite low (though generally not so low as that in the U.S. Congress) and that turnover due to defeat in the general election is even lower (Jewell and Breaux, 1988).[5] With the exceptions of Connecticut and Utah, the incumbent success rate for state legislative seats is as great or even greater than that in the House of Representatives.[6]

The last five columns in Table 7.1 present the percentage of seats in each house of each state's legislature in which an incumbent seeking reelection was not challenged by a candidate in the other major party. The data in these columns show tremendous variation. Two of the eastern states represent examples of extreme positions. In Connecticut very few incumbents have won without major party opposition, a situation not unlike major statewide offices. In Rhode Island, at the other extreme, large numbers of incumbents have faced no major party opposition; far more seats go by default than has been the case in any recent congressional elections. These columns also show interesting variations between houses of the legislature in the same state. Although conventional wisdom would hold that senate seats are "worth more" than house seats, because senates tend to be smaller bodies and legislators represent more people and are hence relatively more visible in policymaking, more senate seats go uncontested than house seats in a number of states. Several hypotheses concerning the prominence and powers of the two houses in different states might usefully be explored to explain this finding. For our purposes, however, the point to be emphasized is that at these levels a number of seats go uncontested, and thus there is no competition.

Meaningfully Contested Elections

Ever since David Mayhew (1974a) first raised the question of the "vanishing marginals," those scholars who study elections have been concerned not just with electoral wins and losses but with the *magnitude* of electoral victory or defeat.[7] Thus another measure of competition is not just whether a candidate wins or loses, not just whether a major

TABLE 7.1
Results of State Legislative Races in Selected States

State	1978–1986 Avg. Percent Incumbents Running	1978–1986 Avg. Percent Incumbents Winning	Percent Uncontested In:				
			1978	1980	1982	1984	1986
Connecticut							
Senate	82	78	5	0	0	0	9
House	80	87	5	15	10	12	20
Rhode Island							
Senate	74	93	49	26	12	19	23
House	78	96	42	37	49	36	34
Delaware							
Senate	84	94	33	40	39	56	56
House	83	89	27	33	37	44	44
Pennsylvania							
Senate	74	94	0	6	18	17	33
House	84	97	6	21	15	19	39
Michigan[a]							
Senate	64	99	34	—	34	—	40
House	79	95	9	21	27	4	3
Ohio							
Senate	81	83	8	10	0	0	17
House	83	96	7	20	5	7	17
Wisconsin							
Senate	75	92	18	34	20	27	7
House	82	93	23	28	15	16	22
Iowa							
Senate	69	89	17	11	20	44	62
House	79	92	32	15	24	31	40
Missouri							
Senate	84	99	13	33	33	62	47
House	84	98	31	51	53	71	56
Kentucky[b]							
Senate	70	96	50	56	62	—	73
House	80	96	61	59	—	55	65
Colorado							
Senate	57	96	50	31	71	55	50
House	70	89	35	34	31	44	40
Utah							
Senate	74	81	14	40	18	27	29
House	72	84	16	11	26	22	24
California							
Senate	81	93	0	0	17	0	6
House	81	97	11	7	16	12	3

[a]The Michigan Senate has nonstaggered four-year terms, whereas all of the other senates have staggered four- or two-year terms.
[b]Due to the fact that Kentucky scheduled legislative elections in odd years until 1984, the figures for 1978 to 1982 actually pertain to elections held from 1979 to 1983.

Source: Table derived from Jewell and Breaux (1988:Tables 1, 2, and 6).

TABLE 7.2
Gubernatorial and Senatorial Races in Which
Winner Outpolled Loser by 3 to 1 or More

Year	Governors			Senators		
	Northern Democrats	Southern Democrats	GOP	Northern Democrats	Southern Democrats	GOP
1978	0	1	0	1	3	1
1980	0	0	0	1	0	0
1982	1	0	0	2	0	0
1984	0	0	0	1	1	2
1986	1	0	0	0	0	0
1988	0	0	0	2	0	0

Source: Table compiled by authors from annual election returns.

party opponent's name was on the ballot, but whether that opponent won a significantly large number of votes to suggest meaningful competition and thus real electoral choices.

Again, it seems instructive to compare data for the more visible elections for state governor and U.S. senator with that for the House of Representatives and state legislature. As a parallel to the earlier discussion about the partisan competition for statewide races, we find not only that these races are contested but also that few have been totally one-sided. Table 7.2 presents data on the number of races for state governor and for U.S. senator in which the winner outpolled his or her major opponent by more than 3 to 1. If this table had been extended back to the 1950s, the data would reveal that during the earlier period, in a number of southern states in which Republicans did field a candidate, they provided only token opposition. But by 1978 real opposition had become the norm. In most states, in most races, candidates are challenging for these offices and running campaigns that attract widespread support. Incumbents lose more of these races than is the case for state legislature or for the House of Representatives; those who win face more serious opposition (Maisel, 1987:Ch. 6; Jewell and Olson, 1988:Ch. 6).

Various measures have been used to indicate serious opposition. For statewide offices we have presented data on lopsided races, because the number of races contested was low and varied from election to election. For congressional and state legislative races, regardless of the measure used, a pattern emerges which reveals that, over the last decade, incumbents' margins of victory have increased. Table 7.3, adapted from Jewell and Breaux (1988) and Jacobson (1987b), illustrates this point by using, as a measure of competition, mean percentage of incumbent votes for the House of Representatives and for seats in selected state legislatures. Jewell and Breaux (1988:502) note that the increase in the incumbents'

TABLE 7.3
Percentage of Votes Won by Incumbents in Congressional
and Selected State Legislative Elections

Legislature	1978	1980	1982	1984	1986
U.S. House	71.8	70.8	71.0	72.8	74.1
Connecticut					
Senate	64.4	59.6	61.5	63.4	68.8
House	65.1	67.9	66.4	63.4	71.6
Rhode Island					
Senate	83.2	74.9	68.9	72.8	72.8
House	83.2	79.7	83.5	76.2	77.4
Delaware					
Senate	73.8	74.0	75.2	80.2	85.6
House	72.9	75.7	78.3	80.7	81.4
Pennsylvania					
Senate	62.2	69.2	70.7	74.4	78.8
House	67.7	73.1	72.4	74.9	81.1
Michigan					
Senate	75.3	—	72.6	—	70.3
House	75.0	74.8	75.7	70.0	73.1
Ohio					
Senate	71.7	65.2	63.9	63.0	72.6
House	68.3	72.9	66.6	69.0	71.6
Wisconsin					
Senate	72.0	73.8	68.5	70.0	68.3
House	72.8	74.6	70.1	71.0	74.2
Iowa					
Senate	66.9	63.0	65.9	76.7	85.2
House	73.7	65.8	70.2	72.9	77.0
Missouri					
Senate	71.6	78.9	74.9	86.6	81.9
House	77.9	83.7	84.4	89.7	84.9
Kentucky[a]					
Senate	83.4	84.3	85.2	—	90.4
House	86.4	85.2	—	83.8	88.4
Colorado					
Senate	86.2	73.0	91.0	83.8	81.2
House	75.7	75.5	74.7	81.0	78.1
Utah					
Senate	71.1	77.0	67.5	77.0	78.6
House	69.3	66.7	73.6	74.2	70.5
California					
Senate	67.4	68.4	70.6	70.4	69.2
House	68.8	68.6	71.9	72.0	70.7

The Michigan Senate has nonstaggered four-year terms, whereas all of the other senates have staggered four- or two-year terms.

[a]Due to the fact that Kentucky scheduled legislative elections in odd years until 1984, the figures for 1978 to 1982 actually pertain to elections held from 1979 to 1983.

Source: Table derived from Jacobson (1987b:32) and Jewell and Breaux (1988:Table 3).

margin of victory seems to occur more often in nonprofessional legislatures, a finding corroborated by the relatively modest increase in
winning margins for the Congress.

No systematic data exist on levels of competition for local offices.
Our clear impression, however, is that the general patterns revealed
earlier would be duplicated and accentuated if we were able to examine
a comprehensive set of returns for elections for county, municipal, and
special district elections. That is, in some areas of the country and for
some offices, two-party competition would be the norm; each major
party would routinely field a candidate, the incumbent would occasionally
lose, and the elections would occasionally be close. However, the more
normal pattern would be for one party or the other to dominate: The
less powerful party would often fail to field complete slates of candidates,
and many elections that are contested would be lopsided.

Our judgment, then, is that the major political parties are inconsistent
in their ability to guarantee competitive elections below the presidential
level in the United States. For the more salient offices—state governor
or U.S. senator—rather intense competition is frequent and total lack of
competition is the exception. For Congress as well as more local elections,
a variety of outcomes are evident—dependent, so it seems, on local
circumstances. If our American electoral system were one in which the
parties at every level simply submitted lists of acceptable candidates for
voter approval, electoral competition would likely exhibit less variation.
But such is not the case in our system of individual (rather than party)
candidacies. In some areas and for some offices, intense competition is
the norm; in other areas and for other offices, any competition at all is
rare. That said, we move on to our next task, which is to isolate the
role that political parties are able to play in finding competitive candidates
to contest for office.

VARIATIONS AMONG THE INSTITUTIONAL CONTEXTS
FOR PARTY ORGANIZATIONS

Endorsement Procedures

Most nominations at the state and local levels are determined by
primary elections.[8] The original purpose of nominating by primary
elections was to permit the voters, not party officials, to make decisions
concerning who would run for office. As V. O. Key wrote twenty-five
years ago, "Throughout the history of American nominating practices
runs a persistent attempt to make feasible popular participation in
nominations and thereby to limit or to destroy the power of party
oligarchies" (Key, 1964:371; see also Maisel, 1987:Ch. 5; Sorauf and

Beck, 1988:Ch. 9; Jewell and Olson, 1988:Ch. 4). But as party officials have a stake in the selection of those party nominees, they have attempted (either formally or informally) to maintain a role in the process.

In a few states, one or both parties retain the party convention as a means of nominating candidates for some offices. More common is the practice of states to permit party organizations to formally endorse candidates for office through local party caucuses or through conventions. Pre-primary endorsements carry with them varying advantages. In Utah and Connecticut, for example, the only way onto the primary ballot is through the acquisition of a certain percentage of the votes in conventions; in Rhode Island and Delaware, the convention endorsee is automatically on the primary ballot whereas other candidates must qualify by petition. Position on the primary ballot, and whether the party endorsee is so designated, also varies by state. Informal endorsement procedures are used in several states that do not have formal mechanisms for a party role. Again, experiences in different states vary significantly. It might be acceptable for a state party organization to endorse a candidate, but local party organizations might refrain from doing so in the same state. Endorsement procedures are a matter of party rules, not state law; thus they are more easily changed, and the role that party officials can and do play alters accordingly.

How effective are endorsement procedures? Again, there is significant variation from state to state, and from locality to locality within states. First, in some states and localities, competition for party nomination is rare. In such cases, the endorsement procedure is effectively determinative, because it is the end result of the party officials' quest to find a candidate to run for an office. In essence, the party officials can say to a potential nominee that they will "guarantee" the nomination (i.e., that no one else will run). In other cases, primary competition is rare because no one would challenge a party endorsee; these nominations might well be worth more than those discussed earlier, but the party role is the same. In still other states and localities, party endorsees are frequently challenged and, on occasion, beaten. In New York State, for example, receiving the party endorsement has been considered a negative factor by some politicians.[9]

Voter Eligibility for Primary Elections

In addition to maintaining a role in the endorsement of potential nominees, party officials have been concerned with determining who in the electorate is eligible to vote in partisan primary elections. In the past, conventional wisdom has held that party officials desire to restrict the primary electorate to those who have a close affiliation with the political party. Thus they favor "closed" primaries in which a voter must be registered in a particular party in order to vote in that party's primary election. Party officials argue that the voters with the greatest stake in a party (i.e., declared partisans) should be able to determine that party's nominees.

Those concerned with politics who are more opposed to the influence of political party—or, stated more positively, those who believe in the widest possible participation in all aspects of the political process—feel that "open" primaries, primary elections in which any registered voter can participate, are more appropriate. Some party officials worry about raiding in open primaries, a practice by which those who favor one political party vote for the weaker candidate in the other party's primary in order to improve the chances of their favored party's candidate in the general election. Although raiding seems an obvious strategy, implementing such a strategy is extremely difficult. Evidence of successful raiding has not been documented, but most party officials, especially leaders in a region's majority party, continue to advocate and to defend a primary system that is closed to all but the party faithful.

Eligibility for voting in primary elections has traditionally been viewed as a function of state law. Twenty-seven states have some form of closed primary, although the point at which one can change from one party to another, and the ability of nonparty enrollees to choose a party at the last minute, varies significantly. Twenty states have primaries generally categorized as open primaries, but, again, these vary as to whether a voter's participation in a party's primary is public information at the time of voting. The line between open and closed primaries is not a distinct one; rather, eligibility is on a continuum from the most closed primaries (those in which enrollment must be accomplished well in advance and cannot easily be changed, and in which independents cannot enroll at the last minute), through primaries that give voters more leeway in changing parties, to the most open primaries (those in which voters choose a party ballot in secret and their choice is never recorded) (see Carr and Scott, 1984). The final three states have unique and very open systems. Washington and Alaska use the "blanket" primary, so called because a single ballot is figuratively as big as a blanket and covers all ("blankets") candidate selection. A voter can vote in either party's primary for each individual office; thus, an individual could vote in the Democratic party primary for governor, the Republican primary for U.S. Senator, the Republican primary for member of Congress, the Democratic primary for state senator, and so on. Under this system, the voter has the most freedom—and can demonstrate the least commitment to one party or the other. Louisiana uses a "nonpartisan" primary, which sounds like a contradiction in terms. All candidates are listed on one ballot, and voters choose one candidate for each office. If any candidate achieves a majority, that candidate is automatically elected. If no candidate receives a majority, a runoff between the top two is held on the general election day. The two candidates for an office on the general election ballot can be of the same or different parties, depending on votes in the primary. Obviously, political party per se has little role in this system.

Until recently, state law determined the type of primary held in each state. If party officials wanted a different type of primary, they had to work through the state legislature to change the law. In 1984 the Republican party of Connecticut challenged that norm. Connecticut Republicans wanted an open primary, not for philosophical reasons but for political ones. In recent decades Connecticut has been a heavily Democratic state with a strong Democratic party organization. The Republicans wanted to attract unaffiliated voters, who constituted roughly one-third of the Connecticut electorate, to their side. They felt that they could do so by giving the unaffiliated voters a say in Republican nominations. The Republicans tried to achieve their goal by changing state law, but they were frustrated by a Democratically controlled legislature in 1984 and by a gubernatorial veto in the next legislative session. They subsequently challenged in court.

In *Tashjian v. Republican Party of Connecticut,* 479 U. S. 208 (1986), the Supreme Court ruled that the state of Connecticut had to allow the Republican party to define its own membership and thus to use an open primary if it so desired. This case is extremely important for defining the role of political parties (Epstein, 1989). Because of this ruling, state parties are now allowed to determine the eligible electorate for party primaries. In so ruling, the Court has given parties a greater say in who their nominees would be.

Epstein (1989:254–260) points out that political scientists who favor strong political parties in the American system of democracy have differed in their response to *Tashjian.* One group of Connecticut political scientists filed an *amicus* brief arguing in favor of closed primaries. They stated, in part, that the closed primary "tends to support the concept of the party as an association of like-minded people" and "that closed primary elections produce other benefits which are conducive to cohesive parties" (Brief of Cibes et al., 1986:23). That, in essence, is the pro-party conventional wisdom. In contrast, another group of political scientists, reflecting the views of the Committee for Party Renewal, a national association of politicians and political scientists searching for ways to revitalize parties as a vital element in American democracy, supported the view of the Republican party, arguing that "political parties can best contribute to American politics if permitted to steer their own courses" (Brief of Burns et al., 1986:4). These political scientists allowed that they might well differ on the merits of open versus closed primaries, but they agreed that the independence of political parties was the most important factor under consideration. Throughout *Tashjian*, that view has prevailed; but its impact on party efforts to control primary electorates— and thus on party efforts to influence who their nominees will be— has yet to be determined.

PARTY EFFORTS TO RECRUIT
MORE COMPETITIVE CANDIDATES

Political party leaders have long understood that one of their most important functions is to recruit candidates for office. Recruitment is often necessary because in the United States decisions on candidacy are ultimately personal decisions. V. O. Key (1956) argued that the rise of political primaries led to the demise of local organizations and that this decline, in turn, would decrease electoral competition and the voters' opportunity to express their preferences at the polls. In the 1970s many observers bemoaned the decline of party organization, and Key's conclusion seemed warranted.

More recently, however, evidence indicates that state and local political party organizations are not so weak as they were once thought to be (Cotter et al., 1984; Gibson et al., 1985). National party organizations, led by the Republican party, have begun to expend great resources in an effort to reinvigorate their local units (Sabato, 1988; Herrnson, 1988). Local political party organizations have continued to grow both in strength and in their ability to perform traditional campaign functions such as recruiting candidates to fill spots on the ballot (Gibson et al., 1989; Frendeis et al., 1990). (See Chapters 2 and 3.)

And these efforts have borne fruit. The probability that the minority party in an area will run a candidate for local offices is a function of the strength of local party organization. Even though minority party candidates might not win, their candidacies contribute to higher vote totals for other members of their party running for offices higher up on the ballot. The connection seems to be that local candidacies make higher-level candidates of a minority party appear more credible (Frendeis et al., 1990). The efforts to revitalize party organizations, including minority party organizations, have had the double impact of increasing the number of seats in which two-party competition is present and of raising the level of competition among candidates for higher offices— precisely the results that pro-party democratic theorists had predicted.

A second method used by parties to increase their ability to compete effectively has been their concentrated efforts to improve the quality of their nominees. The national parties—as well as their respective congressional and senatorial committees—have been actively involved in recruiting candidates for some time. These efforts do not signal a national dominance of local politics. Rather, as each election cycle begins, the staff of the national organizations and their regional political coordinators meet with state and local officials to determine which seats that they are holding might be vulnerable, which seats held by the opposition might be vulnerable, and which seats will be open and hotly contested.

National, state, and local party officials all have a vested interest in finding good candidates for those seats that appear likely to feature close competition. They identify potential candidates and attempt to convince them to run. In the late 1970s and early 1980s, the Republican party went so far as to contribute to primary campaigns for selected candidates. This practice caused some controversy, however, when designated candidates were unsuccessful in winning nominations.

In more recent years the effort has been to assure good potential candidates that the party is interested in their campaign and will help in any way it can. For example, the Democratic Senatorial Campaign Committee helped convince Connecticut Attorney General Joseph Lieberman to challenge incumbent Republican Senator Lowell Weicker, and its Republican counterpart worked to convince Congressman Connie Mack of Florida to seek the Senate seat left open by the retirement of Democrat Lawton Chiles. The most controversial part of party prenomination efforts has been "negative recruitment"—the effort to convince someone considering a race to drop the idea. When parties are successful in negative recruitment, they not only avoid intraparty competition but are also able to begin their assistance to unopposed candidates well in advance of the general election campaign. But when they are not successful, as when the Republicans failed to dissuade Congressman Hal Daub from challenging appointed incumbent David Karnes for the Republican Senate nomination in Nebraska, leftover resentment tends to spill over into the ensuing general election campaign.

Recruitment of candidates is one of the important functions of a campaign organization. It is a critical function at the stage of filling the ballot. But it is also important to ensure, to the extent possible, that party candidates for office can run credible campaigns. Modern party organizations have neither the power nor the inclination to designate all party nominees, as did local party leaders in the age of political bosses. Most nominees are still self-starters. But the party has a stake in encouraging experienced and qualified candidates to seek office under its label. Thus, party officials make it known that they are willing to provide campaign assistance, that they are committed to a race, and, at times, that they would prefer some candidacies over others (Herrnson, 1988:Ch. 3).

A final, relatively new method that party officials can use to improve the quality of their nominees is to define the primary electorate that selects those nominees, as the Republican party did when its actions led to the *Tashjian* case. Since *Tashjian*, a number of state legislatures in closed primary states have passed laws permitting parties to open their primaries should they choose to do this (Epstein, 1989:260–270). The North Carolina Republicans did so choose. In West Virginia, the Republican primary was opened at the request of party leaders when the secretary of state informed each party that they would automatically have that option under the Supreme Court's ruling. But the reaction to the new option has generally been modest.

One can only speculate about other possible reactions to the *Tashjian* decision.[10] For instance, if the true impact of the decision is to free political parties from state domination in defining their membership, would it not be possible for majority parties in open primary states to close their primaries, if they perceived it to be to their political advantage? Could either party in Washington or Alaska void the blanket primary systems used in those states by defining their primary electorate in a more restrictive way? Taken to the logical extreme, could political parties in primary states decide, on their own and in opposition to state legislatures, that they preferred to nominate in convention? Party officials would have to examine the political consequences of any of these moves. Rules that appear to be undemocratic are difficult to justify in a media age, even if they do work to ensure better candidates for office. It is clear, however, that party officials have had options opened to them that were not on the horizon before the *Tashjian* decision.

A MODEL FOR DECISIONMAKING
BY POTENTIAL CANDIDATES

To this point the argument has been that one of the responsibilities of political parties is to guarantee that elections in the United States are competitive. This is a basic concern for a representative democracy, and American parties have been only partially successful in accomplishing the task. But the argument thus far is too simple. Whether an incumbent will face a credible challenger is dependent, in part, on decisions made by *potential candidates* for office, not simply by the parties (Fowler and McClure, 1989). Scholars of political parties and elections have gathered little empirical information to aid us in understanding how potential candidates for office weigh their options; yet we can isolate the variables

FIGURE 7.4
Model of Potential Candidate Decisionmaking Process

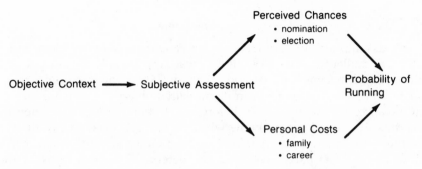

that appear to be relevant and focus on the role that parties play in those decisionmaking calculi.

At this juncture it is important that we draw a distinction among the different paths to party nomination. At one extreme is the traditional group-based concept of candidate recruitment. In this case some external force, normally a political party, tries to influence a potential candidate to run for office. The party, or other external force, attempts to influence the potential candidate's decisionmaking. At the other extreme is candidate self-selection. In this case a potential candidate "emerges" on his or her own and then considers a run for office, assesses chances, and makes decisions independent of political party opinion or other external forces. In between are various "mixed" cases in which potential candidates might be encouraged to run or might "self-recruit," but in either case party and other external forces are part of the decisionmaking process. Our present concern is with the ways in which these decisions are made—and with the role of political party in the decisions.

Figure 7.4 depicts a model of *candidate* decisionmaking. The model assumes that some aspects of a potential contest can be measured objectively, that other factors must be assessed subjectively, and that both sets of assessments determine whether potential candidates will think it worthwhile to run. While determining whether they have a chance of winning, potential candidates must also make judgments about other, more personal factors. Among other things, they must balance the costs associated with losing against the benefits—and quite different costs—of winning. The interplay of these personal factors and the perceived chances of success lead to the eventual decision of whether to run for office. Although this model is quite crude and remains untested, it does spell out many of the factors that enter into a candidate's decisions. In particular, it responds to the question "What causes a person to run for office?" by identifying at least four kinds of influence: the objective context, the subjective context, perceived chances of winning, and personal costs.

The Objective Context

An assumption of this model is that candidates who are likely to be effective challengers for office will be those who are able to view political situations with some sophistication. The context for any race is important; some aspects of that context can be measured objectively and are known in advance. For example, well before an election takes place, potential candidates can and should know what the partisan makeup of a district is; they can ascertain whether citizens tend either to vote straight party tickets or to cross party lines; they can determine whether races for the seat they are seeking have been competitive or one-sided in the past; and, if they already hold another office, they can discover whether the constituency they represent in the office they currently hold overlaps significantly with that of the office they are considering. Potential candidates for office can assess certain aspects of their own background objectively: Have they been able to raise money in the past? Have they been exposed to the issues and demonstrated an ability to handle them? Have they worked with a staff that is capable of running a campaign for a higher office? Early in the decisionmaking process, sophisticated potential challengers consider these and other contextual and institutional variables. Based on this evaluation, they can then reach a preliminary judgment as to whether the race is one that should be contemplated at all. In terms of our model, these factors provide an early indication of the probability that a candidate will seek a specific elective office.

The Subjective Context

Scholars can look at objective indicators and reach objective conclusions. But politicians must make subjective assessments of some of the same indicators (Maisel, 1986). For instance, a prospective candidate may know objectively that she has never run in a race in which she has raised more than $25,000, but she must make a subjective judgment as to whether the same contributors who gave $100 for one race would give much more for a higher-level race. A state legislator may know that his district overlaps with only 20 percent of the state senate district in which he is considering a race, but he must judge whether all of the people in that senatorial district are aware of his state legislative accomplishments.

Indeed, subjective assessments are critical to decisions about possible candidacies. They are essentially political judgments. What does the political environment look like for a candidacy for this position, against these likely opponents, at this time? The timing of these judgments varies from politician to politician, and politicians do not reach these judgments simultaneously but, rather, as they assess relevant information. Moreover, opinions change along with changes in the political environment. The local, state, or national economic context is one of the subjective variables that possible candidates tend to look at. Is this a good year for Democrats? For Republicans? For challengers or incumbents? But identifying that variable is not enough. It is also necessary to determine the point at which the assessment of that variable has an effect on candidate decisionmaking (Jacobson and Kernell, 1983; Bond, Covington, and Fleisher, 1985; Born, 1986). He or she must also ascertain whether local politicians view national factors as having an effect on their immediate political environment—or if it is possible that local interpretations have been applied to national economic indicators. The national economy might be on the rise, but if the local economy is suffering, the latter factor is the relevant one for a politician trying to assess whether economic trends will have an impact on his or her campaign.

Another subjective assessment concerns the strength of the local party organization. Can party officials help a candidate gain the nomination? Can party leaders discourage others from challenging for the nomination? Will they be helpful in a general election race? Will state or national party support be forthcoming? Will state or national leaders help raise money or run the campaign? Can the party be helpful in the post-election period if the campaign is not successful? Will running enhance one's political career within the party? Or will it help only if one wins? Clearly these and related issues can be important to the assessment of whether a candidate will run. Party leaders, at least those who themselves are sophisticated politicians, understand the significance of these factors and can use this understanding to influence potential candidates' decisions.

Perceived Chances of Winning

Our model posits that knowledge of the context of an election and assessments of the political environment affect an aspirant's perception of his or her chances of securing a party nomination and of winning an election. In some instances candidates are quite certain of the accuracy of their perceptions; in other instances they are much less certain. But in either case a potential candidate's perception of the chance of winning is an important variable that determines whether that candidate will in fact choose to run. A political party cannot force attractive, qualified candidates to run for office. Individuals, not parties, therefore control the first threshold in the sequence of activities that ultimately result in the presence or absence of strong competitive candidates.

Personal Costs

The final major variable intervening between perceptions of the political environment and the decision to run for office are the personal costs (and benefits) of seeking office. In this calculus potential candidates must consider a wide range of effects. One set of personal factors encompasses family considerations: additional loss of privacy, the commitment to a campaign, financial costs, the possibility of having to relocate, and so on. The other set of personal factors is career related: having to leave the position currently held, the effect of a campaign on alternative career paths, the impact of a potential loss of subsequent political plans, and the reaction of the party elite to a decision either to run or to forgo a race. Our model suggests that the relationship between these personal costs and the perceived chances of winning is nonrecursive. Indeed, personal costs and benefits may be very sensitive to the perceived chances of winning. For instance, a candidate would not have to worry much about the cost of relocating his or her family if the chances of winning (and of having to move) were remote. On the other hand, a candidate who perceived his or her chances of winning as good might well decide that the costs of relocating were too high to justify entering the race.

Summary of Model

The model we have proposed represents our best understanding of the decisionmaking process that any potential candidate must undoubtedly follow. But the model has not been tested. The importance of the various factors in this process, under what circumstances, is not yet clear. Nor do we know how perceptions are arrived at. These important research questions remain at the top of the agenda of those scholars examining the electoral process.

Nevertheless, our model does illuminate the role that political parties can in fact play in ensuring the existence of genuine competition in American elections. Genuine competition depends on the availability of quality candidates. When incumbents seek reelection to governorships or seats in the U.S. Senate, few have the luxury of running unopposed or of facing challengers who do not provide serious opposition. But those seeking reelection to the U.S. House of Representatives, or to many state legislatures and local positions, are generally not seriously challenged—if indeed they face any opposition at all. They do not face serious opposition because potential candidates for those seats often decide not to run. We do not know precisely how to define the population of potential candidates for any office. To a large extent that is the job of party organization. But once those candidates have been defined— or, as is frequently the case in American elections, once they define themselves—party leaders can have an impact on their decision either to run or not to run only in certain ways. No matter how hard party leaders try to increase their influence, their efforts, our model suggests, will meet with only limited success. A number of the factors important in candidates' determinations are simply beyond the control of political parties.

CONCLUSION

What, then, can one conclude about the role of political parties in the selection of nominees for offices below the presidential level? This essay ends as it began, by emphasizing the diversity of experiences within the American political system. The role that party leaders believe they should play, a role compatible with democratic theory, is to provide competition.

At a minimum, this role involves finding a candidate to run for an office, such that one party's nominee does not attain office without facing an electoral test. But party leaders are not always successful in reaching this goal. Many offices go uncontested each election day. But more than competition is expected. Party leaders want to have candidates on the ballot who have a chance of winning or, at least, who can raise the level of debate in the election campaign and make the eventual winner pay attention. Hence party leaders must find good candidates for office. Yet defining a "good" candidate is an imprecise art. Party leaders must consider, among other qualities, previous electoral experience, visibility or stature within a district, personal wealth or the ability to raise money, articulateness, attractiveness, and intelligence. It must be conceded that many local party officials are amateur volunteers in the rankest sense of amateur and have neither time, inclination, nor ability to fulfill these tasks; but sophisticated local party leaders have a sense of who will be good candidates for the races in their area.

Identifying a potential quality candidate is only the first step, however. Party officials must convince that candidate to seek office—but even their encouragement plays only a small part in the decision calculus of many potential candidates. Their success is incomplete at best. Slates are most likely to be filled with quality candidates when the office is attractive and the chance of victory seems promising. In these cases one often observes candidate emergence, not candidate selection by party officials. The role of party officials is more pronounced, more significant, and more variable in the remaining situations, when they have to work within the existing institutional regulations to convince candidates to seek offices that are not so attractive, in races for which victory seems less likely. Parties were stronger as recruiting organizations before the Progressive reforms led to the near-total acceptance of primary elections as nominating tools. Few would suggest that the nation should return to the era of nominations decided in "smoke-filled" rooms. But various reforms have been suggested to enhance the role of party. The role of political parties in the recruitment process will remain nominal so long as valuable nominations go primarily to self-selected political entrepreneurs. But if those interested in nominations have incentives for seeking party support, because of changes in campaign finance laws or in nominating procedures that enhance the role of party, then party recruitment might well be as viable a route to nomination as the emergence of political self-starters. Such changes would certainly improve the ability of our party system to play the role it should be performing in our electoral process—that of guaranteeing meaningful contests for office at more levels of government in more areas of the country than has been the case in the recent past.

NOTES

1. Kentucky, Louisiana, Mississippi, New Jersey, and Virginia all hold statewide elections in odd-numbered years. In recent years the trend has been for states to move from statewide elections in presidential election years to nonpresidential election years (Maisel, 1987:140–141; Jewell and Olson, 1988:44–47).

2. This essay—and in fact the entire book—does not deal with nonpartisan elections. Although no one would deny the importance of local politics in the vast majority of localities that do not hold partisan elections, the task of examining such elections is clearly separable from the one at hand. (See, for example, Welch and Bledsoe, 1986; Hawley, 1973.)

3. The Thompson case is an exception in many ways. Former Senator Adlai Stevenson III won the Democratic nomination to oppose Thompson but gave up that nomination because two followers of Lyndon Larouche had won primaries to be his running mates on the statewide ticket. The example of the inability of parties to control their own nominations will be discussed later in the essay.

4. These states were chosen for the first release because of the simplicity in analyzing data from single-member districts, but they do not represent a sample of all states (the deep South, for instance, is excluded from these data). However, the data are valuable insofar as they indicate differing trends in the states that can be examined.

5. The second column in Table 7.1 presents the percentages of primary winners who were successful in the general election. The data set does not include primary election results.

6. One can speculate as to why these two states differ so much from the other states for which the data has been released. One hypothesis worth exploring is that political parties play a more prominent structural role in securing nominations in these states than they do in many others—and that this role is

reflected in the extent to which more attractive and successful candidates challenge incumbents. (See Jewell and Olson, 1988:Ch. 4.)

7. More recently, Jacobson (1987a) has once again raised the question of the importance of marginality of victory for predicting subsequent victory or defeat. For our purposes, we include this brief look at marginality as yet another surrogate for effective competition.

8. Certain states still permit party nominations to be determined by party conventions for some offices—or for some offices in one or the other party. Nominations by party officials are often made by minor parties. (See Maisel, 1987:Ch. 5; Sorauf and Beck, 1988:253–255.)

9. Jewell and Olson (1988:94–106) discuss the impact of party endorsement in some detail. (See also Jewell, 1984.)

10. This section draws heavily on Leon Epstein's (1989) thoughtful essay on state regulation of political parties.

8

Structure as Strategy:
Presidential Nominating Politics
in the Post-Reform Era

ELAINE CIULLA KAMARCK

Imagine for a moment that Franklin Delano Roosevelt, Dwight D. Eisenhower, and John F. Kennedy were to join us once again. Furthermore, imagine that they found themselves in the middle of a political strategy session for a presidential campaign. Strategy for the general election would be quite familiar to them. It would revolve around winning the majority of electoral votes. Each state would be categorized as safe for one party or the other, as a lost cause, or as a possible battleground. Candidates and their surrogates would move around the country giving speeches and holding rallies in an attempt to win the crucial battleground states. Much about the general election would be different, of course, but the underlying strategy for accumulating a majority of electoral votes would be very much the same as it had been in their day.

Suppose, however, that our three returned presidents were to find themselves in the midst of a strategy session for the Democratic or Republican nomination. The goal would be the same as it had been for them—to accumulate enough delegates to win the nod at their party's nominating convention. Beyond that, however, the similarities would end, for the strategy for achieving that goal is very different today from what it was in their time.

Imagine Franklin Roosevelt's bewilderment at the use of the term *momentum*. In his day this term was used to describe activity in the convention hall; now it refers to the boost in attention that a candidate gets from primaries and caucuses that take place months before the convention even opens. Imagine Eisenhower's surprise upon hearing that Senator Howard Baker (R-TN) had given up both his job as majority leader of the Senate and his Senate seat *four years* before the presidential election in order to run for president full time. Ike spent the years before the 1952 Republican Convention in Europe with NATO, arriving home in June to campaign for his nomination in July. Imagine Kennedy's puzzlement over the decision made by Walter Mondale, a former Democratic vice-president and favorite of the Democratic party establishment, to enter every single presidential primary. In his day a candidate avoided presidential primaries unless, like Kennedy, he was young, untested, and eager to prove himself to the party establishment.

What our three returned presidents would soon realize is that the strategies for winning the nomination have changed dramatically as the result of underlying changes in the structure of the nominating system. Until the early 1970s, winning the nomination of a major political party was essentially an inside game. Presidential candidates worked at winning the allegiances of the major party leaders, who controlled the minor party leaders, who in turn became delegates to the nominating convention. Presidential primaries were sometimes important, especially if a candidate had to demonstrate vote-getting ability; but to do that he had to keep favorite sons out and draw other national candidates in, a task that was often very difficult. More often than not, the public portion of the nomination campaign—presidential primaries—was not very important to the eventual outcome.

What was important was the semi-public search for delegates—a search that was difficult to observe and often downright mysterious even to careful observers of the process. The nomination system prior to 1972 was, to use Nelson Polsby's term, "a mixed system" (Polsby, 1983:185). The first stage was public and took place in a few contested presidential primaries. The second stage was semi-public at best and involved intense negotiations between serious national candidates and powerful party leaders. James Reston described this stage as follows: "This presidential election is being fought on several levels. The most important of these, so far as nominating candidates is concerned, is the least obvious . . . the underground battle for delegates" (*New York Times*, June 24, 1968, p. 1). Usually the "underground" battle for delegates was fought in the proverbial smoke-filled rooms. Another political reporter, W. H. Lawrence, described the 1960 nomination race as follows: "With the end of the contested presidential primaries, the struggle for the nomination has moved from Main Street to the backrooms of individual party leaders and state conventions dense with the smoke of cheap cigars" (*New York Times*, June 8, 1960, p. 6E).

This process, of courting powerful and not so powerful party leaders in search of a convention majority, was hard to observe and impossible to quantify until the convention itself assembled and started to vote. Thus the race for the nomination used to be very visible during the weeks leading up to and including the convention. More recently, however, the race for the nomination is visible at least a year before the nominating convention and is usually over well before the convention itself ever convenes.

THE POST-REFORM NOMINATION SYSTEM

The presidential nomination system that exists today is the result of two reform movements that occurred at approximately the same time in American politics. Between 1968 and 1972 the Democratic party adopted a series of changes in the process by which delegates to its nominating conventions were chosen. This movement began as a reaction to the contentious 1968 Democratic convention; newcomers opposed to the Vietnam war felt that the party establishment had unfairly thwarted their attempts at participating in the nominating process (Polsby, 1983). At the time, few people (including party professionals) anticipated how profoundly these changes would affect the way that Democrats *and* Republicans elected delegates (Shafer, 1983). Even though the Republican party did not undergo anything even remotely like the reform movement in the Democratic party, so many Democratically dominated state legislatures had to change their laws to comply with the new dictates of the Democratic National Committee that the state Republican parties, more often than not, were inadvertently reformed as well.

The other reform movement began in 1971 with passage of the Federal Election Campaign Act. This law was amended in 1974 as part of the post-Watergate reforms designed to decrease the influence of money in politics, and again in 1979 when it became clear that the law was having unintended negative effects on party activity. The campaign finance reform laws affected both political parties and, like the reforms in delegate selection, had far-reaching implications for the conduct of presidential elections, particularly primary elections.

The effect of these two reform movements was to transform the nomination system into a totally public system where activity at every step of the process could be observed and quantified. In the post-reform system, the search for delegates was conducted in public primaries or caucuses (which became the "functional equivalent" of highly visible primaries), and the search for money took place under the new election law. By limiting the amount of money that any one individual could contribute to a candidate, the new law transformed the quest for money from a quiet search for a few "fat cats" to a public search for thousands of small- and medium-sized contributions. Changes of this magnitude in the underlying structure of the nomination process eventually affected the strategies of presidential hopefuls seeking their party's nomination, but before we can understand these strategies we must understand the structure of the new nominating system.

Primaries and Their "Functional Equivalents"

In the pre-reform era fewer than half of the convention delegates were elected in primaries contested by the major national candidates. In the post-reform era, however, nearly all delegates are elected as the result of contested primaries. A famous quote by former Vice-President Hubert Humphrey sums up the attitude of many presidential hopefuls in the pre-reform era: "[A]ny man who goes into a primary isn't fit to be President. You have to be crazy to go into a primary. A primary now, is worse than the torture of the rack" (quoted in Polsby, 1983:14, and originally, in White, 1961:104).

No one who has watched candidates undergo the grueling process of the modern post-reform nomination process would be surprised to hear Walter Mondale, George Bush, or Michael Dukakis express these sentiments. But for these modern candidates, skipping the primaries is akin to skipping the whole ball game.

The Democratic reformers who made up part of the famous McGovern-Fraser Commission did not set out to increase the number of presidential primaries, but just such an increase was the most immediate and dramatic result of the new rules they had proposed for delegate selection to the 1972 convention.[1] In 1968 there were sixteen states that held some form of presidential primary; in 1972, twenty-three states; in 1976, thirty states; in 1980, thirty-five states; in 1984, thirty states; and in 1988, thirty-four states.

Most observers of the nomination process focus solely on the increase in the number of primaries that followed in the wake of the reform movement—but the increase in *number* is not nearly so important as the change in the *nature* of these primaries. The reform rules' requirement that delegates from a state "fairly reflect the division of preferences expressed by those who participate in the presidential nominating process in each state" greatly increased the importance of each primary by linking a presidential candidate's performance in the primary to the number of delegates that he could get from the state (Democratic National Committee, 1972:12).

Table 8.1 compares presidential primaries in the pre- and post-reform eras. During the former period, primaries did not always dictate which presidential candidate the delegates from that state should support; in other words, if presidential candidates decided to put their names on the ballot (and they more often did not), they could win the primary and not necessarily get any delegates from that state because the primaries

TABLE 8.1

Presidential Preference Polls in Primary Elections: Binding Versus Advisory

	Total Number of Primaries with a Presidential Preference Poll on the Ballot	Preference Poll Is Binding	Preference Poll Is Advisory
1952	10	3	7
1956	10	3	7
1960	11	3	8
1964[a]	12	3	9
1968	9	3	6
Post-Reform Era			
1972	18	12	6
1976[b]	25	17	8
1980[c]	35	33	2
1984[d]	25	19	6
1988[e]	34	28	6

[a]In 1964 the advisory presidential primary in Texas was held for Republicans only.
[b]From 1976 on, the Louisiana "firehouse" (i.e., party-run and party-financed) primary is included.
[c]In 1980 Michigan and South Carolina primaries were for Republicans only; Arkansas had a primary for the Democrats only.
[d]In 1984 the Michigan and Wisconsin primaries were for Republicans only.
[e]In 1988 the South Dakota primary was advisory for the Democrats and was binding for the Republicans, but the Democrats followed its choices when it came to delegate selection.

Sources: 1952 and 1956, David et al. (1960:528–534); 1960, Congressional Quarterly Weekly Report, January 17, 1964, p. 106; 1968 and 1972, Commission on Party Structure and Delegate Selection (1971); 1976, 1980, and 1984, Democratic National Convention, Handbooks of the Democratic National Convention, various dates; 1988, Democratic National Committee, Compliance Assistance Commission Memo, January 25, 1988.

were nonbinding (i.e., advisory). In 1952 Senator Estes Kefauver won the most primaries and yet Governor Adlai Stevenson, who did not enter even one, got the nomination. In 1968, too, Vice-President Hubert Humphrey won the nomination without entering a single primary.

In the modern era, however, if a presidential candidate wants delegates who will vote for him at the convention, he must run in all the primaries that are held. Not only did the number of presidential preference polls increase, but the vast majority became binding on the selection of delegates. By 1980 more than half of all states had a binding presidential preference poll on their ballot.

The reason there were so few presidential preference polls in the pre-reform era is that most presidential primaries were held for the sole purpose of electing delegates to the national convention and these delegates were often not identified as to their presidential preference. Ordinary voters who were not knowledgeable about the politics of the

TABLE 8.2

Primaries in Which Delegates Are Elected Directly on the Ballot

	Total Number of Primaries in Which Delegates Are Elected Directly on the Ballot	Delegates Must Be Identified by Presidential Preference	Delegates May or May Not Run Identified by a Presidential Preference	Delegates May Not Run Pledged to or Identified with a Presidential Preference
1952	15	4	5	6
1956	15	4	5	6
1960	15	2	6	7
1964	15	2	6	7
1968	13	2	4	7
Post-Reform Era				
1972	10	2	5	3
1976[a]	13	2	10	1
1980[b]	3	0	3	0
1984	8	1	7	0
1988[c]	7	1	6	0

[a]In 1976 the New York Legislature decided, at the last minute, to make provisions on the ballot for the names of presidential candidates next to the names of the delegates.
[b]In 1980, in New York, only the Republicans held a delegate primary. They also chose to have all their delegate candidates listed as uncommitted, as did the Illinois and Pennsylvania Republicans.
[c]In 1988, in New York, the Democrats elected delegates on the ballot subject to the results of the binding primary, but the Republicans elected delegates directly.

Sources: See Table 8.1.

local party members running as delegates had no way of knowing how the people they were voting for were going to vote at the convention. But as the number of primaries with binding presidential preference polls increased, two things happened: The practice of electing delegates directly on the ballot became less popular (see Table 8.2), and the practice of allowing delegates to run unidentified by their presidential preference disappeared.

Thus the linkage between presidential primaries and delegate selection is far more important in shaping the structure of the post-reform nominating system than the simple increase in the number of primaries. The results of the presidential primary may or may not tell us who will be attending the nominating convention as a delegate (in many states the actual delegates are elected after the primary), but it *will* tell us exactly how many delegates each presidential candidate on the ballot will get. Hence presidential candidates must now either compete in every primary or risk having no delegates. Indeed, as the primaries have become more important to delegate selection, more and more presidential candidates have begun to compete in them. Not surprisingly, the number

TABLE 8.3
Percentage of Delegates Elected in
Contested Presidential Primaries, by Year

	Democrats	Republicans
1960[a]	19%	no nomination contest
1964[b]	no nomination contest	24%
1968	47%	18%
Post-Reform Era		
1972[c]	78%	no nomination contest
1976[d]	97%	90%
1980[e]	97%	100%
1984[f]	97%	no nomination contest
1988	99%	96%

[a]In 1960, although Humphrey's name was on the ballot in Oregon and thus caused it to be counted as a contested primary, he was effectively out of the race ten days earlier due to the West Virginia primary results.

[b]In 1964, a slate of Goldwater delegates was run in Massachusetts, even though it was Lodge's home state.

[c]In 1972, Alabama and D.C. had favorite-son slates only, and no one contested McGovern in his home state of South Dakota. An insurgent slate was run in New York, but due to the absence of presidential preference on the ballot, it was difficult to contest and is not counted here.

[d]In 1976, Robert Byrd ran as a favorite son in West Virginia and was not contested on the Democratic side. On the Republican side, Reagan skipped New Jersey and Pennsylvania, and no Republicans entered the D.C. primary.

[e]In 1980, Kennedy and Carter did not contest the Michigan primary but competed in caucuses instead.
[f]In 1984, Mondale did not enter the North Dakota primary because it was only a "beauty contest"; he did enter the other three beauty contests in 1984.

Sources: The 1960–1964 data were derived from the data presented in Scammon and McGillivrey (1985). The 1988 data were derived from Pomper (1989).

of delegates elected in contested primaries has risen dramatically in the post-reform era, as Table 8.3 illustrates.

When delegates to national conventions are not elected in primaries, they are elected in caucus systems. In a caucus system, people meet at the local level and elect representatives to the next level—usually the county level. At the county level, the people elected locally meet and elect representatives to the state convention. The state convention then meets to select those who will attend the presidential nominating convention.

Traditionally, many state parties have held conventions to elect delegates to the presidential nominating convention. These conventions used to be closed; that is, only individuals who already held party office could participate in the selection of delegates. But the party reform movement turned these systems of delegate selection into smaller versions of presidential primaries.[2]

Three new requirements—that party meetings having to do with delegate selection be open to anyone who wished to be known as a Democrat; that every participant in the process as well as every candidate for delegate declare his or her presidential preference; and that all first-tier caucuses (i.e., those at the precinct level) be held on the same day—effectively abolished the party caucus and began the process of turning the caucus system itself into the "functional equivalent of a primary."[3]

In the pre-reform era, many party meetings were not open to the public; they were attended by previously elected party officials such as precinct captains or county chairmen. Opening up local meetings to all who called themselves Democrats meant that the local party leaders could often be overruled by newcomers drawn into the party out of enthusiasm for a particular presidential candidate. That's what happened in caucus after caucus in 1972, when the old-time party regulars were beaten by supporters of George McGovern—that is, by young people who were drawn into the party by virtue of McGovern's opposition to the Vietnam War. In 1984 Walter Mondale spent more than $500,000 organizing the state of Maine and won the endorsement of every major Democratic politician in the state. But Senator Gary Hart, riding the momentum of his surprise victory over Mondale in New Hampshire, won the Maine caucuses handily as a brand new group of Democrats turned out to support him. And in 1988 the Reverend Pat Robertson beat sitting Vice-President George Bush in the Iowa caucuses by organizing hundreds of evangelical Christians who had never before participated in the Republican party.

In the pre-reform nominating system, the job of convention delegate was more often than not a reward for long and loyal service to the party. Convention delegates were elected first and expressed their presidential preferences later. In the new nominating system everyone, at every stage of the process, is required to state his or her presidential preference, and the selection of representatives to the next level must reflect the presidential preferences of the people who show up. This means that the most loyal party workers can be bypassed if they have chosen the wrong presidential candidate—which is just what happened in 1972 and 1976, when supporters of outsiders George McGovern and then Jimmy Carter surprised the party establishment in state after state.

Finally, the requirement that first-tier caucuses be held at the same time and on the same day meant that the delegate-selection system, the impact of which had heretofore been difficult to gauge, could now be treated like a primary. When precinct caucuses or county conventions were spread across several weeks or months, most reporters—especially those connected with the national news media—had to wait until the state convention met in order to see which presidential candidate would win the most delegates. Simultaneous precinct caucuses, the requirement that everyone present announce their presidential preference, and, of course, the use of computers and telephones to aggregate lots of data quickly meant that national reporters could descend upon a state such as Iowa and turn their hitherto-ignored precinct caucuses into a primary.

The Iowa precinct caucuses were "discovered" in 1976, when Jimmy Carter "won" them by coming in second to "uncommitted" and beating a field of much better known candidates. Four years earlier most of the press corps had overlooked the Iowa caucuses and in so doing had missed signs that George McGovern was a lot stronger and Senator Edmund Muskie (the reputed frontrunner) a lot weaker than most pundits had assumed. So the press was ready in 1976. As Jules Witcover explains: "For their romance with Muskie the press and television paid heavy alimony after 1972 in terms of their reputation for clairvoyance, let alone clear thinking and evidence at hand. . . . [I]n 1976, if there were going to be early signals, the fourth estate was going to be on the scene en masse to catch them" (Witcover, 1977:200).

The popularity of this new, transformed Democratic caucus system became the envy of the Iowa Republican party. Since its delegate-selection rules were not governed by any state statutes when the Iowa Democratic party was "reformed," the Iowa Republican party wasn't reformed. The result was that, in 1976, the hard-fought battle between President Ford and Ronald Reagan began, as far as the public could see, in New Hampshire, not in Iowa—even though the Iowa Republican caucuses had been held on the same night as the Democratic caucuses that had attracted so much attention. No one paid attention to the Iowa Republican caucuses that year because they were traditional, old-fashioned caucuses that could not be easily counted and interpreted by the national press corps.

The lesson was not lost on the Iowa Republicans who, left out of the limelight in 1976 and eager to share in it in 1980, decided to hold a nonbinding straw poll at each precinct caucus in 1980 and to have the results reported to the Republican State Committee at a location in Des Moines convenient to the national press corps.

Thus, in a relatively short period of time, the process of delegate selection in both political parties was transformed from a process understandable to only the most astute of political observers—and then only toward the end of the process—to a process that was easily quantifiable and therefore accessible to reporters from the earliest moments.

Money and the Need for an Early Start

Reform of the delegate-selection system shifted the focus of attention from the convention to the seven or eight months of primaries and caucuses before the convention; reform of the campaign finance laws shifted attention to the year before the primaries even began. Without going into detail on campaign finance reform, I will say simply that, like delegate-selection reform, it transformed the search for money from a private (or at best a semi-public) undertaking to a highly public, easily quantifiable one.

The reasons are simple. In the pre-reform system a few very rich people could and did bankroll entire campaigns. Sometimes the public knew who these people were; often they did not. After campaign finance reform, the most that any one person could contribute to a presidential nomination campaign was $1,000. Thus candidates had to hold countless cocktail parties, dinners, luncheons, and other events in order to amass the millions of dollars needed to run in every caucus and primary in the country.

Another part of the campaign finance reform bill provided that any contribution up to $250 would be matched by the federal treasury. This meant that large numbers of small contributions suddenly became very valuable, especially if they could be raised through the use of direct mail. But in order for direct mail to work well, the presidential candidate signing the letter had to be well known. With money in lots of fairly small chunks doubling in value (due to the federal match), presidential candidates therefore sought ways to become visible and to appear that they were doing well as early as possible—usually one full year prior to the beginning of the primaries and caucuses.

Another provision of the new campaign finance reform laws required that all presidential candidates make quarterly reports of the money they had raised and spent. These quarterly reports, which are made public, have occasioned news stories on how each presidential candidate is doing. A candidate who raises lots of money begins to be taken seriously, whereas a candidate who raises little money tends to get left out of television stories, newspaper columns, and all the other free press that is so important in campaigns. Media coverage then generates more money, and more money generates more media coverage, and so on and on in a self-fulfilling circle.

This is not to say that money equals success. In 1984 Gary Hart tended to win those contests in which he spent a little bit of money and to lose those contests in which he spent a great deal (Polsby and Wildavsky, 1988:50). But early money not only makes a candidate look like a winner; it also allows him to withstand early disappointments once the nomination season begins. George Bush had $10 million in the bank when he placed third in the Iowa caucuses. Losing so early in the season was clearly a disappointment, but he had plenty of resources with which to withstand a loss. In contrast, a candidate like former

Arizona Governor Bruce Babbitt on the Democratic side had such meager cash reserves that his 1988 campaign was over when he failed in Iowa.

STRATEGIES OF THE POST-REFORM ERA

Sequence as Strategy

The two reform movements and the changes they wrought in the structure of the nomination system created a set of new strategic imperatives for presidential candidates. The most important of these was understanding the role of sequence in winning the nomination. Once primaries and caucuses became binding, presidential candidates had to contest every single one or risk forfeiting delegates. But the new campaign finance laws limited both the amount of money that could be spent in any one state and the total amount of money that could be spent on the entire nomination race to a sum that was less than the total spending permitted in each state.[4] Thus, even if a presidential candidate could raise enough money to spend the maximum in each state, the campaign finance law forced him to pick and choose between states while the new rules for delegate selection were making it all the more important to contest every state.

The result was to make winning early the key to winning the nomination. If a candidate can win several early contests, he will possess "momentum"—and momentum buys things that money cannot buy, such as free media coverage and the perception that the candidate is a winner. Since 1976, when Jimmy Carter's surprise victories in Iowa and New Hampshire demonstrated the power of momentum in no uncertain terms, media coverage of the early contests (especially those in Iowa and New Hampshire) was vastly out of proportion to the size of those states and the number of delegates elected in each.[5] In recent years the major evening news programs have chosen to move their entire shows to Des Moines, Iowa, and to Manchester, New Hampshire, for the week leading up to the delegate-selection contests in those two states—but they paid nowhere near the same amount of attention to Pennsylvania and California, which (though much bigger states) hold primaries late in the season.[6] One reporter counted the number of journalists in Iowa during the 1984 caucuses and discovered that there was one journalist for every one hundred caucus goers (Klose, 1984:A3).

This kind of early media coverage tends to have a powerful effect on voters further down the line. As Larry Bartels has demonstrated, momentum itself, or the perception that the candidate is a winner, influences voters in subsequent primaries independent of other factors such as region and ideology. Unlike nomination contests in the pre-reform years, strategy in the post-reform era relies heavily on the sequence of victories. Bartels sums it up as follows: "The key to success, it appeared, was not to enter the nomination with a broad coalition of political support, but to rely on the dynamics of the campaign itself— particularity in its earliest public phases—to generate support" (Bartels, 1983:170, 172).

As winning early increased in importance, candidates paid more and more attention to the sequence of the early contests. If a candidate had the political power and opportunity to create a calendar to his liking, he did exactly that. Just as Jimmy Carter was the first presidential candidate to understand the significance of exceeding expectations in the Iowa caucuses, he was also the first to understand that the sequence of contests after Iowa would be important.

In 1975 Carter wanted to create the best possible calendar for his candidacy. An early southern contest was important to the overall Carter strategy. He needed to defeat George Wallace early, thereby removing any competition for southern delegates. The best opportunity was in Florida, but a bill in the legislature there threatened to move the primary from early March to late spring. So Carter, his campaign manager, and his lawyer got on a plane to Florida, where they made a successful appeal to the Speaker of the House and the governor to keep the Florida primary early.

In 1979 President Carter could count on a lot more than political friendship to help him create a favorable calendar for his renomination. With White House encouragement, Mississippi, South Carolina, Oklahoma, Georgia, and Alabama—all good states for the president—moved up to early March.

On the Republican side, the campaign of Ronald Reagan was not at all unhappy with the calendar that President Carter was creating—a calendar involving many early southern states. In 1976 Reagan had consistently beaten President Ford in the South, and with any luck Reagan expected to win there once again. But Reagan's campaigners knew that they had to beat Texan John Connally, the only other candidate in the race who had the potential to rival Reagan for southern delegates.

So, under the influence of a young Reagan operative, Lee Atwater (currently chairman of the Republican National Committee), a special state convention was called in which the decision was made that South Carolina would hold its first and only (to that time) Republican presidential primary one week before the rest of the southern primaries. South Carolina was a state in which the Reagan people felt they could beat Connally. After a very heated and expensive primary, Reagan did win. Connally left the race, and Reagan went on to a series of important southern victories.

TABLE 8.4
Determining Steps in the Delegate-Selection Process
for Selected Contested Primary Years[a]

	Pre-March	March	April	May	June
1972 Democrats	7	9	11	18	7
	7%	14%	18%	33%	24%
1976 Democrats	9	8	11	20	8
	9%	17%	25%	29%	20%
1980 Democrats	4	18	9	14	11
	5%	35%	19%	20%	21%
1980 Republicans	12	11	7	15	9
	15%	25%	14%	24%	21%
1984 Democrats[b]	3	29	9	12	5
	6%	36%	17%	21%	13%
1988 Democrats[b]	2	36	7	6	4
	2%	50%	13%	9%	11%
1988 Republicans	3	33	5	6	4
	6%	55%	14%	11%	12%

[a]The first number for each entry is the number of primary or caucus contests in that month. The second number is the percentage of delegates to the nominating convention elected in that month.
[b]Percentages do not add up to 100 percent for the 1984 and 1988 Democrats because of the way in which unpledged party leader and elected official delegates were awarded.

Sources: See Table 8.1.

It is very difficult for presidential candidates to establish the most desirable sequence of contests: Deadlines for establishing the date of a primary or caucus are far in advance of the nomination year, and there are other complicated reasons for which a state chooses to hold a primary or caucus on a certain day. Furthermore, many presidential hopefuls lack the political clout necessary to accomplish such a huge task. But these and other efforts on the part of presidential hopefuls to create a favorable sequence only reinforce the main point—that in the post-reform era presidential candidates have to do well in the earliest contests or face having to drop out of the race altogether. Sequence has indeed become strategy.

The importance of winning early in the new nomination system was not lost on individual state parties. As they looked with envy at the attention and money spent on the early contests, more and more states moved their primaries early in the spring in order to get in on the media and candidate attention that went with being early. Table 8.4 shows the number of contests and the percentage of delegates elected in them month by month for each of the post-reform years.

The percentage of delegates elected in March went up steadily through-out the post-reform years, but it rose sharply in 1988 due to the creation of the Southern Regional primary. In 1986 a group of southern Democratic legislative leaders, concerned that the Democratic party was nominating candidates (such as Walter Mondale) who were too liberal to carry the South, got together and decided to form a southern Super Tuesday. They did so by moving all the southern states' primaries to the second Tuesday in March, specifically in the hopes of giving these states a decisive role in the selection of the Democratic nominee.

Mobilizing the Ideological Extremes

By all accounts, southern Super Tuesday was a failure and it may not be repeated in 1992. It not only failed to produce a southern, more conservative nominee but it gave a boost to two candidates who were, arguably, the most liberal of the seven in the Democratic field—Mas-sachusetts Governor Michael Dukakis and the Reverend Jesse Jackson. Had the crafters of the southern Super Tuesday been more attuned to the history of voting in presidential primaries, however, they may not have been so quick to predict that their new primary would produce a more centrist nominee for the Democratic party.

Voters in presidential primaries have always been more liberal (in the case of the Democrats) or more conservative (in the case of the Republicans) than the rest of the electorate (Lengle, 1981). This factor was not very important in the days when the nomination was largely in the hands of the party professionals. By and large, these people were in the business of winning elections and they judged potential candidates according to whether they could win, not on ideological grounds.

But in the post-reform era, primaries matter and party leaders do not. Presidential primaries attract a very small percentage of all voters—a percentage of people who tend to be more highly educated, more well to do, and more ideologically committed than most voters. Table 8.5 takes data from ABC exit polls in several states and compares the ideological preferences of Democratic and Republican primary voters with those of voters in the general election. In all instances the pattern is the same: The primary electorate is further to the left or the right, depending on the political party, than is the general-election electorate.

Because the primary electorates are so small, a candidate who can mobilize a faction of these loyal party voters has a leg up in seeking the nomination. Jesse Jackson's base in the Democratic party among black voters was very important to his successes in 1984 and 1988. Even though black voters made up only 8 percent of the November electorate, they constituted an average 17 percent of the electorate in the primary

TABLE 8.5
A Comparison of Primary and General Election Voters in 1988,
by Ideology in Selected States

	California	Florida	Illinois	New Jersey	Tennessee	Texas
Proportion of Democratic Primary Voters Who Call Themselves Liberals	45%	30%	38%	36%	30%	34%
Proportion of General Election Voters Who Call Themselves Liberals	30%	21%	25%	28%	18%	21%
Proportion of Republican Primary Voters Who Call Themselves Conservatives	N.D.	60%	55%	N.D.	59%	65%
Proportion of General Election Voters Who Call Themselves Conservatives	N.D.	49%	42%	N.D.	46%	49%

N.D.=No data available

Source: Compiled by the author on the basis of data provided by ABC News (1989).

states. In some states black voters were a very substantial percentage of the primary electorate. In New York they constituted 27 percent of the Democratic primary, and in states with large black populations, such as Mississippi, they constituted nearly half of the Democratic primary electorate.

Being acceptable to the primary electorate is not, however, the same as being acceptable to the general electorate. The successful presidential candidate survives the marathon of primaries and caucuses ever mindful of two audiences: the small audience of party loyalists who participate in the primaries and who hold policy viewpoints far from the center, and the very large and more centrist audience that he will face in the general election.

The preponderance of conservatives in the Republican primary electorates meant that George Bush had to spend most of the year prior to the primaries and caucuses trying to prove his conservative credentials to groups that were suspicious that he was more moderate than Ronald

Reagan. Four years earlier Mondale appealed to the liberal wing of the Democratic party when Gary Hart's come-from-behind campaign threatened to derail his campaign. Mondale's counterattack brought Hart's liberal credentials into question and helped him to mobilize the core group in the Democratic electorate.

In recent years Republican candidates have been better able to handle this transition than their Democratic counterparts, in part because conservatives and moderates outnumber liberals in the electorate by margins of three to one. Thus the Republican candidate doesn't need to convert as many liberals and moderates as the Democrat (ABC News, 1989:19). In the general election Michael Dukakis won the vast majority of self-identified liberals, but he failed to win enough conservative, moderate, and Independent voters to win.

The Delegate Count

Once the initial contests are over, the field of candidates tends to narrow considerably—usually to one or two candidates by the end of March. Presidential candidates continue to receive influxes of federal matching funds as the campaign season progresses; but the law stipulates that, once a candidate fails to win 10 percent of the vote in two consecutive primaries, he can be deemed ineligible for matching funds. Thus candidates who have won very small percentages of the vote have a powerful reason—lack of money—to get out of the race.

Beyond the early contests there are many simultaneous primaries and caucuses, and the delegate count becomes more and more important as a means of interpreting events and of judging who, among the remaining contenders, is closest to winning the nomination. Counting delegates used to be the exclusive domain of party insiders and political professionals who knew all there was to know about the party leaders (major and minor) and could predict how they would behave and whom they would vote for at the nominating convention. At the end of the 1960 primary season John Kennedy had only 134 delegates committed to him, or 18 percent of those he needed to get nominated, as a result of the primaries. Then, as Theodore White described it, the real work began: "Now the rest of the harvest proceeded, state by state, across the nation, fitting itself to the manners and morals of each state's politics like an exercise in the diversity of American life" (White, 1961:161).

In the post-reform era, the delegate count can be conducted even when actual delegates have not been elected. On April 3, 1984, for instance, United Press International reported that Mondale had 729 delegates, Hart had 440, and Jackson had 101. As of that same date, however, if someone had wanted to, he or she could have talked to real live delegates from only six states for a total of 434 delegates—or about one-third the number being reported in the delegate count. But in April no one was interested in talking to real live delegates, so absolute was the certainty that the delegates would simply represent the will of the primary voters.

The translation of the primary vote into a delegate count is accomplished by means of formal allocation rules. Because these rules dictate who wins how many delegates, they have been the source of endless controversy in the Democratic party. Because Republicans do not have centralized rules, and because these rules are often not part of state statutes, the Republican party has not been as affected by the Democratic allocation rules as by some of the Democrats' other rules. Thus there are real and significant differences between the two parties when it comes to the accumulation of a delegate majority.

Simply put, there are two basic ways to award delegates to a presidential candidate: winner take all, and proportional representation. The Republican party tends to use the former and the Democratic party, the latter. Winner-take-all rules award all of the delegates from a state or a congressional district to the candidate who wins the most votes in that state or district. Proportional rules divide the delegates from a state or district as nearly as possible in proportion to the vote that each presidential candidate won in that state or district. The Democratic party has come up with many variations on this theme, but these two rules are the most important for our purposes.[7]

The Democratic party's reform movement encouraged and eventually mandated the use of proportional representation to award delegates to presidential candidates. This development shows up in Figure 8.1, which compares the types of systems used in each party throughout the post-reform years. With the exception of 1972, during which the Democrats encouraged but did not require the use of proportional representation, the Democrats have tended to award delegates to presidential candidates in proportion to the primary vote whereas the Republicans have tended to award delegates to the winner of the state or district.

This difference has important consequences for the two parties. First, proportional representation increases the already-dangerous predisposition of the Democratic party to break down into factions; and, second, it reinforces the importance of a strong showing in the early part of the nomination season for Democratic candidates (Kamarck, 1987). Nelson Polsby argues that reform of the delegate-selection process has worked "disproportionately to the disadvantage of the majority party, the Democrats," who, according to Polsby, are disadvantaged in comparison to the Republicans because of their greater ideological diversity (Polsby, 1983:86).

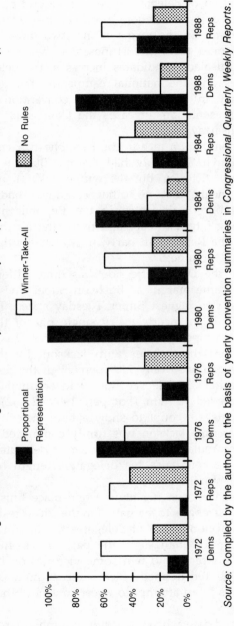

FIGURE 8.1

Percentage of Convention Delegates Elected by Allocation System (by Election Year and Political Party)

Source: Compiled by the author on the basis of yearly convention summaries in *Congressional Quarterly Weekly Reports*.

Unlike losing Republican candidates, a losing Democratic candidate, especially a second-place finisher, can still win delegates. Indeed, a steady accumulation of delegates gives the second-place candidate who is still losing but doing well enough to keep his federal matching funds an incentive to stay in the race for one, two, three, or more rounds, always hoping for a turn in fortunes. As the delegate count of the second- and third-place candidates increases, the delegates pledged to those candidates and the national campaign staff generally urge the candidate to stay in the race until the convention. In other words, proportional representation increases the Democrats' predisposition toward internal disarray.

In 1988 the nomination race in the Republican party was over by the last week in March. Not only had George Bush won an impressive string of primary victories, but the winner-take-all nature of many of those contests meant that no other candidate had accumulated an appreciable number of delegates to the Republican convention. The process of making internal peace and preparing for the general election could begin, in the Republican party, in March—with George Bush the all but annointed nominee.

The story on the Democratic side was quite different. Dukakis did not win by the same margin as Bush on Super Tuesday, even though he had won the two biggest Super Tuesday states, Texas and Florida. Yet, although Bush got nearly every single one of the delegates from those two states, proportional rules dictated that Dukakis had to share the delegates from those states with Jackson. By the end of March Dukakis had accumulated only 21.9 percent of the delegates needed to win the nomination, but George Bush had accumulated 61 percent of the delegates needed to win (Pomper, 1989:42, 62). It took another month for the delegate count to show a bare majority of delegates for Dukakis. By that time Jackson was firmly committed to staying in the race and had accumulated a large number of delegates—a fact that led him to believe he could use his delegate strength to bargain for the vice-presidential nomination.

Jackson may have been the first second-place finisher to attempt to use his delegate strength to bargain for the vice-presidency, but others have used their accumulation of delegates to bargain for planks in the party platform or for changes in the party rules. In 1984 Gary Hart used his delegate strength to win some victories on both platform and rules, and in 1980 Ted Kennedy filed a record number of platform and rules amendments in an attempt to wrest control of the convention from Carter.

The losing candidate who is steadily accumulating delegates needs a rationale for staying in the race, for during the last few contests, the frontrunner and much of the party leadership are urging the loser to end the race as soon as possible. In the process of seeking such a rationale, minor differences between candidates tend to be enlarged and emphasized. Candidates who are not really very far apart become polarized on issues, and the divisions between factions in the party are accentuated at the very point in time when they should be unified—usually to the detriment of Democrats in the general election.

The second effect of a nominating system dominated by proportional representation is, paradoxically, to reinforce the importance of the earliest contests. In a proportional system an early winner can withstand losses later on in the season because he can continue to win delegates even while losing primaries. There are no late bloomers in proportional systems: A candidate who suddenly starts to win or who enters late will find it very difficult to overtake the frontrunner because he can never win large chunks of delegates.

The best example can be found in the 1976 nomination season. Jimmy Carter was the early winner that year, and yet as the spring wore on more and more voters came to have doubts about him (doubts that crystallized in the formation of ABC—Anybody But Carter—groups), and he began to lose primaries. In May and June, Carter suffered a string of defeats, including a defeat in the all-important California primary; but he was still able to accumulate delegates because proportional rules allowed him to claim a share. These delegates, added to those won earlier in the year, gave Carter the nomination in spite of his loss of momentum.

On the Republican side, President Gerald Ford, also an early winner, began (like Carter) to lose contests in the month of May to challenger Ronald Reagan. But due to winner-take-all rules, Ford's losses had serious consequences. In five of the twelve states he had lost to Reagan he won no delegates at all, and in the other states he won very small numbers of delegates. Ford went from being ahead of Reagan in the delegate count to being behind. Even though he eventually won the nomination, Ford was seriously threatened by Reagan all the way up to and including the convention.

In 1976 the controversy was on the Republican side, which lost. And thus we are brought to one final point. Divisive nomination contests in a political party—regardless of the underlying structure—almost always result in the defeat of that party in the general election. Table 8.6 categorizes primaries as to their divisiveness and shows that divisive nomination fights are a significant detriment to a political party.

Two lessons are implicit in this aspect of the nominating system. The first is that political parties should try to avoid systems that add to or generate divisiveness. (The Democrats have yet to learn this lesson.)

TABLE 8.6

Divisive Presidential Primaries and the Fate of the Party in Presidential Elections, 1932–1976[a]

	Divisive Democratic Only	Divisive Both Parties	Divisive Neither Party	Divisive Republican Only
Democratic	14%	45%	57%	60%
Victory	(4)	(5)	(76)	(15)
Republican	86%	55%	43%	40%
Victory	(24)	(6)	(57)	(10)
	100%	100%	100%	100%
N=	(28)	(11)	(133)	(25)

[a]$X^2 = 18.0$; $p < .001$.

Source: Lengle (1980).

The second is that presidential candidates should seek not only to avoid divisiveness in the primary season but also to reach the "magic number" of delegates as soon as possible. In 1984 Mondale successfully tied up the nomination on the day after he lost the California primary. He did this in a last-minute blitz of still-uncommitted delegates and managed to deflect attention from his California defeat onto the fact that he had enough pledged delegates to win the nomination on a first ballot.

The desire to go over the top as far in advance of the convention as possible requires that, when there are different allocation rules in effect, candidates must spend more time and attention in places where they can win more delegates by winning the primary. In other words, winner-take-all systems of delegate allocation are another way for a state to be important in the nomination system without having to select its delegates first.

The Dukakis Super Tuesday strategy was carefully crafted to win congressional districts in states where the delegate harvest would be greatest. For instance, even though Dukakis lost more primaries than he won on Super Tuesday, his delegate count was slightly higher than anyone else's, thus giving him an important edge in the perceptions of those who were trying to interpret the race.

But the most dramatic use of the delegate count occurred during the Mondale campaign in 1984. Reeling from the unexpected victory by Gary Hart in New Hampshire, Mondale went south amid anticipation that his campaign was about to end and lost several important primaries, including the all-important Florida primary. But the vicissitudes of the delegate-selection process allowed Mondale to emerge from Super Tuesday 1984 with many more delegates than Gary Hart. This fact found its way into the hands of the press, which used it, to the dismay of the Hart campaign, to give new life to Mondale's candidacy (Orren, 1985).

The Four-Day Television Commercial

Why is it so important to wrap up the nomination before the convention? Because the post-reform convention has a new role. With rare exceptions, it is no longer the place where the nomination is won. As we have seen, the nomination is won in the primaries and in the caucuses, and the nominee is almost always known prior to the convention. In the pre-reform era, the weeks between the last primary and the opening of the convention were times of intense activity as the leading candidates sought to pin down the votes of delegates who were not already pledged to a presidential candidate. Table 8.7 shows the number of unaffiliated delegates at the end of the primary season in both the pre- and the post-reform years. During the former period, an average of 38 percent of the delegates remained to be wooed in the weeks prior to the convention; during the latter, that number generally dropped significantly.

Another way to look at the same phenomenon is to compare the delegate count for the eventual nominee at the end of the primary season with the first ballot vote for the nominee at the convention. In the pre-reform years, the nominee had barely 50 percent of what he needed to get nominated by the end of the primary season; in the post-reform years, the count at the end of the season tends to be a pretty good predictor of the vote on the first ballot (see Table 8.8).

In the modern nominating system, therefore, the actual nomination function is all but gone from the convention; suspense about the identity of the nominee is a thing of the past. It has been many years since either political party has had a convention that went past the first ballot, so effectively have the primaries and caucuses displaced the convention as the place where the most important decision is made. Other matters of importance still go on at conventions—the party platform and party rules are debated and adopted, for instance—but the big decision is generally made weeks if not months before the convention ever opens.

In the post-reform era, then, the convention has become the place where the general election campaign begins. Byron Shafer, whose book *Bifurcated Politics: Evolution and Reform in the National Party Convention* is an excellent treatment of the post-reform convention, sums up the changes as follows: "[T]he role of the convention in inaugurating the general election campaign grew enormously as the nomination receded. . . . [N]ational news media, especially as embodied in full and national coverage, became the means by which public presentations at the

TABLE 8.7

"Unaffiliated" Delegates at the End of the Primary Season
as a Percentage of the Total Number of Convention Delegates

Year and Party	Percentage and Number of Unaffiliated Delegates
1952 Republican	28% or 336 delegates
1952 Democratic	72% or 884 delegates
1956 Republican	39% or 537 delegates
1960 Democratic	31% or 469 delegates
1964 Republican	26% or 335 delegates
1968 Democratic	29% or 748 delegates

(Average Pre-Reform Years = 38% unaffiliated)

1972 Democratic	23% or 685.25 delegates
1976 Democratic	10% or 295 delegates
1976 Republican	11% or 244 delegates
1980 Democratic	3% or 86 delegates
1980 Republican	5% or 101 delegates
1984 Democratic	7% or 272 delegates
1988 Democratic	11% or 483 delegates
1988 Republican	9% or 210 delegates

(Average Post-Reform Years = 10% unaffiliated)

Sources: Data compiled by the author. 1972 data from June 17, 1972 *Congressional Quarterly*, p. 1465; 1976 Republican data from July 12, 1978 *Congressional Quarterly*, p. 1473; 1976 Democratic data from June 12, 1976 *Congressional Quarterly*, p. 1473; 1980 Republican data from June 14, 1980 *Congressional Quarterly*, p. 1640; 1980 Democratic data from June 14, 1980 *Congressional Quarterly*, p. 1640; 1984 Democratic data from June 9, 1984 *Congressional Quarterly*, p. 1345.

convention could be turned explicitly to the task of advertising the candidate, his party, and their program" (Shafer, 1988:152–154).

Anything that detracts from the party's ability to put its best foot forward—platform fights, rule fights, and ongoing tensions such as those between Ford and Reagan in 1976, Kennedy and Carter in 1980, Hart and Mondale in 1984, and Dukakis and Jackson in 1988—is seen as a major impediment to the use of the convention to begin the general election.

Whereas political parties have become more and more adept at "managing" their conventions, network news executives, under pressure to cut the huge costs involved in covering a convention, have become increasingly reluctant to cover events that are little more than four-day-long advertisements for the party and its nominee. Conventions used to be covered "gavel to gavel," or from the time they opened until the

TABLE 8.8

Relationship Between the Delegate Count at the End of the Primary Season and the Nominee's Vote on the First Ballot at the Convention

	Needed to Nominate	Delegate Count at End of Primary Season for Nominee	First Ballot Vote (Before Shifts)	Ratio of Count to First Ballot Vote
1952 Republicans	604	393	595	.66
1952 Democrats	616	N/A	273	—
1956 Democrats	687	266	905.5	.29
1960 Democrats	761	339.5	806	.42
1964 Republicans	655	560	883	.63
1968 Democrats	1312	662.5	1759.25	.38

(Average Ratio for Pre-Reform Years = .48)

1972 Democrats	1509	1000.25	1728.35	.58
1976 Democrats	1505	1091	2283.5	.49
1976 Republicans	1130	889	1187	.75
1980 Democrats	1666	1783.1	2129	.84
1980 Republicans	998	1551	1939	.80
1984 Democrats	1967	1974	2191	.90
1988 Democrats	2081	2264	2876	.79
1988 Republicans	1139	1669		

(Average Ratio for Post-Reform Years = .73)

Sources: See Table 8.7.

time they closed. In the 1950s and 1960s, in fact, television coverage actually exceeded the amount of time that the convention was in session.

Beginning in 1980, however, coverage by all three networks declined dramatically (Shafer, 1988:276–280). When NBC News announced a plan to cut from its prime-time coverage of the Democratic convention to a "convention without walls" that it was producing itself, there was a predictable outcry from party officials. Joe Angotti, executive producer of the news, said that "[o]ur first and primary responsibility is to cover the news. I'd like nothing better than to throw all this out and cover a real breaking story" (Kamarck, 1988). Threats by the networks to dramatically scale back coverage in the future have become more and more common.

Thus the nominating convention, devoid of its old functions, may have a hard time hanging onto its new functions. The political parties and nominees want to stage the entire affair so as to put the best light on their party, whereas the networks want to cover real news. If some balance is not struck, the conventions could go the way of the electoral college and become a vestigial part of the body politic.

PROSPECTS FOR CHANGE

The basic characteristics of the post-reform nominating system are not likely to change. For the foreseeable future the nominating process will be dominated by highly visible public contests for money and delegates. Though flawed, this system does have one advantage: People perceive it to be fair and open. When polled on the subject, the public has continually favored more primaries (usually national primaries), not fewer primaries. Any attempt to go back in time and give significantly more power to party officials would most likely be perceived as illegitimate by large numbers of voters accustomed to open presidential primaries.

Aside from Congress, which has traditionally been reluctant to get involved in the nomination process, the only agent of change would be the Democratic party, given that the Republicans do not believe in dictating delegate-selection systems to state Republican parties. Having preached the virtues of openness and wide participation for nearly twenty years, the Democrats, no matter how unhappy they are with the results of their recent nominating contests, can ill afford to return the process to smoke-filled rooms.

But the Democrats have made changes that, at the least, will put some checks and balances into the nomination system. One recent change was to make all major party elected officials (especially governors, senators, and members of Congress) automatic voting delegates to the convention. This change was necessary because one of the consequences of party reform was that elected officials, reluctant to compete with constituents for delegate slots, had dropped out of the convention picture.

The "Super Delegates" have not exercised an independent voice in the nomination process thus far. In 1984 many of them endorsed Mondale early, and in 1988 many members of Congress started out with their fellow House member Richard Gephardt and then switched to Dukakis when Gephardt failed in the primaries.

But the inclusion of the Super Delegates remains popular with the Democratic party for several reasons. Some see them as a centrist force that can serve as a counterbalance to the more ideologically extreme activists who tend to dominate the platform and other forums. Others want them there just in case the primaries fail to produce a winner one day and the nomination actually gets decided on the floor of the convention—an unlikely but still possible scenario. In that case the Super Delegates would be expected to exert a leadership role in bringing the convention to a decision, much as they did in the pre-reform era. And, finally, the Super Delegates can provide an element of "peer review" that the primary voters and ordinary delegates cannot provide, inasmuch as many of them will have known and worked with potential presidential candidates.

Another set of changes that are talked about but have not been incorporated into the Democratic party thus far involve deregulating the party rules. Some students of the rules (this author included) believe that the current rules dictate too many details of the delegate-selection process and that in some instances they have become examples of regulation for the sake of regulation. Indeed, there is no real reason to force every state to elect delegates in exactly the same way so long as the process in each state is clear, open, and easy to participate in. If the Democrats allowed for variations among states, one state could check and balance another, and they could all avoid the unanticipated consequences that have ensued every time they have attempted to "reform" the process by writing yet another rule.

Changes in the nomination process should not be tied to an attempt to recapture some prior moment in history, when nominations were decided in the smoke-filled rooms of party leaders. To the extent that changes do occur in the future, they should be made with the goal of building checks and balances into the current system so that it can work to produce the best nominees—of both parties.

NOTES

1. The first and most famous of the party reform commissions was the Commission on Party Structure and Delegate Selection, which met from 1969 to 1972 and was chaired initially by Senator George McGovern and then by Representative Donald Fraser; hence it is known as the McGovern-Fraser Commission. The work of delegate-selection reform was continued in 1972–1973 by the Commission on Delegate Selection and Party Structure, chaired by then Baltimore City Councilwoman Barbara Mikulski. The next commission, the Commission on Presidential Nomination and Party Structure (1975–1978), was chaired by Michigan Democratic Party Chairman Morley Winograd; it was followed by the Commission on Presidential Nomination, chaired by North Carolina Governor James Hunt from 1981 to 1982. The last of the delegate-selection commissions appears to be the Fairness Commission, chaired by former South Carolina party chairman Donald Fowler in 1985–1986.

2. In his book on the reform movement, Byron Shafer (1983:387) makes the following point: "Despite its status as the device by which the largest share of delegates to national party conventions in all of American history had been selected, the party caucus was abolished by rules which were not assembled in any one guideline, which were not presented in the order in which they had

to be assembled, and which did not at any point claim to be making their actual, aggregate, institutional impact."

3. This phrase was coined by Senator Howard Baker (Germond and Witcover, 1985:96).

4. In 1988, for instance, the total amount that any presidential candidate was allowed to spend to get the nomination was $27,660,000, but the sum total of spending permitted in each state in the union was approximately $70,000,000— about two and a half times the first amount.

5. In a famous article, Michael Robinson and Karen McPherson (1977:2) noted that in 1976 New Hampshire received coverage in more than half of all television stories devoted to the nomination season and in more than one-third of all print stories. This pattern of coverage, whereby the two early contests get news attention out of proportion to their size, has persisted in subsequent years.

6. Consequently, in the spring of 1990 a bill was under consideration in California that would move the California primary to the first Tuesday in March.

7. One of the most frequent fights among Democrats is waged over the issue of "threshold"—namely, the percentage of the vote that a presidential candidate must receive in order to be awarded a delegate. Traditionally, the threshold has been at around 15 percent, meaning that a candidate who fails to receive 15 percent of the vote in a district or a state cannot be awarded a delegate. But the threshold is known to have been as high as 25 percent and as low as 5 percent.

9

Campaigns and Money: A Changing Role for the Political Parties?

FRANK J. SORAUF
SCOTT A. WILSON

Depending on one's tolerance for repetition, the observation that the American parties are essentially electoral parties is either a commonplace or a fundamental truth. Whichever it is, the parties have historically been more involved in contesting elections than in governing, more committed to electoral pragmatism than to issues or ideology. They were everywhere in the search for office—developing and recruiting candidates, engineering nominations, running the campaigns, and turning out the vote. In their heyday they were electoral parties by reason of their power and their activities. Virtually nothing of importance in the quest for elective office was beyond their ken and influence.

Much of that has changed, of course. The hordes of canvassers and workers the parties once supplied and the monopoly of campaign expertise they once held have been replaced by new armies of professional consultants, pollsters, media experts, and data managers. The candidate who can raise the cash to rent those professional services is free to run his or her campaign—indeed, the candidate may be as unmarked by party loyalty or service as the campaign is unmarked by party partic-ipation. Especially in races for Congress and governorships the candidate-centered campaign is the norm, and the party struggles to find not a dominant role in it but just a useful place.

The decline of the parties' campaign roles is only a symptom, though a major one, of their more general and widely heralded decline. Indeed, the loss of their traditional roles in American politics is a part of party history. The question, now, concerns the capacity for adaptation, the ability to find a new and constructive role in a changing political

TABLE 9.1

Receipts of the Major Parties, 1978–1988 (in millions of dollars)[a]

	1978	1980	1982	1984	1986	1988
Democratic	$26.4	$37.2	$39.3	$98.5	$64.8	$127.9
Republican	84.5	169.5	215.0	297.9	255.2	263.3
Total	110.9	206.7	254.3	396.4	320.0	391.2

[a]Includes all party committees (national, state, and local).

Source: Federal Election Commission.

environment. Central to that adaptation must be a new electoral role for the parties—a role that goes beyond merely lending their labels to candidates who use them without obligation. For what is an "electoral party" without a substantial role in election campaigns?

THE DIMENSIONS OF PARTY ACTIVITY IN CAMPAIGN FINANCE

In the cash economy of modern campaigning, the parties' capacity for adaptation has inevitably been tested by their ability to raise significant sums of money. To an increasing degree, it is cash that buys the implements and skills of campaign combat, for the parties as well as for the candidates.

In the 1980s the national party committees made substantial progress in fund-raising capacity. By the 1988 election cycle the combined receipts of the party committees were more than 3.5 times greater than those of the 1978 cycle. The aggregate picture thus points to a general increase in the financial prosperity of the parties.

A closer examination of the data in Table 9.1, however, makes clear a sizable disparity in the receipts of the two major parties. Republican committees have been more successful at fund raising than their Democratic counterparts. For the most part, the Republican advantage was achieved by the early and effective use of direct-mail solicitation. In the late 1970s, while Democratic leaders were struggling with a massive debt and the intricacies of party reform, Republican National Committee chairman William Brock directed the attention and resources of his organization to the development of computer-based lists of known contributors and direct-mail programs for soliciting them. These efforts yielded both an immediate surge in the receipts of Republican committees and the enrollment of some 2 million active contributors by the end of 1980 (Reichley, 1985). The Democratic committees started their own direct-mail operations in the early 1980s, and (as the figures in Table 9.1 show) they have managed to reduce the Republican fund-raising advantage in the last two election cycles.

As to whether the Democrats can realistically expect to close the fund-raising gap, the data of Table 9.1 suggest pessimism. The receipts of two national-level Republican committees have indeed declined, but the growth in receipts of their Democratic counterparts has also slowed markedly. The National Republican Congressional Committee (NRCC) has witnessed the most serious decline: a drop in receipts of more than $18.5 million in 1986 and another (albeit smaller) decrease in 1988. Meanwhile, the National Republican Senatorial Committee (NRSC) reported a large decrease (more than $18.5 million) in 1988. Although the Democratic Congressional Campaign Committee (DCCC) and the Democratic Senatorial Campaign Committee (DSCC) have not suffered actual decreases in receipts, they have been unable to maintain their fund-raising momentum. The DCCC raised only $150,000 more in the 1988 election cycle than in the 1986 cycle, a gain made all the more tenuous by the committee's increasing reliance on loans instead of actual contributions (Barnes and Matlack, 1989). The DSCC mustered a healthier $2.9 million increase, but that, too, was noticeably smaller than its $4.5 million gain in 1986.

The data on party receipts speak to the parties' abilities to fund all of their activities. The focus of this essay, however, is on their campaign role, and thus it is necessary to look at direct party spending. Since the data on spending in congressional campaigns are the most complete we have, we shall concentrate on them. Under the provisions of the Federal Election Campaign Act (FECA) and its subsequent amendments, party committees are allowed to invest directly in their candidates' campaigns through two means: direct contributions and coordinated expenditures. Direct contributions are just what their name implies—contributions of cash, equipment, or services that go directly to a candidate's campaign committee for use at its discretion. Coordinated expenditures, also known as "on behalf of" or "441a(d)" expenditures (after the section of the FECA that deals with them), are somewhat different. When making a coordinated expenditure the party committee is free to consult with the receiving candidate, but the committee determines how and for what purposes the money will be spent.

Not surprisingly, the data on direct contributions and coordinated expenditures closely follow the contours of the data on party receipts. Both parties channeled increasing sums of money into congressional campaigns throughout the 1980s. Democratic party committees spent over five times more in the 1988 congressional elections than in those of 1978, whereas Republican committees more than doubled their spending over the same period. Moreover, the disparity between Democratic and Republican fund raising manifests itself in their congressional spending. Republican committees outspent their Democratic rivals by $6.6

TABLE 9.2
Party Committee Spending in Congressional Elections, 1978–1988
(in millions of dollars)[a]

	1978	1980	1982	1984	1986	1988
Democrats						
Contributions	$1.8	$1.6	$1.7	$1.8	$1.6	$1.7
o.b.o. Spending[b]	.3	1.4	3.0	6.0	8.5	9.5
Total	2.1	3.0	4.7	7.8	10.1	11.2
Republicans						
Contributions	4.5	4.4	5.5	4.8	3.4	3.4
o.b.o. Spending[b]	4.1	7.8	14.2	13.1	14.3	14.4
Total	8.6	12.2	19.7	17.9	17.7	17.8
Grand Total	$10.7	$15.2	$24.4	$25.7	$27.8	$29.0

[a]Includes all party committees (national, state, and local) involved in the congressional campaigns.
[b]"On behalf of," or coordinated, expenditures.

Source: Federal Election Commission.

million in 1988—a gap that, like the difference in receipts, has decreased in recent years.

The bulk of party activity in congressional elections is carried out by the four congressional committees, also known as the Hill committees (for Capitol Hill). Whereas the true national committees—the Democratic National Committee (DNC) and the Republican National Committee (RNC)—devote most of their time and resources to presidential campaigning and general party-building activities, the Hill committees concentrate exclusively on House and Senate contests. In 1988, for example, money from the four congressional committees accounted for roughly 91 percent of party spending in congressional elections.

In general, these data on party spending speak to their progress in adjusting to modern electoral politics. One central trend makes this progress especially clear. The increases in party congressional spending have come entirely in coordinated expenditures; direct contributions have even declined somewhat at various points in the years since 1978 (see Table 9.2). There are several reasons behind this development. The FECA's limits on coordinated expenditures are higher than those on contributions. Some candidates also prefer these "on behalf of" expenditures because they do not inflate their own receipt totals. But the primary reason, and the one that makes the growth in coordinated expenditures so important to party adaptation, is the control that party committees have over these expenditures. Determining what purposes an expenditure will serve gives the party more leverage over a candidate's campaign than a simple cash contribution. So, as the parties increase their spending "on behalf of" candidates, they also expand their influence in congressional campaigning.

Comparing the data in Tables 9.1 and 9.2, one can easily see that the combination of direct contributions and coordinated expenditures accounts for a relatively small share of party income. Depending on the year, spending in congressional campaigns constitutes only 8 to 20 percent of the funds raised by the parties, Democratic and Republican alike. Some of this difference surely goes toward a host of organizational expenses—office space, payroll, direct-mail fund-raising costs, and assistance to state and local parties, to name just a few examples. Another significant portion, however, is invested in what Stephen Frantzich (1989) has termed a "service-vendor" capacity. The parties (especially the Hill committees) now offer candidates a wide array of campaign services and expertise, including media production facilities, district polling and research, and fund-raising assistance. In part, therefore, the gap between receipts and campaign spending represents the adaptation of the parties to the service-based nature of contemporary campaigning (Herrnson, 1988).

Despite the progress the parties have made in fund raising and campaign spending, their financial role does not appear very great relative to that of other actors. In the 1988 congressional elections, for instance, all Democratic committees combined made $11,159,001 in direct contributions and coordinated expenditures—a figure that constitutes only 2.3 percent of the $488.5 million spent directly in the congressional campaigns by all candidates, parties, and independent spenders. By contrast, the $17,795,050 spent by Republican committees accounted for about 3.6 percent of the same total spending figure. If one leaves the independent spending aside, the Democratic party total accounts for 4.4 percent of Democratic spending ($252.7 million) and the Republican total, for 8.8 percent of Republican spending ($202.7 million). On the surface, therefore, neither party appeared to be a major force in financing the campaigns.

Whatever these figures say about the strength of parties, they point to the importance of their strategies in making the best use of the resources at their disposal. The provisions and amendments of the FECA do allow the party committees to spend respectable sums in individual campaigns. In House races, the party's national committee and its House Hill committee can each give $5,000 per candidate in direct contributions in both the primary and general elections (for a total of $20,000 per candidate). The statutory limit for coordinated expenditures, which is indexed to inflation, was $23,050 in 1988 for the primary and general elections combined. Thus, each House candidate in the general election could legally receive $43,050 in assistance from his or her national-level party committees. In addition, the state party (which is subject to the same contribution limits as the national committees) may designate the appropriate national committee as the "agent" for its contributions, thus allowing the national-level committee to spend the state's legal limit in addition to its own. For Senate candidates, the national and Hill committees are allowed a combined total of $17,500 in direct contributions per calendar year. The limit per committee for coordinated expenditures is the greater of either two cents times the voting age population of the state or $20,000. As in House elections, these coordinated expenditure limits are indexed to inflation, and agency agreements with the states can be used to augment a national committee's spending limits.

These are statutory limits, of course, and do not represent the actual amounts of party spending. The parties, especially the Democratic party, have not had the resources needed to give the maximum legal amounts to all of their candidates. The point here is that, given their relatively limited resources, these party committees must make effective strategic decisions about which candidates to fund and at what level.

A central feature of the parties' distribution strategy is the concentration of resources in close races. As Gary Jacobson (1981, 1985–1986) and Samuel Kernell (1981) have argued, individuals and some interest groups make contributions to help a particular candidate win and/or to gain access to the winner, but the parties pursue the broad electoral goal of maximizing the size of their contingent in the Congress. Given this objective, the party committees prefer to fund candidates in marginal contests rather than sure winners or losers. The sure winners (most often incumbents) have little need of party assistance; as strong and visible candidates they can raise all the money they need from other sources. Most of the certain losers are also poor investments. Although party spending may give a boost to these candidates, by itself it is unlikely to bring them victory. Quite simply, campaign spending is most influential in races that are otherwise close—races in which the party's strength in the district, national electoral forces, and the characteristics of an individual candidate make for a close election (Jacobson, 1985–1986). For the parties, then, an electorally efficient distribution of resources is one that targets marginal candidates at the expense of those who are either safe or noncompetitive.

Both parties do a reasonably good job of distributing their resources in an electorally efficient manner (see Table 9.3). The average size of a contribution or expenditure increases with the closeness of the candidate's race. Yet a substantial amount of party money does find its way into the campaigns of certain winners and losers. In the House races of 1986, some 48.6 percent of the Democrats' direct contributions and 39.3 percent of their coordinated expenditures went to candidates in noncompetitive

TABLE 9.3
Party Committee Support for House Candidates
in 1986 General Elections, by Competitiveness of Outcome

General Election Vote	Democrats		Republicans	
	Avg. Direct Contribution	Avg. o.b.o. Spending[a]	Avg. Direct Contribution	Avg. o.b.o. Spending[a]
71-100	$546	$970	$2921	$53
58-70	2187	3107	7723	10042
50-57	7178	17991	13144	31829
43-49	7470	14887	16546	38167
31-42	3074	4682	8652	14149
0-30	321	492	1927	1744

[a]"On behalf of," or coordinated, expenditures.

Source: Federal Election Commission.

or safe elections; the comparable figures for the Republicans were 62.4 percent of direct contributions and 46.2 percent of coordinated expenditures. In fact, as the party committees have raised the amounts of their spending in the 1980s, they actually increased the percentage of their spending going to safe and noncompetitive candidates (Wilson, 1989).

In part, this phenomenon simply reflects practical obstacles. Since there is a limited number of candidates in close races, statutory contribution limits can prevent a party committee from spending as much as it would like on·these marginal candidates; the relatively wealthy NRSC, especially, faces this problem. In addition, the parties do not have perfect information on the competitiveness of their candidates' campaigns. As conditions change over the course of the election cycle, races that were once competitive can become one-sided. At least some party money, therefore, goes to the campaigns of safe or noncompetitive candidates because of legal and informational constraints.

More important, the resources of party committees are subject to goals and demands other than seat maximization and electoral efficiency. The committees can pursue some of these objectives by investing in the campaigns of candidates who are noncompetitive in a given election. Potentially good candidates may need a number of attempts at office to gain campaign experience and name recognition, and financial support from the party can be critical in keeping such candidates interested. Support for a hopeless candidate may also help other party candidates on the ballot or support the party building of local party leadership.

At the other end of the spectrum, heavy demands for party resources may be made by the safe candidates, who are most often incumbents. Yet, although they are reelected with surprising frequency (House incumbent reelection rates are consistently more than 95 percent) and by widening margins, most incumbents do not think of themselves as safe candidates (Fenno, 1978; Jacobson, 1980). Moreover, incumbents generally believe in the deterrent value of a large campaign account; an impressive "war chest" may be all that is needed to intimidate would-be challengers. Numerous safe incumbents thus make demands for party money, and they are in a good position to do so. The congressional party committees, after all, are creatures of their respective House or Senate caucuses. So, although the demands of safe incumbents conflict with the party's collective interest in an electorally efficient distribution of its resources, committee leaders invariably accede to at least some of these demands.

Overall, and despite the often conflicting goals and demands with which they are faced, the congressional party committees do concentrate their spending in the campaigns of marginal candidates. (Indeed, they do so far more effectively than the PACs, which in the 1988 congressional campaigns gave 80 percent of their contributions to incumbents, most of it without regard to electoral need.) The party committees also time their spending for the greatest effectiveness, delaying coordinated expenditures until the latter part of the campaign—a time when the outcome of an election is more predictable (Sorauf, 1988). In the final analysis, considerations of strategy point to the importance of financial strength for the parties. Wealthier party committees are better able to deal with a mix of objectives: funding marginal candidates at the desired levels while attending to the needs (real or perceived) of noncompetitive and safe candidates, and providing early "seed money" while saving enough for later, more strategic dispersal.

THE POLITICAL PARTY AS FINANCIAL BROKER

As important as the combination of contributions and coordinated spending may be, it by no means accounts for the entirety of the party role in funding congressional campaigns. It is merely the most overt and identifiable part, largely because it is the part about which the parties must make full reports and disclosures to the Federal Election Commission (FEC). Far less visible are the ways in which the parties function as brokers or intermediaries in raising campaign money—by cuing, channeling, and funneling the money of others to worthy candidates of the party. In these activities the party committee is neither the source nor the final spender of that money, but its role in mobilizing the money is nonetheless crucial to party influence in campaigns.

Of all the forms of financial brokering in which the parties engage, the most widely publicized and the least well understood is the raising of "soft money." Definitions differ greatly, but the greatest number of experts agree that it is money which cannot be contributed under federal law and is thus channeled to less strictly regulated state or local committees for their spending on nonfederal purposes. This channeling—the guiding of the money—can be done by a party committee or a nonparty committee (i.e., a PAC). The best-known case provides the best illustration. In the 1988 presidential campaigns both national party committees, as well as George Bush and Michael Dukakis themselves, raised millions of dollars for state and local party activities, largely registration and get-out-the-vote drives.

Soft money, in other words, is campaign money that moves in the American federal system to the safest haven. Since federal law is more severely regulatory than the laws of virtually all the states, campaign money flows in one direction: to the state jurisdictions with the most permissive limits and the least effective reporting. It is not reported under federal law, and much of it is unreported under state law by the very logic of the "safest haven." Moreover, it is usually "raised" and placed by party committees that cannot legally accept it themselves. The two-party national committees could not have accepted the large sums for themselves in 1988 because of the sources and sizes of the contributions. (On the one hand, contributions from union or corporation assets are illegal under the FECA; on the other, the FECA limits individuals to contributions of $1,000 per candidate per election.) The Bush and Dukakis committees could not have accepted *any* sums because they took public funding for the presidential campaign and thereby agreed not to accept any private money.

As with soft money, "bundling" can be practiced by both party and nonparty committees. It is the practice whereby a committee accepts and transmits the contributions of individuals to candidates specified by the contributors. In the world of PACs the practice is called "earmarking," and, indeed, that is what the regulations of the Federal Election Commission call it. PACs tend not to encourage earmarking, largely because it deprives them of control over the disposition of the money and may even direct money to a candidate whom the PAC does not support. A few PACs, however, have used bundling as a way of organizing contributions to exceed the FECA limit of $5,000 per election on a PAC's contributions to a candidate. Party committees engage in bundling or earmarking chiefly for this latter purpose: to accommodate additional help to candidates when the committee has spent up to its limits on them.

Unlike soft money, earmarking must be reported under federal law by both the intermediary and the recipient. However, the intermediary—the party committee or the PAC—need not count the sums against its own contribution limits unless it "exercises direction or control over the choice of the intended recipient of the contribution." Virtually no intermediaries admit to such control. As for the reports of bundling or earmarking, they remain more or less buried amid the millions of pages of FEC reports. The FEC does not add them up, nor does it index them or bring them together in any accessible way. Only an occasional bit of newspaper reporting brings the subject before the public.

Beyond raising soft and earmarked money, party committees (and PACs) may serve as less formal mobilizers of the cash of others. Much of that informal brokering involves simply giving cues and advice. The Hill committees, for example, routinely urge sympathetic PACs to give money to Candidate X or Candidate Y. Indeed, they have employees whose major duty is to oversee the mobilization of PAC money, even to stage the fabled "meat markets" at which the party's favored challengers make brief attempts to impress potential contributors. Just the mere fact of party support for a candidate is cue enough for some contributors looking for challenger and open-seat candidates with a chance of winning. None of this cue giving, of course, need be reported under either federal or state law.

Given the paucity of data about these activities, it is not easy to estimate their total value to candidates. Various reports on the 1988 presidential campaign estimated that the Democratic and Republican parties each raised between $20 and $25 million in soft money. State and local parties may not legally spend those funds on federal elections (including the presidential ones), but efforts on behalf of a whole ticket or attempts to turn out the vote are not easy to allocate between federal and nonfederal candidates. Critics—Common Cause most prominent among them—have charged that the FEC's allocation formulas (under which the parts of efforts that help federal candidates must be paid for with hard money) are too lenient, that soft money is illegally spent by some state and local parties, and that the soft money is raised in the first place with the intention of affecting a presidential election. Whatever the extent of illegality, it is undeniable that soft money has been raised chiefly in the presidential years and, in major part, with presidential politics in mind.

By contrast, reports of bundling in party committees have not been widespread. The major case in the 1980s was the National Republican Senatorial Committee, which reported approximately $3 million in earmarked money in both 1984 and 1986. After a lengthy review of the 1986 transactions, the Federal Election Commission split 3 to 3 along party lines over whether the $2.8 million raised for twelve candidates (eleven of whom lost) had entered "the direction or control" of the NRSC since the funds had been deposited in NRSC bank accounts. The committee apparently engaged in no bundling in 1988. As for the value of the informal cuing done by the parties, there is no way to put a price on it, even though observers argue that it is by far the most significant indirect party activity in congressional finance.

Whatever the value of these indirect financial operations, one sees in them the effectiveness of the party, precisely because it *is* a political party. Because candidates bear its label on the ballot, voters look to it for guidance in election after election; and because candidates are identified as liberal or conservative by its very name, the party finds itself in a singular position to direct would-be contributors. The extensive national, state, and local structure of the party enables it to maneuver within the interstices of American federalism. And the superiority of its political knowledge and its strategic commitments permit it to make the calculations essential to effective intermediating.

THE STATE AND LOCAL EXPERIENCE

The question concerning the fit of the new financial role for state and local party committees falls easily into two parts: their role in federal election campaigns (both congressional and presidential) and their role in state elections (from gubernatorial down to local). The first role must of course be reported to the FEC, and the latter only under variable state reporting requirements. Understandably, we know far more about the first than the second.

In the 1980s the two parties developed somewhat different roles for state and local parties in federal campaigns. The Republicans pioneered "agency agreements" by which state committees cede all or part of their authority to spend "on behalf of" candidates to a national committee. The Democrats fought that move unsuccessfully both before the FEC and in the federal courts, and by the 1986 and 1988 election cycles the overwhelming number of Republican state committees were delegating their spending quotas in senatorial campaigns to the NRSC. In 1986 the NRSC spent sums approximately twice its limit (i.e., its limit plus the state committee's limit) in twenty-six senatorial races and part of the state limit in at least two others. Only the Idaho Republican committee spent its full alloted sum.

The Democrats have been slower to negotiate such agreements. In 1986 the DSCC spent between 190 and 200 percent of its statutory limit in thirteen senatorial races. It also spent part of the state limit in at least four other cases. No state Democratic committee spent to its full statutory limit. Connecticut's committee, at 58 percent of its limit, was the only one that spent above 50 percent; Florida spending was next, at 38 percent.

What of party spending in state and local elections? The best evidence is unquestionably found in campaigns for state legislatures—campaigns in which, for many years, party roles were substantial because of the limited visibility and political experience of the candidates. By the 1980s the party committees accounted for less than 10 percent of legislative candidate receipts in most of the larger states—for example, 9 percent in Pennsylvania in 1982 and 1.5 percent in California in 1986 (Sorauf, 1988). There is also evidence of declines in party funding. According to the data of the Minnesota Ethical Practices Board, for instance, party committees accounted for 12.4 percent of funds for lower house candidates in 1980; by 1988 the figure was 8.9 percent.

Inevitably, among the fifty states there are other political traditions and additional forms of adaptation to the new politics of cash campaigns. In New Jersey power in the party has shifted from county party organizations to the state committees in legislative elections; state party committees increased their expenditures on legislative candidates by almost 500 percent between 1977 and 1987, accounting for almost a quarter of their receipts in the latter year. The shift from noncash to cash campaigning seems inexorably to produce a centralization of party influence, both within the states and in the American federal system.

With such scraps of data it is not easy to assess the ability of state and local parties to find a substantial place in financing campaigns. Clearly they have no major role in congressional or presidential campaigns. Their cash roles in state campaigns are often substantial in direct outlays, but there is no reason to think that their informal role—cue giving or bundling, for instance—matches that of the national committees. Perhaps the major reason for pessimism about their ability to adapt to cash politics rests in the increasing role of the Democratic National Committee and the Republican National Committee in funding the operation of state parties and the recruitment of state candidates. Indeed, throughout most of the 1980s the RNC funded Republican state legislative candidates in the hope of having a greater Republican impact on the drawing of congressional district lines after the 1990 census.

THE IMPACT OF THE NEW FINANCIAL ROLE

What the new financial role has *not* done for the parties is clearer than what it has done. It has not brought them closer to the model of the programmatic, "responsible" political party. That is, the party committees have not yet tied spending in campaigns to the candidate's position on issues, program or ideology or to the candidate's record of support for party positions. The goals of these committees have been the modest electoral goals of the classically electoral American parties:

to win elections and to maximize the number of elective offices won. The hope that the parties would emerge as the central animating force in American government—that we would have "party government"— seems as remote as ever.

In pursuing more modest electoral goals, the parties have begun to win back some of their lost role in electoral politics. Their ability to raise money and to direct the raising of money from others has made the parties the active players in campaign politics that they were not in the 1960s and 1970s. (That rebound has also resulted, of course, from the development of the parties' capacity to provide campaign technologies and services.) Thus they have "adapted," even recouped a bit, in a campaign politics dominated by candidates and new technologies and technocrats. But how much have they recouped? If one employs the ultimate test—control of the content and strategy of the campaign— the parties are still some distance from the kind of party control they had between the world wars (Heard, 1960).

To some extent, the parties' recapture of a role in electoral campaigns was possible in the 1980s because they lost no further ground in the war of political organizations. The new era of American campaign finance, which dates approximately from the passage of the FECA amendments of 1974, coincided with a rise of interest group power (Schlozman and Tierney, 1986). Inevitably, the campaign instruments of group activity—political action committees (PACs)—experienced the same growth under the fostering provisions of the FECA. There were 1,146 PACs registered with the FEC at the end of 1976 and 4,268 by the end of 1988; their contributions to congressional candidates jumped in the same years from $22.6 million to $156.0 million. PACs entered electoral politics in an ever-expanding way, and through them groups as political organizations made their first massive foray into American electoral politics. The traditional and informal division of labor—parties dominating electoral politics, groups dominating policymaking politics—had been irreparably broken.

Indeed, at the peak of PAC expansion in the early 1980s, it seemed possible that at least some groups would expand their influence in electoral politics beyond the mere channeling of cash. Some PACs and their sponsoring groups began to register new voters and encourage greater voter turnout; a few of the larger PACs began to make contributions not in cash but in campaign services (i.e., "in kind") that permitted them a more active role in the campaigns they supported. But most PACs never followed suit, and no PACs managed to take on the many activities of parties in electoral politics. Most never developed either the political will or the political knowledge and sophistication that once seemed likely to come with experience and affluence. On the contrary, they seem to have become more "risk averse" as they grew and matured; the percentage of their contributions going to challengers and open-seat candidates declined steadily in the 1980s.

There are thus important limits to the capacity of interest groups to act in electoral politics, and the PACs, even in a period of growth and ascendancy, have demonstrated many of them. The PACs do not easily reach the levels of political knowledge and sophistication, the intensity of political purpose, that the parties do, even in their reduced condition. The symbolic and cue-giving value of interest groups—especially for voters—seems more limited in scope, perhaps even in intensity, than that of the parties. Their members have been brought together for very specific and limited political purposes, and disunity threatens whenever the groups venture beyond them. They can limit the parties' hegemony in the electoral arena, but only to a point. It is probably safe to say that the parties' chief rival is still the powerful, autonomous candidate who has the ability to raise substantial cash resources and the consequent ability to rent the imposing new campaign technologies.

Beyond the impact of PACs on the parties' position in the political system, their new role in campaign finance has had a second set of consequences: impacts on the parties themselves. The most obvious of these has been the reemergence of the financial elite. The "new fat cats," as they have been called, are no longer the big contributors but the organizers of the big contribution total. They can no longer give $1 million under federal law, but they can mobilize 1,000 people to give $1,000 each. They can stage receptions or other fund-raising events, arranging not only the events themselves but also the presence of affluent guests. They come from all parts of American life; some are members of distinguished and/or wealthy families, many are captains of commerce and industry, and some are lobbyists, political lawyers, or individuals elsewhere employed in the influence industry.

Nowhere is the return of the money raisers more apparent than in presidential and national committee politics. And no one typifies this return better than Robert A. Farmer, the chairman and chief fund raiser of Michael Dukakis's campaign for the presidency in 1988. A self-made millionaire in publishing from Boston, Farmer oversaw the raising of more than $20 million in Dukakis's campaign for the Democratic nomination and then raised $68 million in hard and soft money for the party in the general election campaign—both record totals in the Democratic party. After Dukakis's loss, Farmer was elected (without opposition) as the treasurer of the Democratic National Committee. No less a pioneer in cash politics was William Brock, who introduced the new political technologies for raising millions of dollars into national party committees.

Thus the need to raise campaign money elevates new individuals and new skills to party leadership. It also readjusts the relationships between various parts of the party, simply because some parts are more successful in raising campaign funds than are others. It is increasingly clear, for example, that the national committees have been far more successful than those at the state and local levels. The agency agreements that permit national committees to use state spending quotas testify to that. So, too, does the increasing practice by the RNC and the DNC of raising money and using it to subsidize state party operations. In the 1950s and before, the money flowed the other way; national committees lived off funds transferred to them by affluent state committees.

Just as significant, the financial role has further empowered the legislative parties, both at the national level and in the states. By the late 1980s the four congressional party committees had taken over the funding of congressional elections from the two party national committees, leaving the RNC and the DNC to fund presidential campaigns and the state parties. Moreover, the four congressional committees had expanded their money-raising capacity at a rate faster than that of the national committees. From 1980 through 1986 the receipts of the two national committees increased 8 percent and those of the four Hill committees, 222 percent. Important political careers were made or nourished in the Hill committees. Representative Tony Coelho turned successful leadership of the DCCC into election to the whip's position in the House Democratic leadership. And in early 1989 the NRCC hired Ed Rollins, the campaign manager of the 1984 Reagan reelection committee, as its executive director; his annual salary of $250,000 signaled the new importance of the Hill committees.

The legislative party, too, has triumphed in many states. Often the legislative caucus of the party directs the fund raising on behalf of the party's legislative candidates, holding fund-raising events, marshaling big contributors, and even beginning direct-mail campaigns for money. In other states there are party committees, detached to some degree from the legislative caucus, that operate much the same way as the Hill committees do in congressional campaigns. And in still other states the major fund-raising responsibility is in the hands of the legislative leadership. The speaker of the California Assembly, Willie Brown, has in each recent election distributed more than a million dollars to fellow Democratic candidates for the legislature. His generosity has helped ensure both a Democratic majority and grateful votes for Brown's speakership.

Whatever the mode, the effect is the same: an increase in the power of the legislative party to fund its own campaigns. That power results from the legislators' discovery of the fund-raising leverage of their incumbency, their electoral invincibility, and their making of public policy. That discovery, more than any other, may well mark the end of any hope for the creation of "responsible parties." It may also mark the greatest impact of the new financial role on the parties themselves.

MONEY AND THE FUTURE OF THE PARTIES

Even though the rate of growth has slowed, the amounts of money going into American campaigns continue to increase. Total spending in all congressional campaigns in 1986 ($450.9 million) was 21 percent greater than spending in 1984 ($374.1 million), and the 1988 figure ($457.7 million) was 2 percent greater than that for 1986. If the parties are to sustain their new role in campaign finance, they will probably have to match *some* increases into the future. Can they?

There is no way to calculate future capacity, but the party fund-raising record since 1984 is mixed. To be sure, the presidential candidates, George Bush and Michael Dukakis, raised record sums for themselves and their parties in 1988. But the failures of 1986 (see Table 9.1) tempered any optimism in the parties, and in 1989 the Democrats began to experience more financial problems. The reasons for those downturns are still under debate, but two explanations enjoy the most support. In the first place, direct-mail solicitations of campaign money have generally fared badly in recent years; a number of the PACs relying on direct mail have done badly, and support for a few (e.g., the National Conservative Political Action Committee, or NCPAC) has completely collapsed. For whatever reasons—oversolicitation of lists, loss of novelty, the poor image and high overhead of some direct-mail operations—it is no longer possible to raise greater and greater sums by mail. Second, the parties (and especially the Democrats) may be suffering from a diminution of ideological, confrontational politics and from a post-Reagan centrism that tempers the reasons for giving money to them.

In short, the financial role for the parties may be as perishable and time rooted as all other party roles have been. Adaptation to earlier change does not protect a party against future change and a subsequent need to adapt. If electoral politics remains centrist and without searing issue or ideological conflict, and if the personae of candidates continue to dominate those politics, the parties may find it harder to raise large sums of money. It is not easy to compete with personable candidates, for it is not easy to personify the abstract collectivity we call a political party. Nor is it easy to compete with PACs in setting out clear issue or ideological positions, especially at a time of centrism in the parties.

Changes in the ground rules governing the getting and spending of money in elections might, however, ease the parties' problems in fund raising. Any substantial restrictions on PAC money, such as President George Bush proposed in the summer of 1989, might direct some political money to party committees. But more substantial, direct legislative aid to the parties seems unlikely, for the truth of the matter is that political parties are not exempt from the popular attitudes that govern the regulation of campaign finance. The public is suspicious about the sources of money, especially "big money," and it will suspect the sources of party money just as surely as the sources of PAC money. It will also be suspicious of the parties for spending large sums and wonder what the parties want for their spending. Certainly their status as political parties has not spared them any criticism for their soft money transactions in 1988. And success in raising money will probably only increase criticism of the party role in campaign finance. "More" in campaign finance wins no more favor with the mass public than "more" in taxes.

So, whether by plan or inadvertence, the parties have ventured on a new accommodation with the new candidate-centered politics of campaigning. But this accommodation is not without its hazards, and, like all other things in party politics, it will certainly not last forever. Moreover, it is an accommodation that works better for some parts of the parties than for others. It has succeeded particularly well for the legislative parties. Greater powers of incumbency have joined with a greater ability to fund the electoral politics of the legislative party. The result, for now, is greater autonomy for legislative parties—greater freedom to frame their own campaign themes and strategies, to set policymaking agendas and positions, without interference from the party organization. As always, it is not the whole political party but only a part of the party that is strengthened.

10

The Press, Political Parties, and the Public-Private Balance in Elections

GARY R. ORREN
WILLIAM G. MAYER

The mass media have done to the campaign system what the invention of accurate artillery did to the feudal kingdom: destroyed the barons and shifted their power to the masses and the prince. While the Reformation removed the intermediary between deity and communicant, the media substitute themselves for the party in an intermediary role, enabling more direct contact between politician and citizen because they transmit more and translate less.

—Stimson Bullitt

Political parties in the United States have always existed on shaky ground. From the earliest days of the republic, Americans have been ambivalent and suspicious toward them, if not downright hostile. Still, parties have performed indispensable functions for the political system. Until recently, for example, they served as the main connecting rods between candidates and voters.

Over the past three decades, however, the party apparatus has atrophied and partisan ties in the electorate have eroded. In the process, many of the functions once basic to the parties have devolved upon other institutions, particularly the media. With each passing election, the media have become bolder and more assertive in appropriating tasks once the exclusive preserve of political professionals and party leaders. As James David Barber puts it, "The media in the United States are the new political parties. The old political parties are gone. What we now have are television and print" (Barber, 1986).

Of course, that is more true for some traditional party roles than for others. Parties once had control over communicating with and educating voters; recruiting, evaluating, and selecting candidates; clarifying electoral choices; and mobilizing voters. In the following pages we sort out which of these functions the parties retain, which have been assumed by the media, which are now the province of individual campaigns, and which are no longer performed by any institution.

As this discussion of electoral functions will reveal, the press—like a political party—is a two-sided institution: It has both a private and a public face. We will examine the ways in which a shifting balance between these two faces has affected the conduct of recent elections. We will also raise the question of what balance is most appropriate.

COMMUNICATING WITH VOTERS

Political parties and the mass media have fought a long battle for dominance in *communicating with and educating the electorate.* The key issue has been this: Who will control the stream of messages that bombards the voters during an election campaign? In other words, who will determine the inputs upon which the citizenry will base its voting decisions?

For most of the nineteenth century, political parties were the dominant instrument of campaign communications and probably of political education generally. From the 1830s on, grassroots party organizations sprang up in every city, county, and rural hamlet in the nation. One of their main functions was to carry the parties' message to the electorate. Party precinct workers went from door to door, selling the merits of the party slate. As Ralph Whitehead once noted, the party organization served as a "labor-intensive communications medium" (Whitehead, 1978:31).

Adding to their effectiveness, such party machines in many locations enjoyed a virtual monopoly on political communications. In city neighborhoods with large immigrant populations that did not speak English, the precinct captain or ward boss became a kind of ambassador to the outside world, interpreting political developments for the new Americans (Handlin, 1952:Chap. 8; Gans, 1962). Needless to say, the information provided this way was far from neutral or objective. Farms and small towns, too, were a lot more isolated in the age before television, radio, and modern highways. So although rural politics in the strong-party era has been less well studied than urban politics, it is safe to say that party organizations served as an important source of political news for many rural residents.

Even where other sources of political news were available, most of them worked with—or for—the party organizations, rather than against them. The 1850 census listed only 5 percent of newspapers as "neutral" or "independent."[1] The other 95 percent were propaganda organs for political parties, nurturing the growth of party organizations and cultivating devoted mass followings. They served as the principal weapons in the intense partisan battles of the age. Scores of campaign newspapers, published strictly for electioneering, sprang up throughout the nation. One of the most successful was Horace Greeley's *Log Cabin*, devoted to perfecting the image of William Henry Harrison.

In fact, the most important editors of this period were essentially politicians who wielded newspapers, fortifying and arousing the party faithful with catchwords and slogans. Many of these editors became leaders of state and local party organizations. Thurlow Weed, for example, used the newspaper he published, the *Albany Evening Journal*, to organize the Whig party in New York. The distinction between the press and the party nearly vanished.

Toward the end of the nineteenth century, however, the partisan press began to wane, and with it the centrality of political parties in communicating with the electorate. Newspapermen started writing about the emergence of a press free from party domination. By 1880, one-fourth of the country's newspapers were independent of party control, and by 1890 about one-third. By 1940 nearly half the papers were independent, and only a quarter had outright partisan ties. And, of course, it was the press itself that led the reform assault against local party machines around the turn of the century. Political leaders like Theodore Roosevelt and Woodrow Wilson used newspapers as a counterforce against party organizations to establish their own direct links with the public.

Today journalism has become a far more professional occupation, bound by an ethic of objectivity. Network television has perfected the nonpartisan approach to news. This has happened partly because of economic pressure to attract the largest possible audience and partly because of regulations requiring balanced reporting and equal time to opposing candidates and parties.

Starting in the Progressive Era, from the mid-1880s to the early 1920s, the strong local party organizations also began to crumble. In this case, the media were not the immediate cause of death. The chief executioners were civil service laws, though in many cases the newly independent press helped lead the fight to enact such laws. Going door to door is not especially interesting work, and the only people who would do it regularly, election after election, were those whose livelihood depended on it. As patronage gave way to civil service, then, local party organizations gradually fell apart.

The last hurrahs of the old party machines occurred at different times in different parts of the country, depending on the local political culture and the resourcefulness of reform leaders. But by 1960 at the latest, party organizations were no longer an important force in large sections of the country. A study carried out in Detroit in 1956, for example, found "a viable Democratic organization in less than half of the precincts, and a working Republican organization in about one-third of the precincts." The state of party organization in Minneapolis in the late 1940s led to a similar verdict: "Roughly 100 of the 634 possible precinct captaincies will be unfilled and not over half the remainder are filled by active precinct workers who can be depended upon at all times" (Eldersveld, 1964:104; Morlan, 1949:485–490). In the national election surveys that the University of Michigan has conducted regularly since 1952, the percentage of American adults who report having been contacted by a party worker has never risen above 25 percent.

But even where the party precinct organizations endured, their monopoly was a thing of the past. The immigrants were gradually assimilated, and rural areas were transformed by revolutions in communications and transportation. Today, a party precinct worker who knocks on a typical American door has to counter the messages that voters have been receiving from television and newspapers. It is not a fair fight, to say the least. In 1980, for example, 86 percent of the Michigan survey sample said they had watched the campaign on television, 71 percent had read campaign stories in the newspaper, 47 percent had heard programs or discussions on radio, and 35 percent had used magazines—but only 24 percent had been contacted by a party worker.

Thus, even if the old precinct organizations were more active, it is questionable how effective they would be. When the typical American adult has watched television for six hours a day for much of his life and thus learned to accept a televised view of reality, how likely is it that he will believe an alternative vision presented by a party precinct worker who visits once or twice before an election? Studies have invariably found that precinct work has little effect on voter choice in major, high-media elections. Using survey data from 1952–1964, Gerald Kramer found that the effect of precinct canvassing in presidential and congressional elections was very small and frequently counterproductive. In one especially good study, Cutright and Rossi conducted extensive surveys of party precinct workers in the city of Gary, Indiana. After controlling for socioeconomic characteristics, the team tried to relate variations in precinct activity to variations in the two-party share of the vote. In the 1956 presidential election, they found that for both Democrats and Republicans, an active committeeman increased his party's share of the vote by only about 4 percent (Kramer, 1970–71:561; Cutright and Rossi, 1958a:177).

Further evidence comes from a survey William Mayer conducted in 1980 in Chicago, then one of the few places in the United States that still had a strong party organization. When asked which of seven sources they relied upon most for information about politics and elections, 73 percent mentioned television, 63 percent named newspapers, and only 7 percent cited their party organization precinct captain. When asked which source they trusted more, the results were: television 43 percent, newspapers 38 percent, precinct captains 3 percent. Asked which they distrusted, 46 percent said precinct captains versus 15 percent for television. Simply put, when faced with a conflict between Walter Cronkite and a local party minion, the average voter sided with Cronkite.

One qualification does need to be added to this picture: Party organization may still be an important force in lower-level elections such as for state legislature or city council and perhaps in some congressional elections as well. Precinct captains can't compete with television anchors, but in these elections they don't need to. The typical state legislative race receives little or no television coverage and may not get much attention in the newspapers, either. With such a dearth of information, the voter may listen to party workers simply because they are the only source available. For example, in the same city where Cutright and Rossi showed that party activity had only a minimal impact on the presidential vote, they found that precinct work accounted for 80 percent of the variation in the Democratic primary vote for offices such as county commissioner and county surveyor (Cutright and Rossi, 1958b:262–269; Wolfinger, 1963:387–398; and Wattenberg, 1984:102–108).

Of course, communication is not just a one-way process. The voters have grievances, demands, and ideas that they want to communicate to political leaders. But here as well, the last thirty years have seen parties supplanted by media. When Franklin Roosevelt wanted to find out what was on the public mind, he often called on party leaders like Ed Kelly in Chicago and Ed Flynn in New York, whose positions and precinct organizations supposedly put them in closer touch with the electorate. Today, the public pulse is monitored largely by opinion polls—some conducted by parties, most by media organizations—or polling firms like Gallup and Harris that sell their results to media clients.

Some readers might interject here that we have ignored an important part of the loop: Parties, it might be argued, also benefit from the mass media. They can use television and newspapers to send their message more effectively to the electorate. But this argument ignores an important distinction: In general, it is not the *parties* but the *candidates* who try to communicate with the voters. And candidates, not surprisingly, are generally uninterested in selling the electorate on the merits of their party as a whole. Modern campaigns, as Robert Agranoff (1972) has noted, are "candidate-centered." Their task is to stress the strengths of their own candidate or to attack the weaknesses of the opponent. In either case, they rarely put much emphasis on partisan ties. Indeed, many modern campaigns—like Jimmy Carter's and Gary Hart's bids for the Democratic presidential nomination—actually ran against the party apparatus, portraying it as out of touch, unresponsive, and illegitimate. If precinct organizations were still the main link to the voters, such candidates would have to make their peace with the party.

One reason precinct organizations are no longer the main link is that they have lost their monopoly on communicating with voters. A new cadre of campaign consultants, independent of political parties, has risen to prominence—if not preeminence—in election campaigns. More and more, campaigns rely on hired guns for advice and services such as advertising, polling, direct mail, and fund raising. The ascendancy of this elite corps of campaign professionals has accompanied, and at the same time hastened, the retreat of party organizations.

Recently the parties, led by the Republicans, have been jumping on the communications bandwagon. They have tried to become major service organizations for campaigns, paying for or supplying polling, advertising, fund raising, and the like. They have even sponsored advertising that promotes the record and virtues of the party. Some observers believe that this new sophistication will resuscitate political parties, as they become repositories of technical expertise and services (Sabato, 1987). But candidates will not readily relinquish their independence and return control to the parties. In the jockeying for campaign supremacy among the media, the consultants, the candidates, and the parties, it is the parties who will come up short.

The substantial literature that has grown up in recent years around modern congressional elections makes much the same point. Members of Congress get reelected by making very personalistic appeals to their local districts. They emphasize the services they have delivered to the voters, the interests and constituencies they stand up for, their effectiveness in guaranteeing the district its fair share of the federal pork barrel—but not their party affiliation. Indeed, the whole purpose of such campaigning is to insulate the representatives from larger national trends, and thus to make sure they will get reelected even if their party's record is unpopular (Fiorina, 1977; Fenno, 1978; Jacobson, 1987).

The media, of course, are not the principal movers behind candidate-centered campaigns. The decisions to downplay partisan themes are taken, in the first instance, by the candidates and their managers. But the media make such campaigns possible. They offer candidates a channel to the electorate that bypasses the party organization. They also focus the public's attention on candidates rather than political parties.

For instance, television made it possible for the first time for millions of Americans to see and hear a live speech by a president, without being in the physical presence of the president. This in itself has bred a new sense of familiarity of citizens with the president, a familiarity that [the presidents] can exploit in their elections campaigns and tenure in office. After all, you cannot televise an entire political party but you can televise an individual candidate. What works best on television is the candidate-centered campaigns, with all the attention to personality, individual character, appearance, poise, and demeanor that mark the television campaign. An older campaign strategy, which centered on party label, and endorsement of party bosses, has not translated nearly as well into the television era (Abramson, Arterton, and Orren, 1988:17).

Print journalism, too, has increasingly focused on candidates. One study that monitored presidential election coverage in five major newspapers and magazines found that candidates were mentioned about twice as often as parties in the 1950s and roughly five times as often in 1980. The press, once the prime reinforcer of partisanship, now highlights candidates instead (Wattenberg, 1984:92–98).

The function of educating the electorate, then, is one that has been usurped almost entirely from political parties. The role has passed to the media and to the individual candidates and campaigns.

SELECTING, EVALUATING, AND RECRUITING CANDIDATES

Just as the parties have lost their monopoly on educating the public, so have they found themselves competing with the media in *selecting candidates*. (See Chapters 7 and 8.) Throughout the nineteenth century and much of the twentieth, controlling nominations was both their central function and their exclusive preserve. Caucuses of party leaders chose the candidates who would bear the party label in the general election. As recently as 1968, a substantial percentage of the delegates to the national party conventions were selected in closed meetings by party leaders or were themselves party leaders serving ex officio.

But parties have gradually been divested of such powers. The mass media, it should be stressed, were only marginally responsible for this transformation.[2] Parties lost control of their nomination processes almost entirely as a result of changes in state laws and national party rules, changes that were often undertaken with the deliberate intention of weakening the party organizations. During the Progressive Era, most states required parties to select their candidates in primary elections that were open to every voter who was willing to show some kind of token allegiance to the party. Between 1968 and 1972, the Democratic party extended the same principle to the selection of national convention delegates.

The result is that formal party organizations have become, in effect, just one more interest group involved in nomination battles. Their powers are largely the same as those granted to every other interest group: They can make endorsements, donate money, recruit volunteers, and try to get their supporters to the polls. In elections where public interest and involvement are low, these activities may prove important. But the higher and more visible the office, the less say parties have about who their candidate will be. As Austin Ranney so aptly put it:

> The party organizations simply are not actors in presidential politics. Indeed, they are little more than custodians of the party-label prize which goes to the winning candidate organization. The parties have long since ceased to be judges *awarding* the prize (Ranney, 1978:239).

Once the parties had been largely removed from the nomination process, it was all but inevitable that the media would rush in to fill the void. Under the old system, the party leaders who made the nomination decisions were usually full-time professionals. Many of them knew and had worked with the major aspirants for the party designation. But when such decisions were made by the public, the media—already dominant in educating and informing the public about the candidates—became instrumental in shaping those decisions. The media have moved well beyond the role of simply providing information, especially in the long, drawn-out contests for presidential nominations. Their reporting of such events has become increasingly interpretive and judgmental.

Reporters now perform the once quintessential party tasks of *evaluating the candidates*, appraising their suitability and setting standards of success and failure. The media effectively determine who the front-runners and the "serious" candidates are. The media issue reports on the candidates' progress (or lack of it) and allocate precious news coverage to some candidates and not to others. They also set the benchmarks, declaring which primaries and caucuses matter and how well a candidate must do to stay viable. The 1988 presidential election demonstrated, particularly in the primaries, just how far the press was prepared to go in supplanting parties as screeners and gatekeepers. In fact, according to some, reporters got so deeply into the role of "character cops" that they shattered some traditional journalistic norms of how far news coverage should intrude into the personal lives of politicians.

A fascinating example of the growing evaluative role of the media, which may well be a sign of things to come, is provided by the campaign advertising of Bruce Babbitt in the 1988 Democratic presidential nomination race. As recently as twenty years ago, an aspirant to the presidency spent much of his time soliciting endorsements from top party officials and office-holders, and then trumpeting them as proof of his fitness and abilities. Today, however, such an endorsement rarely guarantees a candidate more than one additional vote. Indeed, given the popular suspicion and distrust of politicians, a long list of high-level endorsements may even be a liability. It allows opponents to portray the candidate as a tool of the bosses and the special interests. So the Babbitt campaign opted for a very different strategy. Its advertisements in Iowa boasted about the favorable reviews that Babbitt had received in various newspapers and magazines. Babbitt's endorsements came not from fellow politicians but from reporters and columnists.

Even the power to *recruit candidates* has slipped through the parties' fingers. Historically, this function was performed mainly by local and state party organizations and to a lesser extent by national parties. Much like officers of a private fraternity, party leaders cultivated possible newcomers, groomed them as they moved up the organizational ladder, observed them as they served political apprenticeships, and ultimately tapped those they thought could most effectively carry the party banner in an election. Political parties were an enlisting and training ground for political careers.

The dismantling of parties and the rise of the electronic media have turned the decision to announce into a private affair, almost entirely the province of the individual office seeker. Even though they play virtually no role in attracting or encouraging a potential candidate to get into the race, the media can confer celebrity status overnight. This capability gives people with little political experience, and sometimes scant public recognition, the confidence to throw their hats into the ring. It is not surprising, then, how many recent presidential elections have been won by "outsider" candidates—weak partisans and relative political newcomers like Dwight Eisenhower, John Kennedy, Jimmy Carter, and Ronald Reagan (Orren, 1985:29).

Consider the sharp contrast between the political careers of Franklin Roosevelt, who rose during the parties' heyday, and Ronald Reagan.[3]

Roosevelt entered party politics shortly after graduating from law school, then climbed through the ranks of the Democratic party. In 1910 the county party organization of his native Dutchess County urged him to run for the New York State Senate and helped him win the nomination at the county convention. In 1912 Roosevelt worked on behalf of Woodrow Wilson at the Democratic national convention and was rewarded with an appointment as assistant secretary of the navy. Eight years later, after carefully cultivating Democratic politicians, he was chosen as the party's vice-presidential nominee. In 1928 at the Democratic national convention he delivered his "Happy Warrior" nomination speech for Al Smith. That same year he was drafted and made the party's gubernatorial nominee at the New York state convention. His closest advisers in that campaign, which he won, were the Democratic leader in the state assembly, Democratic State Committee Secretary James A. Farley, and Bronx Democratic boss Edward J. Flynn. In 1932, as the governor of the country's largest state, he was nominated for and elected president.

Ronald Reagan, by contrast, took a job as a radio announcer after college, a path that led him to a Hollywood movie career. As president of the Screen Actors Guild in the 1940s, Reagan was a New Deal Democrat who supported local and national Democratic candidates. In the 1950s he left Hollywood for corporate public relations. He became a spokesman for General Electric and the U.S. Borax Company, hosting television programs they sponsored and representing them throughout the country. As his thinking turned in a conservative direction, Reagan began to get involved in Republican campaigns in California, and he joined the GOP in 1962. He served as cochairman of the California committee for Barry Goldwater in 1964. Two years later, he successfully ran for governor of California. Reagan was aided in this effort by Spencer-Roberts, a political public relations firm that managed his campaign and launched a direct mail appeal to raise money and support. After two terms as governor, he challenged a sitting Republican incumbent president, Gerald Ford, for the party's presidential nomination in 1976. He narrowly failed in that attempt, but was successful four years later and eventually went on to win the general election.

Franklin Roosevelt's political career relied heavily on the machinery and personnel of the political party and included many years of party service. The party apparatus was essential to his decision to enter politics and his subsequent decisions to seek higher office. Ronald Reagan relied instead on the machinery and personnel of public relations, and the decision to enter politics and eventually run for office was his own.

WHERE PARTIES PREVAIL

Despite their strong influence over the outcome of elections, the media cannot take over all the traditional functions of the parties. With the deluge of information they issue, for example, the media cannot possibly simplify electoral choices the way the parties can.

When political scientists began to conduct empirical studies of the American electorate, one of their first major discoveries was how poorly the average voter measured up to the standards of democracy expounded in civics books and Fourth of July speeches. The typical voter, they found, was not especially interested in government and politics; was not very well informed, even about the major issues and candidates of the day; and didn't have a coherent ideology that might allow him to assess new policies or draw connections across disparate issues (see Campbell et al., 1960).

So how could democracy survive? How could the voters live up to the demands of self-government? Most political scientists believed that political parties played a crucial role in filling the gap. Parties acted, as Anthony Downs (1957) noted, as an information-economizing device. In less technical language, they helped to frame or *clarify the choices* available to the voter.

Parties performed this function in one of the three possible ways, depending on how one viewed the structure of the voting decision. According to one line of thinking, parties were important because they were enduring elements in the political world, unlike candidates and factions who appeared and disappeared with each new election. As a result, each party gradually came to be associated in the public mind with a stable cluster of policies and principles. The voters used past performance as a way of predicting what each party might do in the future (Key, 1966; Fiorina, 1981). The legacy of the New Deal was not just that many voters came to love or hate Franklin Roosevelt. They also learned that the Democratic party as a whole was more sympathetic to governmental intervention, social welfare, and labor unions, while the Republicans advocated the causes of limited government, the free market, and business. Thus, when a new candidate, like Adlai Stevenson or John Kennedy, appeared on the scene, the candidate's party attachment allowed voters to learn something about where he stood on the issues without conducting a lengthy inquiry into the newcomer's policy pronouncements.

Other studies of voting behavior have envisioned an even simpler decision process: The voters would use party labels not as a symbol for a set of policies, but as a way of holding a particular group of officeholders responsible for their performance. The voters might not know which candidate was more in favor of an expanded welfare state and they might not even have an opinion about whether such policies were desirable. But they did know whether they were satisfied or dissatisfied with the way things were—whether incumbents had succeeded in providing prosperity and peace. If satisfied, they would vote to keep the incumbent party in power; if sufficiently upset, they would throw out one partisan team and turn over the reins of government to the opposition. Of course, this kind of retrospective evaluation can sometimes occur in nonpartisan elections. But the presence of political parties made it considerably more effective. Parties guaranteed that an incumbent would be held responsible even if he decided not to run again; denied the opportunity to vent their anger on Harry Truman or Lyndon Johnson, the voters could reasonably see Adlai Stevenson or Hubert Humphrey as standing for a continuation of that record, while Dwight Eisenhower and Richard Nixon promised a more decisive break with the past. Party labels also allowed the voters to extend their rancor (or their pleasure) to different offices on the same ballot: someone who was really dissatisfied in 1980, for example, could vote not only for Ronald Reagan, but also for a Republican senator and representative.

A third theory of how the parties assist the electoral decision is even less optimistic about the voters' capacities. Most Americans, it is argued, possess some kind of party allegiance. This identification often has little or no substantive content; in most cases, it is simply inherited from one's parents. Nevertheless, party identification plays a major role in shaping voters' decisions. This third version of the party-voting linkage presents a decidedly ambivalent picture of the American electorate. The voters' decisions are not especially rational, but at least they aren't dangerous. For party identification serves as an anchor that restrains most Americans from supporting the kinds of demagogues and "flash parties" that have often disrupted European democracies.

Regardless of which way parties have helped voters to clarify choices, this is a function that the media cannot perform. As Thomas Patterson has noted, "They are in the news business, not the political business, and, as a result, their norms and imperatives are not those required for the effective organization of electoral coalitions and debate. The press' values produce a news agenda that bears little relationship to the choices at stake in an election" (Patterson, 1989:107).

Another reason the media cannot clarify choices is that, as far as the average voter is concerned, they provide too much information: thousands of column inches and television news stories about campaign events, policy speeches, and candidates' character and abilities. Stimson Bullitt put it cleverly and accurately in the epigraph that heads this chapter: the media transmit more and translate less. The key attribute of political parties was that they helped the voters sort through all of the hubbub and focus on a few central differences.

How well do parties perform this clarifying function in the new media age? Our verdict is different for each of the three versions of how parties clarify choices. If, as in the first theory, a party is viewed as a symbol for a distinct set of policies and principles, there is evidence that the parties clarify choices *better* than they did thirty years ago. To serve this function, the parties do not need extensive grassroots organizations. Nor do they need strong party identification among voters. Even the staunchest independent may use the party labels to help identify Michael Dukakis as a liberal and George Bush as a conservative. All that is required is that those candidates who run under a party's label advocate a roughly similar set of values and programs. American parties have long been criticized, of course, for being too broad and heterogeneous, but this criticism is substantially less true today than it was in the 1950s. The most conservative elements of the Democratic party have either died off or joined the Republicans, while the small number of liberal Republicans have migrated to the Democrats. The issue activists who have played such an important role in recent intraparty battles are more ideologically motivated and more extreme than the rank-and-file. The result, according to Gerald Pomper, is that the voters have a much clearer idea about where the parties stand on the important issues of the day (Pomper, 1972).

As for the second theory of how parties clarify choices—retrospective voting—the electorate can still vote on the basis of an incumbent's past performance. But the weakening of party ties has made such retrospective decisions considerably more difficult, for in many cases the voters are no longer sure where to affix responsibility for a particular problem. When the U.S. economy collapsed in the early 1930s, for example, the electorate not only voted out Herbert Hoover, but also elected a Democratic Congress and Democratic state governments to help carry out Franklin Roosevelt's programs. Although the voters might have disagreed about whether the New Deal worked, there was little doubt as to which party deserved the credit or blame. Hard economic times in the late 1970s, by contrast, brought in a Republican president and a narrow GOP majority in the Senate, but left the House of Representatives securely in Democratic hands. One result of this divided government was that, when the federal deficit ballooned in the early 1980s, most voters had trouble deciding where to point a finger.

But of all the theories, the evidence is clearest for the third. Since 1964, identification with the two major parties has dropped significantly, and the number of independents has grown. Those who maintain a party identification, moreover, use it less as a voting guide. Even among strong partisans, there has been a significant increase in defections, ticket-splitting, and issue voting. Partisanship, then, is a less effective compass to political choice than it once was.

Mobilizing the voters is another function better suited to parties than to the media. Parties traditionally got out the votes in two different ways. First, party precinct organizations were designed not just to sell the party's message but also to make sure that its supporters actually showed up at the polls. Even in the age of television, traditional precinct work still appears to be effective in this regard. Kramer (1970–1971) found that a call or visit from a party worker, while unlikely to change the partisan direction of a person's vote, had a substantial effect on whether a person voted at all. Numerous other studies have come to the same conclusion. Regardless of how actively a party precinct organization tries to mobilize voters, there is evidence that people who identify with a party are more likely to vote than people who do not.

But as party organizations weaken and more Americans lose their party identification, voter turnout continues to dwindle (Orren, 1987:99). Unfortunately, this is a case where the media, while helping to undermine parties, cannot substitute for them. Others have tried to fill the void. A variety of interest groups (civil rights, labor, religious, civic) and government agencies work hard to register voters and encourage them to exercise their right. Candidate campaigns take pains to get their supporters to the polls. Still, after the dust settles, and despite pockets of success, disappointingly few people vote. None of these efforts has replaced the former mobilizing power of political parties.

So far, we have spoken of six electoral functions that parties have traditionally performed. Of course, party functions do not end once the election is over. Parties also play an important role in governing and policymaking. Most political scientists agree that parties must aggregate interests, formulate policies, and coordinate the activities of different office-holders and branches of government.

The problem is that how well the parties perform these functions depends on how well they accomplish their electoral mission. Elected officials accord their greatest attention to those individuals and organizations who helped them get elected in the first place and whose continued support is necessary to their reelection. As the saying goes, they dance with the one who brought them there. As politicians rely less on partisan backing and more on the communications media, parties are left with fewer carrots and sticks with which to persuade them to say no to predatory interest groups or to adopt the position staked out by party leaders.

The failure to appreciate this point has, in our judgment, led to a strange duality in much of the popular commentary on political parties. On the one hand, pundits have often lamented the weakened position of the parties in government, which, they say, causes policy stalemate and gives growing power to special interest groups. Yet most of these same critics shudder at the thought of granting parties the resources and powers they need in the electoral arena. They express outrage at the slightest sign that the parties are trying to check the spread of presidential primaries or reward the party faithful with jobs or contracts. In our view, they can't have it both ways; weak electoral parties ensure weak governing parties.

The link between the media and American politics has always been close. Indeed, important changes in the organization and technology of the press have gone hand in hand with changes in election campaigns

TABLE 10.1
Key Intermediary Functions in Elections

Function	Formerly Performed by	Currently Performed by
Communicating with voters	Political parties	News media Candidate campaigns (and their consultants)
Evaluating candidates	Political parties	News media
Selecting party nominees	Political parties	Voters
Recruiting candidates	Political parties	No group or institution (individuals decide on their own)
Mobilizing voters	Political parties	Political parties } very Interest groups } weakly Candidate campaigns }
Clarifying electoral choices	Political parties	Political parties (weakly)

throughout American history (Abramson, Arterton, and Orren, 1988:66–91). Over the past three decades, as the power of traditional intermediary institutions like political parties has been eclipsed, this linkage has grown even stronger and the media have assumed a commanding role in elections. As Harry Holloway and John George have written, "A society with weak parties, countless factions, and a demanding, if somewhat cynical, electorate is one in which there is much for the media to do" (Holloway and George, 1979:239).

Table 10.1 summarizes our discussion of who is now performing which traditional party functions. The mass media have largely supplanted political parties as the conduit through which candidates communicate with voters and through which voters become educated on election issues. Individual campaigns have taken over much of this function as well. They now control such activities as fund raising, field operations, polling, press relations, getting out the vote, and especially advertising.

The media have also become the principal institution that evaluates the candidates and their standing in the races, judging whether they are strong or weak, worthy or unworthy, doing well or doing poorly.

Nevertheless, there are ways in which the media cannot fill the parties' shoes. As direct primaries have increasingly drawn the public into the nomination process, the function of selecting candidates has passed to the voters themselves. Moreover, two of the functions once reserved for parties are no longer performed by any institution, at least not vigorously. Candidate recruitment is virtually a thing of the past. And while psychological attachment to a party still has some power to get people to the polls, voter mobilization is not a hallmark of contemporary American politics.

To a greater extent, the parties continue to clarify and structure electoral choices for voters. They do this less effectively than they once did. Yet even in a country where distinctions between parties are relatively weak, the party label still serves as a symbol for a cluster of policies and principles that yields helpful cues to the voters.

THE PUBLIC-PRIVATE BALANCING ACT

As the preceding discussion should suggest, political parties and the media, as intermediary agencies, are inevitably two-sided institutions. They have both a public and a private face; they are, one might say, *semipublic institutions*. In order to link the public to political leaders and government, these institutions must be privately organized and operated. (Otherwise, they would simply be creatures of the very leaders or government they were trying to influence.) But they also play a vital role in the political and governing process and serve important public functions.

In the case of political parties, this public-private duality has taken shape gradually since the nineteenth century. Originally, parties were little more than aggregations of like-minded individuals who came together to promote various interests and policies and to gain the benefits of political power. Parties were never mentioned in the Constitution and not in state law until the late 1800s. Eventually, however, many Americans came to feel that, since the parties exercised such important political power, they should be regulated by the government. The first step in this direction came with the adoption of the partisan version of the Australian ballot (a ballot marked in secret and printed, distributed, and counted by public authorities) in the 1880s, in which state governments officially recognized party-nominated slates of candidates. Having bestowed legal status on the parties, the states next found it necessary to determine who was entitled to the party label, which led to the adoption of the party primary in the early 1900s. "By 1920," wrote Austin Ranney, "most states had adopted a succession of mandatory statutes regulating every major aspect of the parties' structures and operations" (Ranney, 1975:81). This trend probably reached its zenith in 1944, when the U.S. Supreme Court, in outlawing the whites-only primary, declared that a party whose nomination system was prescribed in state law became, in effect, "an agency of the state."[4]

The courts thereby announced that political parties were institutions that performed important public functions. But if parties become too closely regulated by government, if they really are nothing more than creatures of the state, then they lose the flexibility and self-governing capacity that are necessary to represent public demands and grievances.

And so, more recently, the pendulum has started to swing back in the opposite direction as the Supreme Court has affirmed the private status of political parties. In a series of decisions handed down over the last two decades, the Supreme Court has consistently upheld the superiority of national party rules over state laws, declaring that "a political party's choice among the various ways of determining the makeup of a state's delegation to the party's national convention is protected by the Constitution."[5]

Within the Democratic party, controversial battles and debates over presidential nomination rules have also reflected this public vs. private duality. Party reformers who criticized the "smoke-filled room" traditions of the party tried to make the presidential selection process more public and more accountable. They sought to broaden participation and make room for divergent points of view. Party regulars, on the other hand, defended rules and procedures that enhanced the influence of party professionals and strengthened peer review. They hoped to keep the selection of nominees essentially an internal affair.

The mass media also exhibit both a public and a private face. As with political parties, Supreme Court rulings support both faces of the media. For example, the Court has recognized that the press plays a unique and critical role in a self-governing democracy by providing the information necessary for the public to make intelligent political choices.[6] Moreover, as the Court has noted, the press provides a "powerful antidote to any abuses of power by government officials" and helps keep them "responsible to the people whom they were elected to serve."[7] However, the Court has also made clear that the government cannot *require* the press to perform these public functions. Newspapers, for instance, are private entities, not "common carriers" obligated to accept the messages of anyone who wants space in the news columns or on the editorial page.[8] In short, the First Amendment does not permit government to meddle in the process by which newspaper editors decide what and what not to publish. By and large, the same is true of broadcasters, although the Court has upheld statutes and regulations by the Federal Communications Commission (FCC) that require licensees to provide air time to others under certain narrow circumstances.[9]

Media professionals disagree whether the press is more public or more private. For example, a raging debate over the proper role of television news recently broke out at NBC (Lundberg, 1989). On one side stood those who saw network news as a public service that should be shielded from the financial imperatives of other businesses. The news division, in their view, ought to be subsidized by the profits of the network's entertainment division. On the other side were those who claimed that the news media are private businesses subject to the demands of the marketplace. The news department must carry its own financial weight.

In a democracy, intermediaries like political parties and the press are neither wholly public nor wholly private. Indeed, the appropriate question is not whether they are more public or more private but where they should fall on the public-private continuum to best perform their mediating functions. One's assessment of how well political parties and the media are doing their jobs depends largely on how satisfied or dissatisfied one is with their positions on this continuum.

Elections are among the most public activities in a democracy. However, we conduct them these days in the most private of ways. Much of our discomfort with recent campaigns can be traced to this privatized style of electioneering.[10] It pervades almost every aspect of contemporary electoral politics, resulting in an "electronic plebiscitary democracy."

> The most striking feature of the system of electronic plebiscitary democracy is direct, continuous, highly intense communication between Presidents (and would-be Presidents) at one end, and scores of millions of people at the other. The politicians reach the people via polls. In this relationship, the politicians act almost solely in their capacity as popular leaders and scarcely at all in their capacity as party officials or government managers. The people act almost solely in their capacity as atomized individual television-watchers, and scarcely at all in their capacity as citizens of states and communities or members of political parties or other voluntary associations (*New Republic,* 1984).

The privatization of modern campaigns is especially evident in the role of television. Public rallies and speeches have given way to televised appearances in which candidates speak directly to individual voters in the privacy of their homes. The viewers' attention is focused squarely on the personal qualities of the candidates. The spotlight shines brightly on day-to-day squabbles among the candidates and even brighter on their gaffes. The bulk of the coverage is about who's in the lead, and more recently, about the inside strategy and tactics of the candidates. The main casualty of this preoccupation with personality and process is serious public discourse. Little effort is made to connect the campaign to the central issues of the day—the issues that will shape the way people are governed after election day.

Unlike other Western democracies, the United States leaves the ownership and control of television largely in private hands. For the most part, broadcast media are privately owned and commercially financed. In these advertiser-driven media, pressure for audience ratings is intense. Indeed, commercial television today can no longer afford the luxury of insulating the news from the ratings. Inevitably, entertainment values intrude in all programming, including the news, which more and more is produced to hook and please the audience.

Campaigns exploit this to the hilt. According to Michael Deaver, Ronald Reagan's former aide and image maker: "The media, while they won't admit it, are not in the news business; they're in entertainment. We tried to create the most entertaining, visually attractive scene to fill that box, so that the networks would have to use it" (Russert, 1990). The campaigns ration the media's access to the candidates, providing instead alluring photo opportunities and dramatic visuals.

Succumbing to the need for tight structure and fast pacing to beat the competition, networks and local stations chop the candidates' words into shorter and shorter sound bites. In the twenty years since 1968, the typical sound bite in presidential campaigns has shrunk from forty-three seconds to a mere nine (Hallin, 1990).

Privatized democracy also finds expression in the candidates' and the media's reliance on public opinion polls. More and more, citizens' involvement is reduced to the passive and private act of registering their opinions in a poll, a shallow form of participation at best. Even more troubling is the hold that polls have over news coverage. Not only does poll-based information command a substantial and growing portion of the news, but the amount and content of coverage that candidates receive is to a large extent determined by their standing in the polls (Patterson, 1989:104–107).

Our system defends the right of private entrepreneurs to sell consulting services to campaigns. Today every would-be prince wants a gang of these Machiavellis on the campaign payroll. These technical experts, who set the strategy, message, and tone of so many campaigns, are not attached to more permanent, public, and hence more accountable, organizations like political parties. Reinforcing privatized democracy, they sell services like polling, direct mail, and paid advertising that establish direct pipelines between campaigns and voters. In most democracies, candidates cannot purchase advertising time. In the United States, they can, and the results have been less than encouraging. Increasingly, the airwaves are filled with highly personal, crudely manipulative attack ads designed to sully an opponent's reputation. By and large, the press has permitted the admen to set the campaign agenda and dialogue with these ads. And although the ads are sometimes misleading or false, and of dubious relevance to the office at stake, the press has not vigorously dissected them or held their authors accountable.

The chorus of lamentations about deficiencies in the selection of leaders grows louder with each passing election. Everyone has their favorite complaints. Yet the problem lies deeper than any particular shortcoming. It can be traced to the process of intermediation itself.

Political columnist David Broder and network executive Timothy Russert have recently been crusading to get the U.S. media to assume greater public responsibility in covering election campaigns. They have issued a plea for a more vigilant press corps. As they envision it, the press would help keep the news agenda focused on relevant and nontrivial issues; scrutinize nonelected consultants; carefully monitor, dissect, and criticize campaign advertising; insist on more substantive candidate debates; and demand regular and routine access to the candidates in press conferences (Broder, 1990; Russert, 1990). Other journalists have urged that the networks provide free air time in the evening to candidates or parties during campaigns, a common practice in other democratic countries. With this more public posture, the press would hardly be a neutral messenger that simply reports the news as it occurs.

If adopted, these ideas might go some way toward reducing the excessive privatization that has marked recent campaigns. But two caveats are worth bearing in mind. First, one ought to ask how realistic many of these proposals are. In the heat of the 1992 campaign, will the media actually live up to such high standards? In the end, the news media are private, profit-making businesses that hope to attract large audiences. Their behavior is governed by news and entertainment values, not political values. As Thomas Patterson has put it, "The issue for the press is not which candidates would be good for a majority of the country but which are material for good news stories" (Patterson, 1989:100). Although many observers criticized the media's obsession with polling in 1988, there are few signs that any major media organizations are planning to stem this tide in 1992.

The other caveat is that even if they do police election campaigns more aggressively, the media will somehow have to be held accountable. If the press becomes more assertive, more prescriptive, and more judgmental, then how can we redress the possible errors and abuses of a powerful and unelected elite? Expecting news organizations to monitor each other seems a vain hope. According to some, the media already are the Fourth Estate, yet they are not subject to the kinds of checks and balances that restrain the other three. Calls for an accountable press, however, understandably make journalists and defenders of the press nervous. While it seems natural enough to hold candidates or intermediaries like political parties accountable, the idea of applying such restraints to the news media is not easily reconciled with the cherished ideal of a free press.

The decline of parties has made the media the most powerful intermediary in American politics. The press must now face head-on a question it has too often tried to avoid: What public purposes should it serve while preserving its status as a private, nongovernmental institution?

NOTES

Our thanks to Carla Lim, Scott Matheson, John Watkins, and Ali Webb for their help in preparing this chapter.

1. The following discussion of the partisan press and its decline relies on Abramson, Arterton, and Orren (1988: 10–16, 80–86).

2. Television coverage of the 1968 Democratic convention helped to create the perception in many people's minds that the nomination system needed reforming, and thus led to the creation of the first party reform commission, the McGovern-Fraser Commission. Television also enhanced the legitimacy of primaries by presenting their results as the authentic voice of "the people."

3. This contrast appears in Salmore and Salmore (1989: 2–4) based upon biographical material in Burns, 1956 and Cannon, 1982.

4. *Smith* v. *Allwright,* 321 U.S. 649 (1944).

5. *Democratic Party* v. *Wisconsin ex rel LaFollette,* 450 U.S. 123 (1981); *Cousins* v. *Wigoda,* 419 U.S. 477 (1975).

6. *New York Times Co.* v. *Sullivan,* 376 U.S. 254 (1964); *Saxbe* v. *Washington Post Co.,* 417 U.S. 843 (1974) (Powell, J., dissenting); *Houchins* v. *KOED, Inc.,* 438 U.S. 1 (1978) (Stevens, J., dissenting); see also Meiklejohn, 1948; Emerson, 1970.

7. *Mills* v. *Alabama,* 384 U.S. 214 (1966); see also Stewart, 1975; Blasi, 1977.

8. *Miami Herald* v. *Tornillo,* 418 U.S. 241 (1974); *Chicago Joint Board, Amalgamated Clothing Workers of America* v. *Chicago Tribune Co.,* 435 F.2d 470 (7th Cir. 1970), *cert. denied,* 402 U.S. 973 (1971); *Schuck* v. *Carroll Daily Herald,* 247 N.W. 813 (Iowa 1933).

9. *Red Lion Broadcasting Co.* v. *FCC,* 395 U.S. 367 (1969); *CBS, Inc.* v. *FCC,* 453 U.S. 367 (1981).

10. This point is discussed at length in Abramson, Arterton, and Orren (1988), which we draw upon here.

PART FIVE

The Parties in Government

11

The Congressional Party: Evolving Organizational, Agenda-Setting, and Policy Roles

BARBARA SINCLAIR

According to the theory of party government, the winning party is expected to organize the government, set the policy agenda, and enact that agenda into law. In the United States, the congressional parties have traditionally played an important role in organizing the legislature, but the governmental structure and the sort of parties it has fostered have often made it difficult for congressional party leaders to perform the policy functions. Because members of Congress have never owed their election to strong centralized parties, numerical majorities do not translate directly into policy majorities. Although almost all members of Congress are elected under the banner of one or the other of the two major parties, individual members are not bound either to work or to vote with their fellow party members.

Most observers agree that a constellation of changes in the Congress during the 1970s greatly exacerbated the already severe problems confronting congressional party leaders. The dispersion of influence within the Congress and changes in the electoral arena that further reduced the influence of parties on members' reelection chances, they argued, made strong party leadership impossible.

Yet the mid- and late 1980s witnessed the emergence of strong, policy-oriented majority party leadership in the House of Representatives. When compared to its predecessors of the last half-century, the current majority party leadership is more involved and more decisive in organizing the party and the chamber, setting the policy agenda, shaping legislation, and determining legislative outcomes. The purpose of this essay is to describe the expanded role of the leadership and the party and to explain its emergence.

The essay begins with a brief sketch of the restricted role of party and party leadership in the 1950s and 1960s. Included in this section is a discussion of the changes in Congress during the 1970s that were widely interpreted as further constraining the exercise of party leadership. A description of the expanded role of the current majority party leadership in the House, as well as an analysis of the emergence of strong, policy-oriented leadership, constitutes the second section and the heart of the essay. The third section is devoted to Senate comparisons: Has the role of the party leadership and the importance of parties changed in the Senate as well? The final section attempts to provide a systematic answer to a key question: Why has a stronger congressional party emerged in a weak party era?

PARTIES AND PARTY LEADERSHIP DURING THE COMMITTEE GOVERNMENT AND EARLY POST-REFORM ERA

The period from approximately 1920 through 1970 can be characterized as an era of committee government in the House of Representatives (Fenno, 1965, 1973). Legislation was the product of a number of autonomous committees headed by powerful chairmen who derived their positions from their seniority on the committees. The chairmen's great organizational and procedural powers over their committees, as well as the norm of reciprocity that dictated mutual deference among committees, protected most legislation from serious challenge on the floor of the House.

Within this system, the role of the majority party leadership was restricted. Both the Speaker's meager institutional resources and party factionalism (especially in the case of the Democrats, who were in the majority for most of the period after 1930 and continuously from 1955 on) limited the scope of the party leadership's involvement and influence. Committee assignments, then as now, were made through the congressional party, thus potentially providing the leadership with its most significant role in organizing the party and the chamber. During the committee government era, the seniority rule for choosing committee chairmen and the norm guaranteeing members the right to stay on a committee once assigned to it limited the leadership's role. The party leadership did exert considerable influence over the initial assignment of members to committees, but even here the leaders' role was restricted inasmuch as the party leaders did not serve on the "committee on committees."

Since Franklin Roosevelt's time, whenever the president and the congressional majority have been of the same party, the president has set the policy agenda of the majority party and the Congress. During the committee government era, when control of Congress and the White House was divided, the majority party's policy agenda consisted of whatever emerged from the autonomous committees. The House Democratic party lacked any mechanism either for developing a party agenda or for imposing one upon powerful committee chairmen. In the 1950s the ideological split between northern and southern Democrats would, in any case, have made agreement upon an agenda impossible.

The party leadership's role in the policy process was largely restricted to facilitating passage at the floor stage of legislation written by autonomous committees (Ripley, 1967). Party leaders seldom if ever interceded in committee to shape legislation; the chairmen's power and norms of deference to committee worked against such involvement.

Even the leadership's role at the floor stage was somewhat restricted. Although the Speaker as presiding officer had considerable control over the flow of legislation to and on the floor, the independence of the Rules Committee during this period meant that the party leadership's control over the scheduling of legislation for floor consideration was only partial. As a result of intercommittee reciprocity, most committees could expect to pass much of their legislation on the floor without great difficulty; accordingly, committees and their chairs did not often require help from the leadership. Yet in the case of those highly controversial issues that were fought out on the floor, the leadership often confronted a deep north-south split and had great difficulty in successfully building winning coalitions.

Elections in the late 1950s and the 1960s brought into the House a large number of liberal northern Democrats who found this system ill-suited to the advancement of their goals. The powerful committee chairmen were largely conservative southerners; they (not the party leadership or the party as a whole) set the policy agenda and determined the substance of legislation. The chairmen thwarted the liberals' policy goals by blocking liberal legislation, and frustrated the liberals' desire to participate meaningfully in the legislative process by running their committees in an autocratic way (Bolling, 1965).

In the late 1960s and early 1970s reform-minded members succeeded in instituting a series of changes in chamber and party rules that transformed the House. Sunshine reforms opened up most committee markups and conference committee meetings to the media and the public. The supply of resources available to Congress and its members (especially staff) was expanded and distributed much more broadly among members. A series of rules changes shifted influence from committee chairmen to subcommittee chairmen and rank-and-file members. The subcommittee bill of rights removed from committee chairmen the power to appoint subcommittee chairmen and gave it to the Democratic caucus of the committee; it guaranteed subcommittees automatic referral of legislation as well as adequate budget and staff. Members were limited to chairing no more than one subcommittee each (Dodd and Oppenheimer, 1977).

Some of the rules changes of the 1970s had centralizing potential. The requirement that committee chairmen and the chairmen of Appropriations subcommittees win majority approval in the Democratic caucus was intended to make them responsive to a party majority. The Speaker was given the right to nominate Democratic members of the Rules Committee subject only to ratification by the caucus. The committee-assignment function was shifted to the new Steering and Policy Committee, which the Speaker chairs and a number of whose members he appoints. The new multiple referral rules gave the Speaker authority to set a deadline for reporting when legislation is referred to more than one committee. Moreover, the budget process, too, has centralizing potential (Ellwood and Thurber, 1981). These various rules changes either directly augmented the party leadership's resources or gave it new leverage. Yet many scholars argued that, on balance, the reforms of the 1970s weakened the party leadership and reduced party influence (Cooper and Brady, 1981; Smith and Deering, 1984; Waldman, 1980; Oppenheimer, 1981b; and Rohde and Shepsle, 1987).

Augmented resources, rules changes, and the attendant changes in norms increased the number of significant actors in the legislative process and thus made the environment in which the leadership operated much less predictable. Members' desires to participate fully in the legislative process, their new staff resources, the recorded teller vote, and the reduced power of committee chairmen led to a huge increase in amendments offered on the floor. Intercommittee reciprocity no longer protected legislation from floor attack, and the leadership's task of building winning coalitions at the floor stage became a much more formidable challenge. The reforms dispersed legislative decisionmaking power to about 150 highly active subcommittees, the scholars argued, and the leadership lacked the resources to coordinate the resulting fractured process. The party leaders' ability to influence their members declined still further as members increasingly perceived their reelection to be primarily dependent upon their own efforts and decreasingly dependent upon party success.

THE EMERGENCE OF STRONG, POLICY-ORIENTED LEADERSHIP IN THE LATE 1980s

In the 1970s and early 1980s the party leadership was often portrayed as incapable of coping with the reformed House. By the 100th Congress (1987–1988), however, it was being hailed by journalists as strong, policy oriented, and successful (Hook, 1987; Cohen, 1987) and excoriated by Republicans as tyrannical (Cheney, 1989). As we shall see in the following discussion of the leadership's expanded role, its development can be linked to the altered political context of the 1980s combined with the reforms of the 1970s.

Organizing the Party and the Chamber

The political parties have traditionally organized the House of Representatives. The Speaker, the chamber's presiding officer, is chosen by the majority party, and the assignment of members to committees is carried out through the parties. All committees are chaired by majority party members, and the majority party holds a majority of the seats on all committees.

Every two years, after the elections and before the new Congress convenes, the members of each of the two parties meet. The Democratic Caucus, as the organization of all House Democrats is called, nominates a candidate for Speaker and elects both a floor leader and a whip. So long as the Democrats maintain their majority in the chamber, their candidate will be elected Speaker on the first day of the Congress, inasmuch as the speakership vote is always a straight party-line vote. The Republican Conference, the organization of all House Republicans, chooses its candidate for Speaker, who will become the minority floor leader; it also elects a whip.

During the committee government era, rules and customs gave the Speaker a variety of opportunities to influence the organization of the party and the chamber. For example, the Speaker appointed all majority party members to select committees and special committees as well as to a number of commissions. The reforms of the 1970s, however, greatly augmented the leadership's role. In 1975 the committee-assignment function was shifted from the Democratic members of the Ways and Means Committee to the new Steering and Policy Committee, which is chaired by the Speaker. The thirty-one members of the committee include the core leadership (Speaker, majority leader, whip, and chief deputy whip) and eight individuals appointed by the Speaker. By custom, a freshman, a woman, and a black are included among the eight. As Speaker (1977–1986), Tip O'Neill allowed the groups representing those members to choose their representative, but Jim Wright in 1987 reasserted the Speaker's prerogative to make the choices himself.

Before 1975 the Speaker could influence the assignments made by a "committee on committees" on which he did not serve. Now, although he cannot dictate, the Speaker is the dominant influence. Norms of fairness that require some attention to seniority and considerable attention to geographical balance constrain the leadership's discretion in making assignments to the most desirable committees. Nevertheless, the leaders can and do use their influence to ensure that loyalists are appointed to those committees most important to the party program. Before a Democrat receives an appointment to the key money committees (Ways and Means, Appropriations, and Budget), the Speaker usually has a talk with the candidate to make sure he or she understands and can assume the obligation to support the party position in a crunch.

Leaders also use their influence over committee assignments to do favors for members—sometimes as a reward, and sometimes to amass chits useful in the future. When Jim Chapman received a coveted Appropriations assignment in late 1988, the leadership was rewarding him for casting a politically difficult vote that gave the leadership victory on a key element of its program. It was also sending a clear message to the Democratic membership that a willingness to take risks for the party would be rewarded.

In 1975 the Speaker was given the power to nominate at the beginning of each Congress the chairman and all the Democratic members of the Rules Committee, subject only to ratification by the caucus. The primary route by which major legislation reaches the floor is via rules from the Rules Committee. These rules allow legislation to be taken up out of order; they also govern the amount of debate time and, sometimes, the amendments permitted. Accordingly, the leadership controls floor scheduling only so long as the Rules Committee is a reliable ally. During much of the period of committee government, the Rules Committee was controlled by a bipartisan conservative coalition. To get legislation supported by a majority of Democrats to the floor, the Speaker was forced to bargain with the committee, and his resources for doing so were limited.

By the early 1970s changes in its membership had transformed the Rules Committee from an independent obstructionist force to a usually reliable ally (Oppenheimer, 1981a). Both the 1975 rules change and the way in which speakers have used their appointive powers have made the committee an arm of the leadership. Reliability as well as political institutional sagacity have been the criteria of choice. In addition to appointing members upon whom they can depend, O'Neill and Wright have guarded against the development of norms constricting the Speaker's discretion. When the California delegation endorsed one of its members to succeed a departing Californian on the Rules Committee, O'Neill publicly stated that he considered such state delegation endorsements illegitimate and appointed a different Californian. Both Speakers have insisted on going through the formalities of reappointing Rules members in full at the beginning of a Congress so as to remind them that the Speaker has no obligation to reappoint.

During the committee government era, the party organization was skeletal by today's standards. When Sam Rayburn was Speaker (1940–1946, 1949–1952, 1955–1961), the caucus met only at the beginning of a congress and then only to ratify decisions made elsewhere. In Rayburn's view, meetings would only provide a forum for the factions in the party to confront each other directly and would thereby worsen the intraparty split. A Steering Committee existed on paper but never met. The whip system—which consisted of a whip, a deputy whip, and approximately eighteen regionally elected zone whips—was not very active. It seldom systematically gathered information on Democrats' voting intentions and never engaged in organized persuasion efforts. Because the zone whips were chosen by the members of their regional zones, the leadership could not depend on their being loyal to the party position.

Since Rayburn's day, party organization has become much more elaborate, with many of the new positions being filled by leadership appointment (Dodd, 1979; Sinclair, 1983). The whip system underwent a major expansion in the 1970s and 1980s. To solve the problem of unreliable zone whips, the leadership appointed some at-large whips. As the House environment became increasingly unpredictable during the 1970s, more such whips were added to aid the leadership in information gathering and voter mobilization. Then, as more Democrats perceived that it was beneficial to be a whip, the system expanded further. Such appointments became favors that the leaders could dispense to their members. As of the 101st Congress (1989–1990), the whip system consisted of the whip, a chief deputy whip, fifteen deputy whips, three task force chairmen, sixty-five at-large whips, and eighteen zone whips. All but the zone whips were leadership appointees.

The majority party leadership's role in organizing the party and the chamber is extensive by any standard and much greater than the role of the party leadership during the committee government era. Rules changes during the 1970s that promoted this greater role were motivated by the reformers' desire to make independent power centers, such as the Rules Committee and the "committee on committees," more responsive to party majorities. The expansion of the whip system, however, was the leadership's response to the more unpredictable environment.

This increased role represents a major expansion of leadership resources. It provides the leaders with many opportunities to do favors for members. As leaders do not control the members' reelection chances, they must persuade—not command. Although explicit quid pro quos are seldom involved, the leaders' persuasion efforts are certainly facilitated by the supply of favors they can dispense. More important, the leadership's role in organizing party and chamber allows it to influence outcomes through the choice of personnel and provides it with tools crucial to its expanded policy role.

Setting the Agenda

In December 1986, immediately after being chosen as the Democrats' nominee for Speaker, Jim Wright outlined a policy agenda for the majority party and the House. Deficit reduction achieved in part through a tax increase received the most press attention, but clean water legislation, a highway bill, trade legislation, welfare reform, and a farm bill were also included. In his acceptance speech on January 6, 1987, and in his televised reply to Reagan's state of the union address on January 31, Wright further specified and publicized the agenda, adding aid to education and insurance against catastrophic illness.

Over the course of the 100th Congress, the Speaker continued to call attention to and raise expectations of action on these items in a variety of public and in-House forums. He used his powers as Speaker to ensure that these bills were given preferential consideration in the chamber. As items were enacted they were repeatedly cited as accomplishments, and some new issues were added to the agenda. By and large, however, the Speaker kept the focus upon the original agenda, and by the end of the 100th Congress every item on that agenda had become law.

Special political conditions facilitated the Speaker's aggressive agenda setting. President Reagan had been weakened by the Iran-Contra scandal, the loss of a Senate majority, and his lame-duck status. The House Democrats believed that they finally had the opportunity to pass legislation that had been stymied during six years of the Reagan administration—if they were disciplined enough to exploit the opportunity. They very much wanted to establish a record of effective governance going into the 1988 elections. In short, the House Democrats wanted policy leadership.

Agenda setting is a key aspect of policy leadership. In drawing up his priorities for the congress, the Speaker consulted with other members and also relied upon his judgment about what legislation members really wanted and needed to advance their goals, on the one hand, and what would pass, on the other. The resulting agenda contained items important to all segments of the party; a majority of these items had broad support throughout the party.

Though particularly bold in the 100th Congress, the leadership's role in agenda setting had been developing throughout the 1980s. Actually, in response to pressure from liberals who objected to the party's policy agenda being simply the result of the decisions of twenty-odd autonomous committees, Speaker Albert in 1975 had attempted to set a party agenda (see *Congressional Record,* January 14, 1975, p. 19). But splits within the Democratic party doomed that effort (see *Congressional Quarterly Weekly Report,* June 28, 1975, pp. 1332–1333). In 1981, after Reagan had won the presidency and the Republicans (surprisingly) had won control of the Senate, O'Neill used his initial speech upon being elected Speaker to pledge cooperation with the new president (see *Congressional Record,* January 5, 1981, p. 96). In 1983 and 1985, by contrast, O'Neill laid out the outlines of a Democratic agenda that was an alternative to the president's (see *Congressional Record,* January 3, 1983, p. H4; January 3, 1985, p. H3). The Democrats' televised reply to Reagan's annual state of the union address was increasingly used during the 1980s to highlight alternative approaches although these were not usually presented as the official leadership agenda.

In 1989 the Democratic leadership responded to the political dictates of deference to a newly elected president's legislative wishes by promising full cooperation. The Speaker nevertheless set out a Democratic alternative agenda. Although it was not as extensive or specific as the 100th Congress agenda, the leadership's engagement in counteragenda setting in the first year of a new president's term suggests that this has now become a normal rather than extraordinary leadership activity.

With divided control increasingly perceived as the normal situation, Democrats have become more concerned about preventing presidential dominance of agenda setting. Given the constraints on policy innovation imposed by the big deficits, effective counteragenda setting must be centralized. Hence the party leaders must be the central players. House Democrats expect their leaders to consult extensively, but they also expect them to engage in agenda setting rather than leaving that matter to the committees and subcommittees. Of course, House Democrats also expect the political needs and policy goals of the Democratic membership to be the primary determinants of the agenda that their leaders put together.

Shaping Legislation

Contemporary party leaders more frequently play a role in shaping the substance of legislation than did their predecessors of the committee government era. When party leaders do intervene in a process that used to be a committee monopoly, they do so as agents of the Democratic membership. That is, they do so primarily in order to advance legislation high on the Democratic agenda and to make sure it and other important legislation reflects the policy preferences of the Democratic membership.

The party leadership itself now sometimes directly negotiates over substance with other key actors such as Senate leaders and the president.

In September 1987 when the Gramm-Rudman budget-balancing legislation was being rewritten, in November 1987 when a two-year budget agreement between Congress and the White House was being worked out, and in December 1987 when the continuing resolution to fund the entire government for most of 1988 was at issue, the key players for the House were not the committee chairmen but the party leadership. In negotiations with the Bush administration on a contra aid package and on the budget in 1989, party leaders again played central roles.

In each of these cases, decisions highly consequential to the party and the membership as a whole were at stake; most involved broadly encompassing omnibus legislation and negotiations with cabinet-level administration officials. Under such circumstances, the party leadership perforce gets involved; it alone has the legitimacy that derives from being the elected agent of the majority party. As such, the leadership has a basis for speaking for and making agreements on behalf of the majority that other entities lack.

The leadership sometimes plays a direct role in within-House negotiations as well. In 1987 the Speaker brokered the compromise version of the catastrophic health insurance bill. The two committees to which the legislation was referred, Ways and Means and Commerce, produced versions that conflicted in a number of areas; but the majority members of both realized that, to pass the legislation on the floor, they needed to agree upon one bill. In 1988 the party leadership decided to make passage of antidrug legislation a top priority. As provisions of the bill fell into the jurisdiction of a large number of different committees, the Speaker delegated to the Majority Leader the job of coordinating the work of those committees and putting together the composite bill.

Sometimes the leadership will set guidelines or parameters. In 1987, for example, the Speaker strongly influenced the budget resolution both by proposing the basic formula for achieving the necessary savings and by insisting that provision be made to fund the programs that made up the Democratic agenda that he had formulated (see Palazzolo, 1989). He then told the Ways and Means Committee that the tax bill it had reported to carry out the budget agreement needed to be progressive in character.

A great deal of the leaders' influence on legislative substance is the result of their behind-the-scenes efforts to get members at loggerheads to compromise and to persuade committee leaders to be responsive to majority sentiment in the party. During the Reagan administration, for example, the conservative chairman of the Defense Appropriations Subcommittee was regularly prevailed upon to include Democratic majority–supported arms control amendments in his defense funding bill so as to protect them from presidential vetoes. And for several years, a number of younger members had attempted to change the appeals process for veterans' benefits but had been stymied by opposition from the chairman of the Veterans Affairs Committee. The Speaker called a meeting of the chairman and the younger members and, after a lengthy discussion, the chairman promised to move on the bill.

Finally, the leadership may influence substantive outcomes through the decisions it makes on matters of process. When bills are sequentially referred to several committees (an increasingly common occurrence), the Speaker sets deadlines for when all but the first committee must report the legislation. The amount of time allowed often affects the result, especially near the end of a congress. In the fall of 1988 the Judiciary Committee was given a very short sequential referral of the veterans' appeal board legislation, leaving enough time for that bill to complete the legislative process; but a more generous time limit for reporting back the banking bill contributed to that legislation's demise. Decisions about when legislation is considered on the floor and about the ground rules for floor consideration can also have a major impact, as we shall see shortly.

The expanded role of the party leadership in shaping legislation was made possible by the 1970s reforms that reduced the power and independence of committee chairmen. Weakened by the subcommittee bill of rights, which reduced their control over their committees' agenda, organization, and staffing, chairmen were made dependent upon a secret ballot majority vote in the Democratic caucus for their position. Accordingly, chairmen had to become responsive to the caucus majority and the party leadership insofar as it speaks for that majority.

Changes in the legislative process have made that expanded role necessary. In 1975 the House instituted a rule allowing the referral of legislation to more than one committee, and in the 1980s an increasing proportion of major legislation was multiply referred (Davidson, Oleszek, and Kephart, 1988; Collie and Cooper, 1989). When several committees are involved in the drafting of legislation, a coordinating and integrating entity becomes essential. As a result of the huge budget deficit (which constrained legislative choices) and the deep ideological divisions between congressional Democrats and the White House, especially during the Reagan years, Congress had to do much of its legislating through the passage of a small number of huge omnibus bills. The unpalatable decisions made necessary by the deficits have been easier to pass when combined into a package in which all members share the pain. Moreover, such bills are difficult for a president to veto and could thus be used to further Democratic objectives that Reagan opposed. Given the number of issues and committees involved in these omnibus measures, as well as the stakes for the party, not only a coordinating entity but one that can speak for the party as a whole is needed to make such a process function.

As a consequence of the leadership's expanded role in shaping the substance of legislation, the policy preferences of party majorities undoubtedly have more influence on major legislation than they did during the committee government era. To be sure, most legislation is still written in committee without any party leadership involvement. Furthermore, when the leadership does bring the policy preferences of the Democratic membership to bear in the process, it is usually the leadership's reading of those preferences. Although the Democratic caucus is available as a forum on which majorities can formally express their views through the passage of resolutions, it is seldom used in that way. Leaders do have many opportunities for learning what their members want, and the legitimacy of their involvement in the shaping of legislation depends upon their representing members' preferences with reasonable accuracy. Most of the time, leaders do act as faithful agents of the party majority.

Committees are much less insulated now than they were during the committee government era. In order to retain their positions, committee chairmen must be responsive to party majorities. As will be shown in the next section, committees must also be responsive if they wish to receive the help they need to pass their legislation.

Influencing Outcomes

Superintending the House floor and shepherding legislation to passage at the floor stage are the core of the party leadership's responsibilities as traditionally defined. In recent years, the leadership has become more active at this stage of the legislative process as well. As the norm of intercommittee reciprocity declined during the 1970s and members offered increasing numbers of amendments on the floor, committees faced a much greater challenge in passing their bills on the floor (Bach and Smith, 1988:28–29). If the bill at issue was a major controversial one, the committee majority often could not engineer passage on its own. Partly as a result of the 1970s reforms and partly in response to the problems they created, the party leadership obtained a command over resources that it can use to give committee majorities the help they need.

Since the Rules Committee has become an arm of the leadership, party leaders truly control the scheduling of legislation for floor consideration. The capacity to decide when a bill will be considered is an important strategic resource because it can affect outcomes. Thus the leadership can delay a bill until sufficient support for passage has developed or, more rarely, move legislation quickly before opposition has time to coalesce.

The special orders or rules reported by the Rules Committee govern the amending process on the legislation at issue; a rule may, for example, ban all amendments or allow only certain amendments. In response to the expanded amending activity on the House floor, the party leadership in the 1980s increased its use of rules that restrict amendments. From the 95th Congress (1977–1978) to the 100th Congress (1987–1988), restrictive rules increased from 12 to 43 percent of all rules (Cheney, 1989:43).

A rule must be approved by a majority of the House membership. Given that restrictive rules do limit members' freedom to offer amendments, it is reasonable to ask why majorities vote for such rules. (During the 100th Congress only 5 of 165 rules were defeated.) The answer is that restrictive rules save members' most precious resource—time—and move the legislative agenda. As amending activity increased in the 1970s, some bills were on the floor for days while others died because of lack of floor time. Furthermore, some of the amending activity was clearly aimed at obstructing the legislative process. In addition, minority party members became adept at fashioning amendments intended to embarrass majority Democrats. In 1983, for example, Republicans offered a prohibition on loans to communist countries as an amendment to a bill financing the U.S. contribution to the International Monetary Fund (see *Washington Post*, October 22, 1983). In fact, the IMF cannot accept funds under such conditions, and the Reagan administration opposed the amendment. That the amendment was simply a Republican political ploy was demonstrated the next day, when the National Republican Congressional Committee distributed press releases in the districts of twenty-one junior Democrats accusing them of "voting to give loans to communist dictatorships" and of having cast "a vote to support communism." Outraged, the party leadership used its scheduling power to pull the bill off the floor and refused to reschedule it until Reagan had sent a letter of thanks to each of the Democrats who had supported his position. Restrictive rules can sometimes protect members against such no-win votes.

Rules can also be used to structure the choice situation that members face on the floor so as to advantage the outcome favored by the leadership. In a case of welfare reform legislation in 1988, for example, the rule allowed an amendment that cut the bill's price tag moderately but not one that proposed a more draconian cut. Members who believed that, for reelection reasons, they had to vote for some cut were given the opportunity to do so. The rule for consideration of the minimum wage bill in spring 1989 also protected the committee majority's compromise proposal by favoring it in terms of the order in which votes were to be taken and by not allowing an amendment specifying a completely different approach (see *Congressional Quarterly Weekly Report,* March 15, 1989, p. 641).

Through adept use of its control over scheduling and over the character of rules, the party leadership can significantly increase a bill's chances of passing intact on the floor. The leadership's involvement in shaping the substance of legislation at the pre-floor stage is often aimed at producing legislation with support broad enough to pass the chamber. Nevertheless, on major controversial legislation, a floor-vote mobilization effort is often required.

On legislation of consequence, the party leadership conducts a whip count to ascertain the level of support among Democrats. Shortly before the leadership intends to bring the legislation to the floor, the regional whips are usually instructed to ask the members in their zones how they intend to vote. If the count indicates insufficient support, due either to opposition or to a large number of undecided votes, a task force is formed. All the whips and the Democratic members of the committee of origin who supported the bill are invited to take part. The task force, working from the initial count, distributes the names of all Democrats not listed as supporting the party position among its members. The members' task is to talk to those Democrats, to ascertain their voting intention, and to persuade a number sufficient for victory to support the party position.

During the 100th Congress, task forces functioned in about seventy instances and about 60 percent of the House Democrats served on one or more task forces. The task force device and the expanded whip system of which it is a part make it possible for the party leadership to mount much more frequent and extensive vote-mobilization efforts than was possible for earlier party leaderships. Task forces also provide members with opportunities to participate broadly in the legislative process— opportunities especially attractive to junior members who do not yet chair a subcommittee. In this way, they channel members' energies into efforts that help the party.

The party leadership, then, can significantly help committees pass their legislation on the floor. But the price for this aid is committee responsiveness to the party agenda and to party majority preferences on legislative substance. The party contingents on most committees are relatively representative of the party membership, and the need for caucus approval works to keep committee chairmen responsive to party sentiment. Accordingly, most committees can be expected to produce legislation reasonably satisfactory to most Democrats in any given case. Nevertheless, the committee majority's need for leadership to help pass its legislation does heighten its responsiveness to the leadership and the party majority. If the committee has put together legislation acceptable to a strong majority of Democrats, the leadership will work to protect that legislation from being picked apart on the floor and will use its command over rules and the vote mobilization apparatus to do so. The party majority's position is probably more determinative of the substance of legislation that passes the House than it used to be. Certainly the old bipartisan conservative coalition appears much less frequently than it did in the 1970s or early 1980s (Ehrenhalt, 1987).

In recent years, the relationship between party and committee leaders has tended to be cooperative. During the 100th Congress, the agenda enunciated by the Speaker was for the most part strongly supported by the relevant committee Democrats and, in some cases, grew out of previous committee work. In most cases, committees welcomed the priority given to their legislation and worked hard to meet the Speaker's schedule for reporting their bills. Throughout the process, most of the committee majorities were sensitive to their party colleagues' policy preferences and wrote legislation acceptable to a substantial majority of Democrats. In return, they received important help from the party leadership in passing their legislation on the floor.

This cooperative relationship paid off with legislative success. During the 100th Congress, every item on the Speaker's initial agenda became law—in some cases, over the president's veto. Important legislation that was added to the agenda in the second year—such as the Civil Rights Restoration Act, a drug bill, legislation to control ocean dumping, and legislation on AIDs—was also enacted. When the party leadership worked a vote, it very seldom lost.

These legislative successes were built on a foundation of extraordinarily high Democratic voting cohesion. During the 100th Congress, the typical Democrat voted with a majority of his or her party colleagues on 88 percent of those votes that divided Democrats and Republicans. This average party unity score is the highest for Democrats from 1925 to the present. For the period 1951–1970, the House Democrats' average party unity score was 77.6; this figure fell to 73.8 for the period 1971–1982. After the 1982 election, the score began to rise and averaged 85.3 for the period 1983–1988. During these last three congresses, the proportion of roll calls on which a majority of Democrats voted against a majority of Republicans also increased, averaging 55.4 percent compared with 37.2 percent during the period 1971–1982.

This extraordinary Democratic voting cohesion is, to some extent, a tribute to party and committee leaders' skill in writing broadly attactive legislation and in mobilizing votes. However, since current party leaders, like those of the committee government era, can influence their members' reelection chances only at the margins, their ability to change members' voting intentions is also at the margins. As the favors that leaders can do for their members are valued, members will vote the party when they can; they will not do so, however, if it is likely to be costly in terms of reelection.

What, then accounts for the high Democratic voting cohesion? If low cohesion is a function of members being pulled in different directions by their disparate districts, an increase in district homogeneity might well account for an increase in cohesion. In fact, much of the increase in Democratic cohesion is the result of increased party support by southern Democrats. During the 100th Congress, southern Democrats supported the party position on about 80 percent of partisan roll calls, whereas the average support of northern Democrats was a little more than 90 percent. Compare that with the average difference between the two groups of about 38 points for the period 1965–1976 and 24 points for the period 1977–1984 (see *Congressional Quarterly Weekly Report,* January 16, 1988, and November 19, 1988; Rohde, 1988).

Since the late 1960s the constituencies of southern Democrats have become more like those of their northern colleagues (Rohde, 1988). In part, this convergence is the result of processes such as the urbanization of the South. More important, with the passage of the voting Rights Act and growing Republican strength in the South, blacks have become a critical element of many southern Democrats' election support. Hence the policy views of the electoral coalitions supporting many southern Democrats are not drastically different from those of the average northern Democrat.

As southern electoral coalitions changed, incumbent southern Democrats began to modify their voting behavior and newly elected southerners tended to be national Democrats (Sinclair, 1982:Chs. 7–8). Thus the House Democratic party became considerably less ideologically heterogeneous. The big budget deficits of the 1980s, which constricted the feasible issue space by making expensive new social programs impossible, probably also made intraparty agreements easier to reach. In any case, the Democratic party's increased homogeneity was almost certainly a prerequisite for the emergence of strong, policy-oriented leadership. It made possible a party agenda that included some items really important to almost every Democrat and, at the same time, was one that all Democrats could live with. In its dealings with committees, party leadership could not meaningfully require deference to a broad majority's preferences. Repeated success in mobilizing floor votes was also made possible.

Parties and Party Leaders in the Senate

In the Senate, too, the parties organize the chamber. Each party elects both a floor leader and a whip from among its membership. Senators receive their committee assignments from party committees.

The Senate majority leader is the leader of the majority party in the Senate but, unlike the Speaker, he is not the chamber's presiding officer. In any event, the presiding officer of the Senate has much less discretion than his House counterpart. The only important resource that the Senate rules give to the majority leader to aid him with his core tasks of scheduling legislation and floor leadership is the right to be recognized first when a number of senators are seeking recognition on the Senate floor.

Institutional rules give the majority party leadership few special resources, but they bestow great powers on rank-and-file senators. In most cases, any senator can offer an unlimited number of amendments to a piece of legislation on the Senate floor, and those amendments need not even be germane. A senator can hold the Senate floor indefinitely unless cloture is invoked; cloture requires an extraordinary majority of sixty votes.

During the late 1960s and the 1970s the Senate increased the supply of staff and of desirable committee assignments and began to distribute those resources much more equally among its members. Norms dictating specialization and a highly restrained use of the great powers that the Senate rules confer upon the individual lost their hold. As a consequence the typical 1990s senator becomes involved in a broad range of issues, including some that do not fall within the jurisdiction of his committees. He is active both in the committee room and on the Senate floor (Sinclair, 1989).

In the Senate, unlike the House, rule and norm changes that increased rank-and-file members' opportunities to participate were not accompanied by leadership-strengthening changes. The Senate majority party leader, always institutionally weaker than the Speaker of the House, was given no significant new powers for coping with the more active, assertive, and hence less predictable membership.

A single senator can disrupt the work of the Senate by, for example, exercising his right of unlimited debate or objecting to the unanimous consent requests through which the Senate does most of its work. Clearly, a partisan majority of any size can bring legislative activity to a standstill. The Senate necessarily operates in a more bipartisan fashion than does the House. As the majority leader makes decisions on the floor scheduling of legislation, he confers on an almost continuous basis with the minority leader and, in fact, touches base with all interested senators. In the negotiation of unanimous consent agreements, which the Senate often uses to set the ground rules for the consideration of legislation on the floor, the majority leader must obtain the assent not only of the minority leadership but of all interested senators as well. An objection from any one senator would kill such an agreement.

Like their House counterparts, Senate committees in the 1970s faced a more complex and unpredictable floor situation as the number of amendments rapidly increased. The political environment of the 1980s, with its high-intensity ideological politics, its deficit constraints, and, after 1986, its divided control further complicated the situation confronting committee majorities. Yet the majority party leadership's limited control over the floor agenda and its lack of a device such as House special orders (rules) for advantageously structuring the choice situation have severely limited the help that the party leadership can give committees in passing their legislation on the floor.

In the House, the majority party leadership's new influence over the substance of legislation stems in good part from its ability to give committees this help. But the Senate majority leader, who lacks that capacity, has not gained the same influence. The majority leader spends a great deal of time attempting to work out differences among senators through direct negotiation or the facilitation of negotiation. In negotiations with key actors outside the chamber on such major matters as the budget, a continuing resolution, Contra aid, or an omnibus drug bill, the Senate majority leader will play a role. Like his House counterparts, he commands the legitimacy derived from being the elected leader of the majority party. Yet, compared to his House counterparts, he defers more to committee chairmen and to other interested senators. Since he can help them less than the House leaders can help their House counterparts, he is able to influence them less as well.

Leadership agenda setting depends in part on the leaders' capacity to engineer passage of their priority legislation. During the 100th Congress, the narrow Democratic margin in the Senate accentuated the problems created by Senate rules. It was probably for this reason that the Senate Democratic leadership deferred to the House leadership in agenda setting. During much of 1987 Senate Minority Leader Dole pursued a filibuster strategy of blocking Democratic initiatives through extended debate. For a variety of reasons the Republicans abandoned that strategy, and all of the initial Democratic agenda enunciated by Speaker Wright eventually passed the Senate and became law. Other important legislation—especially a minimum-wage increase and a child-care bill—died in the Senate in 1988 as a result of the Democrats' inability to muster the 60 votes necessary to cut off debate.

When Senate Democrats chose George Mitchell of Maine as their new majority leader for the 101st Congress, they were signaling their desire for an effective media spokesman as well as for an inside player. President Reagan's brilliant use of the media in pursuing a course that threatened the Democrats' policy, reelection, and power goals persuaded Democrats in both houses of the need for a media strategy of their own to counter the president and the Republican party. Party images, the policy agenda, and the terms in which issues are debated can all be influenced through the media. When the 1988 election brought continued divided control, Senate Democrats saw the spokesman role as even more important.

One aspect of that role is agenda setting, and Mitchell responded to his members' desires for Senate Democrats to have a greater impact on the congressional agenda by commissioning the Senate Democratic Policy Committee to draft a consensus agenda. Such activities are likely to continue and become bolder but, so long as the Democratic margin is narrow, party and leadership agenda-setting activities are likely to be limited by the difficulty of passing the items, given Senate rules.

The Senate has not seen the development of the strong, policy-oriented party leadership that occurred in the House during the 1980s. In the Senate, as in the House, the heterogeneity of the Democrats' election constituencies has declined. Most of the southern Democrats, whose election in 1986 returned control of the chamber to the Democratic party, depend upon black votes. However, the Senate majority party leadership's meager resources for helping the Democratic membership, committee majorities, and committee leaders to protect their legislation from amendments and to pass it on the floor do not provide the same leverage as that supplied by the House leadership's much more potent resources.

Although the Senate party leadership has not become significantly stronger, party has become somewhat more important in the Senate during the 1980s. National politics in the 1980s was, for political elites especially, a politics of high intensity and high stakes. The possibility of realignment was in the air during much of the decade, scaring Democrats and exhilarating Republicans. The alterations in partisan control of the Senate enhanced the sense of shared fate among the party contingents. Many Democrats considered President Reagan's legislative proposals to be abhorrent from both a policy and a constituency perspective. The decline in the heterogeneity of the Democrats' election constituency facilitated intraparty cooperation, and their regaining of Senate control made some policy victories seem possible if they worked together. Though enunciated by the House leadership, the Democratic agenda during the 100th Congress was suited to the needs of the more homogeneous Senate Democrats as well. Through cooperative effort, Senate Democrats passed the entire agenda, though in some cases with great difficulty.

The increased partisanship was evident in Senate voting behavior. Although the percentage of all roll calls evoking a partisan division increased only modestly from 41.6 in 1969–1980 to 45.1 in 1981–1988, important votes were much more frequently partisan—about 80 percent in 1981–1985, according to the *National Journal*'s selection of important votes (Hurley, 1989:131). On party votes during the 1980s, the Senate's majority party maintained high party cohesion. Republicans voted with their party 81.2 percent of the time on average in 1981–1986, compared with 71.9 in 1969–1980. During the 100th Congress, Senate Democrats supported their party's position on 85.1 percent of the roll calls, compared with 74.3 percent in 1969–1980 and 76.2 percent in 1981–1986.

A STRONG CONGRESSIONAL PARTY
IN A WEAK PARTY ERA

To summarize, and to formalize the argument somewhat, I contend that strong, policy-oriented party leadership emerged in the House in the 1980s because the costs and benefits to Democratic members of such leadership—and of the behavior on their part that makes such leadership possible—have changed significantly. The reforms of the 1970s, especially when combined with the constraints of the 1980s political environment, greatly increased the difficulty of enacting legislation—particularly legislation favored by Democrats. The majority party leadership possesses resources that, if acquiesced to by Democratic members (through their votes for restrictive rules, for example), can significantly increase the probability of legislative success. Hence the costs of weak leadership in terms of legislative outputs forgone—to the Democratic membership, to Democratic committee contingents, and to Democratic committee leaders— were considerably higher in the 1980s than in previous decades. Political circumstances at the beginning of the 100th Congress highlighted the benefits of strong leadership and the costs of weak leadership for the Democrats. With the Senate again under Democratic control and the Reagan presidency weakened, House Democrats perceived an opportunity to pass major legislation that had been stymied throughout the six years of the Reagan administration. Taking advantage of that opportunity, most realized, would require strong leadership.

Changes that reduced the costs of strong leadership also occurred during the 1980s. Most important, the effective ideological homogeneity of the Democratic membership increased as the election constituencies of southern Democrats became more like those of their northern party colleagues and as the big deficits shrank the feasible issue space. No appreciable segment of the Democratic membership need fear that, as a consequence of the exercise of strong, policy-oriented leadership, their reelection chances will be reduced. In addition, the 1980s political environment, especially the deficit situation, made free-lance policy entrepreneurship as practiced in the 1970s much less feasible for liberals. Independent advocacy of new programs, especially if they are costly, has little chance of success. Accordingly, when Democratic members practice the sort of restraint that makes strong leadership possible (by giving up the right to offer floor amendments on selected legislation, for example), they are not giving up very much.

In the 1990s, then, the great majority of House Democrats currently gain as individuals from strong party leadership; such leadership increases the probability that the legislation they favor will become law. So long as gains are achieved by the majority of the membership, leadership is likely to remain strong. The leadership upheavals that House Democrats experienced in June of 1989 resulted in some change in leadership style. Speaker Tom Foley is more conciliatory and less aggressively partisan than former Speaker Jim Wright was. The leadership's roles, however, remain the same: agenda setting, shaping legislation, and influencing floor outcomes.

So long as the House majority party leadership remains strong, it will amplify the influence of party in the chamber. A strong leadership can bestow valuable favors on its members, thus increasing their incentive for going along whenever they can. A strong leadership that controls resources for facilitating floor passage makes it more likely that, on controversial legislation, legislative compromises will be made within the party rather than across party lines.

The Senate Democratic membership has become less ideologically heterogeneous as the election constituencies of southern Democrats have changed. The political environment in the aftermath of the 1986 election was conducive to partisanship for the Senate as well as for the House. The result in the Senate was more partisan behavior, including but not restricted to voting behavior. However, significantly stronger majority party leadership was not a consequence, because the Senate party leadership did not possess the initial resources necessary to significantly increase the probability of legislative success and thereby advance the goals of its membership. Thus senators have no incentive to act in such a way as to make stronger leadership possible.

The Senate, then, lacks the strong leadership that can amplify the influence of party. The extent of partisanship is primarily a function of factors in the immediate political environment and a question of whether they cut along or across party lines. But in the House, too, the extent of partisanship ultimately depends upon the extent to which the members of a party, whose reelection is much more dependent upon their own constituency-pleasing efforts than upon the party's record, see their individual interests as coinciding.

NOTES

This essay is based in part upon a fifteen-month period of participant observation in the office of the Speaker and in part upon interviews with members and staff. I am grateful to Jim Wright and his staff for giving me an unprecedented opportunity to see leadership in operation from the inside, and to all those people who took some of their precious time to talk with me. This research was supported by intramural grant funds from the Academic Senate University of California, Riverside, as well as by a grant from the Dirken Congressional Leadership Research Center.

12

Coalitions in the U.S. Congress

DAVID W. BRADY

In the United States, though not in most other Western democracies, analysis of political coalitions is complicated by variation in the nature of the groups that divide or come together to form temporary alliances. To talk of coalitions in the British party system is to refer to ideological faction within parties, whereas the Japanese party system has factions within parties that are not ideological but personal. In Germany one describes the two or more *parties* that must agree on policies and ministerial posts in order to form a coalition government. In the United States, however, factions within the two major parties sometimes form coalitions to set party policy, while at other times cross-party coalitions are formed on the basis of common interests.

Contemporary commentators speak of the Roosevelt-Truman (New Deal) coalition of northeasterners and southerners that won five consecutive presidential elections between 1932 and 1948. By contrast, the Conservative Coalition in Congress refers to Republicans voting with southern Democrats against northern Democrats. The urban-rural coalition is composed of rural and urban representatives, regardless of their party affiliation, who combine forces to pass legislation that favors price supports for farmers and food stamps for the urban poor (Ferejohn, 1986). In this essay, coalitions are viewed as both cooperating factions within the parties and as cross-party policy blocs.

The American electoral system is also relatively unusual in that the executive and legislative branches may be controlled by different parties. Although the United States is not the only country with this feature, few governments are designed to permit divided control of its branches as readily as ours does. There are exceptions, of course: During his first term, French President Mitterrand, a Socialist, had a National Assembly controlled by Chirac and the Conservatives; and, as of 1990, the Korean government had a president from the Democratic Justice party (DJP) as well as a legislature dominated by a coalition group that did not include the DJP. But divided government in the United States has been the norm since 1950. It is important to note the features of the U.S. system that permit split control of government.

This essay begins with a discussion of some of the constitutional and institutional features that affect parties in America—features that, in turn, have led to the development of coalitions within and among parties. The argument here is that if we had a constitutional system that encouraged responsible parties, then a study of coalitions in Congress would describe the factions within the two major parties and discuss the ways in which these factions affected the parties' electoral and policy positions. However, since the American system does not encourage responsible parties, it is necessary to show how coalitions in the United States are both electoral and policy coalitions—and how the operative electoral and legislative coalitions differ. For example, the electoral coalitions that make one party the majority in Congress do not ensure a majority position on issues such as tax rates, farm price supports, or affirmative-action policy. Indeed, one can explain coalitions in American government by showing how electoral and policymaking activities in America are disjoint.

CONSTITUTIONAL CONSTRAINTS ON AMERICAN PARTIES

The major features of the American Constitution that distinguish it from most other democratic countries are federalism, separation of powers, and checks and balances. Federalism for the founding generation helped to ensure that the Congress and the president would reflect and recognize the social, economic, and religious differences among states and regions. Federalism institutionalized the differences inherent in a growing, widespread, diverse population (recall *Federalist*, No. 51). The doctrines of separation of powers and checks and balances have resulted in an American system of government that is characterized by "separate powers sharing functions," which is in contradistinction to other Western democracies in which power is centralized and functions are specific.

Although many aspects of the doctrines of federalism, separation of powers, and checks and balances have changed so as to make the system more democratic and centralized, the American system of government remains fragmented and cumbersome. Shortly after the Constitution took effect, difficulties inherent in governing within its framework presented themselves. Alexander Hamilton, Washington's secretary of the treasury, could not implement the policies he considered necessary without appropriate legislation. Thus, he commenced work on building organized support in Congress for Washington's policies; in effect, he became the leader of the pro-national faction in the Congress. Over time, the factions that had opposing views regarding the direction the national government should take developed into political parties. The goal of these nascent parties was to elect others to Congress who shared their views, in order to form a majority for the policies they favored. Yet, even though American parties were founded as a means to make governing less cumbersome, the same forces that produced them—federalism, separation of powers, checks and balances, and single-member districts with plurality winners—also worked to limit their strength.

The most basic effect of a federal form of government on the American party system is that, instead of one national two-party system, we have fifty state party systems. Each state's party system has demographic, ideological, structural, and electoral peculiarities. For instance, the Democratic party in the electorate and as an organization in New York is distinct from the Democratic party in the electorate and as an organization in Georgia. The same fact applies to the components of the Republican party in these states. The heterogeneity of the state party systems is such that, at the level of party in government, unlike-minded men and women bearing the same party label have come together in the U.S. Congress. Put another way, the federal system has brought built-in differences among states and regions to the Congress. Although this arrangement may be useful in maintaining system equilibrium, it has more often formed an extremely poor basis on which to build coherent congressional parties; in effect, it has encouraged cross-party coalitions. The New Deal coalition of rural southern agricultural interests and urban northern industrial interests is a case in point. Long after this coalition had passed its major policy changes and the reasons for its formation no longer obtained, it continued to serve as the basis of the electoral coalition for the Democratic party. Even with a successful electoral coalition, however, the party was often divided on major policy issues.[1] In fact, on a number of major policy issues, such as civil rights and social welfare, the components of the New Deal coalition were poles apart. American political history abounds with examples of successful electoral coalitions that could not keep their members from forming cross-party legislative coalitions. Parties formed out of numerous and diverse state party systems tend to emphasize electoral success and to minimize policy cohesion.

The separation of powers and the system of checks and balances have contributed, as well, to the fragmentary, disjointed status of American parties. When sectional, coalitional parties are given the opportunity to seek numerous offices (both elective and appointive) in the various branches, they become further fractionalized. Thus, for example, one faction of the party may dominate presidential politics and another, congressional politics; and since both have powers over the courts, an equal division of court appointments may result. The Democratic party from 1876 to at least 1976 was characterized by just such an arrangement. The northern wing dominated presidential politics and elections, the southern wing dominated congressional leadership posts, and both wings influenced court appointments. Such a system may enhance representation of differences, but it does little to facilitate coherent party majorities capable of cohesive policymaking.

The constitutional arrangement of single-member-district plurality elections has also contributed to the fragmentation of the party system. House members elected on local issues by a localized party in the electorate generally build local party (or personal) organizations (Mann, 1978; Fenno, 1978; Mayhew, 1974a; Fiorina, 1989). Once elected representatives—owing little loyalty to national party leaders—can behave in nonpartisan ways with few personal consequences. Indeed, throughout most of the Congress's history, party leaders have been able only to persuade, not to force, members to vote "correctly." Party leadership, without even the threat of sanctions, is likely to be unsuccessful in building consistent partisan majorities. It is thus not surprising that the highest levels of voting along party lines in the history of the Congress occurred at a time (1890–1910) when the Speaker's sanctions over members were greatest and the Senate was run by a hierarchy that also had powerful sanctions. In turn, representatives elected by local majorities can work and vote on behalf of those interests regardless of the national party position; congressional leaders do not "persuade" from a position of power.

Local and state diversity is institutionalized in the American system of government in such a way as to allow that diversity to work its way up, almost unchanged, from party in the electorate through party organizations to the congressional parties. Thus, at the top as at the bottom, the American party system reflects the cumbersome fractionalism of the American system of government. It also facilitates cross-party coalitions. The fragmentation of the parties in the electorate and in government carries over into the organization of the legislature. In the following section the effect of this fragmentation on House organization is given as an example.

House Organization

Like all such organizations, the House of Representatives had adapted to social change by creating internal structures designed both to meet the pressures or demands from its various constituencies and to perform its policymaking function.[2] To the enormous range of interests in the United States and the concomitant pressures they generate, the House has responded with a division of labor. The result is a highly complicated committee system. When the country was in its infancy and government was limited, the House formed ad hoc committees; however, by the Jacksonian era, a standing committee system was in place. As the country grew more industrial and complicated, the House responded by expanding and enlarging the committee system. Early in this process, committees were established to deal with such policy domains as war, post offices, and roads, and the ways and means to raise revenues to support the government.

These committees—or "little legislatures," as George Goodwin (1970) described them—were organized around governmental policy functions; they were and still are decentralized decisionmaking structures. Both the making of Reconstruction policy after the Civil War and Wilson's claim that "congressional government is committee government" attest to the power of committees at relatively early times (Wilson, 1885; see also Bogue, 1980, and Benedict, 1974). Decentralizing power to committees was a necessary response to pressures for government action in certain policy areas; to the extent that the committees decided policy, however party leaders were limited. As decentralized decisionmaking mechanisms, committees are dominated by members elected to represent local interests. The fact that members can choose (within limits) the committees they serve on determines to a large extent the direction that the committees' policy choices will take. This is essentially what William Riker (1983) means by "congealed preferences." The decentralized committee system, which allows members to represent local interests, has become a powerful force that encourages members from different parties to cross party lines in order to achieve policy results. Throughout the 1950s, for example, a coalition of conservative Democrats and Republicans on the House Rules Committee was able to block or weaken civil rights legislation favored by northern Democrats.

What the division of labor pulls apart in organizations, integrative mechanisms must pull together. In the House the major integrative mechanism is the majority congressional party. And as we have seen, congressional parties are limited by the governmental structure established by the Constitution as well as by the fact that members are elected by local parties (or groups) on the basis of local issues. Members responsible to and punishable only by local electorates tend to be responsive to constituents, not parties. Under such conditions, party strength tends to be low and coalitional strength high. Even when party voting was at its peak in the U.S. House of Representatives, it was low compared to that of other Western democracies. Even under ideal conditions the congressional parties in the House have limited integrative capacity. Under normal conditions policy decisions are thus likely to reflect localized committee interests, thereby limiting the national party leaders' attempts to build coherent congressional majorities. House voting patterns show that different coalitions are active on different policy issues (Clausen, 1973; Sinclair, 1982). Coalitions cut across regional party as well as social and economic lines, making the party leaders' job a "ceaseless maneuvering to find coalitions capable of governing" in specific policy areas (Key, 1952).

Two other features of the American institutional arrangement should be emphasized as well. First, the Constitution provides for the separate election of a president and Congress; thus the electoral institution makes it possible to have divided government. The rules in most democracies make divided government highly unlikely. In the United Kingdom and Japan, for example, the prime ministers are members of parliament elected by their fellow legislators as chief executives. Divided control is possible in such cases only if enough Conservatives or Liberal Democrats vote with Labor or Liberals to elect the prime minister. The fact that divided government has become the norm in the United States since 1950 is important because it ensures a special role for coalitions in Congress. President Bush cannot pass any of his policy proposals without some support from Democratic members of Congress, and the Democrats cannot pass their policies over the president's veto without some Republican support. In short, divided government both implies and necessitates cross-party coalitions.

Second, the American Constitution ensured what Nelson Polsby (1975) has called a "transformative legislature." That is, the sharing of power between separate institutions (with the ability to check each other) helps ensure that what happens in Congress actually affects the direction of public policy. In most legislatures, committees (if they exist) do not significantly affect the direction of policy. In the U.S. Congress, however, committees do matter. Similarly, voting in most legislatures is party-responsible voting. The parliamentary party member, for instance, votes the government or opposition-party position on crucial policy votes. But in Congress, party leaders have to exert themselves to get party members to support them, and often they fail. During the 101st Congress, the Democratic leadership pressed hard to get Democrats to vote against a capital-gains tax reduction that President Bush preferred. In the final House vote, some seventy Democrats voted with the Republicans in favor of a capital gains reduction. This outcome would not have occurred on similar votes in most other democracies.

In sum, American institutional arrangements have constrained party responsibility, encouraged divided government, and made the legislature an important actor in the policy process. The combination of these features makes cross-party coalitions especially important in Congress;

indeed, without analyzing such coalitions, we cannot account for the direction of American public policy. But the institutional arrangements of the American system alone do not explain the importance of coalitions. One must also consider citizen preferences. If U.S. citizens wanted a strong party system, they could change the rules so as to strengthen parties; or, conversely, they could elect a Congress that would be of the same party as the president. But since they have not changed the rules, nor do they often elect presidents and Congresses of the same party, it must be the case that their preferences are consistent with weak parties and divided government. The number and complexity of explanations offered to account for the relationship between citizen preferences, institutions, and government action ranges from Marx's ideology of false consciousness to Friedman's invisible hand solutions. I shall not try to resolve this broad issue; rather, I will focus on the electoral connection.

CROSS-PARTY COALITIONS

The prevalence in the U.S. Congress of cross-party policy coalitions is largely attributable to the electoral base of U.S. parties. The fact that liberals such as Ted Kennedy and George McGovern share the same party label as conservatives such as Sam Nunn and James Eastland helps to explain the existence of coalitions that feature Democrats and Republicans who vote alike. The intraparty heterogeneity of preferences leads directly to voting blocs that weaken party responsibility in the U.S. Congress. The coalitions are of two kinds: One is broadly ideological whereas the other is issue or policy specific. The Conservative Coalition is an example of a broad ideological coalition that has formed across a wide range of issues. The policy-specific coalitions are more diverse and numerous; the aforementioned urban-rural coalition is but one example. Policy-specific coalitions can be based on members' constituent interests, or, as in the case of the pro-Israel coalition, on members' preferences or ideology.

Homogeneous and Cohesive Parties

The development of congressional coalitions is obvious when we compare the current arrangement with that which existed in 1890–1910, when parties were relatively cohesive and strong. During that earlier period the number of cross-party coalitions was low; by tracing their rise, we can determine the extent to which that rise was associated with electoral results.

Both the U.S. House of Representatives and the Senate at the end of the nineteenth century were partisan, centralized, and hierarchical. The

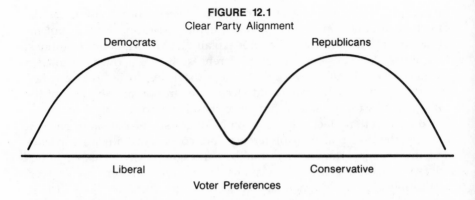

FIGURE 12.1
Clear Party Alignment

Democrats   Republicans

Liberal   Conservative

Voter Preferences

congressional majority party for most of this period (i.e., the Republican party) was controlled by a small number of leaders who occupied both party and committee leadership positions, thus making power centralized and hierarchical in that members took their voting cues from these party leaders (Brady, 1973). Voting on the floor and in committees was highly partisan. For example, during the 55th and 56th Congresses (1897–1901), more than 90 percent of the roll-call votes were a majority of one party voting against a majority of the other party. In addition, more than half of all roll calls in these Congresses were 90 percent of one party versus 90 percent of the other. Thus it is fair to claim that, at the turn of the century, congressional parties more closely resembled European parties than contemporary American parties.

How did we evolve from a system in which congressional parties were strong and cross-party coalitions were nonexistent or weak to one in which cross-party coalitions are strong and parties are weak and/or unimportant (Broder, 1971)? The argument here is that, at the turn of the century, American parties were internally homogeneous and the two major parties had opposing views on appropriate governmental policy. The Republicans largely represented northern industrial districts, whereas the Democrats largely represented rural and southern districts. The Republicans, in calling for policies that favored continued industrial development, proposed tariffs to protect American industries, the gold standard (which favored Eastern monied interests and was the European standard), and the expansion of American interests abroad. The Democrats, who represented different constituencies, were opposed to the Republican ideas. They favored free trade, the coinage of silver at a 16 to 1 ratio with gold, and an isolationist foreign policy. In short, constituent preferences were in line with the parties (see Figure 12.1).

FIGURE 12.2
Overlapping Party Alignment

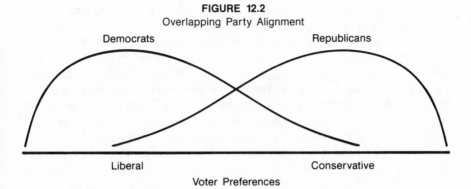

Democrats   Republicans

Liberal   Conservative
Voter Preferences

Heterogeneous Parties and Cross-Party Coalitions

As intraparty heterogeneity was introduced into the congressional parties, cross-party coalitions—both ideological and policy specific—resulted. In other words, as the distribution of preferences and the party alignment changed (as shown in Figure 12.2), the probability of interparty coalitions increased. In contrast to the data in Figure 12.1, some Democrats were now closer to the Republicans than to the Democratic median and some Republicans were closer to the Democrats than to the Republican median. If we were to include more than one policy dimension in the model, we would see even more cross-party similarity. With the addition of a foreign policy factor, for instance, some Democrats might have shown up as economic liberals but foreign policy conservatives. In short, as the number of policy dimensions is expanded, the possibility of cross-party coalitions increases dramatically. The central point is clear: When intraparty hetereogeneity exists, voting patterns and public policy change.

The rise of the Progressives in the early twentieth century introduced hetereogeneity of preference into the majority Republican party. Progressives such as Robert Lafollette (R-WI), Albert Cummins (R-IA), and George Norris (R-NE) disagreed with Republican stalwarts such as Speaker Joseph Cannon (IL) and Senator Nelson Aldrich (RI) over issues such as income tax, government regulation of industry and banking, tariff schedules, and electoral reform. There were similar splits between southern and northern Democrats over immigration and civil rights policy. The combined result of this intraparty hetereogeneity was a cross-party coalition of Democrats and Progressive Republicans that effectively changed the leadership in the House and Senate and permitted the passage of policies associated with President Woodrow Wilson (Holt, 1967).

Under the alignment shown in Figure 12.1, the House and Senate were organized to accommodate a strong and unified majority party's policy agenda. In the House, for example, Boss Reed (the Speaker in 1891–1990 and 1985–1999) and Czar Cannon (the Speaker in 1901–1909) appointed committees, controlled the Rules Committee, and had the right to recognize anyone they chose to speak on the floor. In 1910–1911 a coalition of Progressive Republicans and Democrats stripped the Speaker of his appointive power, dropped him as chair of Rules, and restricted his floor powers. They did so largely because they believed that, with centralized Speaker control, they could not get their policies passed. In sum, after the Progressive reforms in the House and Senate, both bodies were organized to accommodate parties that had intraparty differences. This is not to say that party was irrelevant but simply that it was less important and had fewer sanctions over members' legislative careers.

In the 1920s the major cross-party coalition was the so-called farm bloc—a coalition of Republicans and Democrats representing agricultural interests. The American economy had developed rapidly after World War I, although agriculture continued to be depressed (because of overproduction and thus low prices) throughout the decade. Representatives and senators from farm districts and states proposed price supports and parity payments, among other policies, to alleviate the effects of the depressed agriculture sector. The most hotly debated proposal was the McNary-Haugen policy proposal. At various times either the House or the Senate passed versions of this proposal; but the president vetoed it, and it did not become public policy. Nevertheless, the farm bloc was a powerful force in the U.S. Congress, and it was cross partisan.

The Great Depression brought Franklin Roosevelt and the Democrats to power, and from 1933 until 1938 they acted in a cohesive fashion. Levels of party unity and party voting increased during this era (Brady, 1988). Roosevelt and the Democrats achieved this unity and purpose by establishing what Theodore Lowi (1979) called "interest group liberalism." In each relevant policy area, that is, the affected parties were the relevant actors. The National Industrial Recovery Act tried to set quotas, prices, and wages by allowing each industry to define its equilibrium point. Agricultural policy was established by allowing the different commodities (corn, tobacco, sugar, rice, etc.) to work out their own arrangements regarding parity, price supports, and production levels; and much the same held for labor and other affected interests.

This arrangement was restricted by the rise of the Conservative Coalition in 1938. In 1937 Roosevelt had proposed the Fair Labor Standards Act to the Congress. Among its features was a set of provisions that would have reduced southern industry's ability to attract investment due to lower wage rates. Moreover, increasing union membership in the South would have equalized wages, thus stripping the South of its major economic advantage—cheap labor. Southern Democrats were opposed to the Fair Labor Standards Act because it adversely affected powerful interests in their states and districts. Many Republicans were opposed as well, on the grounds of both constituent interests and philosophy. The Republicans and southern Democrats combined to block passage of the act, and thus was born the Conservative Coalition. From 1938 to 1965 the Conservative Coalition was a dominant force in the Congress. It was able to stop or seriously water down the passage of Medicare, Civil Rights and Fair Housing legislation; increases in government management of the economy; welfare policies such as Food Stamps and Aid to Families with Dependent Children; and other legislation.

All of the cross-party coalitions from 1920 to 1965 were broadly ideological and sought to enact policies consistent with the constituents' broad interests. Parties still mattered on some important issues (Mayhew, 1966), and members of Congress and senators were still elected primarily on the basis of their party affiliation. In the late 1950s and early 1960s representatives and senators came to be elected less often according to party affiliation than on the basis of the personal vote. In the next section the development of the personal vote is traced and its rise is shown to be concomitant with an infusion of cross-party coalitions that are policy specific in a narrow sense.

The Personal Vote

Two prominent studies of the Congress have identified elections as determinative factors not only in the behavior of members but in the structure of Congress itself and, more broadly, in the nature of national politics and policy (Mayhew, 1974b; Fiorina, 1989). A connective thread in this literature is the subject of incumbency. Mayhew (1974a) and Erikson (1972) found that, as of the mid-1960s, incumbent members of Congress began winning by larger margins, thus reducing the number of competitive districts in congressional elections. Fiorina (1989) built on these earlier findings by arguing that increases in incumbents' domination of elections affected the policy choices made by the Congress. In essence, his point was that members of Congress supported big government and bureaucracy so as to provide their constituents with goods and services, for which they took credit.

But some scholars, most notably Garand and Gross (1984), took exception to the incumbency theories. They argued that, beginning as early as the late 1980s, a three-point advantage was associated with incumbency. They also maintained that there was a greater incumbency advantage in the 1920s than in the 1970s. Thus their work showed that the apparent pro-incumbent shift in the 1960s was only an increase in incumbency advantage and not the source of the advantage. Garand and Gross failed, however, to distinguish between partisan incumbent advantage (which arose from the demographic or organizational strength of the incumbent's party in the district) and personal incumbency advantage (which was directly related to incumbency itself [Alford and Brady, 1987]). In other words, some districts are Republican or Democratic because they are populated by groups that are strongly Republican (e.g., whites with incomes over $75,000 per year) or strongly Democratic (e.g., blue-collar union workers). We need to distinguish between the vote that is strictly partisan and the vote that belongs to the incumbent due to services the representative has performed or to the incumbent's name recognition or other personal factors.

The standard measures of the personal vote attributable to the incumbent are retirement slump and sophomore surge. In each measure the personal advantage of incumbency is taken to be the difference between a party's vote share in an open-seat contest and the vote margin of an incumbent of that party in an immediately adjacent election. For example, a Republican incumbent runs for reelection in 1948, wins 58 percent of the vote, and retires before the 1950 election, creating an open seat. In the 1950 election the Republican candidate wins with 56 percent of the vote, runs for reelection in 1952, and captures 59 percent of the vote. The 1940 and 1950 elections produce a 1950 retirement slump estimate of −2 percentage points (the 1950 open-seat margin of 56 percent minus the 1948 pre-retirement margin of 58 percent). The 1950 and 1952 elections produce a 1952 sophomore surge estimate of +3 percentage points (the 1952 first incumbent reelection margin of 59 percent minus the 1950 open seat margin of 56 percent).

This approach to measuring incumbency advantage provides two benefits. By focusing on a single district and a set of adjacent elections, it largely controls for district characteristics. Differentiating an incumbent performance from an open-seat performance removes from gross incumbency advantage that portion due to partisan advantage, as reflected by the party's performance in an open-seat contest. The remainder is the net personal advantage enjoyed by the incumbent, above and beyond that available by virtue of the partisan or party organizational strength of the district itself. It is this concept of personal incumbency advantage on which most of the incumbency literature, and the related work in the congressional literature, implicitly turns.

Table 12.1 and Figure 12.3 present the data for sophomore surge and retirement slump over the period 1846–1986. In each case the value for a given election year was derived by computing the mean slump or

TABLE 12.1
Retirement Slump and Sophomore Surge in
All House Elections with Major Party Oppostion,
1846–1986

Year	Retirement Slump	Sophomore Surge
1846	0.05	−1.10
1848	−2.50	−1.80
1850	−0.20	1.10
1856	−0.50	−0.80
1858	−1.20	−3.30
1860	−0.20	−2.40
1866	−1.30	0.25
1868	0.20	−0.60
1870	−6.20	−2.90
1876	−4.80	−3.30
1878	0.70	2.60
1880	−4.40	−3.00
1886	−1.80	1.50
1888	1.80	−1.70
1890	−1.70	−0.70
1896	−3.20	0.15
1898	1.60	2.15
1900	0.65	−0.65
1906	−0.45	−0.70
1908	−3.50	−1.25
1910	−0.70	1.40
1916	−0.58	0.85
1918	0.90	1.50
1920	−2.50	−4.00
1926	−0.48	2.00
1928	−6.70	−2.95
1930	2.25	1.85
1936	−3.10	−1.30
1938	−0.35	−1.33
1940	−1.50	0.03
1948	−3.00	−1.20
1950	−0.85	1.08
1956	−3.30	1.30
1958	1.40	1.90
1960	−6.90	0.70
1966	−6.35	4.90
1968	−6.70	5.80
1970	−5.85	7.70
1976	−7.15	6.45
1978	−11.80	6.55
1980	−6.80	9.20
1986	−9.30	6.40

Source: Table compiled by author on the basis of annual election returns.

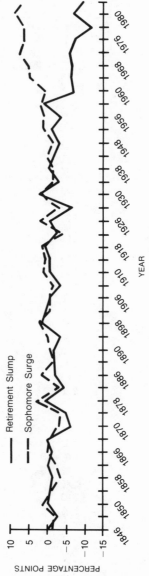

FIGURE 12.3

Sophomore Surge and Retirement Slump in All House Elections
with Major Party Opposition

Retirement Slump

Sophomore Surge

PERCENTAGE POINTS

YEAR

Source: Figure compiled by the author on the basis of annual election returns.

surge value for each party separately and then averaging together the two party surges or slumps irrespective of their individual *n*'s.

Any remaining doubt as to the historically unique nature of incumbency advantage in the post–World War II era should be put to rest by Figure 12.3. Prior to 1945 there was little evidence to indicate any, even short-term, personal advantage to incumbency. Had there been such an advantage, we would expect a sophomore surge to have been positive and retirement slump to have been negative. But at that time these trends occurred only 9 times out of 31 elections (i.e., 28 percent of the total, compared to an expected 25 percent due purely to chance), whereas after 1945 they occurred in 10 out of 12 elections. Moreover, slump and surge in the pre-1945 period never occurred in the expected direction for any adjacent pair of elections.

If we use a somewhat more rigorous test for the existence of personal incumbency advantage, such that both slump and surge occur in the expected direction and both equal or exceed their respective standard errors (though hardly a stringent test by the usual statistical standards), the pattern is even more distinct. This standard was not met even once until 1966 and, in every election since then, both slump and surge have been more than twice their standard errors. Personal incumbency advantage, a fluctuation that figures so prominently in the congressional literature of the last twenty years, scarcely predates that literature.

The data presented thus far pertain to the House of Representatives. The data for the Senate are more difficult to interpret because there are only 33 or 34 elections per election year, compared to 435 House elections. If, however, the data on Senate elections are aggregated by decade, the number of elections rises to around 350. The results show that there is evidence for personal incumbency advantage in Senate elections.[3] The magnitude of both retirement slump and sophomore surge is lower in the Senate than in the House. The timing of the rise of the personal vote is similar to that found in the House. Thus the same conclusions drawn for the House results can be drawn for the Senate, albeit somewhat more weakly.

Since the rise in the personal vote during the mid-1960s, incumbents have been winning reelections by wider margins. In the current Congress, members are nominated in primaries during which they must raise their own funds, organize and staff the campaign machine, and distinguish themselves from opponents of their party. After winning the nomination, they rely on their personal organization and fund-raising abilities. Thus the role of the political parties has declined. In short, from the nomination through the election, members come to rely on personal resources at the expense of political parties. No other democratic political system has an electoral mechanism in which members are so independent of the party organization. Hence party is more effective and important in other countries.

Members of Congress elected on their own owe little to the party leaders on the Hill. At best, the leadership can coordinate the preferences of their members; they have little or no ability to cajole or force members to vote with the party. As long as members can please their constituents, neither the national party nor the congressional party can affect their electoral career. Senator Phil Gramm (R-TX) is a classic example. Gramm was initially elected to the U.S. House of Representatives as a Democrat from College Station, the home of Texas A&M University. His voting record was very conservative. In 1981–1982 he voted with President Reagan more than 95 percent of the time. In fact, he jointly proposed with Delbert Latta (R-OH) the now-famous budget-cutting resolution. The Democratic leadership sought to punish him in the next Congress by denying him a spot on the Budget Committee. When the Democratic congressional caucus supported their leaders, Gramm resigned his seat, changed his affiliation to Republican, and won a special election in his district to fill the seat he had "vacated." In the 1984 election, he ran and won a Senate seat as a Republican. In sum, Gramm was not hurt by the Democrats' attempt to reprimand him for his voting record.

The point of this story is that, given weak parties and strong legislator-constituent relationships, cross-party coalitions are perfectly understandable. Members can vote with members in the other party who share their ideology. The Conservative Coalition voting scores published yearly by the *Congressional Quarterly* attest to the pervasiveness of a major ideological coalition. In addition to cross-party ideological coalitions, there are cross-party coalitions based on district interest. During the energy crisis of the 1970s, a coalition of midwestern and eastern representatives formed to keep oil and energy prices low and to ensure that their constituents would not have to bear an undue share of the costs associated with the crisis. As John Ferejohn (1986) has shown, an urban and rural coalition has formed around price supports and food stamps. That is, rural representatives vote for food stamps to aid urban poor and, in exchange, urban representatives vote for price supports that aid rural communities.

Yet another type of coalition has formed around specific interests. Since the 1960s the number of special-interest caucuses in Congress has risen. Before 1970 there were 3 such caucuses, by 1980 there were 60, and in 1987 there were 120. The Congressional Black Caucus, Congressional Women's Caucus, Congressional Hispanic Caucus, Irish Caucus, Coal Caucus, Copper Caucus, and many others have been formed. These caucuses meet on occasion, have staffs, present research papers, and in general try to influence relevant public policies. Although it is true that some of these caucuses are populated by members of only one party (e.g., the Black Caucus), their existence apart from the party system is a further indication of the importance of coalitions in the contemporary Congress.

My listing of ideological, general, and special-interest coalitions is not meant to imply that representatives vote general (i.e., ideological) interests over their constituents' interests. Rather, my point is that representatives and senators can form coalitions with members of the other party if they can sell it to their constituents. Thus, in an important sense American public policy is less party oriented than is public policy in other countries. In the American system special interests have a better chance to affect policy than do comparable special interests in other countries. The reason, in part, is that political parties can protect members from special interests by bundling policies and controlling nominations. In Britain, for example, a group like the National Rifle Association could not affect public policy as readily as it does in the United States. Within limits, British political parties control the nomination of members. Thus, they can ensure that the electorate never sees a candidate who favors gun control. Voters in Britain can choose between a party that favors policies A, B, C, D, and E and a party that favors V, W, X, Y, and Z. If the voters favor A, B, C, D, and Z, they will likely choose the first party. Because of the primaries in the United States, however, the parties cannot protect members from interests who favor Z. Thus the National Rifle Association is a powerful force in American politics, whereas it would not be so in other countries. In the United States, members of Congress must balance each interest in their district—in part because they are unprotected in primaries.

CONCLUSION

I began by asserting that the major difference between congressional coalitions in the United States and coalitions in other countries was that U.S. elections and policy were disjointed. Beginning in the Progressive era, political parties came to be composed of members who held different views. From the 1920s through the 1950s a number of cross-party coalitions emerged, the farm bloc and the Conservative Coalition being the most important. With the rise of the personal vote, the hold of party over member was further diminished, and there was a concomitant rise in the number of general and special-interest coalitions. Understanding the contemporary Congress's legislative record is thus increasingly a task of understanding the cross-party coalitions that form and re-form across a broad number of issues.

This scenario would seem to be somewhat contradicted by recent studies that show an increase in levels of party voting in the Congress, but that trend should not be overemphasized. Even with the rise in party voting, there is no doubt that legislative parties are weaker and cross-party coalitions are stronger in the United States than in other democracies. Furthermore, in order to claim that the rise in party voting is meaningful, one must know the extent to which policy content has been changed. In European party government, cabinets propose policies that regular members vote for in parliament and voters then choose between parties. If the increase in party voting in the U.S. Congress is attributable to the leaders' better coordination of members' preferences, then, in principle, there is a difference. That is, party positions are determined by calculating each member's preferences, and policy differences between parties are minimized by giving voters less to choose between. Thus party strength in Europe as well as Japan, and, more important, in the United States at the turn of the century, is clearly very different from party strength in the United States today.

NOTES

1. This phenomenon is deeply rooted in the American federal system. The Republican party was divided on the gold-silver question prior to 1896 and on the question of welfare and government management of the economy in the post–Franklin D. Roosevelt period.

2. In the following section, I rely on the work of Joseph Cooper (1975).

3. These data were taken from Alford and Hibbing (1983).

13

Partisan Presidential Leadership: The President's Appointees

G. CALVIN MACKENZIE

Politics is about control. Who controls the policymaking process, and to what end? In a democracy, the legitimate exercise of political power falls to those who win free elections. One of the benefits of victory is the authority to control appointments to those executive offices that are not filled by election but which contribute substantially to the determination of public policy.

Throughout much of American history, political parties have served as wholesalers in this democratic process. In choosing a president, the American people also choose a political party to run the executive branch. From 1800, when Thomas Jefferson's election signaled a transfer of power from the Federalists to the Democratic Republicans, until 1988, when George Bush's election implied a continuation of Republican control, parties have been a primary conduit for the translation of electoral victories into public policies. As the election of Jefferson portended the appointment of Democratic Republicans and their policy preferences, so the election of George Bush heralded the appointment of Republicans and their policy preferences.

To the casual observer, not much has changed. The tides that sweep into government after each election are party tides, carrying in the new president's co-partisans and carrying out the co-partisans of the old. But that surface appearance masks a set of important changes in the role that political parties now play in the staffing of presidential administrations and in appointments to the federal judiciary. Although party still seems to be the glue that holds administrations together, its consistency is much thinner than ever before and its holding power is greatly reduced. What endures is the party label; what has changed is the meaning of the label and the influence of the party organizations in presidential personnel decisions. Elections are still about control but, now more than ever before, they are about policy control rather than party control.

This essay will examine the changes that have occurred in party impacts on federal executive staffing in this century.[1] It begins with a look at the pre–New Deal experience and follows with an explanation of the New Deal and postwar evolution. Finally, it illuminates the reasons for the change in party role and influence, and explains the impact of that change on the governing process.

PARTIES IN GOVERNMENT: STAFFING THE EXECUTIVE BRANCH

The Birth of Parties

The Constitution, and the debates from which it sprang, anticipated no role for political parties in staffing the government. In fact, the framers of the Constitution did not very seriously contemplate the emergence of political parties, nor did they envision a government of such size that positions could not be filled by the president's personal acquaintances. There was little need for them to worry about the details of the appointment process, for they had not worried very much about the details of the executive or judicial branches.

The framers seemed to believe that a single person—the president— would make wiser personnel choices than any collective body sharing the appointment power. And, although they established the Senate's right of advice and consent as a check against defective appointments, they thought they had created a process that the president would dominate. As Alexander Hamilton pointed out in the 76th *Federalist*, that was their clear intent.

> [O]ne man of discernment is better fitted to analise and estimate the peculiar qualities adapted to particular offices, than a body of men of equal, or perhaps even of superior discernment.
>
> The sole and undivided responsibility of one man will naturally beget a livelier sense of duty and a more exact regard to reputation. He will on this account feel himself under stronger obligations, and more interested to investigate with care the qualities requisite to the stations to be filled, and to prefer with impartiality the persons who may have the fairest pretensions to them. . . . [I]n every exercise of the power of appointing to offices by an assembly of men, we must expect to see a full display of all the private party likings and dislikes, partialities and antipathies, attachments and animosities, which are felt by those who compose the assembly. The choice which may at any time happen to be made under such circumstances will of course be the result either of a victory gained

by one party over the other, or of a compromise between the parties.
. . . In the first, the qualifications best adapted to uniting the suffrages
of the party will be more considered than those which fit the person for
the station. In the last the coalition will commonly turn upon some
interested equivalent—"Give us the man we wish for this office, and you
shall have the one you wish for that." This will be the usual condition
of the bargain. And it will rarely happen that the advancement of the
public service will be the primary object either of party victories or of
party negociations. (Cooke, 1961:510–511)

In filling appointive positions, George Washington relied (as the
framers had anticipated) on people of whom he had personal knowledge.
Thomas Jefferson, Henry Knox, Edmund Randolph, and Alexander Hamilton filled the cabinet slots; Thomas Pinckney was appointed ambassador
to Great Britain and Gouverneur Morris to France; and John Jay became
the first chief justice. Washington's circle of acquaintances was large,
and the number of positions he needed to fill was small.

When required to fill federal positions of primarily local importance,
such as customs collectors or postmasters, Washington found it convenient
to defer to the judgment of senators from the relevant states. This practice
quickly acquired the veneer of custom when the first Senate rejected
Washington's appointment of Benjamin Fishbourn to be naval officer for
the port of Savannah, Georgia. Fishbourn was fully qualified for the
post, but the two senators from Georgia preferred another candidate
and succeeded in convincing their colleagues to reject the Fishbourn
nomination. (Mackenzie, 1981:93) Hence was born the concept of "senatorial courtesy," by which senators are granted significant influence
over presidential appointments within their home states. (When parties
later emerged, the courtesy was usually granted only to senators of the
president's party.)

Although most of Washington's appointees shared his views on
important issues, there was little sense of them and him as members
of the same political party. Even as disagreements began to emerge on
major issues of the day—the Jay treaty and the financing of state debts,
for example—they produced cleavages that only slowly formed into
lasting factions. Washington sought men of experience and judgment
to aid him in running the government. Whatever political litmus test
he might have applied was informal and primitive.

That changed rather rapidly, however, following Washington's retirement and the election of John Adams. With Washington gone, politics
became more bare-knuckled and political factions hardened. Adams's
appointees took on a clearly defined political coloration: Only Federalists
need apply. On the eve of his departure from government and the

transfer of power to the Jeffersonians, Adams sought to pack the government with Federalist appointments to many lower-level positions. Jefferson and his secretary of state, James Madison, tried to block these midnight appointments. The Supreme Court, in the great case of *Marbury v. Madison*, permitted them to do so. The battle was joined, and appointments would forever after be a chief prize of partisan politics.

The Spoils System

Partisan control of presidential appointments reached its zenith with the election of Andrew Jackson in 1828. His approach to appointments came to be known as the "spoils system," following the old adage that "to the victor belong the spoils." In the case of victors in presidential elections, the primary "spoils" were federal jobs.

In truth, Jackson did not invent the spoils system, nor was he the first president to put it into practice. But he was so vigorous in using his appointment powers to place his own loyalists in government offices and so shameless about doing so that his presidency is usually characterized as a watershed in the development of federal personnel practices. Jackson's presidency was all the more noteworthy, perhaps, because it resulted in a significant change in the kinds of people who staffed the federal government. Earlier presidents, in seeking fit candidates for office, had often turned to members of the country's wealthier families, and throughout the first six presidencies there was a distinct upper-class cast to the executive branch. But the turn toward popular democracy that Jackson's election signified found expression in his appointees, many of whom had little wealth or education.

To political observers of the time, this fact suggested not only that Jackson intended to sweep out all previous office holders in favor of his own supporters but also that political loyalty was to be the principal measure of fitness for office. Jobs in government began to be viewed as rewards for political services to the successful candidate.

Not coincidentally, this was a period of intense partisanship in American politics. Parties were becoming national political organizations and began to hold quadrennial national nominating conventions. Connections among partisans at the local, state, and national levels were becoming tighter. The trickle of immigration was also just beginning and would soon turn into one of the great floods in human history. As politicians sought the support of these new groups, increasing numbers of recent immigrants were finding work in government offices or party organizations. Before long, pressure to expand the number of government jobs, and to make as many of them as possible available for political appointment, began to build. The state and local political machines were growing, and they developed hearty appetites for government jobs (see White, 1954, 1958; Van Riper, 1958; Fish, 1904).

One consequence of these political developments was that government jobs were becoming an increasingly valuable currency. Political leaders and members of Congress began to contest with the president for control over the appointment process. Presidents came to realize that the well-timed appointment of a political supporter of a member of Congress or a party boss could often produce votes for legislation in Congress. Trading of this sort took place in earnest.

This was also a time when U.S. senators were chosen by their state legislatures, not by direct election. Since most of those senators were beholden for their offices to the leaders of their party, not to the people directly, they were eager to assist in whatever way they could to acquire federal government jobs for party members in their states. This situation only added to the pressure to treat the appointment process as a supplement to party politics rather than as a mechanism for attracting the country's most talented people into the public service. Political credentials were usually more valuable in seeking a federal job than talent or administrative experience.

Not surprisingly, the quality of the federal service during most of the nineteenth century was, at best, uneven. A great many positions were filled by appointees—sometimes called "spoilsmen"—who lacked any apparent substantive qualifications. The government survived this practice in part, at least, because it was not engaged in many activities that required significant technical or management skills. In fact, most of the technical specialities that now exist in government agencies were unknown in the nineteenth century: astrophysics, econometrics, environmental analysis, and so on.[2] The principal preoccupations of government in the nineteenth century were the conduct of a small number of routine functions that required little skill or experience: delivering the mail, collecting customs duties and taxes, building roads and canals. In many cases, a political hack could do these jobs about as well as anyone else. What was good for the party, therefore, was not always terrible for the government.

Nevertheless, the spoils system began to produce the seeds of its own destruction. The principal failing, of course, was that many of the people employed by the government were neither the most talented nor the most qualified available. In many cases, in fact, they were totally without qualifications other than their political connections. The spoils system was also a hungry monster, a constant source of pressure for the creation of new government jobs intended to provide for more political appointments and to lighten the burden on office holders so that they could devote more of their time to political activities.

Moreover, the spoils system invited corruption of all sorts because appointees were neither constrained by a sense of the honor of public service nor confined by any ethical notions of holding a public trust. They had their jobs because their party won an election and attained political power. And so long as they held that power, there were few real limits on how they could exercise it. Knowing that their horizon extended only to the next election, appointees were also driven to take advantage of their offices as hastily as they could, for they might soon be out of a job. If the sun was to shine only briefly, they felt compelled to make hay all the more quickly.

Another troubling aspect of the spoils system was the pressure it put on the president to devote substantial amounts of time to filling low-level positions in the federal government. Presidents in the nineteenth century had none of the elaborate White House staff structure that exists today. There was no one to whom they could delegate responsibility for handling patronage matters. Thus many hours were consumed brokering conflicting demands for appointments to individual offices. A story about President Lincoln suggests the plague-like quality of these pressures. The White House was a public building for much of the nineteenth century, and there were few restrictions on access to the main lobby. Job seekers often came there hoping for a moment or two with the president to plead their case. Lincoln found it very uncomfortable to pass through the lobby on the way to his office because his very presence often set off a flurry of such pleading. Once, when he was suffering from a bad cold, he said to his secretary as he was about to enter the lobby, "Now, at last, I have something I can give them."

The Creation of the Civil Service

Efforts to reform the personnel staffing process of the federal government appeared as early as the 1850s and gathered steam after the Civil War. Rutherford B. Hayes was elected president in 1876, having campaigned for civil service reform. He made little headway against congressional resistance during the next four years, however. His successor, James A. Garfield, had been a supporter of reform while serving in Congress. He was assassinated four months after his inauguration—in the legend of the time, by a "disappointed federal job seeker"—and reformers used his slaying as evidence of the rottenness of the spoils system and the acute need for reform. Two years later, in 1883, Congress passed the Pendleton Act, which created the federal civil service system.

This was hardly the death of the spoils system. Civil service protection spread slowly among government jobs. The majority remained subject to political appointment for years yet to come. Some categories continued

TABLE 13.1
Growth of the Federal Civil Service System

Year	Total Civilian Employment	Percentage Under the Merit System
1821	6,914	
1831	11,491	
1841	18,038	
1851	26,274	
1861	36,672	
1871	51,020	
1881	100,020	
1891	157,442	21.5%
1901	239,456	44.3
1911	395,905	57.5
1921	561,142	79.9
1931	609,746	76.8
1941	1,437,682	68.9
1951	2,482,666	86.4
1961	2,435,804	86.1
1970	2,921,909	81.9
1975	2,741,000	83.1
1980	2,772,000	78.5
1987	3,075,097	81.0

Sources: Data derived from Stanley and Niemi (1988:218); U.S. Department of Commerce (1987:309–311); and Young and Mace (1989:238).

to be filled through political appointment until well into the twentieth century. Local postmasters, for example, remained political appointees until 1970. And even the most vigorous of the reformers recognized that some positions would always be political in character and thus could never be blanketed under the coverage of a merit-based civil service. But a significant change had begun in 1883 and, as Table 13.1 indicates, it continued to spread in the century that followed.

The Pendleton Act, including its subsequent refinements, accomplished several ends. First, it set the principle that government jobs should be open and available to all citizens and should be filled by those who successfully demonstrate that they are best qualified for the position. Second, it established the policy that examinations were the best and most objective way to determine those qualifications. Third, it provided civil servants with protections against political removal and established a pattern of continuity: Civil servants would continue in office even as the presidency changed hands. And, fourth, to supervise this system and protect its neutrality from politics, the act created a Civil Service Commission whose membership would have to reflect a degree of partisan balance.[3]

Growing out of the success of the reform movement was a new question, the debate over which has continued into our own time. Once the principle was established that some positions in the government should be filled on the basis of merit rather than politics, arguments ensued about where the line should be drawn. Which positions should be granted civil service protection and which should continue to be treated as political appointments? The spread of civil service protection indicated in Table 13.1 suggests that a steadily growing percentage of federal offices have been placed outside of the political stream. But what of those offices left unprotected by the merit system? How were they to be filled? And by whom? That is the topic of the rest of this essay.

PRESIDENTIAL APPOINTMENTS IN
THE TWENTIETH CENTURY

The 1900–1932 Period

Except that a slowly increasing number of government jobs were coming under the coverage of the civil service, the appointment process in the first third of the twentieth century varied little from what it had been in the second half of the nineteenth. The positions outside the civil service were still filled by means of a process in which political parties played an important role and appointments were still viewed as a reward for political services.

This is not to suggest that all presidential appointees lacked substantive qualifications for federal service. Many of those who had been party activists had also built impressive records of public service and would have merited high-level positions even without party sponsorship. Names like Charles Evans Hughes and William Jennings Bryan would have appeared on most lists of highly qualified eligibles for cabinet or other top positions in government. Presidents, too, retained the latitude to select appointees who had no significant record of party service, whose primary qualification was talent or experience. In this category were people like Josephus Daniels, Andrew Mellon, and Henry Stimson.

But partisan pressures in the appointment process were ever present. In putting together their cabinets, for example, presidents felt constrained to select people who represented different factions or regional elements in their party (Fenno, 1959:78–88). In this sense, Woodrow Wilson's cabinet was not very different from Abraham Lincoln's. Though strong-willed and independent leaders, both felt compelled to respect partisan concerns in staffing the top positions in their administrations.

Throughout this period, the national party organizations played an important role in identifying candidates for presidential appointments.

It was quite common, in fact, for the head of the president's party to hold a position in the cabinet, usually as Postmaster General. This made sense, not only because the Post Office Department was the principal consumer of patronage appointments but also because a cabinet post provided a vantage point from which the party leader could work with the president and other cabinet secretaries to ensure a steady flow of partisan loyalists into federal posts throughout the government.

The party role was critical to the functioning of the government because there was at the time no alternative source of candidates for appointment. Each cabinet secretary had his own acquaintances and contacts, but few of them knew enough politicians to fill all the available positions in their departments with people who would be loyal to the administration, pass muster with appropriate members of Congress, and satisfy the political litmus tests of party leaders in the states and cities where they might serve. The party could help with all of that.

Some of the individuals brought forward to fill appointive positions may well have been unqualified political hacks, but many of the appointees who came through the party channel were skilled and qualified. The parties themselves performed valuable services; this was by no means merely a turkey trot. More important, partisan control of the appointment process usually guaranteed the construction of an administration that was broadly representative of the elements of the president's party and thus, in some important ways, was in touch with the American people it was intended to serve. Equally important, the parties served as an employment agency upon which the government was heavily reliant. Indeed, they provided a steady stream of politically approved candidates for federal offices. That was a function of no small significance in a government that lacked any other tested means of recruitment for positions outside the civil service.

The 1933–1952 Period

Following the pattern of his predecessors, Franklin Roosevelt appointed James Farley, the leader of the Democratic party, to serve as Postmaster General and to superintend the selection of lower-level appointments in the first Roosevelt administration. Farley directed a patronage operation that bore a close resemblance to those of the previous half-century.

Despite the familiar look of FDR's patronage operation, however, changes were set in motion by the New Deal that would have lasting consequences for the staffing of presidential administrations. Three of those deserve some mention here.

The first was the very nature of the politics of the New Deal. The coalition that brought Franklin Roosevelt to office was composed of a broad diversity of groups and views. It provided FDR a sweeping victory by drawing support from Americans who disagreed with each other about important matters, yet agreed on the need to elect a president of their own party. But the New Deal coalition soon proved as useless for running a government as it had been useful for winning elections. Even with the most delicate kind of balancing act, it was no small task to construct an administration of intellectuals and union members, northern liberals and southern conservatives, progressives and racists. The task was complicated all the more by the intensity of the new administration's efforts not merely to redirect but to *reconstruct* public policy in the United States. It simply could not be reliably assumed that Democratic appointees would fully support all the dimensions of the president's program.

Hence, Roosevelt and his senior advisers increasingly began to end-run the Democratic party patronage system in filling key positions in the government. More and more, the people closest to the president— James Rowe, Louis Howe, Harry Hopkins, and others—began to run their own recruitment programs. Typically they would identify bright young men who were already serving in government or were anxious to do so and cultivate them with the kind of ad hoc assignments that prepared them for more important managerial positions. These men were either lifelong or recently converted Democrats, but they tended not to be people with any history of party activism. It was the passions of the time and their commitment to the New Deal that inspired their interest in politics, not a pattern of service to local or state political machines.

The need for such people grew increasingly apparent as the consequence of a second change wrought by the New Deal. The government was growing. Total federal employment was 604,000 in 1933. It had nearly doubled by the end of the decade. The New Deal seemed to be spawning new agencies and programs almost daily. The result was a voracious need not merely for people to fill newly created slots but for skilled managers and creative program specialists to attend to problems at least as complicated as any the federal government had ever before tackled.

This complexity also had the effect of diminishing the importance of the party patronage system as a source of appointees. It became increasingly apparent that the party faithful did not always include the kinds of people required to operate technical agencies such as the Securities and Exchange Commission and the Agriculture Adjustment Administration. So Roosevelt turned to other sources and occasionally even risked the wrath of party leaders in so doing.

A third change in the New Deal years—the growing importance of the White House staff—fed off of the momentum of the first two. As the energy of the federal government came to be centered in the president (as was dramatically the case during the New Deal), the need for more support for the president became increasingly apparent. In 1936 Roosevelt appointed a committee headed by his friend Louis Brownlow to study the organization of the executive branch and to make recommendations. The report of the Brownlow Committee described the need for vigorous executive leadership to make a modern democracy work. But it also pointed out that "the President needs help" in this enterprise. It went on to recommend both the creation of an Executive Office of the President (EOP) and the establishment of presidential authority to appoint a small personal staff that would assist in the management of the government (U.S. President's Committee on Administrative Management, 1937). In 1939 the Congress acted affirmatively on most of the recommendations of the Brownlow Committee.

In the past, presidents had little choice but to rely on their party's patronage operation because they lacked the staff necessary to run a personnel-recruitment operation of their own. With the creation of the EOP, however, that began to change. Embedded in the recommendations of the Brownlow Committee was a philosophy of public management that threatened the importance of party patronage. Political control of the government, in the view of Brownlow and his many supporters in the schools of public administration, had come to mean policy control, not merely party control. It was no longer enough for a president to staff his administration with members of his own party and to let them work with co-partisans in Congress to superintend the routines of government. Instead, the president needed managerial support through broader control of the budget, government organization, and personnel selection to move public policy in the direction that he had set—a direction that, presumably, had earned the endorsement of the American electorate.

This gradual evolution in management philosophy clearly suggested that the president and his personal staff needed to play a larger role in recruiting appointees who supported the president's policy priorities and possessed the skills and creativity necessary to develop and implement them. In that scheme, government jobs could not be viewed primarily as rewards for party loyalty, and recruitment could not be left primarily to party patronage operations.

None of these changes took place overnight; instead, they slowly found their way into the operations of the presidency. Loyal Democrats continued to claim positions in the Roosevelt and, later, the Truman administrations. The pressure to fill vacancies with the party faithful did not abate. The Democratic National Committee continued to operate a full-service employment agency, but most appointments to important positions no longer came via this route.

The strains on the patronage operation grew more acute after Roosevelt's death. Truman found himself in an odd position. Though a Democrat like Roosevelt, he needed to forge his own identity as president. Members of his party often had difficulty in transferring their loyalties from the dead president to the new one, especially since many of them thought Truman was several cuts below Roosevelt in stature.

The 1948 election campaign widened the fissures in the Democratic party all the more. The southern wing of the party split off to support then Democratic Governor Strom Thurmond of South Carolina. The so-called Progressive wing had its own candidate in Henry Wallace. After winning reelection, Truman found that he had to temper his faith, slender as it already had become, in the ability of the Democratic party to provide candidates for appointment who were certain to be loyal to him and the important policies of his presidency.

Truman did what any reasonable leader would have done under the circumstances. He relied less heavily on candidates recommended by the party and built his own recruitment process. The latter never passed much beyond the primitive stage, and the former continued to play an important role. But change was under way, and its full impacts would emerge in the administrations that followed.

The 1952–1968 Period

Dwight Eisenhower was the least partisan president of the twentieth century, and he came to office with fewer debts to his party than any of his predecessors. Although Republicans had not controlled the presidency for twenty years, it cannot be said that Eisenhower's election signified the beginning of a flood of old-line Republican loyalists into federal offices. Eisenhower's chief of staff, Sherman Adams, reported that the president was often indignant at what he considered to be political interference in his appointments and that he "avoided giving the Republican National Committee any responsibility for the selection of government officials, a duty the commiteee would have been happy to assume" (Adams, 1961:125). Charles F. Willis, Jr., an Eisenhower aide who worked on personnel matters, noted that the president "seemed to react against intense political pressure, more than anything else that I noticed, adversely, and I think that his appointments and the people he surrounded himself with at the top level reflected that he considered quality rather than political know-how" (Willis, 1968:28).

Eisenhower did intend to oust as many New Dealers and Fair Dealers as he could, but he sought to replace them with people who subscribed to his own brand of Republicanism. Being a Republican, even a lifelong member of the party faithful, was not enough to get a job in the Eisenhower administration—as soon became evident to Republicans across the country.

Although the new administration worked closely with Republican National Committee Chairman Leonard Hall and did in fact place a number of party loyalists, appointments to top-level positions were much more heavily influenced by a group of the president's close friends. During the 1952 transition, Lucius Clay, Herbert Brownell, and Harold Talbott commissioned the New York consulting firm of McKinsey and Company to do a study identifying the most important positions in the government. At that time, and in the years that followed, they were an important source of suggestions and advice to Eisenhower on matters of government staffing.

The composition of the Eisenhower administration quickly came to reflect the diminished role of the president's party as a source of senior-level personnel. A majority of Eisenhower's first cabinet had no significant history of Republican party activism. The subcabinet looked much the same, having drawn heavily on the practical talents of the business and legal communities, with only a smattering of officials whose primary credentials were partisan or political (Mann, 1965:293).

Eisenhower's second term marked an even more important turning point in the transition away from party dominance of the appointment process. The Twenty-Second Amendment, limiting presidents to two terms in office, had been ratified in 1951. Eisenhower was the first president to whom it applied, and his reelection in 1956 made him the first president ever to enter a term as a lame duck. Since he could not run again for reelection, there was less incentive for Eisenhower to be making appointments with an eye toward building partisan electoral support: He was freer than ever to distance himself from patronage pressures.

That freedom was reflected in the significant initiatives that developed during Eisenhower's second term for management of the personnel function in the presidency rather than in the party. The Eisenhower White House was the first to respond to a modern president's need for centralized control over executive branch personnel by seeking to construct procedures and organizational structures to serve that objective. The position of Special Assistant for Personnel Management was created, and the first elements of a systematic recruitment operation were put in place (Kaufman, 1965:66).

This momentum toward centralized presidential control of the appointment process and away from reliance on party patronage accelerated in the Kennedy and Johnson administrations. Kennedy, like Eisenhower, had won the presidential nomination by setting up his own organization and capturing the party. His was not a life of deeply committed partisanship, nor did he grant the Democratic party organization much credit for his narrow victory in the 1960 election. So Kennedy felt little compulsion to staff his administration with party loyalists to whom he might have had any debt or obligation. From the very start, he and his staff operated their own personnel-recruitment operation.

After Kennedy's assassination, Lyndon Johnson continued the practice of operating a White House personnel office. He designated John Macy, then chairman of the Civil Service Commission, to handle presidential appointments as well. Macy expanded the personnel office and began to systematize its procedures, even employing computers to maintain records on thousands of potential appointees.

Under both Kennedy and Johnson, the White House personnel office worked with the Democratic National Committee, in varying degrees of cooperation. But the participation of the party was clearly subsidiary. Most of the time the National Committee's role was to determine that candidates for appointment selected by the White House would not incur the opposition of party leaders in their home states. The White House also conducted checks with home-state Democratic senators and members of Congress to avoid opposition from them. But as Dan H. Fenn, Jr., an assistant to Kennedy on personnel matters, has noted: "The kind of people we were looking for weren't the kind of people who were active in party activities" (Fenn, 1976).

These checks, which came to be known as clearances, emerged as a routine of the appointment process and provided a role for the party, albeit a limited one. Although party officials were a steady source of suggestions regarding potential nominees, genuine control over personnel selection had shifted to the White House. This process had begun in the early days of the New Deal; it accelerated as the size of the White House staff grew. The party ceased to have an initiative role in the appointment process and clearly no longer operated that process as it once had. The party had become a check point and, with but few exceptions, not much more. As Hugh Heclo has indicated, its influence was reduced to the exercise of "'negative clearance'; that is, nursing political referrals and clearing official appointments in order to placate those political leaders in Congress and in state, local, or other organizations who might otherwise take exception" (Heclo, 1977:71). The party no longer drove the appointment process, but its disapproval of an appointment could bring that process to a temporary halt.

1969 and Beyond

The movement to centralize control over presidential appointments reached new levels of sophistication and success in the administration of Richard Nixon and those that followed. Nixon himself never had much interest in personnel selection, but the people to whom he delegated that task tended to be experienced professional managers who saw it as a critical ingredient in efforts to establish control over the executive branch.

In the years after 1969, the White House Personnel Office (later called the Presidential Personnel Office) became an important component of the White House Office and grew in size. It now routinely employs more than thirty people, and often swells to more than fifty at particularly busy times. Appointment procedures have been systematized and routinized. Computers play an important role in tracking the progress of appointments. And clearances with leaders of the president's party, relevant members of Congress, officials in the agency to which an appointment is to be made, and policy specialists in the administration are regular features of almost every appointment decision (Mackenzie, 1981; Bonafede, 1987).

But the most important characteristic of the modern appointment process, and the one that most critically affects the influence of political parties, has been the creation of a genuine and aggressive recruitment or outreach capability within the White House staff. Party influence in appointments remained significant so long as the White House lacked the ability to identify qualified candidates on its own. Then the president and his staff had little choice but to respond to recommendations and suggestions that, as the terminology of the time had it, came in "over the transom." It is an iron law of politics that "you can't beat someone with no one," and of football that "the best defense is a good offense." Both apply in the appointment process as well.

The thrust of most of the contemporary development of White House personnel operations has been to grasp the initiative, to relieve presidents from reliance on external sources for their appointees. Primary among those sources historically was the president's own political party organization, but the successful establishment of a recruiting capability in the White House has left the parties with little remaining control over a function they once dominated.

PARTIES AND PRESIDENTIAL LEADERSHIP:
AN ACCELERATING EVOLUTION

The years after World War II have been a time of diminishing influence for the national party organizations in the operations of the presidency. This was a trend with prewar antecedents, but its pace accelerated after the war. There is no simple explanation for the change. In fact, it resulted from a confluence of other changes occurring both inside and outside of the government in those years. The most important of those are summarized here.

The Game Changed

Party influence was always greatest with respect to appointments to positions outside of Washington. When an appointee was to serve as, say, customs collector for the port of Philadelphia or as postmaster in Butte, local party officials generally had a determining influence in choosing the person to fill the slot. Even though this was technically a presidential appointment, presidents readily deferred to the leaders of their party in the local area. Until relatively recent times there were tens of thousands of such positions, and they were a significant part of the political rewards system for party workers. A person who had spent years as party organizer, poll watcher, and minor office holder could reasonably expect to cap a political career with an appointment to a sinecure as a local official of the federal government.

But after World War II, largely at the behest of an increasingly vocal public service–reform movement, many of these positions were taken out of the patronage stream and placed under some form of civil service coverage. What was good for the party was increasingly bad for the delivery of government services. And the reformers thought the solution was to take some of the politics out of appointments to these administrative offices.

The Number of Important Presidential Appointments Grew

From the beginning of the New Deal onward, the number of senior-level positions in the federal government grew. New cabinet departments and independent agencies were added, and old ones expanded as hordes of new programs were created. The bureaucracy thickened and new administrative layers were added to the federal government. Departments that might have had two or three presidential appointees before World War II now have a dozen or more. The Department of Defense, which came into being after World War II, has almost fifty senior positions filled by presidential appointment. And the Department of Education, created in 1979, has more than thirty (U.S. House of Representatives, Committee on Post Office and Civil Service, 1988).[4]

Many of these new positions (e.g., those of Under Secretary of Commerce for Oceans and Atmosphere, Assistant Secretary of Defense for Research and Technology, and Director of the Office of Energy Research) required appointees with a high level of technical or scientific competence because they bore responsibility for complex government programs. The kinds of people needed to fill these positions were unlikely to be found hanging out at party headquarters on election night.

As a consequence of the growth and increasing sophistication of the government's senior appointive positions, presidents needed to develop their own personnel-recruitment operations. It became apparent during the New Deal that party channels would simply not be adequate to provide the number and kinds of talented appointees that an increasingly active government required.

The magnitude of that inadequacy grew larger in the years that followed. In response, successive administrations developed and then refined their own systems and procedures for staffing the senior levels of the executive branch. Parties had once played a central role in this process; by the end of the second decade after World War II, however, their role was essentially peripheral. Members of the president's party continued to fill most of the appointed positions, but their identification, selection, and recruitment were conducted at some distance from the formal organization of the president's party.

The Power Situation Changed

As the federal government came to play a larger role in American life, appointees who developed and implemented programs became more powerful. Consider the contrast between 1932 and the present. The federal government in 1932 did *not* provide aid to education, run a national pension system, provide health care for the elderly, fund the national highway system, regulate financial markets, shoot rockets into space, or serve as democracy's policeman around the world. It does all of those things and many more today, and it spends more than a trillion dollars each year in the process.

Management of those programs and of the distribution of the funds they involve affords a great deal of power to presidential appointees. Decisions regarding who fills those positions matter more than ever before. And the groups in American society affected by the choices made by these appointees have become increasingly unwilling to leave them to purely patronage appointees. They have sought instead to put pressure on presidents to select appointees with the necessary technical skills and experience and with particular policy views. Party loyalty and service have been largely irrelevant to these calculations.

As appointments became more important, parties became less important in filling them. Throughout much of American history, the principal contests for power were outside of government, in elections where the parties were strongest. With the beginning of the New Deal, the power struggle increasingly took place within government, in the modern bureaucratic state where the parties were weakest. When the terrain shifted, the locus of power shifted as well.

Changes Outside the Appointment Process

Nothing in government occurs in a vacuum. In fact, government is a great social mirror: What happens there usually reflects what is happening elsewhere in society. That is certainly true of the changes that have taken place in the appointment process during this century. The influence of political parties diminished in the appointment process because their influence was also diminishing elsewhere. Parties could claim a potent role in presidential appointment decisions only so long as they were able to exert influence elsewhere in American politics— that is, by controlling the candidate-nominating process, delivering votes, and maintaining their hegemony over critical political skills. But that role, too, was changing during the middle decades of this century, as other essays in this book have amply demonstrated.

Parties lost their primacy as organizers of American political life. Direct primaries took control of the nominating process out of the hands of party leaders and gave it to voters. Candidates devised ways to raise their own money, build their own organizations, do their own advertising. They hired political consultants to provide the kinds of skills that parties had traditionally provided. As fewer Americans identified strongly with the two major parties, it became harder and harder for the parties to deliver votes.

The long-term impact of all this was that parties had fewer debts to call due in the appointment process. Presidents had less and less reason to feel obligated to their parties and party workers for their own elections and, hence, less incentive to appoint those workers to federal offices to meet such obligations. Once parties began to lose control of the electoral process, they lost control of the appointment process as well.

Simultaneous with the decline in party fortunes was an explosion in the number of national special-interest groups. Counting the number of national interest groups is no small task, but Ronald Hrebenar and Ruth Scott identified 14,726 national nonprofit organizations in 1980, a 43 percent increase over 1968 (Hrebenar and Scott, 1982:8). This figure, of course, omits profit-seeking corporations, which are themselves increasingly active political entities.

These groups were both much more substantive and much more focused than the major political parties. They were typically concerned with a relatively narrow set of policies, and they represented the people most directly affected by the shape of those policies. Thus they were able to concentrate their attention and political influence on the small number of presidential appointments that mattered most to them. They were also able to work closely with the congressional committee and subcommittee chairs who were most interested in those programs and who controlled their appropriations. These were often politically potent combinations that generated considerably more influence over presidential appointments than broad-based coalition parties were able to generate. In the competition for influence over appointments, interest groups became increasingly successful, often at the expense of the political parties.

The decentralization of power in the Congress also worked against the interests of the parties in the appointment process. During the early decades of this century, real political power in Congress was concentrated in the hands of a relatively small number of institutional party leaders and committee chairs. Local political bosses and national party leaders regularly worked with them to influence the president's appointment decisions. If the leader of the Democratic National Committee or the mayor of Chicago called Sam Rayburn, the Speaker of the House, and asked him to try to get the president to appoint a particular Democrat to the Federal Communications Commission, it would have been hard for the president to deny the request. Sam Rayburn was a key factor in determining the fate of the president's legislative program. Keeping him happy was usually much more important than any particular appointment.

After the middle of the century, however, the party leaders and committee chairs increasingly lost their grip on power in Congress. Younger members generated reforms that spread power around, to the subcommittee level in the House and to individual members in the Senate. The political calculus became much more complex, and it was much more difficult for local bosses or leaders of the national party organization to use the congressional lever to influence presidential appointment decisions. Individual members of Congress were less beholden and less connected to the national party in any case, having built their own personal political organizations and having developed their own sources of campaign funds. Their interest in presidential appointments was much more ad hoc and personal in character: They sought appointments for their friends, supporters, and staff members, not for traditional party workers. As parties became less important to the job security of members of Congress, incentives diminished for members to use their influence in the appointment process for purposes broader than their own personal objectives.

So the political landscape underwent broad transitions after World War II. Senior-level appointments grew more important as national political power moved to Washington. Lower-level appointments were transferred in large numbers to the civil service. The presidency became a larger and increasingly sophisticated institution with unprecedented management capabilities. The electoral process was no longer the sole realm of political party organizations. Interest groups sprang up everywhere and rapidly gained political potency. A decentralized Congress was less able and less willing to serve purely partisan interests in the appointment process. Individually and collectively, these changes eroded the influence once exercised by parties on the staffing of the executive branch of the federal government.

THE CONTINUING PROBLEM OF POLITICAL CONTROL

Two important trends have been the dominant themes of this essay. One is also the dominant theme of this book: that parties are not what they used to be. In virtually every aspect of American political life, organized political parties play a smaller role now than they did at the beginning of the century. That is certainly true, as we have sought to demonstrate, in presidential appointments to administrative positions.

The other trend, more directly relevant to the topic of this essay, has been the steady and successful effort to isolate public employment from political pressure, to create a federal work force that is "protected" from the tides of political passion in the country and among the electorate. At the beginning of this century, there were 240,000 federal civilian employees. Of these, more than half were political appointees of one form or another. As of 1990, there are 3 million federal employees. Of these, only a few thousand are actually filled by political appointment.

Thus a peculiar but familiar reality is suggested: that Americans are suspicious of politics and parties. For many of them, politics is a dirty business, and one that can easily mess up government. Accordingly, there has been substantial public support for efforts to depoliticize the personnel-selection process in government, to eliminate all the pejoratives: cronyism and nepotism and the spoils system.

But Americans are also highly skeptical of bureaucrats, and so they respond positively to campaigning politicians who bash bureaucrats and promise to put government back into the hands of the people. The most popular American politician of recent times, Ronald Reagan, was a master of this strategy. "Government," he often said, "is the problem, not the solution."

Hence there exists a kind of public schizophrenia that deeply complicates the task of presidential leadership. Americans want a government that is isolated and protected from the worst aspects of partisan politics. But they also want a government that is controlled not by "faceless bureaucrats" but by elected leaders who will keep it responsive to popular concerns. Those are contradictory goals. How is it possible to have a government that is simultaneously free of politics and under political control? The answer, of course, is that it is not possible. And, as a consequence, conflict between these competing objectives constantly pervades the personnel process.

When parties were the dominant influence in presidential personnel selection, the reigning notion was that getting control of the government meant establishing partisan control. The way to implement the will of the electorate was to fill as many positions as possible with members of the president's party. By filling all, or a large number, of the federal offices with the president's co-partisans, the government would move in the directions he had laid out.

It wasn't a bad theory, except that it didn't work in practice, especially after 1932. It didn't work for two reasons primarily. First, it couldn't work in the United States because of the nature of American political parties. The large national parties whose candidates won presidential elections were constructed of delicate coalitions. They rarely offered the electorate a very detailed or refined set of policy objectives. Their primary task was to win the elections, and to do that they clung to the center, trimming specifics to develop the broadest possible mass appeal. Even in the most intense periods of party conflict in the United States, it was difficult for most voters to perceive very broad *policy* differences between the parties. Parties provided few meaningful clues to what exactly the government would do if their candidate were elected.

There was thus little reliability in the notion that staffing the government with members of the same party would provide a unified sense of direction under presidential leadership. In fact, members of the same party often disagreed with one another, and with their own president, on a great many matters of policy. In many cases, all they shared was a party label. The spoils system and its successors constituted a very shaky foundation for getting control of the government through coherent policy leadership from the White House.

Even if American political parties had been more ideologically and substantively unified, the aforementioned theory would have failed in implementation. Partisan domination of the appointments process was never viewed by party leaders as a system for aiding the president in establishing policy leadership. It was treated as a vehicle for party, not presidential, purposes. The principal goal underlying the suggestion of party candidates for appointment was to sustain the vigor and the regional and ideological balance of the party, not to find loyal or effective supporters of the president's program. As indicated earlier, many presidential appointments were controlled by the local party organizations, which had little interest in national policy. They sought to get federal jobs to reward their own faithful servants and to prevent the federal government from upsetting their local control.

For both these reasons, party participation in presidential appointments failed to serve the purpose of aiding the incumbent administration in establishing policy leadership over the government. And in this century, as we have seen, American presidents began to reject that participation. Slowly but steadily they found ways to construct their own appointment processes that were increasingly distanced from party influence. In the past few decades, party influence on appointments has faded almost to the vanishing point.

Presidents still struggle to "get control of the government." Few of them fully succeed. But no recent American president has sought party help in accomplishing this critical objective. And for good reason. American political parties were rarely very helpful in this respect when they were relevant and potent. They would be even less valuable today with their potency on the wane and their relevance to the task of governing very much in doubt.

NOTES

1. Partisanship in judicial appointments will not be discussed in this essay because of space constraints. Interested readers are referred to the excellent work that Sheldon Goldman has done on this topic.

2. The reader should note that a few technical specialties had begun to emerge in the nineteenth century, primarily in the areas of public health and agriculture. Even at the height of the spoils system, these positions were often treated as exceptions and were filled by the same people from one administration to the next, without regard to political loyalties.

3. In 1979 the Civil Service Commission was abolished and replaced by two new agencies: the Office of Personnel Management and the Merit Systems Protection Board.

4. The numbers in this paragraph refer to so-called PAS appointments: presidential appointments that require Senate confirmation.

PART SIX

Toward the Future

14

Can a Partisan Be Bipartisan? Party Politics in the Bush Administration

E. J. DIONNE, JR.

George Bush has an unusual pedigree for an American president. As the only president ever to serve as both county chairman and national chairman of his party, Mr. Bush seemed to be just the person to preside over a highly partisan presidency. Here, at last, is a Republican president who appeared incapable of *not* thinking about how his actions would affect the fortunes of his party's candidates all the way down the ticket. The folks who make the party run matter to George Bush; they were, after all, the people who helped nominate him. And by naming Lee Atwater, his campaign manager, as chairman of the Republican National Committee, Mr. Bush signaled a personal concern for the workings of the party apparatus. For years, the party organization had played a subordinate role to that of the White House's political office. Now, by placing one of his most important political advisers at the head of the national committee, Mr. Bush was declaring that, at last, the party would mean something again (Dionne, 1989:30).

It is clearly true that the Bush presidency, in its first year at least, was highly political—sometimes all too obviously so. The president's travel schedule suggested that his would be a campaigning presidency. The use of media gimmicks seemed to get out of hand when it was learned that, to provide the president with a dramatic prop for a major speech on drugs, law enforcement officials had lured a crack dealer into Lafayette Park in front of the White House so they could seize some crack just a few hundred yards away from the Oval Office itself. But in principle there is nothing wrong with a campaigning president; and, in the current era, as Sidney Blumenthal has argued, the "permanent campaign" is simply a fact of life (Blumenthal, 1980).

The major issues that George Bush emphasized in his first year were clearly selected with an eye toward their impact on the partisan balance. In light of opinion polls showing that drugs were a major concern to Americans, it was not surprising that the president would highlight his war against them. Moreover, since the drug issue is a crime issue, an emphasis on drugs had the potential of keeping alive a major partisan theme from the 1988 Bush campaign: that Republicans were tougher on crime than Democrats. Nor was it surprising that the president chose to lead a (brief) crusade against flag burners. Patriotism has been a refuge for right-of-center political parties all over the world for generations. A president who got so much mileage from the pledge of allegiance during his election campaign could be expected to show the flag at the first opportunity.

But there was far more subtlety to the Bush political strategy than flags and crack alone. For in highlighting two other issues, education and the environment, the Bush administration went after the Democrats on their strongest ground.

Among the important findings of public opinion polls in the final years of the Reagan administration was a renewal of public support for an activist government. Voters were still not wild about taxes—a finding that George Bush certainly took to heart. But they did sense that after years of laissez-faire politics/government, it might be time again for a period of modest public engagement. In a sprightly formation, Paul Taylor of the *Washington Post* suggested that the "me generation" might be transforming itself into the "we generation." At the least, there was a new uneasiness over the relationship between "me" and "we."

Few understood this transformation better than Mr. Bush's able free-lance speechwriter, Peggy Noonan. As a former Democrat, she instinctively saw what ardent free marketeers did not: that for all the talk of a new age of selfishness, Americans still longed for a sense of community and mutuality. Out of this grew phrases that became clichés (the highest compliment to a speechwriter) including "a kinder, gentler nation" and "a thousand points of light." The latter was a reference to the work of voluntary agencies that was a bit too mystical for Michael Dukakis to understand.

Education and the environment were areas where Mr. Bush could show—or claim to show—that he believed in the kind words Ms. Noonan had written for him. In the case of education, he could do this without spending more money, by attacking liberal failure and emphasizing the need for local governments to do more. On the environment, the president was willing to take several steps to the left of Ronald Reagan, knowing that the middle-class voters for whom the environment was top priority were just the sorts of people the Republicans needed to secure their base. It was also no accident that the environment and education were two areas in which the Democrats usually got high marks from the public. Take those issues away from the Democrats and what would they have left?

Richard Darman, the president's budget director, carried the attack on the Democrats one step farther in his talk of cultural "now now-ism." Here again, the Bush administration was moving shrewdly to steal another Democratic idea. Democratic presidential aspirants, especially Senator Joseph R. Biden, Jr., and Representative Richard A. Gephardt, noticed the public's unease about the nation's future and its sense that individuals had become too selfish. They sometimes tried to give the issue a class edge by contrasting the millions made by the arbitrageurs and investment bankers in the "paper economy" with the hard work of employees and entrepreneurs who made far less trying to produce "real" things.

Mr. Darman changed hardly a comma in these Democratic speeches. He attacked national selfishness head on, trying to make it a Republican cause. Democrats said this wholesale larceny of their ideas was shameless. They also conceded it was good politics.

This, then, is the background to the next period of American politics, a time when the battle between the two parties will be over ideas (or what pass for "ideas") and themes. And the fighting will be far more subtle than it was in the Reagan era. Mr. Bush has prudently decided that appearing too partisan, too often, ill suits a president. Hence his incessant appeals to "bipartisanship." And he contributes further to his nonpartisan image by putting so much emphasis on what were once thought of as "Democratic" issues. This makes many conservatives nervous. Yet make no mistake: The Bush administration is trying hard, and with at least some success, to continue the wrecking job on the Democrats that Ronald Reagan performed so well. In the Reagan era, Republicans sought to outflank the Democrats by polarizing the electorate. In the Bush era, Republicans are seeking to undermine the Democrats' foundations by co-opting as many of their themes as necessary and, if possible, by giving them a conservative twist. It is a kinder, gentler approach to the pursuit of partisan advantage. But it is the pursuit of partisan advantage all the same.

CHANGING POLITICAL IDEAS
AND REPUBLICAN SUCCESS

One can easily overemphasize the importance of ideas in American politics, especially since politicians tend to look at ideas not for their intrinsic merits but, rather, as weapons in an ongoing battle. And the average voter tends to make pragmatic rather than ideological judgments at the polls. When they elected Ronald Reagan, that most ideological of presidents, most voters explained their choice by referring to the failures of the Carter presidency. Who needed ideology to explain a vote for which 20 percent interest rates and the hostages in Iran provided ample justification? V. O. Key was quite correct in his classic formulation that elections are retrospective referenda on the performance of the party in power—and that is just what the 1980 election was (Key, 1966).

But to say that the judgments rendered in any given election can be explained in pragmatic terms is not to deny the longer-term shifts that take place in the country's political thinking. There is an interaction— a "dialectic," if you will—among a party's performance in office, its marshaling of the available political ideas, and the voters' own assessments of "what works." Over the long run, voters can change their philosophical orientation by changing their minds about "what works."

For example, the Great Depression was a disaster for the Republicans not just because Herbert Hoover was sitting in the White House when the stock market crashed but also because the Depression itself undermined public confidence in the business class that had effectively run the country in the 1920s. In the 1930s, the businessmen were replaced by planners, politicians, and intellectuals. Laissez-faire economics was replaced by that slightly convoluted version of social democracy, New Dealism (Brinkley, 1990: 85–121; Schneider, 1988:51–98). The sharp shift away from pure free-market ideology was so profound that even Richard Nixon came to declare that all of us had become Keynesians.

The 1970s did to liberals and the Democrats what the 1920s did to businessmen and the Republicans. But this is *not* to say that there was a broad shift to the right on all issues. Thomas Ferguson and Joel Rogers were quite correct when they argued in 1986 that "poll after poll demonstrates that the basic structure of public opinion in the United States has remained relatively stable in recent years" (Ferguson and Rogers, 1986). For the most part, voters did not reject government benefits—especially the ones that government had given them. The change was more subtle. Government, once viewed in a largely positive light, came to be viewed in a more negative light. Conservatives, once viewed as heartless and cranky, came to be seen as realists whose values were those of the majority in the country. Liberals, the folks who gave us the New Deal and our victory in World War II, came to be seen as impractical souls who picked the pockets of the middle class. Humphrey Bogart, the warm-hearted tough guy who beat out Ronald Reagan for the lead role in *Casablanca*, once symbolized what it meant to be a liberal Democrat. The beautiful friendship between the mass of voters and Democratic liberalism that Bogart represented is over.

Nowhere is this fact more striking than in the two parties' use of the symbols of class. The classic New Deal slogan, "If you want to live like a Republican, vote Democratic," almost perfectly captured what voters wanted and gauged both the extent and the limits of class resentment in the country. The slogan did not attack the rich as such, nor did it imply that average voters had anything against being rich themselves. Indeed, it acknowledged that most people would, on balance, prefer to be rich and to "live like Republicans." At the same time, the slogan did appeal to class resentments, though in an optimistic way, by implying that most people did not, in fact, live like Republicans and needed to do something about it. The Democrats became the party of all those who had little and aspired to more.

Currently, the Republicans might themselves run under the slogan, "If you want to live like a Republican, vote Republican." If the earlier Democratic slogan implied that the middle and bottom might ally together against the top, Republican strategy these days aims at uniting the top and the middle against the bottom. High tax rates on the middle class ensure that this strategy will appeal to a great many voters.

The Republicans have also been able to marshal class resentments to an extraordinary degree by arguing that the real class war was not over money but over "values." To (white) working-class voters, the Republicans argue that their values on such issues as crime, the family, self-discipline, and work are much closer to the norm than the values of the Democrats. Republicans seek to cast the class enemy not as the rich but as an upper-middle-class elite (represented by people like journalists and professors) that disdains the values of "ordinary people." The heartbeat of America, the Republicans argue, does not throb in Harvard Yard. That this argument could be made effectively even by a prep school–educated, old-family Yale graduate like George Bush suggests just how powerful it is.

The Democrats have thus been hurt both by the shift in the sense of "what works" (to many voters, government doesn't) and by the transformation in which people see as "the elite" (intellectuals; not businesspeople).

No account of the Republicans' electoral success since 1964 is complete without mention of racial politics. White resentment against Democratic support for measures on behalf of blacks has clearly helped build the Republican base. White racism, it should be noted, is not as widespread as liberals sometimes fear, and the polls have shown measurable improvements over the last three decades in white attitudes toward blacks. But there can be no doubt that the race issue has helped Republicans to create something like a "solid South" for their presidential candidates. Even when George Bush trailed Michael Dukakis badly in the polls, he remained competitive in the South. In the northern cities, the Republican base vote among middle- and working-class whites—especially among Roman Catholics—is much higher now than it was in 1960, in part because of the race issue. Even in victory in 1976, Jimmy Carter ran behind traditional Democratic voting levels in the white neighborhoods of northern cities. Between his high point in the polls after the Democratic Convention and election day, Michael Dukakis suffered some of his most severe losses among Catholics (Phillips, 1970; Edsall, 1988:3–49; Clymer and Frankovic, 1981; Orren, 1978:183–270; Dionne, 1988:A1).

But if the issues and the key constituency groups have been moving so strongly against the Democrats, how have they survived so well in Congress? And how effectively can the Democrats fight the Republicans from their congressional bastion?

THE DEMOCRATS' SEARCH FOR WINNING ISSUES

By operating from a congressional base, the Democrats suffer from two basic difficulties. These might be summarized as tactical and strategic.

The tactical difficulty is that the resources and approaches that allow individual Democrats to hold onto congressional seats cannot be translated into presidential politics. Very simply, Democratic members of Congress can "cheat." They can abandon individual party positions whenever it is convenient for them to do so—as sixty-four House Democrats did on the capital gains tax in late 1988. Morever, individual members of Congress have routinely made peace with the dominant interest groups in their districts or states—even though these groups, notably in business and industry, have been predominantly Republican at the national level. Such peace-making efforts guarantee incumbent Democrats large campaign treasuries that, in turn, almost guarantee their reelection.

The strategic difficulty is that the American political system generally forces highly partisan congressional leaders to pay a high cost for partisan opposition. Generally, voters want the president and Congress to work together. Congressional leaders who oppose the president with partisan fervor are usually labeled "politicians." Those who work amicably with the White House are usually labeled "statesmen" or "stateswomen." This rule breaks down only when a president becomes highly unpopular, in which case members of his own party begin to bolt, giving opposition a fine, bipartisan sheen.

In addition, it is difficult for any party, and especially for the heterogeneous Democrats, to achieve the consensus required to run an effectively partisan campaign from Congress. Few issues have demonstrated this more clearly than the question of whether taxes should be raised to cut the federal budget deficit. Even among Democrats who agreed on the need for tax increases, there have been sharp divisions over which taxes to raise. And the tax issue criss-crosses ideological lines. Ronald H. Brown, the Democratic national chairman, is quite clearly a liberal. Yet he lambasted Democratic congressional leaders who responded to President Bush's drug proposals by calling for higher taxes to pay for more programs. Mr. Brown is not opposed to tax increases on principle. He just thinks that making higher taxes a battle cry is terrible politics. (The Democrats had similar difficulties coming to agreement on one of their most popular issues—child care.)

The Democrats also suffer from having to do too many things at once. If the Democrats are ever to build a presidential majority, they will need to post gains in two groups—roughly speaking, the younger non–blue collar workers and the older blue collar workers. The Democrats maintain a certain appeal to both groups, but for contradictory reasons. The younger group generally holds liberal attitudes on the environment and on social issues, notably abortion, but it is ideologically agnostic or conservative on economic issues. The older group still generally likes New Deal economics but has strayed from the Democrats on the social issues and race.

The Democrats' challenge is to find a message that wins votes from both groups. This is not necessarily as difficult as it seems. The younger, non–blue collar workers are by no means all rich; they are most assuredly not all "yuppies." Thus, some of the Democrats' talk about class inequality and "fairness" could appeal to such voters, if given a properly modern and "forward-looking" caste. The older group is not uniformly conservative, and Democratic talk about "community" (notably Mario Cuomo's rendition of the "family of America") can be given a traditional twist that resonates with the values of the small town and the old neighborhood.

But contradictions abound. A pro-choice message on abortion is broadly appealing but may send the wrong message to the older voters. Stanley Greenberg and Celinda Lake, polltakers who favor abortion rights, have argued that the issue must be handled with care, lest the Democrats come to look like the party of "permissiveness." Even voters who are wary of government interference with abortion generally don't like "permissiveness." The older, blue collar voters the Democrats need to target favor permissiveness less than almost anyone. And too much talk about inequality and fairness can lead voters in both groups to suspect the Democrats of harboring dreams of huge tax increases. As William Schneider has argued, "fairness" is a powerful theme when the many feel threatened economically—during a recession. But when the many feel relatively secure about their pocketbooks, "fairness" sounds like a way of taking money away from the majority to give to the poorest. It is a noble sentiment, perhaps, but not always a popular one. The rebellion of wealthier elderly people against paying higher taxes for catastrophic health insurance for their poorer senior-citizen brethren is a sobering story for advocates of redistribution.

In their search for new issues, Democrats are struggling to find their way back to an old approach that worked so well for them in the past: taxing a minority of rich Republicans to pay for programs for the vast majority of middle-class and poor people, who would gratefully vote Democratic. The Democrats' most ingenious solution so far is "mandated benefits." Essentially, Democrats would require business to pay for programs that they might, in other times, charge off to the taxpayers. Such benefits include day care, health insurance, and mandated leave for the parents of newborns. The minimum wage—a way of forcing businesses that hire the working poor to lift them out of poverty—also falls into this category. Generally speaking, all these programs are popular; most people would love to have business give them benefits. The difficulty is that the tactical imperatives of Democratic members of Congress often prevent them from embracing such programs wholeheartedly. The many Democratic incumbents who have warm relationships with their local business communities feel the most pressure from their business friends on just these issues. And small business, a potent force in local politics, hates mandated benefits even more than large business, which already provides many of them anyway.

The other difficulty is that mandated benefits may represent an idea whose time has already come and gone. Economic forces are pushing large business to urge that the benefits they already pay for, notably health care, be effectively "socialized" so as to pass the costs back to government and the taxpayers. Just at the point when mandated benefits seem to be so promising politically, they are becoming increasingly difficult to achieve economically.

Another popular approach among Democrats, establishing a kind of welfare state for the middle class, has run smack into the nation's fiscal difficulties. It is undoubtedly true that a substantial majority of the electorate would like the government to enact programs to assist first-time homebuyers and to guarantee access to college to all students who can get in. But such programs would be costly. Even loan schemes that appear to be "self-financing" ultimately have large costs, either at the startup point or later on, when the bills for the houses and the tuitions come due.

The Democrats' overall difficulty is that their basic rationale as the party of the average man and woman requires balancing acts that most Democrats seem incapable of carrying out. Taxing the rich is generally popular, but it runs up against the congressional party's base of financial support. Holding the line on taxes is also popular, but this keeps the

Democrats from supporting new government programs that would win them votes. Having business pay for popular policies also impinges on the party's financial base and may raise serious economic problems. Doing nothing at all may be the course of least safety, since it allows George Bush to steal issues and votes at the margins. Mr. Bush's big advantage is that he and his party represent the status quo and are thus not expected to change matters very much. The Democrats are supposed to be the party of change—but they don't know how to pay for it.

There is a deeper dilemma for the Democrats: Their role in American politics is akin to that of the European social democratic parties. They are the party of mild redistribution and active government. Thus, nothing would help the Democrats more than increasing the public's confidence in the government's ability to get good things done. Yet with George Bush in the White House, making government work means making *Republican* government work. In this situation, the gains of effective government might as easily accrue to George Bush and his party as to the Democrats.

THE POLITICAL DANGERS OF "PARTISAN BIPARTISANSHIP"

The Democrats can still draw hope from the old adage that there is nothing wrong with their party that a sharp economic downturn can't cure. And they can draw sustenance from an even more comforting thought: that the Republicans face as many contradictions in trying to sustain a presidential majority as the Democrats face in trying to build one of their own.

Nothing illustrates this point better than the contortions Republican politicians underwent after the Supreme Court expanded the rights of states to regulate abortion in the 1988 *Webster* decision. Until *Webster*, opposition to abortion was an almost costless stance for Republicans. Voters who were strongly opposed to abortion voted Republican as their best option for overturning legal abortion. Yet voters who favored legal abortion, especially among the well-to-do, voted Republican without much fear that the status quo on abortion would change very much; the Supreme Court had taken care of that. Suddenly, these Republican-leaning but ardently pro-choice voters saw a right that they had taken for granted come under threat. And they showed signs of defecting in large numbers to the Democrats. As Roger Stone, a conservative Republican political consultant, put it in late 1988:

There is a growing centrist coalition in the country—and the abortion issue is bringing black clouds over the Republican coalition. What has happened is the yuppie element in our coalition, soon to be if not today the dominant group in our culture, likes the Republican message on economics, opportunity, foreign policy and doesn't like the Republican message on social issues. (Hoffman, 1989:A7)

The Republicans, no less than the Democrats, need to perform balancing acts. In the Republicans' case, that entails balancing off the older, poorer, socially conservative constituency (notably the religious conservatives) against the young, the socially hip, and the better-off. In trying to do this in 1989, Republican candidates for governor in both Virginia and New Jersey showed how clumsy such a process can look when it is carried out in public. In the case of abortion, an issue that is supposed to draw on individuals' deepest moral convictions, the cost of appearing too opportunistic can be high indeed.

The Republicans' stumbling on abortion helped the Democrats win both the Virginia and New Jersey governorships. And, after the election, Republican National Chairman Lee Atwater, seeking to accommodate pro-choice Republicans, annoyed many pro-life Republicans.

Even in defeat, Michael Dukakis showed in 1988 that it was possible for the Democrats to expand their share both among the younger middle class and among older working-class and rural voters. Mr. Dukakis drastically cut the Republicans' victory margin in California by posting major gains in middle-class areas all over the state, and he carried such quintessentially middle-class liberal states as Oregon and Washington. Yet he also cut the Republicans' margins sharply in states such as Illinois, Iowa, Missouri, Montana, and Kansas by appealing to the economic discontent of the less well-off.

For all its manifest strengths, Mr. Bush's strategy of "partisan bipartisanship" leaves him vulnerable on several fronts. It has little appeal for the staunch conservatives inside the Republican party, on whom Republican presidents need to rely when their administrations fall onto hard times. Early on, Mr. Bush faced serious carping from the right, which does not view him as the heroic figure that Ronald Reagan was. The continuing pressure from the right could complicate Mr. Bush's efforts to reach out to the center, forcing him into stands that contradict the image of moderation he so prizes.

And by fighting the Democrats on their own ground—on education and the environment especially—Mr. Bush runs a substantial risk of failure. To show real movement on education, he may ultimately run up against a difficult choice: either to embrace some of the more radical "privatization" proposals urged by such party thinkers as House Whip Newt Gingrich, or to spend more money as Democrats urge. The education issue is sufficiently complicated that Mr. Bush may slip by with his favored method of splitting differences. But in doing so, he may lose some of the initiative. On the environment, Mr. Bush has shown a willingness to make genuinely hard choices. But his efforts to satisfy environmentalists will always run up against the demands of the Republicans' business constituents.

The broader danger for Mr. Bush and the Republicans is that "prudence," "caution," and "competence" provide them with no secure philosophical moorings. As a consequence, the administration is more vulnerable to accusations that it is engaged in pure "gimmickry." In the Reagan administration, the gimmicks at least seemed to have a broader purpose. Mr. Bush, by contrast, is in danger of appearing to lack any purpose other than maintaining power. Given that what he is trying to maintain is a relatively conservative regime, his supporters argue that his approach is in fact one based on principle. But over time, the Bush strategy's lack of dynamism could open the way for a Democratic campaign similar to John F. Kennedy's nonideological call in 1960 "to get the country moving again." Those who preside over seemingly purposeless administrations are easily dismissed by the voters as mere time-servers.

PARTY POLITICS AND THE END OF THE COLD WAR

The tumultuous changes in the Soviet Union and Central Europe will drastically alter the American political dialogue and party politics. The changes give all kinds of political writing, from the newspaper article to the academic essay, a highly perishable quality. It is impossible to say for sure where Europe is going; it is, if anything, more difficult to say how America will react.

The popular view is that the end of the Cold War will be bad news for conservatives. Anticommunism, as conservative strategist David Keene put it, is "the glue that holds the movement together." Most of the well-off economic conservatives share with their socially conservative comrades a hatred for the Soviet Union and all its works. They might disagree on abortion and still bash the communists. The end of the Cold War could eliminate that common ground (Barrett, 1990).

The transformation of the Soviet Union, moreover, effectively removes from the political agenda an issue that has hurt the Democrats since 1972: their image as "the party of weakness." What was "McGovernism," after all, except the belief that the Soviet Union was not as dangerous as conservatives thought it was, and that military spending could therefore be cut sharply? Mikhail Gorbachev has made that view popular across the political spectrum. As Richard Nixon might put it, we are all McGovernites now.

With the Soviet Union fading as an enemy, America's economic competitors, notably Japan, will loom larger. Economic nationalism, a theme that comes more naturally to economically interventionist Democrats than to free-market Republicans, could replace anticommunism as a broad national sentiment.

Mr. Bush seemed to be failing a test that he himself had said presidents should pass. In a speech criticizing Mr. Dukakis in late August 1988, Mr. Bush declared: "The American people expect someone in the driver's seat who will tell them where our foreign policy was going, not someone who won't." In the new atmosphere, it was not clear that Mr. Bush himself knew where American foreign policy was going. The country itself was certainly confused about the future, and national confusion always creates opportunities for the opposition—if it is creative enough to bring some order to the chaos.

Some Democrats certainly feel this way, and they believe they can use George Bush's reactive approach to the changes in the East against him. In early 1990 Representative Richard A. Gephardt, the Democratic majority leader, called Mr. Bush's approach to foreign affairs "a policy adrift, without vision, without imagination, without a guiding light save precious polls." The situation, in Mr. Gephardt's view, is ripe for a Democratic call for change and action.

But what action? It is here that the Republicans may yet be better off without the Cold War than they were with it. The end of the Cold War, far from exacerbating old splits in the Republican coalition, could ease some new divisions that began to develop at the end of the Reagan administration. Even before the momentous events of 1989, popular support for military spending had waned. The level of support for direct American military intervention abroad was low even during the Reagan years. Only quick and successful operations such as Grenada and Panama won broad popular support. Beneath the surface, there were real divisions on foreign policy within the Republican coalition. Many of the Republicans' well-educated supporters were not only liberal on social issues but also relatively anti-interventionist on foreign policy. Most of them, after all, were of the Vietnam generation. Such voters often responded to new-style Democrats such as Senators Bill Bradley of New Jersey and Tim Wirth of Colorado.

The end of the Cold War will render irrelevant such Republican foreign policy splits. Now, the Republicans can freely respond to the public mood and cut military spending *themselves*. At just the point when it seemed impossible for George Bush to close the budget deficit without a tax increase, the "peace dividend" loomed as a relatively easy solution. The Republicans could also use the peace dividend to open up a new debate that might help their cause: Should the money cut from the defense budget be used for new programs, as the Democrats would wish, or should it be given back to the taxpayers? Barely was the Berlin Wall down when one of the Republicans' shrewdest strategists,

Senator Phil Gramm of Texas, began a personal campaign to turn the peace dividend into a tax cut (Pines, 1990:A29).

The Democrats faced an elementary political problem: The Cold War ended while the Republicans were in the White House and, at least initially, Bush handled the transition with considerable skill. Most important, nothing Mr. Bush did retarded the changes in Central and Eastern Europe that everyone had welcomed. In an extremely complicated situation, not making a mistake can be the most important thing. The Democrats might call for a "grand vision," but Bush's prudence was a response to the widespread feeling that *no one* really knew yet how to respond to so many changes happening so quickly. Mr. Gephardt himself illustrated the Democrats' difficulty in offering real alternatives to the Bush policy. When Mr. Gephardt proposed that the United States give direct aid to the Soviet Union, he was criticized not just by Republicans but also by leading Democrats—notably, Senator Bradley. Mr. Gephardt's inability to come up with something better may have been less a comment on him than on the paucity of grand visions generally.

It is almost certainly true that over the long run, the end of the Cold War will benefit the Democrats by ridding the political agenda of the national security issues that so hurt their party and divided it so badly. Moreover, the Democrats ought to be able to gain some ground on the new issues of international economics, if only because America's competitive difficulties raise questions about how much the Reagan-Bush years really helped the American economy. But the long run can be a very long time. It took the Republicans twenty years to win a presidential election after Herbert Hoover lost the White House.

Ultimately, of course, it is a mistake to speak of "the end of the Cold War" as a discrete event. The end of the Cold War is an ongoing process. The United States and the Soviet Union will spend many years negotiating the terms on which it will be concluded. Events in the Soviet Union, furthermore, are largely (though not entirely) out of America's control. Still, assuming a reasonable amount of competence on the part of the Bush administration, one might contend that precisely because the end of the Cold War is an event of such immense proportions, it will produce little immediate political change at home. American voters, no less than the writers of essays, may need much more time before they reach firm conclusions about such an important turn in history.

CONCLUSION:
THE BUSH STRATEGY AND POLITICS OF THE 1990s

Turning back to party politics, we might conclude that the future hangs less on what each party does to the other than on what each does to itself. Within both parties, there are rich traditions of factionalism and division. Within both, the competing factions speak incessantly about how their adversaries will bring their party to ruin. Within the Republican party, conservatives argue that only enthusiastic adherence to (conservative) principle will maintain the party in power. After all, Gerald Ford, the moderate, lost and Ronald Reagan, the believer, won. Moderate and liberal Republicans argue that Ronald Reagan won precisely because he campaigned and governed much closer to the center than he talked. In the Democratic party, many liberals argue that only a more aggressive economic populism will staunch the defection of less well-off voters to the Republicans or to abstention. Moderates and conservatives argue that "special interests" (usually meaning blacks, labor, and feminists) hold too much power in the party and that Democrats need to move closer to "the values" of the country (meaning more conservative values, especially on defense and the social issues).

Such arguments are likely to continue in the Bush years, but they will be increasingly irrelevant to what actually happens in political campaigns. For when it comes to organizing campaigns, power in American politics is being concentrated in an increasingly small number of hands. The central party committees—the national committees and the House and Senate campaign committees—play an ever more important role in organizing political campaigns, especially the crucial campaigns for open seats in the Senate and House. And although the Republicans continue to raise more money than the Democrats, the latter have been able to make their central campaign committees highly competitive.

In addition, both parties have developed relatively small groups of "brand name" consultants who square off against each other in election after election, and in state after state. The consultants develop their own specialties, and individual consultants often develop primacy in particular states. To pick just one example: In California the Democratic teams of Doak and Shrum, media specialists, and Hickman-Maslin, polltakers, moved together from the successful Alan Cranston for Senate campaign in 1986 to the unsuccessful Leo McCarthy for Senate campaign in 1988 to the Attorney General John Van de Kamp for Governor campaign in 1990. The consultants are also coming to play an increasingly important role in shaping both presidential and congressional strategy, in the off-years as well as during election campaigns. The fact that so much political talk in the country is about "themes" and "messages" is a tribute to the growing influence of consultants, not only within their own field of expertise but also on ordinary discourse.

It is common journalistic and academic practice to bemoan the rise of the consultants, especially their penchant for "negative campaigning." And with good reason. A strong case can be made that the growth of negative campaigning has depressed voter turnout and, more dangerous still, diminished public confidence in the competence of democratic government. If food producers said the scurrilous things about one another's products that candidates routinely say about the opponents, much of the country would stop eating anything except home-grown produce.

The rise of consultants has also made American politics less democratic in certain visible ways. In the first place, the consultants are expensive, thus increasing the role of money in politics and decreasing the chance that less well-off candidates will win. Second, the consultants tend to hold much of the decisionmaking power within campaigns and even exercise a remarkable amount of control over what candidates say. As a result, the chances of a spontaneous airing of heretical ideas are diminished, the impact of other organized political groups is limited, and the influence of volunteers and amateurs (in other words, average citizens) on electoral politics is reduced.

There are, however, some countervailing trends. The notion that a campaign should spend all of its money on direct mail and television is now widely contested. Michael Dukakis invested heavily in an elaborate field operation in California, based on such old-fashioned concepts as door-to-door campaigning. In the 1989 Democratic mayoral primary in New York, David Dinkins relied heavily and successfully on a substantial field operation based in significant part on the trade union movement. And activists on both sides of the abortion issue have shown that political volunteers can have a major impact on electoral outcomes.

The impact of the consultants cannot be dismissed as entirely negative. Both the centralization of campaign knowledge and the free exchange of ideas among consultants have given an increasing coherence to each party's message. Consultants literally export ideas that work, from one state to another. A Democratic campaign for governor in Pennsylvania increasingly resembles a Democratic campaign for governor in Kentucky, and each party's congressional campaigns often look much the same from one district to another.

And even if some of the ideas exported across district lines are trivial (male candidates often look good when they score in a basketball game played with a group of teenagers), others are substantive. Republicans are identified as the party that opposes tax increases, not just because Mr. Bush asked that his lips be read but also because, in district after district, the advertising of Republican congressional candidates placed a heavy emphasis on the tax issue. Democratic candidates have come to emphasize their support for programs on behalf of children, not just because doing so is noble but also because the research of several

Democratic polltakers has shown that popular support for Democratic-style programs was greatest when the programs pertained to children.

Thus, if the consultants can be faulted for taking some of the surprise out of politics, they can also be praised for doing just that. As a consequence of the testing of party messages and themes from election to election, both parties may be able to develop increasingly consistent public images over the years as the consultants come to agree on what works. Such a politics is really no more cynical than "waving the bloody shirt" was for Republicans after the Civil War or attacking Herbert Hoover was for Democrats after the Depression. And consultants know better than almost anyone the limits of their craft. In 1988 George Bush appealed to voters in the center but knew he needed to tend carefully to his conservative base, lest his campaign be disrupted by conservative attacks or undermined by low conservative turnout. In the South, even the most conservative Democrats understand the importance of black voters to their electoral success and know that moving too far to the right on civil rights will doom their candidacies. Which is to say that even the most cynical consultant is limited to some degree by the nature of his candidate and by the image, history, and base constituency of his candidate's party.

But at least until the end of the Bush administration, coherence will come much easier to the Republicans than to the Democrats. Not only is there broader agreement among Republicans over what their party needs to do, but a president can be far more successful in molding his party's image than any collection of even the most skilled congressional leaders, aided by the most adept consultants. For Mr. Bush, success under the banner of bipartisanship is likely to be the best partisan formula of all—a happy marriage for a conservative who actually likes government and likes getting along with his opponents. Democrats are still searching for a purpose and a method for their partisanship. In the meantime, their best hope is to use the very shrewdness of the Bush strategy to get voters to ask whether their president stands for anything at all.

15

The Evolution of Political Parties: Toward the 21st Century

L. SANDY MAISEL

Nearly fifty years ago, E. E. Schattschneider (1942:1) wrote that "[t]he rise of political parties is indubitably one of the principal distinguishing marks of modern government. The parties, in fact, have played a major role as makers of governments; more especially they have been the makers of democratic government. It should be flatly stated at the outset that . . . the political parties created democracy and that modern democracy is unthinkable save in terms of the parties." A decade later the American Political Science Association (1950) issued a special report that was critical of the state of American political parties and called for a more responsible party system. As the 1970s began, the *Washington Post*'s award-winning columnist and reporter David Broder, proclaimed in a widely circulated book that *The Party's Over* (1971). But, most recently, political scientist Larry Sabato discussed the reactions of political parties to the crisis they had faced in *The Party's Just Begun* (1988).

Political analysts have blamed parties for the evils of our society, decried the ways in which they perform their roles, and despaired over whether the nation could progress without them. They have sounded the death knell for parties (at times in mourning and at times in jubilation) and declared their resurrection. But scholars and journalists, activists and analysts, have not ignored political parties—and they have not been neutral toward them. The persistence of American political parties over nearly the entire history of the nation and the prominence given their role by all commentators on American democracy are vivid testimonies to their resilience.

Perhaps political parties can best be understood in terms of organizational theory. They arose to meet certain needs of the polity but, as time has passed, they have achieved a life of their own, responding to criticism, abandoning some roles and fulfilling new ones, changing with the system and the political environment in which they exist. Value-laden appraisals miss the point. Political parties per se are not inherently good or evil. Rather, they are functional. They are extra-constitutional institutions that bridge gaps in the constitutional structure of American democracy.

At times their roles are clear and at times cloudy. At times they perform their roles well and at times poorly. At times their roles have been central and at times peripheral. They persist and adapt to changing conditions because, like all such organizations, they are composed of individuals who have a stake in their survival. The key to understanding political parties, and to speculating about their future, is to view the parts as well as the sum of the parts. Who has a stake in the different roles that political parties fulfill? Who is involved in defining their role—from within the parties and from without?

Virtually all textbooks on political parties begin with a definition of what a party is (Sorauf, 1980:17; Maisel, 1987:10). But perhaps we should recall what V. O. Key (1964:200) concluded on the subject of definition: "Pat definitions may simplify discussion, but they do not necessarily promote understanding. A search for the fundamental nature of party is complicated by the fact that 'party' is a word of many meanings. . . . The nature of parties must be sought through an appreciation of their role in the process of governance." It seems appropriate to keep that warning in mind as we speculate about the directions that political parties are going to take as the nation embarks on its third century.

THE CURRENT CONTEXT

The Leading Players

We begin our assessment by looking at those most involved in today's partisan politics. Certainly individuals are important in shaping institutions; in today's context the relationship of leading politicians to the political parties—because it is so different from that in the recent past—seems particularly worthy of note.

Students taking introductory courses are frequently told that one of the president's extra-constitutional roles is to serve as leader of his political party. But that role is as leader of his party in government; presidents have not typically been involved with their party's organization. The division of party roles into party organization, party in the electorate, and party in government has parallels in the individuals who perform each role. Only rarely in the last half-century has an elected government official played a key role in party organization. The exceptions that prove the rule have been in those communities that have retained the last vestiges of dominant party machines, in which the party boss has at times been a mayor or a county leader. Similarly, the vast majority of voters loyal to one party or another have little or no interest in working for the party, much less in serving in office.

Of course, a close connection between party organization and party in the government has always existed. Elected officials have run as candidates of organized political parties, whether the "organization" had any role in securing those nominations or not (see Chapters 7 and 8 of this volume). Once in office, elected officials become "celebrities" at party functions. But that is very different from playing an active role in working on the structure of the party.

More often the party has become a political tool of incumbents, helping them to gain reelection and serving as a way to enhance their political careers and those of their supporters. Presidents have nominated their allies to chair the national committee, and the party organization has become a political arm of the White House. The same has been true for governors and, to a lesser extent, legislators at the national, state, and local levels. It should also be recalled that few elected officials have come up through the party organization; the careers of elected politicians, particularly those of prominent national politicians, have typically been independent of party careers.

Against that background it is noteworthy that George Bush came to the White House with the perspective of one who has served as chairman of the Republican National Committee. As E. J. Dionne points out (in Chapter 14), Bush's party background is not a defining characteristic; but it does lead one to question whether organizing party activities, working for all Republicans and not just himself, and defining a winning coalition for the Republican party will be more important to him than they have been to his predecessors.

Of particular interest is the number of other contemporary leaders whose careers have bridged the various partisan roles. Senate Minority Leader Robert Dole (R-KS), like Bush, is a former chair of the Republican National Committee (RNC). Senator George Mitchell (D-ME), the majority leader, served as chair of the Maine State Democratic party and as a member of the Democratic National Committee and its Executive Committee; moreover, while the Republicans were in power during the Nixon administration, he was narrowly defeated by Robert Strauss in a bid to become the party's leader.

Furthermore, Mitchell's drive to Senate leadership was decisively aided by the role he played as head of the Democratic Senate Campaign Committee. The Hill committees of both parties are now viewed as important players in the political arena (recall Chapter 3). Mitchell's rise to Senate leadership and that of Tony Coelho (D-CA) in the House (before his resignation under the threat of an ethics investigation) have led aspiring congressional figures to see chairing the congressional campaign committees as a step on a career ladder in ways never before envisioned.

The current chairs of the two national committees also come to their roles with unique perspectives. Traditionally, party chairs have been supporters of the president who have worked within the party organization, either nationally or in their own state (e.g., John White for the Democrats and Richard Richards for the Republicans), or they have been political figures tied to their party's national leader (e.g., Democrat Kenneth Curtis, an early Carter supporter who had been governor of Maine, and George Bush, a former representative defeated in a race to become senator from Texas when appointed RNC chair), or they have been political fund raisers (e.g., Democrat Robert Strauss and Republican Frank Fahrenkopf).

Before assuming his position as Republican National Committee chairman, Lee Atwater was a political consultant—the very essence of an institutional rival to party organization as an influence in the electoral process. Democrat Ron Brown's career was as an establishment Washington lawyer and lobbyist and as an adviser first to Senator Ted Kennedy (D-MA) and then to Jesse Jackson, who in turn were quintessential examples of candidates whose rise toward power and celebrity status were aided more by the media than by party regulars.

Thus, to a greater extent than has ever before been the case in the era of modern campaigning, those in partisan leadership roles in the government and in formal organizations know politics and the roles of the political parties from a number of different perspectives. The leaders of the two parties in the government have experience in party organization as well as in more personalized campaigning. The four congressional campaign committees (the Hill committees) stand at the intersection of the worlds of party organization, modern campaigning, and governing. The leaders of the party organizations came to their current roles with backgrounds in other institutions that have competed with party for influence over electoral politics. All of these leaders have a commitment to political party—to partisan politics. One question, then, is how these commitments are played out in terms of the role that party plays in the political and governing processes. Another is whether the views of these leaders will be broader than those of individuals whose entire careers had been involved with only one aspect of what political parties have been called upon to do.

The Roles of Party Today

Party Organization. The earlier essays in this book have detailed various aspects of the roles performed by political parties in the 1980s. Consider first the formal party organizations. Perhaps they can best be described as institutions responding to changes and searching for roles. Although the national committees were never reputed to be powerful (recall that Cotter and Hennessy [1964] entitled their book on the national committees *Politics Without Power*), state and local party leaders were extremely influential in nominating politics at all levels of government. Because many areas were dominated by one or the other of the political parties, this control over the nomination process often meant control over elections. In those areas in which the two parties contested elections, party organization provided important tools for candidates' campaigns. Before the era of television and computers, before high-tech campaigning, electioneering was done largely on the street—and political parties provided the foot soldiers for their candidates' campaigns.

But many changes occurred quite quickly, and parties were somewhat slow to respond. Two changes stand out: the spread of the direct primary as the principal means of nominating candidates and the advent of new campaign techniques, emphasizing mass media approaches to the voters, candidate appeals through television and radio, computer-generated mailings, and targetted messages. Because of the first change, political parties lost control over the nominating process; party-designated candidates could be and were challenged by independent entrepreneurs who were seeking the party label and using the new techniques of campaigning. The new techniques carried over into the general election, with party organization playing a greatly reduced role.

The party organizations began to respond, although the two national parties responded differently. The Republicans, under the leadership of National Chairman William Brock, decided that they would become important players in electoral politics. To do so, they needed to provide services that the candidates wanted. And to provide services, the national party needed money. The Republicans established a highly successful direct-mail operation, raising the vast sums that are necessary to mount a modern campaign operation. Then they systematically set about providing services that would help all Republican candidates. They established schools to train campaign staffs; they undertook negative research on incumbent Democrats to help Republican challengers; they developed media messages that could be adapted to various localities; and they helped their candidates with survey research as well as fund raising—essentially, with many of the services otherwise provided by consultants.

The Republicans at the national level became active in recruiting candidates to run for the Senate and the Congress and even for seats in state legislatures. They used promises of needed services and financial assistance to recruit quality candidates, and they set national strategies and targets. In short, they proceeded as a modern campaign organization.

While the Republicans were building this impressive campaign apparatus, the Democrats were saddled with a large deficit and were divided by procedural quarrels. They spent much of the 1970s in troublesome debates over party rules, particularly those governing the presidential nomination. The changes in party rules that resulted (as discussed below) were important and contributed to the nationalizing of the Democratic party; but they also consumed time and energy and left the Democrats noticeably behind the Republicans in fund raising and the ability to provide services to their candidates. Under Chairman Charles Manatt, the Democrats began to emulate their Republican counterparts, but the effort was clearly one of catching up, not of matching performance.

At the local and state levels, parties have also looked for ways to influence elections. They began to provide services to candidates, achieving economies of scale by working for all of their candidates in a certain area. The Republican party has aided state and local organizations as they play this new role; again, the Democrats, because they lack a financial base, have not been able to match Republican efforts. Although state and local party organizations have not regained control of the nominating process, they do retain a role as players in the electoral game, because they developed resources that the candidates could use. This role, in turn, has established a connection between victorious candidates and party organization. Few candidates want to be dubbed "candidates of the organization," but as state and local parties gain in organizational and financial strength (see Chapter 2), candidates increasingly take them into account.

One aspect of the work of party organization that is often overlooked concerns the building of party platforms. These statements of how the party feels about the issues of the day theoretically link the organization (which has the responsibility for writing the platforms) to the electorate (which can look to the platforms to see how the party will address the issues of the day) and to elected party leaders (whose job it is to implement the platforms). Some claim that platforms are meaningless documents, but Gerald Pomper (1972) has demonstrated that they distinguish the major parties in meaningful ways. Moreover, recent evidence (see Chapter 4) suggests that the differences among the party activists who write the platforms might well be widening—and that these differences could affect the electorate's view of the parties in the future.

Parties and the Voters. But what about the voters? How do they relate to political parties? When Campbell, Converse, Miller, and Stokes wrote *The American Voter* (1960), the model of voting behavior they described sought to explain party affiliation, because party affiliation was the best predictor of vote. By the time Nie, Verba, and Petrocik wrote *The Changing American Voter* (1976), however, strength of party affiliation was on the decline and issues, as such, seemed more important to more voters. As Bob Dylan sang, "The times, they were a changin'." Vietnam and a series of social issues—as well as a long period of time since the cataclysmic events that shaped the New Deal coalition—strained voter allegiance. The candidates of the two parties did not necessarily reflect citizens' feelings about the salient issues of the day, and the citizens responded accordingly.

But more was happening than that. Candidates for different offices were campaigning in different ways. Presidential candidates were being associated with the party whose banner they carried—or, perhaps more correctly put, the parties began to be viewed in terms of the candidates who ran under their banner. The Democrats were the party of George McGovern (i.e., liberal) and then Jimmy Carter (i.e., weak); the Republicans were the party of Ronald Reagan (i.e., strong and conservative, fiscally and socially). Reagan might not have been involved with party organization, but he did work hard to rebuild the image of the Republican party in terms of his own policy agenda. As Warren Miller has demonstrated in Chapter 5, the voters read these signals and reacted to them.

But candidates for other offices, even when they used some of the resources of the party organization, campaigned as individuals. They developed their own images, their own relationships with the voters. Many of them never revealed their party affiliation on any campaign advertising. The message was, "You know and like me! Vote for me! It doesn't matter what party you are in!" The high rate of return for incumbents seeking reelection, prevalent not only among members of Congress but also among candidates for local offices, is testimony to the success of this strategy. It further attests to the separation of party affiliation and the vote. As Fiorina notes in Chapter 6, the factor that most distinguishes today's elections from those of a half-century ago is ticket splitting. Whereas many states once provided party levers so that citizens could vote for all of one party's candidates with a minimum of effort, straight-party voting is now the exception, not the rule. Candidates encourage voters to vote for individuals rather than the party, except where majority party candidates in areas of strong one-party dominance are concerned. If voters feel an allegiance to one party or the other, that allegiance does not carry over as a cue for voting below the presidential level.

Parties in the Electoral Process. Political parties have always played many roles, but the primary role has been one involving the electoral process. In the 1980s their success in this role has been mixed. The party role in the nominating process is symptomatic of the problem faced by parties.

When a nomination is not highly valued (e.g., the nomination to run against an entrenched incumbent), the party role can be dominant. In that situation, in fact, the role of party is to recruit a candidate, to find someone to run, and to support that candidate. Where party organization is strongest, fewest seats go uncontested. Too often, however, party organization is weak in a particular area and many offices go uncontested. As competition is the key to democracy, this role for party is an important one and should not be dismissed. However, even in the case of attracting candidates for less sought-after nominations in areas with effective party organizations, the role of party is not decisive. Decisions regarding candidacy are essentially individual decisions. Strong party leaders can say to a sought-after candidate, "The nomination is yours, if you want it." But the same party leader often cannot convince a potential candidate that the benefits of running a campaign and of serving in office are worth the personal, political, and financial costs.

When a party's nomination is highly valued, the role that party can play is even less decisive because a number of candidates are likely to want to run under the party label. In many areas of the country, party organization must stay neutral in nominating contests. In others, the influence varies from considerable, to minimal, even to negative. But in all cases, individual candidates running their own campaigns can appeal directly to the voters. Until the recent Supreme Court decision in *Tashjian v. Republican Party of Connecticut*, 479 U. S. 208 (1986), parties were unable to define their own membership—that is, to determine the electorate in their primaries. Even with the Court ruling, most state parties are content to let state law specify party membership criteria; many choose to be inclusive, allowing anyone who wants to vote in their primary to do so, rather than exclusive, limiting primary participation to those who have allegiance to the party. Thus, the party role in determining these nominations, a decision critical to the electoral process, is limited by the decisions of potential candidates, the campaigns run by those candidates who decide to seek nomination, and the choice made by a primary electorate, which most frequently is not limited to those with strong allegiance to the party. It is difficult not to conclude that the party role in state and local nominations is a weak one (see Chapter 7).

Much the same can be said for presidential nominations. As noted earlier, the Democratic party has exerted a good deal of time and effort toward the goal of nationalizing the nominating process. Reform commission has followed reform commission in a continuing effort to increase participation, provide for fair representation, and guarantee procedural fairness. As Elaine Kamarck demonstrates in Chapter 8, national party rules in the Democratic party now structure the contest, with obvious implications for candidate strategy. To a certain extent, because many party reforms have resulted in changes in state law, the Republican party nominating contest has been affected as well.

But to say that party rules affect the nominating contest is not to say that party dominates the nominations. One of the clearest conclusions to be drawn from the recent spate of Democratic reform commissions is that the consequences of party reform are often difficult to predict. Party rules cannot keep candidates out of the process. They cannot determine who will adopt the most successful strategy or who will reach the voters with the most effective message. Campaign strategists, like losing generals, too often adopt strategies that have been successful in the past, but without realizing that the political climate has changed. Those interested in reforming party rules can fall prey to the same difficulties. Some rule changes—such as those calling for open and timely participation—have been adopted for philosophical reasons. And they have largely achieved their goals, though with often unintended and unpredicted consequences. Other reforms—such as those calling for a reduction in the time period during which convention delegates could be chosen (while allowing for some exceptions)—had political goals in mind. Again, as often as not, the results were neither predicted nor intended. For these reasons, party seemed to have as little control over presidential nominations in the 1980s as over decisions reached by primary voters at the state and local levels.

If party does not play the dominant role in determining nominations, has its role been enhanced in general election campaigns? Again the answer seems to be mixed. On the one hand, political campaigning is certainly no longer the "pound-the-pavement, glad-handing" enterprise it once was. The era of the ward boss and the precinct leader who delivered the votes of loyal party followers (and patronage recipients) is long gone. On the other hand, party organizations seem to be adjusting to the cash economy of modern campaigns, as noted by Sorauf and Wilson in Chapter 9.

One can see the role that party plays in a number of different ways. National party committees, including the two parties' Hill committees, are now collecting larger sums of money, donating them to campaigns to the extent possible and permissible, and passing them on to state and local committees when that is possible. Whereas the presidential campaigns have been federally funded for the last four elections, individuals in 1988 who had raised money for Bush and Dukakis during the nominating battles had also raised money for the national committees during the general election, thus extending and seemingly legitimating a practice begun in 1980 and continued in 1984. The money raised in this manner could be used for the general election so long as it was spent on activities that benefited the entire ticket. The money raised by fund raisers for the individual candidates was ultimately spent on party-building activities, because those activities were seen as aiding the presidential candidates. If the process seems circular, that's because it is. But the net result is increased "old-style" politics at the local level, run by political operatives who are frequently drawn in by the presidential candidates but who work for local organizations. And it seems clear that local candidates as well as those at the top of the ticket benefit from this increased activity.

What are the messages given out by these campaigns? For a time in the early 1980s, the Republicans experimented with a series of "Vote Republican" commercials, the most prominent of which featured an actor portraying Democratic House Speaker Thomas ("Tip") O'Neill (MA), who was driving a car and ran out of gas despite frequent warnings. Although the commercials were artistically successful, Democratic incumbents were reelected to Congress in record numbers. Apparently the ad campaign was a failure.

Much more frequently, party cooperation comes in the form of themes developed for one campaign that are picked up by co-partisans. In such cases, the transmitting agent is the political advertising consultant rather than a party official. Neither the Bush nor the Dukakis campaign in 1988 hit on a theme that carried over effectively to others running on the same party label. In the gubernatorial and mayoral elections of 1989, however, a number of Democratic candidates were successful in running pro-choice campaigns, inasmuch as they struck a responsive chord in an electorate energized by the Supreme Court's *Webster v. Reproductive Health Center* decision. Is abortion a party issue, then—that is the kind of issue that will attract a strong following among the electorate? As a political issue, abortion can be determinative in individual campaigns, but it is not likely to be the sort of issue that would divide the parties in a systematic way over a period of time. Rather, one must conclude that the political parties per se are still looking for a role in general elections. They may have found a role as part of the cash economy of elections, but candidates still raise the vast majority of their money independent of party and run their campaigns based on issues that appeal to their particular electorates, regardless of how the party feels about those issues.

Party in the Government. Those favoring a "responsible party model" feel that the party in power should be able to legislate its program—to govern. Though rare in the United States, the passage of such legislation has occurred in many constitutional democracies. In fact, since 1952, when Dwight Eisenhower was elected in the first campaign that made significant use of television advertising, the party that has controlled the White House has also controlled both houses of the Congress for only fourteen out of thirty-eight years. Divided government has become the norm, not the exception.

How have the parties responded to this situation? Even asking that question raises more questions. What is meant by "party" in that context? How can one have "party government," if that is taken to mean the victorious party has the ability to implement its program and the two branches of the government are controlled by opposing parties? "Party government" implies that the victorious party has demonstrated majority support and can then rule—but that concept is foreign to modern American democracy.

Local candidates are elected locally; they build local coalitions and represent local interests. For much of what they do, their horizons do not extend beyond the boundaries of the local district. Presidential candidates, by contrast, are elected nationally. Some claim that presidential elections reflect popular assessments of the job of the incumbent (Fiorina, 1981); others are less certain. But presidential candidates also campaign as individuals. And they campaign against their opponents as individuals. The 1988 campaign rhetoric was long on Pledge of Allegiance, Willie Horton, and Boston Harbor and short on differing views of the future of the nation. It was clear that Ronald Reagan's priorities and vision were different from those of Jimmy Carter in 1980—and that Walter Mondale in 1984 differed from Reagan on issue after issue. It might have been clear that George Bush was the heir to Reagan in 1988—and voters might well have supported him for that reason—but one had to look quite hard at the rhetoric of his campaign to see how he intended to govern.

Thus the American national government features a Congress made up of representatives and senators elected as individuals, judged on the basis of their service to and relations with their constituents, and a president elected in a national campaign, based on image and short on ideas for future policies. How does party function in such a setting?

Recent party leaders in Congress have tried to regain the majority-building mechanisms that were lost among the decentralizing reforms of the 1970s. As the end of the 1970s neared, the House of Representatives was ruled by more than 200 subcommittees, each run by a chair who was protective of his or her own turf. The subcommittee reforms and efforts to break the grip of seniority leaders resulted in a wide dissemination of power but an inability to act. Beginning in 1977 Speaker O'Neill sought to regain some semblance of control. Recognizing that in order to move the legislative agenda forward the Speaker needed additional powers, the members assented to broadening the Speaker's appointive powers, allowing him to control the Rules Committee, permitting multiple referral of pieces of legislation and the establishment of task forces to handle certain key issues. O'Neill was a Speaker who knew the House and knew politics, but he was not very concerned about specific policies. He used his powers to aid others with their legislative proposals. In his short and doomed Speakership, as Barbara Sinclair notes in Chapter 11, Jim Wright (D-TX) gave evidence that he was going to use the newly expanded powers of his office to forward a Democratic policy agenda for which he was to be the chief spokesperson. However, although we caught glimpses of how this role might work, Wright's short tenure and forced resignation prevented it from reaching fruition.

Republican party leaders had the opportunity to work with a forceful, ideological leader of their party throughout the decade of the 1980s. In the Senate, they did so with majority control throughout the first six years of the Reagan administration. The Republican experience demonstrated how a united party can come together behind a legislative program. Reagan lobbied hard with his co-partisans. He worked closely with Howard Baker (R-TN) and Bob Dole (R-KS), the Republican leaders in the Senate, and with Bob Michel (R-IL), the House minority leader. He achieved remarkable success in terms of the support that his programs received from Republicans in Congress.

But the Republican successes early in the Reagan years were not repeated at the end of Reagan's first term, nor during his second term. Again, the limits of party government—and of party as an organizing element within the government—are apparent. When Reagan was successful in implementing his legislative agenda, he was successful in the House because of a cross-party coalition (recall Chapter 12). Democrats supported his budget-cutting proposals because they felt that Reagan was in tune with their constituents. After the 1982 congressional election, during which Democrats who felt threatened were reelected, support for Reagan's program diminished. Legislative entrepreneurs created cross-party coalitions, legislators claimed that the elections gave no mandate for policy to the president, and the president struggled to translate his personal popularity into legislative achievements.

How does a president govern in these circumstances? As Cal Mackenzie points out in Chapter 13, a president does so by staffing an administration with personal followers. But the political party is simply not very helpful in this task. A president does not want to reward hard work at political organizing. He wants to find individuals who believe as he does and who have the talent to implement his programs and to forward his ideas. If a president wants to change the way the government is functioning in a radical way, as Ronald Reagan sought to do, then he must extend his reach deep into the bureaucracy—again, as Reagan sought to do. The appointments constituted not "Republican patronage" but "Reagan patronage." Given the heterogeneity of the parties (and this is more true of the Democrats than of the Republicans), presidents want their personal followers in positions of power. Whereas parties once performed as giant personnel agencies for the government, they now serve as ad hoc organizations established in each new administration to guarantee implementation of the new leader's wishes.

Some semblances of party in government still appear. The Hill committees provide a link between the party and incumbent legislators who are supported in reelection bids. But the link is not a strong one. It does not replace personal ties to constituents. Legislative leaders have asserted new authority, but the rank-and-file members look to their constituents' interests first. The president is the leader of his party in government, but the members owe their allegiance more to the president than to the party. And, most significantly, neither party can govern, in the sense of presenting a program to the electorate, gaining office, and implementing that program.

TOWARD THE 21ST CENTURY

The picture of political parties that emerges as the twentieth century draws to a close is thus a mixed one. Party—in all senses of the term—has attempted to adapt to changing situations. But these attempts have not been totally successful. Change has been an important part of the history of parties, in terms of the roles performed by parties, the centrality of that role for governing (recall Chapter 1), and the procedures followed by political parties.

The final report of the Democratic party's McGovern-Fraser Commission, the Commission on Party Structure and Delegate Selection appointed after the debacle at the 1968 presidential nominating convention, approvingly quoted Lord Thomas Babington Macaulay, the British poet and statesman who worked to revise the colonial penal system in the nineteenth century: "We reform that we may preserve." And so it has been with party leaders in recent decades.

As noted earlier, however, reform has been of two types. Political parties have proved remarkably successful at reforming party practices that have become passé: The machine is gone; smoke-filled rooms are gone; male domination is gone. The existence of party as an organization has been preserved by such reforms. Indeed, party leaders have responded to the dissatisfaction that has threatened their existence, and the threat has abated.

The other, more basic sense of reform pertains to party renewal. In this enterprise, parties have been less successful. Renewal involves building parties into better-structured, more active, more effective, and more policy-oriented organizations. This effort has begun, but only just begun. Parties have adopted an electoral role and have built an organization to perform it. (The Republicans have been more successful than the Democrats in this regard.) The effort was started in Washington and is only slowly spreading to the states and local units. But as the essays in this book make clear, building an electoral role is only one part of renewing a party structure. What has been missing is a sense of the role of political party in the governing process. And that involves a systematic division of the two parties on the issues that affect the electorate.

Is such a renewal possible? In the early 1970s those people looking to renew the Democratic party called for party conferences to discuss policy matters in between presidential nominating conventions. These so-called midterm conferences were designed to invigorate the national party—and, through the delegate-selection process, state and local parties, too—as a forum for discussing the critical issues of the day. In 1985, after only two such conferences, the Democratic National Committee moved quickly (but quietly) to end the practice, fearing that the appearance of divisiveness, the inevitable result of discussing critical issues, would hurt the party's chances to present a unified front and regain the Senate in 1986 and the White House in 1988. So discussion of issues was removed from the Democratic party agenda in favor of winning elections. The Democrats did regain the Senate in 1986, but they lost the presidency once again in 1988, during a campaign in which the electorate did not know what the party stood for.

Meaningful party renewal depends on the willingness of partisan leaders to distinguish their party from the other one. In responding to criticism that he had not been sufficiently partisan in his first year as Senate majority leader, George Mitchell stated, "I reject the view that I should oppose for the sake of opposition and confront for the sake of confrontation" (Harkavy, 1989). Yet the Democratic leadership in both houses of Congress, unsuccessfully in the House but successfully in the Senate, opposed President Bush's effort to reduce the capital gains tax on the specifically partisan grounds that this proposal would aid the affluent and not those more in need.

The question of the role of party in the twenty-first century is thus one of issues. If party is to be meaningful, if the two-party system is to play a more central role than it has for decades, then the voters must come to understand that a candidate's party affiliation will have an impact on the performance of that candidate in office. They must also understand that Republican and Democratic leaders differ on the issues important to the public—and that elected officials will stand by these differences.

The Democrats have not been willing to stand by these differences, largely because the differences have been defined in recent years in terms of losing positions for Democratic candidates. Thus, Democrats lose presidential elections and win at other levels by running personal or office-specific campaigns. No party renewal in any meaningful sense is possible with such strategies.

Will this trend continue? The shortest, simplest, and safest answer is to say that one cannot predict. After all, who in 1988 could have predicted the events in Eastern Europe during 1989? But we do know some things. We know that the campaign techniques of the future will not revert to those of the past. We know that the 1990 Census will bring significant redistricting for congressional and state legislative seats by the 1992 election. We know that the issues of the first Bush administration will be key issues in 1992—and that these may well define the agenda for the rest of this century and into the next. And we know that the Democrats must respond to this challenge or continue to lose, certainly at the presidential level and perhaps, after redistricting, at the congressional level as well.

The Democratic party has been associated with two principal issue clusters. Domestically they have been associated with the expansion of the government, with a broader federal role. But this role has become increasingly unpopular. In terms of foreign policy, the Democrats have been viewed as weak on communism, as the less able defenders of the American way of life. At the risk of being accused of looking into a crystal ball, one can paint a scenario, based on the events of George Bush's first year in office, that afford the Democrats a position distinct from that of the Republicans, but not a losing position.

First, the events in Eastern Europe in the fall and early winter of 1989 dramatically changed the view that Americans have of foreign policy. It may still be too early to claim that the Cold War is over, but as Dante Fascell (D-FL), the chair of the House Foreign Affairs Committee, stated, "Every night for forty years we walked into the bedroom, opened the closet, and looked under the bed to see if we could find a Communist.

And one day we walked in, and he was in our bed, smiling. It's very confusing" (Oreskes, 1989). Yet that confusion helps the Democrats. As a nation we might not be ready to welcome the Russians with open arms as long-lost friends, but we are ready to ease tensions. President Bush was criticized for the slowness of his response to the events in Poland and elsewhere in Eastern Europe. Clearly an opening exists for a Democratic foreign policy that is balanced but responsive. At the least, a distinct Republican advantage may have been lost. As Lee Atwater said, "If our candidates are foolish enough to campaign as if the Cold War were still on, they'll get hurt" (Oreskes, 1989).

Similarly, the debates over the capital gains tax reduction and over governmental policy on abortion signal a different slant in domestic politics. The Democrats are no longer defending an increased role for the federal government. They are no longer taking unpopular stands on cutting social issues. Rather, they are saying, in the case of the abortion debate, "Keep the government out of individual decisions!" and, in the case of the capital gains tax debate, "This is a benefit just for the rich, not for the middle class." The challenge for the Democrats is to take issue stands that distinguish them from the Republicans on key economic and social issues but bring a majority into the Democratic fold. They have to stress the opportunity for all (not just the underclass) to succeed and get ahead; they have to talk about individual rights but must couple that with responsibility.

President Bush's cautious approach in his first year, combined with the extraordinary events in Eastern Europe, seems to have opened a window of opportunity for Democratic politicians. Democratic leaders in the government and in the party organization appear poised to debate some of the new issues on new terms. If they are successful in doing so (as Senator Mitchell was with the capital gains tax debate in 1989, and as many Democratic politicians seem to have been in reflecting the public's view when they criticized the president's response to events in Eastern Europe), if these emerging issues do indeed become the issues of the 1990s and beyond, and if the two parties present differing visions of the twenty-first century, then party renewal in a meaningful sense is possible.

Political party *qua* party was an institution on the decline when the electorate was last split on how the government should respond to pressing issues. Accordingly, the New Deal resulted in partisan realignment, but not party renewal. As new campaign techniques emerged, as individual politicians learned to defend their electoral bases without resort to issues, parties became less and less relevant for more and more kinds of political actions. Parties as organizations have begun to react to this diminished role. They stand ready to play a key role in a new electoral alignment; indeed, that part of renewal is well under way. What remains unclear is whether issues have arisen or will yet arise that divide the electorate in such a fundamental way that party can reemerge as relevant to voters for a range of offices and for politicians as they seek to govern.

Acronyms

ACIR	Advisory Commission on Intergovernmental Relations
DCCC	Democratic Congressional Campaign Committee
DJP	Democratic Justice party
DNC	Democratic National Committee
DSCC	Democratic Senatorial Campaign Committee
EOP	Executive Office of the President
ERA	Equal Rights Amendment
FCC	Federal Communications Commission
FEC	Federal Election Commission
FECA	Federal Election Campaign Act
IMF	International Monetary Fund
NCPAC	National Conservative Political Action Committee
NRCC	National Republican Congressional Committee
NRSC	National Republican Senatorial Committee
PACs	political action committees
RNC	Republican National Committee

References

ABC News. 1989. *The 88 Vote*. New York: ABC News.

Abramson, Jeffrey B., F. Christopher Arterton, and Gary R. Orren. 1988. *The Electronic Commonwealth: The Impact of New Media Technologies on Democratic Politics*. New York: Basic Books.

Adamany, David. 1984. "Political Parties in the 1980s." In Michael J. Malbin, ed., *Money and Politics in the United States*. Chatham, NJ: Chatham House.

Adams, Sherman. 1961. *Firsthand Report*. New York: Harper and Brothers.

Advisory Commission on Intergovernmental Relations. 1986. *The Transformation in American Politics: Implications for Federalism*. Washington, DC: Advisory Committee on Intergovernmental Relations.

Agranoff, Robert. 1972. "Introduction: The New Style Campaigning." In Robert Agranoff, ed., *The New Style in Election Campaigns*. Boston: Holbrook.

Albany Argus. 1846. November 3.

Alexander, Herbert E. 1984. *Financing Politics*. Washington, DC: Congressional Quarterly.

Alford, John, and David Brady. 1989. "Personal and Partisan Advantage in U.S. Congressional Elections, 1846–1986." In Lawrence C. Dodd and Bruce I. Oppenheimer, eds., *Congress Reconsidered*, 4th edition. Washington, DC: Congressional Quarterly Press.

Alford, John, and John Hibbing. 1983. "Incumbency Advantage in Senate Elections." Paper presented at the Annual Meeting of the Midwest Political Science Association, Chicago.

Allwright, Smith v. 1944. 321 U.S. 649.

American Political Science Association, Committee on Political Parties. 1950. *Toward a More Responsible Two-Party System*. New York: Rinehart.

Andersen, Kristi. 1979. *Creation of a Democratic Majority: 1928–1936*. Chicago: University of Chicago Press.

Babcock, Charles R. 1988. "Being There Unnecessary for Republican Victories." *Washington Post*, November 25.

Bach, Stanley, and Steven S. Smith. 1988. *Managing Uncertainty in the House of Representatives*. Washington, DC: Brookings Institution.

Baer, Denise L., and David A. Bositis. 1988. *Elite Cadres and Party Coalitions*. New York: Greenwood Press.

Balz, Dan. 1990a. "Democrats Split Over Plans To Close Donation Loophole." *Washington Post*, March 2.

_____ . 1990b. "When Party Cash Crosses State Lines." *Washington Post,* February 7.

Banner James. 1970. *To the Hartford Convention: The Federalists and the Origins of Party Politics in Massachusetts, 1789–1815.* New York: Alfred A. Knopf.

Banning, Lance. 1978. *The Jeffersonian Persuasion: Evolution of a Party Ideology.* Ithaca: Cornell University Press.

Barber, James David. 1986. Private communication.

Barnes, James. 1989. "Reinventing the RNC." *National Journal,* January 14.

Barnes, James, and Carol Matlack. 1989. "Running in the Red." *National Journal,* July 8.

Barnes, James, and Richard E. Cohen. 1988. "Unity—Will It Last?" *National Journal,* September 30.

Barrett, Lawrence I. 1990. "Can the Right Survive Success?" *Time,* March 19.

Bartels, Larry. 1983. *Presidential Primaries and the Dynamics of Public Choice.* Ph.D. dissertation submitted to the University of California, Berkeley.

Bates, Richard, Executive Director, DCCC. 1989. Personal interview. January 9.

Beck, Paul Allen. 1984. "The Electoral Cycle and Patterns of American Politics." In Richard G. Niemi and Herbert F. Weisberg, eds., *Controversies in American Voting Behavior.* Washington, DC: Congressional Quarterly.

_____ . 1979. "The Electoral Cycle and Patterns of American Politics." 9 *British Journal of Political Science* 129.

_____ . 1977. "Partisan Dealignment in the Postwar South." 71 *American Political Science Review* 477.

Benedict, Michael. 1974. *A Compromise of Principle: Congressional Republicans and Reconstruction, 1863–1896.* New York: Norton.

Benson, Lee. 1981. "Discussion." In Patricia Bonomi, ed., *The American Constitutional System Under Strong and Weak Parties.* New York: Praeger Publishers.

_____ . 1961. *The Concept of Jacksonian Democracy: New York as a Test Case.* Princeton: Princeton University Press.

_____ . 1955. *Merchants, Farmers, and Railroads: Railroad Regulation and New York Politics, 1850–1887.* Cambridge: Harvard University Press.

Benson, Lee, Joel H. Silbey, and Phyllis F. Field. 1978. "Toward a Theory of Stability and Change in American Voting Behavior: New York State, 1792–1970 as a Test Case." In Joel H. Silbey, Allan G. Bogue, and William H. Flanigan, eds., *The History of American Electoral Behavior.* Princeton: Princeton University Press.

Berke, Richard I. 1988. "True Tales of Spending in the Presidential Race." *New York Times,* December 11.

Beth, Richard S. 1984. "Recent Research on 'Incumbency Advantage' in House Elections: Part II." 11 *Congress and the Presidency* 211.

_____ . 1981–1982. "'Incumbency Advantage' and Incumbency Resources: Recent Articles." 9 *Congress and the Presidency* 119.

Bibby, John F. 1986. "Political Party Trends in 1985: The Continuing but Constrained Advance of the National Party." 16 *Publius* 90.

_____ . 1983. "State House Elections at Midterm." In Thomas E. Mann and Norman J. Ornstein, eds., *The American Elections of 1982.* Washington, DC: American Enterprise Institute.

———. 1981. "Party Renewal in the National Republican Party." In Gerald M. Pomper, ed., *Party Renewal in America: Theory in Practice.* New York: Praeger Publishers.

———. 1979. "Political Parties and Federalism: The Republican National Committee Involvement in Gubernatorial and Legislative Elections." 9 *Publius* 22.

Black, Earl, and Merle Black. 1987. *Politics and Society in the South.* Cambridge: Harvard University Press.

Blasi, Vince. 1977. "The Checking Value in First Amendment Theory." *American Bar Foundation Research Journal* 521–649.

Blumenthal, Sidney. 1980. *The Permanent Campaign: Inside the World of Elite Political Operatives.* Boston: Beacon Press.

Bogue, Allan. 1980. *The Earnest Men.* Ithaca: Cornell University Press.

Bohmer, David. 1978. "The Maryland Electorate and the Concept of a Party System in the Early National Period." In Joel H. Silbey, Allan G. Bogue, and William H. Flanigan, *The History of American Electoral Behavior.* Princeton: Princeton University Press.

Bolling, Richard. 1965. *House Out of Order.* New York: Dutton.

Bonafede, Dom. 1987. "The White House Personnel Office from Roosevelt to Reagan." In G. Calvin Mackenzie, ed., *The In and Outers.* Baltimore: Johns Hopkins University Press.

Bond, Jon R., Cary Covington, and Richard Fleisher. 1985. "Explaining Challenger Quality in Congressional Elections." 47 *Journal of Politics* 510.

Born, Richard. 1986. "Strategic Politicians and Unresponsive Voters." 80 *American Political Science Review* 599.

Brady, David W. 1988. *Critical Elections and Congressional Policy Making.* Stanford: Stanford University Press.

———. 1973. *Congressional Voting in a Partisan Era.* Lawrence: University Press of Kansas.

Brief of James MacGregor Burns, Barbara Burrell, William Crotty, James S. Fay, Roman B. Hedges, John S. Jackson III, Everett C. Ladd, Kay Lawson, and Gerald M. Pomper. 1986. *Tashjian v. Republican Party of Connecticut,* 479 U.S. 208.

Brief of William J. Cibes, Jr., Clyde McKee, Sarah McCally Morehouse, and Wayne R. Swanson. 1986. *Tashjian v. Republican Party of Connecticut,* 479 U.S. 208.

Brinkley, Alan. 1990. "The New Deal and the Idea of the State." In Steve Fraser and Gary Gerstle, eds., *The Rise and Fall of the New Deal Order, 1930–1980.* Princeton: Princeton University Press.

Broder, David S. 1990. "Five Ways to Put Some Sanity Back In Elections." *Washington Post.* January 14.

———. 1986. "The Force." *Washington Post,* April 2.

———. 1971. *The Party's Over: The Failure of American Politics.* New York: Harper and Row.

Bruce, Harold R. 1927. *American Parties and Politics.* New York: Henry Holt.

Bullitt, Stimson. 1977. *To Be a Politician.* Rev. ed. New Haven: Yale University Press.

Burnham, Walter Dean. 1982. *The Current Crisis in American Politics*. New York: Oxford University Press.

———. 1975. "American Politics in the 1970s: Beyond Party?" In Louis Maisel and Paul M. Sacks, eds., *The Future of Political Parties*. Beverly Hills: Sage Publications.

———. 1973. *Politics/America: The Cutting Edge of Change*. New York: D. Van Nostrand.

———. 1970. *Critical Elections and the Mainsprings of American Politics*. New York: Norton.

———. 1965. "The Changing Shape of the American Political Universe." 59 *American Political Science Review* 7.

Burns, James MacGregor. 1956. *Roosevelt: The Lion and the Fox*. New York: Harcourt, Brace.

Campbell, Angus, Philip E. Converse, Warren E. Miller, and Donald E. Stokes. 1960. *The American Voter*. New York: John Wiley and Sons.

Campbell, James E. 1986. "Presidential Coattails and Midterm Losses in State Legislative Elections." 80 *American Political Science Review* 45.

Cannon, Lou. 1982. *Reagan*. New York: Putnam.

Carmines, Edward G. 1986. "The Logic of Partisan Transformations." Paper presented at the Annual Meeting of the American Political Science Association, New Orleans.

Carmines, Edward G., Steven H. Renten, and James A. Stimson. 1984. "Events and Alignments: The Party Image Link." In Richard G. Niemi and Herbert F. Weisberg, eds., *Controversies in American Voting Behavior*. Washington, DC: Congressional Quarterly Press.

Carr, Craig L., and Gary L. Scott. 1984. "The Logic of State Primary Classification Schemes." 12 *American Politics Quarterly* 465.

Chalmers, Wally, Executive Director, DNC. 1989. Personal interview, January 12.

Chambers, William N. 1963. *Political Parties in a New Nation: The American Experience, 1776–1809*. New York: Oxford University Press.

Chambers, William N., and Walter Dean Burnham. 1975. *The American Party System: Stages of Political Development*. New York: Oxford University Press.

Cheney, Richard B. 1989. "An Unruly House." 11 *Public Opinion* 41.

Chlopak, Robert, Executive Director, DSCC. 1989. Personal interview, January 12.

Chubb, John E. 1988. "Institutions, the Economy and the Dynamics of State Elections." 82 *American Political Science Review* 118.

Clausen, Aage. 1973. *How Congressmen Decide*. New York: St. Martin's Press.

Clubb, Jerome M., William H. Flanigan, and Nancy H. Zingale. 1980. *Partisan Realignment: Voters, Parties, and Government in American History*. Beverly Hills: Sage.

Clymer, Adam, and Kathleen A. Frankovic. 1981. "The Realities of Realignment." 4 *Public Opinion* 42.

Cohen, Richard E. 1987. "Quick-Starting Speaker." *National Journal*, May 30.

Collie, Melissa P., and Joseph Cooper. 1989. "Multiple Referral and the New Committee System in the House of Representatives." In Lawrence C. Dodd

References 331

and Bruce I. Oppenheimer, eds., *Congress Reconsidered*, 4th edition. Washington, DC: Congressional Quarterly Press.

Commission on Party Structure and Delegate Selection. 1971. *Mandate for Change.* Washington, DC: Democratic National Committee.

Converse, Philip E. 1976. *The Dynamics of Party Support.* Beverly Hills: Sage Publications.

Converse, Philip E., Aage R. Clausen, and Warren E. Miller. 1965. "Electoral Myth and Reality: The 1964 Election." 59 *American Political Science Review* 321.

Conway, M. Margaret. 1983. "Republican Party Nationalization, Campaign Activities, and Their Implications for the Political System." 13 *Publius* 1.

Cook, Rhodes. 1981. "Chorus of Democratic Voices Urges New Policies, Methods." *Congressional Quarterly Weekly Report*, January 17.

_____. 1988. "'88 Vote: Stress Persuasion over Registration." *Congressional Quarterly Weekly Report*, October 1.

Cooke, Jacob E. 1961. *The Federalist.* New York: Meridian.

Cooper, Joseph. 1975. "Strengthening the Congress: An Organizational Analysis." 12 *Harvard Journal on Legislation* 307.

Cooper, Joseph, and David W. Brady. 1981. "Institutional Context and Leadership Style: The House from Cannon to Rayburn." 75 *American Political Science Review* 411.

Cotter, Cornelius P., James L. Gibson, John F. Bibby, and Robert J. Huckshorn. 1984. *Party Organizations in American Politics.* New York: Praeger Publishers.

Cotter, Cornelius, and Bernard C. Hennessy. 1964. *Politics Without Power: The National Party Committees.* New York: Atherton Press.

Crotty, William. 1985. *The Party Game.* New York: W. H. Freeman.

_____. 1984. *American Parties in Decline.* Boston: Little, Brown.

_____. 1983. *Party Reform.* New York: Longman.

Cutright, Phillips, and Peter Rossi. 1958a. "Grass Roots Politicians and the Vote." 23 *American Sociological Review* 177.

_____. 1958b. "Party Organization in Primary Elections." 64 *American Journal of Sociology* 262.

Dahl, Robert. 1956. *A Preface to Democratic Theory.* Chicago: University of Chicago Press.

David, Paul T., Ralph M. Goldman, and Richard C. Bain. 1960. *The Politics of National Party Conventions.* Washington, DC: Brookings Institution.

Davidson, Roger H., Walter J. Oleszek, and Thomas Kephart. 1988. "One Bill, Many Committees: Multiple Referrals in the U.S. House of Representatives." 13 *Legislative Studies Quarterly* 3.

Dean, John, Director of the Office of Voter Participation, DNC. 1989. Personal interview, January 12.

Deckard, Barbara Sinclair. 1976. "Political Upheaval and Congressional Voting." 38 *Journal of Politics* 326.

Democratic National Committee. 1972. *Report of the Committee on Rules for the 1972 Democratic National Committee.* Washington, DC: Democratic National Committee.

Dionne, E. J., Jr. 1989. "Attack Shows G.O.P. Strategy Shift." *New York Times*, June 11.

———. 1988. "Dukakis Campaign Battling in Last Democratic Trench." *New York Times*, October 20.

Dodd, Lawrence C. 1979. "The Expanded Roles of the House Democratic Whip System: the 93rd and 94th Congresses." 7 *Congressional Studies* 27.

Dodd, Lawrence C., and Bruce I. Oppenheimer. 1977. *Congress Reconsidered*. New York: Praeger Publishers.

Downs, Anthony. 1957. *An Economic Theory of Democracy*. New York: Harper and Row.

Drew, Elizabeth. 1983. *Politics and Money: The New Road to Corruption*. New York: Macmillan.

Edsall, Thomas B. 1989. "Branching out with Burgeoning Influence." *Washington Post*, January 17.

———. 1988. "The Reagan Legacy." In Sidney Blumenthal and Thomas Byrne Edsall, eds., *The Reagan Legacy*. New York: Pantheon Books.

Edwards, George C. III. 1983. *The Public Presidency*. New York: St. Martin's Press.

Ehrenhalt, Alan. 1987. "Changing South Perils Conservative Coalition." *Congressional Quarterly Weekly Report*, August 1.

Eldersveld, Samuel J. 1964. *Political Parties: A Behavioral Analysis*. Chicago: Rand McNally.

Ellwood, John W., and James A. Thurber. 1981. "The Politics of the Congressional Budget Process Re-examined." In Lawrence C. Dodd and Bruce I. Oppenheimer, eds., *Congress Reconsidered*, 2nd edition. Washington, DC: Congressional Quarterly Press.

Emerson, Thomas I. 1970. *The System of Freedom of Expression*. New York: Random House.

Epstein, Leon D. 1989. "Will American Political Parties Be Privatized?" 5 *Journal of Law and Politics* 239.

———. 1986. *Political Parties in the American Mold*. Madison: University of Wisconsin Press.

Erikson, Robert. 1972. "The Advantages of Incumbency." 3 *Polity* 395.

Federal Election Commission. 1989. FEC Press Release, March 27.

———. 1988a. FEC Press Release, February 5.

———. 1988b. FEC Press Release, November 8.

———. 1984. FEC Record, March 10.

Fenn, Dan H., Jr. 1976. Interview with the author. Waltham, MA, March 26.

Fenno, Richard F., Jr. 1978. *Home Style: House Members in Their Own Districts*. Boston: Little, Brown.

———. 1973. *Congressmen in Committees*. Boston: Little, Brown.

———. 1965. "The Internal Distribution of Influence: The House." In David B. Truman, ed., *The Congress and America's Future*. Englewood Cliffs, NJ: Prentice-Hall.

———. 1959. *The President's Cabinet*. New York: Vintage.

Ferejohn, John A. 1986. "Logrolling in an Institutional Context: A Case Study of Food Stamp Regulation." In Gerald Wright, Leroy Reiselbach, and Lawrence Dodd, eds., *Congress and Policy Change*. New York: Agathon.

Ferejohn, John A., and Randall Calvert. 1984. "Presidential Coattails in Historical Perspective." 28 *American Journal of Political Science* 127.

Ferejohn, John A., and Morris P. Fiorina. 1985. "Incumbency and Realignment in Congressional Elections." In John E. Chubb and Paul E. Peterson, eds., *The New Directions in American Politics*. Washington, DC: Brookings Institution.

Ferguson, Thomas, and Joel Rogers. 1986. *Right Turn*. New York: Hill and Wang.

Fiorina, Morris P. 1990. "An Era of Divided Government." In Bruce Cain and Gillian Peele, eds., *Developments in American Politics*. London: Macmillan.

———. 1989. *Congress: Keystone of the Washington Establishment*. New Haven: Yale University Press.

———. 1981. *Retrospective Voting in American National Elections*. New Haven: Yale University Press.

———. 1977. *Congress, Keystone of the Washington Establishment*. New Haven: Yale University Press.

Fischer, David Hackett. 1965. *The Revolution of American Conservatism: The Federalist Party in the Era of Jeffersonian Democracy*. New York: Oxford University Press.

Fish, Carl R. 1904. *The Civil Service and the Patronage*. Cambridge: Harvard University Press.

Fleming, Thomas, and Paul Gottfried. 1988. *The Conservative Movement*. Boston: Twayne Publishers.

Formisano, Ronald P. 1983. *The Transformation of Political Culture: Massachusetts Parties, 1790s–1840s*. New York: Oxford University Press.

———. 1981. "Federalists and Republicans: Parties, Yes—System, No." In Paul Kleppner et al., *The Evolution of American Electoral Systems*. Westport, CT: Greenwood Press.

———. 1974. "Deferential-Participant Politics: The Early Republic's Political Culture, 1789–1890." 68 *American Political Science Review* 473.

———. 1971. *The Birth of Mass Political Parties: Michigan, 1827–1861*. Princeton: Princeton University Press.

Fowler, Linda L., and Robert D. McClure. 1989. *Political Ambition: Who Decides to Run for Congress*. New Haven: Yale University Press.

Fowler, Linda L., and L. Sandy Maisel. 1990. "The Changing Supply of Competitive Candidates in House Elections, 1982–1988." In Glenn R. Parker, ed., *Changing Perspectives on Congress*. Knoxville: University of Tennessee Press.

Franklin, Charles H., and John E. Jackson. 1983. "The Dynamics of Party Identification." 77 *American Political Science Review* 457.

Frantzich, Stephen E. 1989. *Political Parties in the Technological Age*. New York: Longman.

Frendeis, John P., James L. Gibson, and Laura L. Vertz. 1990. "The Electoral Relevance of Local Party Organizations." 84 *American Political Science Review* 225.

Gans, Herbert C. 1982. *The Urban Villagers: Group and Class in the Life of Italian-Americans*. New York: Free Press.

Garand, James C., and Donald A. Gross. 1984. "Changes in the Vote Margins of Congressional Candidates: A Specification of Historical Trends." 78 *American Political Science Review* 17.

Germond, Jack W., and Jules Witcover. 1985. *Wake Us When It's Over: Presidential Politics of 1984*. New York: Macmillan.

Gibson, James L., Cornelius P. Cotter, John F. Bibby, and Robert J. Huckshorn. 1985. "Whither the Local Parties? A Cross-Sectional and Longitudinal Analysis of the Strength of Party Organizations." 29 *American Journal of Political Science* 139.

Gibson, James L., John P. Frendeis, and Laura L. Vertz. 1989. "Party Dynamics in the 1980s: Changes in County Party Organizational Strength 1980–1984." 32 *American Journal of Political Science* 67.

Gienapp, William. 1987. *The Origins of the Republican Party, 1852–1856*. New York: Oxford University Press.

―――. 1982. "'Politics Seem to Enter into Everything': Political Culture in the North, 1840–1860." In Stephen Maizlish and John Kushma, eds., *Essays on American Antebellum Politics, 1840–1860*. College Station: Texas A&M University Press.

Gierzynski, Anthony, and Malcolm Jewell. 1989. "Legislative Campaign Committee Activity: A Comparative State Analysis." Paper presented at the Annual Meeting of the Midwest Political Science Association, Chicago.

Godwin, R. Kenneth. 1988. *One Billion Dollars of Influence: The Direct Marketing of Politics*. Chatham, NJ: Chatham House.

Goodman, Paul. 1964. *The Democratic-Republicans of Massachusetts*. Cambridge: Harvard University Press.

Goodwin, George. 1970. *The Little Legislature: Committees in Congress*. Amherst: University of Massachusetts Press.

Gottfried, Paul, and Thomas Fleming. 1988. *The Conservative Movement*. Boston: Twayne Publishers.

Graber, Doris A. 1984. *The Mass Media and American Politics*. Washington, DC: Congressional Quarterly Press.

Grove, Lloyd. 1988. "Putting the Spin on the Party Line." *Washington Post*, July 18.

Hallin, Daniel. 1990. "Sound Bite News." In Gary R. Orren, ed., *Blurring the Lines: Elections and the Media in America*. New York: The Free Press, forthcoming.

Handlin, Oscar. 1952. *The Uprooted*. Boston: Little, Brown.

Harkavy, Jerry. 1989. "Mitchell Reflects on Anniversary as Senate Leader." *Central Maine Morning Sentinel*, November 29.

Hawley, Willis D. 1973. *Nonpartisan Elections and the Case for Party Politics*. New York: Wiley.

Hays, Samuel P. 1959. *Conservation and the Gospel of Efficiency: The Progressive Conservation Movement*. Cambridge: Harvard University Press.

―――. 1957. *The Response to Industrializationism, 1877–1914*. Chicago: University of Chicago Press.

Heard, Alexander. 1960. *The Costs of Democracy*. Chapel Hill: University of North Carolina Press.

Heclo, Hugh. 1977. *A Government of Strangers*. Washington, DC: Brookings Institution.

Herrnson, Paul S. 1989. "National Party Decision-Making, Strategies, and Resource Distribution in Congressional Elections." 42 *Western Political Quarterly* 301.

———. 1988. *Party Campaigning in the 1980s*. Cambridge: Harvard University Press.

Herrnson, Paul S., and David Menefee-Libey. 1988. "The Transformation of American Political Parties." Paper presented at the Annual Meeting of the Midwest Political Science Association, Chicago.

Hoffman, David. 1989. "Bush Makes Rare Bow to GOP's Conservatives." *Washington Post*, October 18.

Hofstadter, Richard. 1969. *The Idea of the Party System: The Rise of Legitimate Opposition in the United States, 1780–1840*. Berkeley: University of California Press.

Holloway, Harry, and John George. 1979. *Public Opinion: Coalitions, Elites, and Masses*. New York: St. Martin's.

Holt, James. 1967. *Congressional Insurgents and the Party System, 1909–1916*. Cambridge: Harvard University Press.

Holt, Michael. 1978. *The Political Crisis of the 1850s*. New York: John Wiley and Sons.

———. 1973. "The Antimasonic and Know Nothing Parties." In Arthur M. Schlesinger, Jr., ed., *History of U.S. Political Parties*. New York: Chelsea House.

Hook, Janet. 1987. "Speaker Jim Wright Takes Charge in the House." *Congressional Quarterly Weekly Report*, July 11.

Howe, Daniel Walker. 1979. *The Political Culture of the American Whigs*. Chicago: University of Chicago Press.

Hrebenar, Ronald J., and Ruth K. Scott. 1982. *Interest Group Politics in America*. Englewood Cliffs, NJ: Prentice-Hall.

Huckhorn, Robert J. 1976. *Party Leadership in the States*. Amherst: University of Massachusetts Press.

Huntington, Samuel. 1965. "Political Development and Political Decay." 17 *World Politics* 386.

Hurley, Patricia A. 1989. "Parties and Coalitions in Congress." In Christopher J. Deering, ed., *Congressional Politics*. Chicago: Dorsey Press.

Jackson, Brooks. 1988. *Honest Graft: Big Money and the American Political Process*. New York: Knopf.

Jackson, John E. 1975. "Issues, Party Choices, and Presidential Votes." 19 *American Journal of Political Science* 161.

Jacobson, Gary. 1987a. "The Marginals Never Vanished: Incumbency and Competition in Elections to the U.S. House of Representatives, 1952–82." 31 *American Journal of Political Science* 126.

———. 1987b. *The Politics of Congressional Elections*, 2nd edition. Boston: Little, Brown.

———. 1985–1986. "Party Organization and Distribution of Campaign Resources: Republicans and Democrats in 1982." 100 *Political Science Quarterly* 603.

————. 1985. "Parties and PACs in Congressional Elections." In Lawrence C. Dodd and Bruce I. Oppenheimer, eds., *Congress Reconsidered*. Washington, DC: Congressional Quarterly Press.

————. 1980. *Money in Congressional Elections*. New Haven: Yale University Press.

Jacobson, Gary, and Samuel Kernell. 1981 (2nd edition, 1983). *Strategy and Choice in Congressional Elections*. New Haven: Yale University Press.

Jennings, M. Kent, and Richard Niemi. 1981. *Generations and Politics*. Princeton: Princeton University Press.

Jensen, Richard. 1981. "The Last Party System: Decay of Consensus, 1932–1980." In Paul Kleppner, ed., *Evolution of Electoral Systems*. Westport, CT: Greenwood Press.

————. 1978. "Party Coalitions and the Search for Modern Values, 1820–1970." In Seymour Martin Lipset, ed., *Emerging Coalitions in American Politics*. San Francisco: Institute for Contemporary Studies.

————. 1971. *The Winning of the Midwest: Social and Political Conflict, 1888–1896*. Chicago: University of Chicago Press.

Jewell, Malcolm E. 1984. *Parties and Primaries*. New York: Praeger Publishers.

Jewell, Malcolm E., and David Breaux. 1988. "The Effect of Incumbency on State Legislative Elections." 13 *Legislative Studies Quarterly* 495.

Jewell, Malcolm E., and David M. Olson. 1988. *Political Parties and Elections in American States*, 3rd edition. Chicago: Dorsey Press.

Jones, Ruth S. 1984. "Financing State Elections." In Michael J. Malbin, ed., *Money and Politics in the United States: Financing Elections in the 1980s*. Chatham, NJ: Chatham House.

Jones, Ruth S., and Thomas J. Borris. 1985. "Strategic Contributing in Legislative Campaigns: The Case of Minnesota." 10 *Legislative Studies Quarterly* 89.

Kamarck, Elaine Ciulla. 1988. "Who Will Control Coverage of the Conventions?" *Newsday*, July 11.

————. 1987. "Delegate Allocation Rules in Presidential Nominating Systems: A Comparison Between the Democrats and the Republicans." 4 *Journal of Law and Politics* 275.

Kaufman, Herbert. 1965. "The Growth of the Federal Personnel System." In Wallace S. Sayre, ed., *The Federal Government Service*. Englewood Cliffs, NJ: Prentice-Hall.

Kayden, Xandra, and Eddie Mahe, Jr. 1985. *The Party Goes On*. New York: Basic Books.

Keefe, William J. 1976. *Parties, Politics, and Public Policy in America*. Hinsdale, IL: Dryden Press.

Keith, Bruce E., et al. 1987. "The Myth of the Independent Voter." Unpublished manuscript, University of California, Berkeley.

Kent, Frank R. 1923. *The Great Game of Politics*. New York: Doubleday.

Kernell, Samuel. 1986. *Going Public: New Strategies of Presidential Leadership*. Washington, DC: Congressional Quarterly Press.

Kerr, Peter. 1988. "Campaign Donations Overwhelm Monitoring Agencies in the States." *The New York Times*, December 27.

Key, V.O. Jr. 1966. *The Responsible Electorate.* Cambridge: Harvard University Press.

———. 1961. *Public Opinion and American Democracy.* New York: Alfred A. Knopf.

———. 1956. *American State Politics: An Introduction.* New York: Knopf.

———. 1955. "A Theory of Critical Elections." 17 *Journal of Politics* 3.

———. 1952 (3rd edition; 1958, 4th edition; 1964, 5th edition). *Politics, Parties, and Pressure Groups.* New York: Crowell.

Kilday, Anne Marie, and Mark Edgar. 1988. "Bentsen Forces on the Move." *Dallas Morning News,* October 16.

King, Anthony. 1978. *The New American Political System.* Washington, DC: American Enterprise Institute.

Kleppner, Paul. 1979. *The Third Electoral System, 1853–1892: Parties, Voters and Political Cultures.* Chapel Hill: University of North Carolina Press.

Kleppner, Paul, et al. 1981. *The Evolution of American Electoral Systems.* Westport, CT: Greenwood Press.

Klinge, Kenneth, Political Director, DSCC. 1989. Personal interview, January 12.

Klose, Kevin. 1984. "Up From Obscurity: Ratio of Journalists to Iowa Caucus Goers Hits One to One Hundred." *Washington Post,* February 20.

Kontnik, Ginnie, Director, Harriman Communications Center. 1989. Personal interview, January 6.

Kousser, J. Morgan. 1974. *The Shaping of Southern Politics: Suffrage Restriction and the Establishment of the One-Party South, 1880–1910.* New Haven: Yale University Press.

Kramer, Gerald H. 1970–1971. "The Effects of Precinct-Level Canvassing on Voter Behavior." 34 *Public Opinion Quarterly* 561.

Ladd, Everett C. 1985. "As the Realignment Turns: A Drama in Many Acts." 7 *Public Opinion* 2.

Ladd, Everett C., with Charles D. Hadley. 1975. *Transformations of the American Party System.* New York: W. W. Norton.

Lengle, James. 1981. *Representation and Presidential Primaries: The Democratic Party in the Post Reform Era.* Westport, CT: Greenwood Press.

———. 1980. "Divisive Presidential Primaries and Party Electoral Prospects: 1932–1980." 8 *American Politics Quarterly* 261.

Loftus, Tom. 1985. "The New 'Political Parties' in State Legislatures." 58 *State Government* 108.

Louisville Journal. 1852. September 8.

Lowi, Theodore J. 1979. *The End of Liberalism: The Second Republic in the United States.* New York: Norton.

Lundberg, Kirsten. 1989. "General Electric and the National Broadcasting Co.: A Clash of Cultures." Kennedy School Case Program. Cambridge: Kennedy School of Government, Harvard University.

Lynn, Frank. 1987. "Part-Time Legislature Finds Little Time to Ponder Ethics." *New York Times,* March 1.

Mackenzie, G. Calvin. 1981. *The Politics of Presidential Appointments.* New York: Free Press.

Maddox, John, Deputy Director of the Executive Division, NRCC. 1989. Personal interview, January 5.

Maisel, L. Sandy. 1987. *Parties and Elections in America: The Electoral Process.* New York: Random House.

———. 1986. *From Obscurity to Oblivion: Running in the Congressional Primary.* Knoxville: University of Tennessee Press.

Malbin, Michael J. 1975. "Republicans Prepare Plan to Rebuild Party for 1976." *National Journal,* March 1.

Mann, Dean E. 1965. *The Assistant Secretaries: Problems and Processes of Appointment.* Washington, DC: Brookings Institution.

Mann, Thomas E. 1978. *Unsafe at any Margin.* Washington, DC: American Enterprise Institute.

Mayhew, David R. 1986. *Placing Parties in American Politics.* Princeton: Princeton University Press.

———. 1974a. "Congressional Elections: The Case of the Vanishing Marginals," 6 *Polity* 295.

———. 1974b. *Congress: The Electoral Connection.* New Haven: Yale University Press.

———. 1966. *Party Loyalty Among Congressmen.* New Haven: Yale University Press.

McClosky, Herbert, Paul J. Hoffman, and Rosemary O'Hara. 1960. "Issue Conflict and Consensus Among Party Leaders and Followers." 54 *American Political Science Review* 406.

McCormick, Richard L. 1986. *The Party Period and Public Policy: American Politics from the Age of Jackson to the Progressives Era.* New York: Oxford University Press.

———. 1981. *From Realignment to Reform: Political Change in New York State, 1893–1910.* Ithaca: Cornell University Press.

———. 1979. "The Party Period and Public Policy: An Exploratory Hypothesis." 66 *Journal of American History* 279.

McCormick, Richard P. 1982. *The Presidential Game: The Origins of American Presidential Politics.* New York: Oxford University Press.

———. 1967. *The Second American Party System: Party Formation in the Jacksonian Era.* Chapel Hill: University of North Carolina Press.

McCurry, Michael, Communications Director, DNC. 1989. Personal interview, January 11.

McGerr, Michael. 1986. *The Decline of Popular Politics.* New York: Oxford University Press.

McSeveney, Samuel T. 1971. *The Politics of Depression: Voting Behavior in the Northeast, 1893–1896.* New York: Oxford University Press.

McWilliams, Wilson Carey. 1981. "Parties as Civic Associations." In Gerald M. Pomper, ed., *Party Renewal in America.* New York: Praeger Publishers.

Meiklejohn, Alexander. 1948. *Free Speech and Its Relation to Self-Government.* New York: Harper & Brothers.

Merriam, Charles E. 1923. *The American Party System.* New York: Macmillan.

Messick, Deborah, Deputy of Communications, RNC. 1989. Personal interview, January 13.

Miller, Warren E. 1986. "Party Identification and Political Belief Systems: Changes in Partisanship in the United States, 1980–84." 5 *Electoral Studies* 101.

Miller, Warren E., and M. Kent Jennings. 1986. *Parties in Transition.* New York: Russell Sage.

Morlan, Robert L. 1949. "City Politics: Free Style." 37 *National Municipal Review* 485.

New Republic. 1984. "The Electronic Plebiscite." Editorial, October 29, p. 8.

Nichols, Roy F. 1967. *The Invention of the American Political Parties.* New York: Macmillan.

Nie, Norman H., Sidney Verba, and John R. Petrocik. 1976 (Enlarged edition, 1979). *The Changing American Voter.* Cambridge: Harvard University Press.

O'Donnell, Thomas, Political Director, DCCC. 1989. Personal interview, January 11.

Oppenheimer, Bruce I. 1981a. "The Changing Relationship Between House Leadership and the Committee on Rules." In Frank H. Mackaman, ed., *Understanding Congressional Leadership.* Washington, DC: Congressional Quarterly Press.

———. 1981b. "Congress and the New Obstructionism: Developing an Energy Program." In Lawrence C. Dodd and Bruce I. Oppenheimer, eds., *Congress Reconsidered,* 2nd edition. Washington, DC: Congressional Quarterly Press.

Oreskes, Michael. 1989. "Cold War No Longer Wins Votes." *New York Times* News Service, December 3.

Ornstein, Norman J., Thomas E. Mann, and Michael J. Malbin. 1987. *Vital Statistics on Congress, 1987–1988.* Washington, DC: Congressional Quarterly Press.

Orren, Gary R. 1987. "The Linkage of Policy to Participation." In Alexander Heard and Michael Nelson, eds., *Presidential Selection.* Durham: Duke University Press.

———. 1985. "The Nomination Process: Vicissitudes of Candidate Selection." In Michael Nelson, ed., *The Elections of 1984.* Washington, DC: American Enterprise Institute.

———. 1982. "The Changing Styles of American Party Politics." In Joel L. Fleishman, ed., *The Future of American Political Parties.* Englewood Cliffs, NJ: Prentice-Hall.

———. 1981. "Presidential Campaign Finance: Its Impact and Future." 4 *Common Sense* 50.

———. 1978. "Candidate Style and Voter Alignment in 1976." In Seymour Martin Lipset, ed., *Emerging Coalitions in American Politics.* San Francisco: Institute for Contemporary Studies.

Orren, Gary, and Nelson Polsby, eds. 1987. *Media and Momentum: The New Hampshire Primary and Nomination Politics.* Chatham, NJ: Chatham House.

Ostrogorski, M. 1964. *Democracy and the Organization of Political Parties,* Volume 2: *The United States.* Garden City, NY: Anchor Books.

Palazzolo, Dan. 1989. "The Speaker's Relationship with the House Budget Committee." Paper presented at the Annual Meeting of the Midwest Political Science Association, Chicago.

Patterson, Thomas E. 1989. "The Press and Its Missed Assignment." In Michael Nelson, ed., *The Elections of 1988*. Washington, DC: Congressional Quarterly.
Pessel, Peter, Producer, NRCC. 1989. Personal interview, January 13.
Phillips, Kevin P. 1970. *The Emerging Republican Majority*. Garden City, NY: Anchor Books.
Pines, Burton Yale. 1990. "Go Ahead, Slash the Military." *New York Times*, March 14.
Polsby, Nelson W. 1983. *Consequences of Party Reform*. New York: Oxford University Press.
———. 1975. "Legislatures." In Fred I. Greenstein and Nelson W. Polsby, eds., *Handbook of Political Science*. Reading: Addison-Wesley.
Polsby, Nelson W., and Aaron Wildavsky. 1984, 1988. *Presidential Elections*. New York: Charles Scribner's Sons.
Pomper, Gerald M. 1989. "The Presidential Nominations." In Gerald M. Pomper, ed., *The Election of 1988: Reports and Interpretations*. Chatham, NJ: Chatham House.
———. 1972. "From Confusion to Clarity: Issues and American Voters, 1956–1968." 66 *American Political Science Review* 415.
Poole, Keith T., and Howard Rosenthal. 1984. "The Polarization of American Politics." 46 *Journal of Politics* 1061.
Price, David E. 1984. *Bringing Back the Parties*. Washington, DC: Congressional Quarterly Press.
Ranney, Austin. 1983. *Channels of Power*. New York: Basic Books.
———. 1978a. *The Federalization of Presidential Primaries*. Washington, DC: American Enterprise Institute.
———. 1978b. "The Political Parties: Reform and Decline." In Anthony King, ed., *The New American Political System*. Washington, DC: American Enterprise Institute.
———. 1975. *Curing the Mischiefs of Faction*. Berkeley: University of California Press.
Rapoport, Ronald B., Alan I. Abramowitz, and John McGlennon. 1986. *The Life of the Parties*. Lexington: University Press of Kentucky.
Register of Debates. 1826. United States Congress, Nineteenth Congress, 1st Session.
Reichley, A. James. 1985. "The Rise of National Parties." In John E. Chubb and Paul Peterson, eds., *The New Direction in American Politics*. Washington, DC: Brookings Institution.
Remini, Robert. 1951. *Martin Van Buren and the Making of the Democratic Party*. New York: Columbia University Press.
Republican National Committee. 1989. *1988 Chairman's Report*. Washington, DC: Republican National Committee.
———. 1986. *1986 Chairman's Report*. Washington, DC: Republican National Committee.
Riker, William. 1983. *Liberalism Against Populism*. San Francisco: W. H. Freeman.
Rintye, Peter, PAC Director, NRCC. 1989. Personal interview, January 5.
Ripley, Randall. 1967. *Party Leaders in the House of Representatives*. Washington, DC: Brookings Institution.

Robinson, Michael J. 1981. "The Media in 1980: Was the Message the Message?" In Austin Ranney, ed., *The American Elections of 1980*. Washington, DC: American Enterprise Institute.

Robinson, Michael J., and Karen McPherson. 1977. "Television News Coverage Before the 1976 New Hampshire Primary: The Focus of Network Journalism." 21 *Journal of Broadcasting* 2.

Rodgers, Daniel T. 1982. "In Search of Progressivism." 10 *Reviews in American History* 113.

Rohde, David W. 1989. "'Something's Happening Here; What It Is Ain't Exactly Clear': Southern Democrats in the House of Representatives." In Morris P. Fiorina and David W. Rohde, eds., *Home Style and Washington Work*. Ann Arbor: University of Michigan Press.

———. 1988. "Variations in Partisanship in the House of Representatives: Southern Democrats, Realignment and Agenda Change." Paper presented at the Annual Meeting of the American Political Science Association, Washington, DC.

Rohde, David W., and Kenneth A. Shepsle. 1987. "Leaders and Followers in the House of Representatives: Reflections on Woodrow Wilson's *Congressional Government*." 14 *Congress and the Presidency* 111.

Roseboom, Eugene H. 1970. *A History of Presidential Elections*. New York: Macmillan.

Rusk, Jerrold G. 1970. "The Effects of the Australian Ballot Reform on Split Ticket Voting, 1876–1908." 64 *American Political Science Review* 1220.

Russert, Timothy. 1990. "For '92, the Networks Have to Do Better." *The New York Times*, March 4.

Sabato, Larry J. 1988. *The Party's Just Begun: Shaping Political Parties for America's Future*. Glenview, IL: Scott, Foresman.

———. 1984. *PAC Power*. New York: Norton.

———. 1981. *The Rise of the Political Consultants: New Ways of Winning Elections*. New York: Basic Books.

Sait, Edward M. 1927. *American Political Parties and Elections*. New York: Century Company.

Salmore, Barbara G., and Stephen A. Salmore. 1989. *Candidates, Parties, and Campaigns: Electoral Politics in America*. Washington, D.C.: Congressional Quarterly.

Scammon, Richard C., and Alice V. McGillivrey, eds. 1985. *American Votes: A Handbook of Contemporary Election Statistics*. Washington, DC: Congressional Quarterly Press.

Schattschneider, E. E. 1942. *Party Government*. New York: Holt, Rinehart, and Winston.

Schlesinger, Joseph A. 1985. "The New American Party System." 79 *American Political Science Review* 1151.

Schlozman, Kay L., and John T. Tierney. 1986. *Organized Interests and American Democracy*. New York: Harper and Row.

Schneider, William. 1988. "The Political Legacy of the Reagan Years." In Sidney Blumenthal and Thomas Byrne Edsall, eds., *The Reagan Legacy*. New York: Pantheon Books.

Shade, William G. 1981. "Political Pluralism and Party Development: The Creation of a Modern Party System, 1815–1852." In Paul Kleppner et al., *Evolution of American Electoral Systems*. Westport, CT: Greenwood.

Shafer, Byron E. 1988. *Bifurcated Politics: Evolution and Reform in the National Party Convention*. Cambridge: Harvard University Press.

———. 1983. *Quiet Revolution: The Struggle for the Democratic Party and the Shaping of Post Reform Politics*. New York: Russell Sage Foundation.

Shalope, Robert. 1972. "Toward a Republican Synthesis: The Emergence of An Understanding of Republicanism in American Historiography." 29 *William and Mary Quarterly* 49.

Shanks, J. Merrill, and Warren E. Miller. 1989. "Alternative Interpretations of the 1988 Election: Policy Direction, Current Conditions, Presidential Performance, and Candidate Traits." Paper presented at the Annual Meeting of the American Political Science Association, Atlanta.

Shively, W. Phillips. 1979. "The Development of Party Identification Among Adults: Explorations of a Functional Model." 73 *American Political Science Review* 1039.

Silbey, Joel H. 1991. *The American Political Nation, 1838–1893*. Stanford: Stanford University Press.

———. 1985. *The Partisan Imperative: The Dynamics of American Politics Before the Civil War*. New York: Oxford University Press.

———. 1977. *A Respectable Minority: The Democratic Party in the Civil War Era, 1860–1868*. New York: W. W. Norton & Co.

———. 1967. *The Shrine of Party: Congressional Voting Behavior, 1841–1852*. Pittsburgh: University of Pittsburgh Press.

Sinclair, Barbara. 1989. *The Transformation of the U.S. Senate*. Baltimore: Johns Hopkins University Press.

———. 1983. *Majority Leadership in the U.S. House*. Baltimore: Johns Hopkins University Press.

———. 1982. *Congressional Realignment, 1925–1978*. Austin: University of Texas Press.

Smith v. Allwright. 1944. 321 U.S. 649.

Smith, Steven S., and Christopher J. Deering. 1984. *Committees in Congress*. Washington, DC: Congressional Quarterly Press.

Sorauf, Frank J. 1988. *Money in American Elections*. Glenview, IL: Scott, Foresman.

———. 1980. "Political Parties and Political Action Committees: Two Life Cycles." 22 *Arizona Law Review* 445.

———. 1964 (1980, 4th edition; 1988 [with Paul Allen Beck], 6th edition). *Political Parties in the American System*. Glenview and Boston: Scott, Foresman/ Little, Brown.

Squire, Peverill. 1989. "Competition and Uncontested Seats in U.S. House Elections." 14 *Legislative Studies Quarterly* 281.

Stanley, Harold W., and Richard G. Niemi. 1988. *Vital Statistics on American Politics*. Washington, DC: Congressional Quarterly Press.

Stewart, Potter. 1975. "Or of the Press." 26 *Hastings Law Journal* 631.

Stokes, Donald E., and Warren E. Miller. 1962. "Party Government and the Saliency of Congress." 26 *Public Opinion Quarterly* 531.

Stone, Walter J., and Alan I. Abramowitz. 1983. "Winning May Not Be Everything, But It's More than We Thought." 77 *American Political Science Review* 945.

Stone, Walter J., Alan I. Abramowitz, and Ronald B. Rapoport. 1989a. "How Representative Are the Iowa Caucuses?" In Peverill Squire, ed., *The Iowa Caucuses and the Presidential Nominating Process.* Boulder, CO: Westview Press.

_____. 1989b. "Candidate Support in Presidential Nomination Campaigns." Boulder, CO: Center for the Study of American Politics, University of Colorado.

Stonecash, Jeffrey M. 1988. "Working at the Margins: Campaign Finance and Strategy in New York Assembly Elections." 13 *Legislative Studies Quarterly* 477.

Sundquist, James L. 1988. "Needed: A Political Theory for the New Era of Coalition Government in the United States." 103 *Political Science Quarterly* 613.

Taylor, Paul. 1988a. "Testing the Electoral College 'Lock.'" *Washington Post,* September 18.

_____. 1988b. "GOP Strategist 'Carpet Bombs' Buckeye State." *Washington Post,* November 4.

Thompson, Pamela S. 1988. "The Selling of the Candidate." *The Political Report,* July 22.

Thornton, J. Mills. 1978. *Politics and Power in a Slave Society, Alabama, 1800–1860.* Baton Rouge: Louisiana State University Press.

U.S. Department of Commerce. 1987. *Statistical Abstract of the United States, 1987.* Washington, DC: Government Printing Office.

U.S. House of Representatives, Committee on Post Office and Civil Service. 1988. *Policy and Supporting Positions.* Washington, DC: Government Printing Office.

U.S. President's Committee on Administrative Management. 1937. *Report of the Committee, with Studies of Administrative Management in the Federal Government.* Washington, DC: Government Printing Office.

Van Riper, Paul P. 1958. *History of the United States Civil Service.* New York: Harper and Row.

Victor, Jayne, Deputy Director of the Local Elections Division, RNC. 1989. Presentation to the Committee for Party Renewal, January 10.

Visclosky, Annamarie. 1989. Business Manager, Harriman Communications Center. Personal interview, January 6.

Waldman, Sidney. 1980. "Majority Leadership in the House of Representatives." 95 *Political Science Quarterly* 373.

Wallace, Michael. 1973. "Ideologies of Party in the Early Republic." Unpublished Ph.D. dissertation, Columbia University.

_____. 1968. "Changing Concepts of Party in the United States: New York, 1815–1828." 74 *American Historical Review* 453.

Ward, Stephen, PAC Director, DCCC. 1989. Personal interview, January 6.

Watson, Harry L. 1981. *Jacksonian Politics and Community Conflict.* Baton Rouge: Louisiana State University Press.

Wattenberg, Martin P. 1990. *The Decline of American Political Parties, 1952–1988.* Cambridge: Harvard University Press.

_____. 1986. *The Decline of American Political Parties, 1952–1984.* Cambridge: Harvard University Press.

_____. 1984. *The Decline of American Political Parties, 1952–1980.* Cambridge: Harvard University Press.

Watts, Steven, 1987. *The Republic Reborn: War and the Making of Liberal America, 1790–1820.* Baltimore: Johns Hopkins University Press.

"Week in Review." 1980. *New York Times,* August 3.

Weisbrot, Robert. 1990. *Freedom Bound: A History of America's Civil Rights Movement.* New York: Norton.

Wekkin, Gary D. 1985. "Political Parties and Intergovernmental Relations in 1984." 15 *Publius* 19.

Welch, Susan, and Timothy Bledsoe. 1986. "The Partisan Consequences of Nonpartisan Elections and the Changing Nature of Urban Politics." 30 *American Journal of Political Science* 128.

White, Leonard D. 1958. *The Republican Era.* New York: Macmillan.

_____. 1954. *The Jacksonians.* New York: Macmillan.

White, Theodore H. 1961. *The Making of the President, 1960.* New York: New American Library.

Whitehead, Ralph. 1978. "Mayor Daley's Personal Media." *Illinois Issues,* March.

Wiebe, Robert. 1967. *The Search for Order, 1877–1920.* New York: Hill and Wang.

Williamson, Chilton. 1960. *American Suffrage: From Property to Democracy, 1760–1860.* Princeton: Princeton University Press.

Willis, Charles F., Jr. 1968. Oral history interview with John T. Mason, Jr., March 15. Columbia University.

Wilson, James Q. 1962. *The Amateur Democrat.* Chicago: University of Chicago Press.

Wilson, Scott A. 1989. *Congressional Party Committees and the Distribution of Campaign Resources.* Summa Cum Laude thesis, University of Minnesota.

Wilson, Woodrow. 1885. *Congressional Government.* Baltimore.

Witcover, Jules. 1977. *Marathon: The Pursuit of the Presidency 1972–1976.* New York: Viking Press.

Wolfinger, Raymond E. 1963. "The Influence of Precinct Work on Voting Behavior." 27 *Public Opinion Quarterly* 387.

Young, Joseph, and Don Mace. 1989. *Federal Employees' Almanac, 1989.* Falls Church, VA: Federal Employees' News Digest, Inc.

About the Book and Editor

In recent years, journalists and scholars alike have sounded the death knell for political parties—only to resurrect them when the parties refused to die. *The Parties Respond* takes a more balanced view, for parties are composed of many parts and perform different roles: as organizational entities and groups of political activists, as objects of citizen loyalty and cue-givers for voters, and as fierce (if variably successful) competitors with campaign financiers, media moguls, and independent elected officials. Even as it reviews these role adaptations of the 1980s, *The Parties Respond* points us in the directions the parties are sure to take in the 1990s and beyond.

Fifteen original essays written especially for this volume reflect the best and most current scholarship in the field. The essays, prepared with a student audience in mind, are organized in the way courses on parties and elections are taught. Included among the contributors are the authors of three of the most widely adopted texts on parties. Maisel has drawn together leading scholars in all aspects of parties research: "rising stars," well-known insiders, and experienced participants. The mix of perspectives and approaches ensures a stimulating and provocative analysis of contemporary American parties.

This compact yet comprehensive volume can provide the core of reading for a course on political parties and elections or it can supplement one of the leading texts. The distinguished lineup of contributors promises to make this book essential reading for novice and serious students of parties alike.

L. Sandy Maisel is Charles A. Dana Professor of American Democratic Institutions and chair of the Department of Government at Colby College and has studied American politics as a participant and a scholar. His own unsuccessful campaign for Congress is documented in his important study of primary elections, *From Obscurity to Oblivion: Running in the Congressional Primary.* In addition to being the author of numerous articles, Maisel is also the author of one of the leading texts on parties, general editor of the forthcoming *Encyclopedia of American Political Parties and Elections,* and now hard at work on his true passion, a cookbook for those who love to eat but hate spending hours in the kitchen.

About the Contributors

Alan I. Abramowitz is professor of political science at Emory University. A student of congressional as well as presidential elections, he is the author of a large number of articles, coauthor and coeditor of *Life of the Parties: Activists in Presidential Politics*, and coauthor of *Nomination Politics: Party Activists and Presidential Choice*.

John F. Bibby is professor of political science at the University of Wisconsin, Milwaukee. A former staff member of the Republican National Committee, he is coauthor of *Vital Statistics on Congress* and *Party Organizations in American Politics* and author of *Politics, Parties, and Elections in America*.

David W. Brady is the Bowen H. and Janice Arthur McCoy Professor of Political Science, Business, and the Environment in the Graduate School of Business as well as professor in the Department of Political Science at Stanford University. He is more widely known, however, for his jump shot from the top of the key, his aggressive play at the net, and his deft flycasting. His most recent book, *Critical Elections and Congressional Policy Making*, won the 1989 Richard F. Fenno Prize as the best book published in the area of legislative studies.

E. J. Dionne, Jr., is a reporter on the national staff of the *Washington Post*. He was a visiting scholar at the University of Virginia's Center for Public Service and is the author of a forthcoming book on contemporary problems of liberalism and conservatism.

Morris P. Fiorina is professor of government at Harvard University and chairman of the Board of Overseers of the National Election Study. Among his works in the area of electoral behavior are *Retrospective Voting in American National Elections* and *The Personal Vote: Constituency Service and Electoral Independence*. The latter won the 1988 Richard F. Fenno Prize for the best book on legislative studies.

Linda L. Fowler is associate professor of political science in the Maxwell School at Syracuse University. Current chair of the Legislative Studies Section of the American Political Science Association, she is coauthor of *Political Ambition: Who Decides to Run for Congress*.

Paul S. Herrnson is assistant professor in the Department of Government and Politics at the University of Maryland. His recent book, *Party Campaigning in* *the 1980s,* builds on his continuing research into the campaign activities of the national party organizations.

Ruth S. Jones is professor and chair of the Department of Political Science at Arizona State University; in 1989–1990 she served as the executive on loan to the Arizona State Board of Regents. She is an acknowledged expert in and author of a number of articles on state campaign financing and on sources of campaign funds.

Elaine Ciulla Kamarck is senior fellow of the Progressive Policy Institute in Washington, D.C. Earlier she served on the staffs of the Winograd Commission, the 1980 Platform Committee for the Democratic party, and the 1984 Mondale for President and 1988 Babbitt for President campaigns.

G. Calvin Mackenzie is professor of government at Colby College and the director of the Presidential Appointee Project of the National Academy of Public Administration. Among his many publications in the area of presidential staffing are *The Politics of Presidential Appointments* and *The In and Outers.*

L. Sandy Maisel is Charles A. Dana Professor of American Democratic Institutions, chair of the Department of Government, and director of the Washington Program at Colby College. A former candidate for Congress and Democratic Party activist, he is the author of *From Obscurity to Oblivion: Running in the Congressional Primary* and *Parties and Elections in America: The Electoral Process* as well as general editor of the forthcoming *Encyclopedia of American Political Parties and Elections.*

William G. Mayer received his Ph.D. in political science from Harvard in 1989. He is now completing a book on changes in American public opinion between 1960 and 1988.

Warren E. Miller is Regents Professor of Political Science at Arizona State University and senior research scientist at the Center for Political Studies and adjunct professor of political science at the University of Michigan. Among his widely cited works are *Without Consent: Mass-Elite Linkages in Presidential Politics* and the seminal study of voting behavior, *The American Voter: Parties in Transition.*

Gary R. Orren is professor of public policy and associate director of the Joan Shorenstein Barone Center on the Press, Politics, and Public Policy at the John F. Kennedy School of Government at Harvard University. His recent publications include *Media and Momentum: The New Hampshire Primary and Nomination Politics* and *The Electronic Commonwealth: The Impact of New Media Technologies on Democratic Politics.*

Ronald B. Rapoport is associate professor of government at the College of William and Mary. His long-term study of party activists at state nominating conventions has resulted in a number of articles as well as two books including *Life of the Parties: Activists in Presidential Politics.*

Joel H. Silbey is the President White Professor of History at Cornell University. He is the author or editor of numerous articles in books in American political history, including *The Partisan Imperative: The Dynamics of American Political History Before the Civil War.*

Barbara Sinclair is professor of political science at the University of California, Riverside. A former American Political Science Association Congressional Fellow and frequent participant-observer of the Congress, she is the author of *Congressional Realignment, 1925–1978, Majority Party Leadership in the U.S. House,* and many other works in this area.

Frank J. Sorauf is professor of political science and former dean of the College of Liberal Arts at the University of Minnesota. A leading scholar of campaign finance in an age of reform and regulation, he is the author of *What Price PACs?, Money in American Elections,* and *Party Politics in America.*

Walter J. Stone is associate professor of political science and research associate of the Institute of Behavioral Sciences at the University of Colorado. A frequent contributor to professional journals, he is also the author of *Nomination Politics: Party Activists and Presidential Choice* and *Republic At Risk: Self-Interest in American Politics.*

Scott A. Wilson graduated *summa cum laude* from the University of Minnesota and is currently a graduate student in political science at Stanford University.

Index